DEFINING YOUR OWN SUCCESS

BREASTFEEDING AFTER BREAST REDUCTION SURGERY

DEFINING YOUR OWN SUCCESS

BREASTFEEDING AFTER BREAST REDUCTION SURGERY

DIANA WEST

LA LECHE LEAGUE INTERNATIONAL
SCHAUMBURG, ILLINOIS

First edition, August 2001
© 2001 La Leche League International

All rights reserved
Printed in the United States of America

Edited by Katherine Solan and Judy Torgus
Book and Cover design Digital Concepts, LLC
Cover illustration by Subhadra Tidball
Illustrations and photos by Subhadra Tidball
Lact-Aid illustrations courtesy of Lact-Aid, Inc.

Softcover ISBN 0912500-86-7
Hardcover ISBN 0912500-89-1
Library of Congress Card Number 2001091587

La Leche League International
1400 N. Meacham Road
Schaumburg, Illinois 60173-4840 USA
www. lalecheleague.org

I dedicate this book to the great women in my life who have made this book possible:

My aunt, Patricia Marti, who breastfed in a world that was not accepting of it because she knew it was the best gift she could give her children;

My late mother, Mary Ellis Duty, who was inspired by her older sister Pat to breastfeed her children, each for over a year, in an environment of misinformation and disdain;

My grandmother, Lois Duty, who could not breastfeed her children because her doctor erroneously proclaimed her milk to be too "blue," but who gave me a warm comment of support at a very critical moment; and to

My mother-in-law, Sharon West, who breastfed her children and whole-heartedly supported my strenuous efforts to do so, especially in my first days of BFAR.

I also dedicate this book to the great men in my life:

My father, Davis, who has been my dearest friend for all of my life;

My brother, John, who has been my most loyal champion;

My father-in-law, Lanny, whom I deeply admire and who has been an ardent supporter of my efforts to breastfeed;

My husband, Brad, who sacrificed and supported me every page of the way— without his love and devotion, I could never have finished this project;

My son, Alex, who opened my eyes and my heart to the importance of breast-feeding;

My son, Ben, who fulfilled the yearnings of my heart for a breastfeeding relationship and confirmed that BFAR is definitely possible; and to

My son, Quinn, who developed and grew in utero as I wrote this book, becoming twins with it in the process.

Finally, I dedicate this book to all past, current, and future members of the BFAR email list. You are an amazing group of women and I never cease to be deeply impressed by your efforts for your children. They are fortunate babies, indeed.

CONTENTS

FOREWORD

This is an important book. It is a book that is needed. It brings into focus many issues about breastfeeding that have not been sufficiently thought about, such as the value of partial breastfeeding and how to accomplish this. Given that no other book has been written from this unique perspective, it is a book that is not only for women who have had breast reduction and wish to breastfeed but it is also for the health care professionals who treat them and care for them.

Frequently mothers are told that if they are not producing enough milk, they might as well stop breastfeeding, that breastfeeding in such circumstances is not worth it. This is incredibly irresponsible advice, given the abundance of studies showing that even if there are less pronounced health benefits for mother and baby when the mother is supplementing her own milk supply with artificial baby milk (formula, modified cow's milk), the benefits are still there, and the partially breastfed baby is healthier than the exclusively formula-fed baby.

Furthermore, there is much more to breastfeeding than the milk, much more. Breastfeeding is a relationship between two people. Feeding at the breast has always been nature's way of ensuring a special connection between a mother and her child that is essential to the baby's physical, mental, and emotional development. The physical contact between a mother and baby renews and builds the emotional connection between them in a way that cannot be duplicated. It is a pity that so many women give up breastfeeding before they have understood it as more than just another way of feeding a baby.

The woman who has had breast reduction surgery may not be able to produce all the milk the baby needs. She may not even be able to produce more than a small percentage of the milk the baby needs. But is this a reason not to breastfeed? True, breastfeeding can be difficult at first, even without a woman's having had this type of surgery. But with good support the difficulties can usually be overcome. This is true in the case of the woman who has had breast reduction. Breastfeeding can also come naturally, as easy as "rolling off a log" as one of my patients said to me. Although a mother who is breastfeeding after a breast reduction surgery will probably encounter her share of challenges, there is no reason for some or even all of the experience not to come just as naturally to her as it does to many other mothers. If the supplementer at the breast is seen as just another group of alveoli, and the tube as just another duct, and the mother doesn't set the amount of milk she is producing as her ultimate measurement of success, breastfeeding can be as wonderful an experience for the mother who has had breast reduction as it can be for any other woman.

In the breastfeeding clinics where I work, I have seen many women who have had breast reduction surgery. Some have managed to breastfeed exclusively. Most do have to supplement, but have still managed to enjoy the unique experience that breastfeeding can bring to a mother and child. With the information available in this book, I hope to be able to counsel the mothers I see in the future better than I have in the past, and I think the mothers will be able to take the information available in this book to help them get through some of the initial difficulties and uncertainties and go on to a wonderful breastfeeding experience.

Jack Newman, MD, FRCPC, Toronto, Ontario, May 2001

ACKNOWLEDGEMENTS

It is my great pleasure to acknowledge the significant contributions of many great friends and professional associates who each added to and transformed this book on a heretofore unknown subject into the comprehensive resource that it became.

First, I would like to thank Carol Maranta who shared my vision of the need for a book about BFAR and worked many long hours with me to develop an outline and consider the BFAR issues from every perspective.

Second, I would like to thank Ginger Sall, Chairman of the LLLI Board of Directors, who was the first person at LLLI to speak to me about my idea for the book at a local LLL conference in Frederick, Maryland, in 1997. I'll never forget her remarkably poignant question, "Everyone has a book inside of them. Is this yours?" Judy Torgus also deserves a tremendous expression of appreciation for her belief in the need for a book on this topic, her hard work in developing the project from inception to final product, and her championing of its new ideas. Katherine Solan, my always optimistic and very skilled editor, compels a heartfelt note of thanks. She has impressed me deeply with her keen insights and organizational mastery.

I would like to thank Dr. Kathleen Auerbach for her generous mentoring in the book's early stages and invaluable contributions of content in the latter; Dr. Jack Newman for his belief in and ready support of this project; my midwife and co-instructor Diana Taylor for her insights from the midwifery perspective; Dr. Gregory Dick, a plastic surgeon, for his support of breastfeeding after reduction mammoplasty and review of the surgical discussions; Carla D'Anna, IBCLC, for her very valuable contributions to the body of BFAR knowledge, including a comprehensive review of the project in varying stages; Cher Sealy, IBCLC, for her keen personal insights as both a lactation consultant and BFAR mother and her professional review of the manuscript; Jan Ellen Brown, IBCLC, for her warm agreement to review the manuscript on short notice and for the valuable feedback she returned; Barbara Heiser, IBCLC, for her enthusiastic support of the project over its several years' duration and her unhesitating willingness to review the manuscript even in the midst of her own monumental projects; Jane Hearren, RN, for kindness and very valuable review of the galactagogue section of the manuscript; and Diane O'Brien Juve for sharing her uniquely successful approach to pumping with BFAR mothers.

There are many long-time members of the BFAR email list who generously volunteered their time and expertise to this project, and who each deserve my most sincere gratitude. Victoria Avakian, RN, Maya Shetreat, MD, and Kelly Hayday, MD, offered valuable insights into the clinical application of BFAR. Tracy Johnson and her husband, Theron Johnson, PhD, filled gaps in my knowledge of biochemistry and Susan Fuller deepened my understanding of reflux in the context of BFAR. Sarah Sullivan, an LLL Leader, kindly answered email from BFAR mothers seeking personal advice so that I could concentrate on writing the book. Jenifer Ackerman, Victoria Avakian, Vanessa Buchthal, Lara Cowan-Vesper, Wendy Jackson, Tracy Johnson, Patti Ryan, Carol Maranta, Janna Skura Mintz, Louise Shapiro, Sarah Sullivan and Misha Woodruff shared their personal stories of BFAR, deeply enriching the book.

Additional thanks go to many special women of the BFAR and BFAR mothers email list who gave this project such constant and tremendous support, and who were always willing to help me with ideas and feedback when I most needed them: Mari Adams, Kinga Barwig, Sloan Becker, Dina Dreifuerst, Jennifer Haymore, Lisa Israel, Amy Jones, Jasmine Larimer, Kathleen Prouty, Kristy Rodney, Melissa Ruffing, Sue Mirman, Heather Scrimsher, Chris Simon, Anne Marie van Osch, Annabelle Wall, and my friend Karen Wolfson. To all the other members of the BFAR email lists that helped and supported me, but who are not mentioned here, I thank you with all my heart.

Finally, I would like to extend a very special note of appreciation to my dear friends Taina Litwak and Lauri Fontaine, who faithfully encouraged and supported me during every stage of the project, and who sometimes lovingly cared for my children so that I could have uninterrupted time to write.

INTRODUCTION

When asked whether it is possible to breastfeed after breast reduction surgery, most people will automatically answer that it probably is not. Many women who have had breast reduction surgery do not even consider breastfeeding and bottle-feed their babies from birth onward. Other women who have had breast reductions try to breast-feed, but are ultimately unable to, perhaps because the surgical damage to the breast was too severe. But often it is simply that these women lacked adequate information and support. Increasingly, however, women who have had breast reduction surgeries are defying conventional wisdom and successfully breastfeeding their babies.

In addition to co-founding a resource center for breastfeeding after breast reduction surgery and working with hundreds of breastfeeding women in my capacity as a La Leche League Leader, I breastfed my three children with increasing success. My professional and personal experiences have convinced me that it is possible to breastfeed after breast reduction surgery if three factors are present:

- At least one breast and nipple;
- Information; and
- Support.

While the first is obviously necessary, I firmly believe it is the latter two factors, information and support, that are the most critical predictors of a post-surgical woman's chances of developing a satisfying breastfeeding relationship. Far more women are forced to abandon breastfeeding in favor of formula-feeding not because these women are physically incapable of producing milk, but because no one around them knows enough about the issues involved to be able to educate them or fully support their efforts.

If you are one of those women who was told that breastfeeding was impossible after breast reduction, you may be pleasantly surprised to learn that the ability to produce milk, in and of itself, is not a criteria for having a successful breastfeeding relationship. This book defines a breastfeeding relationship as one in which the baby is fed a regular portion of his nutritional requirement at the breast. So, although many post-breast-surgical women may need to supplement in varying degrees, at or away from the breast, there are few instances wherein breastfeeding cannot be a very important and beneficial part of the mother-child relationship.

Among women who have had breast reduction surgery and are now breastfeeding, it is often said that "We each define our own success." As it is used here, "success" is not an absolute term referring to a continuum of less to more milk produced. Rather, it is defined by the degree of satisfaction each woman and her baby derive from the breastfeeding relationship they create together. It is not determined by the amount of milk a woman produces. Each woman's experience of success will be different; some may be able to breastfeed exclusively, while others may need to supplement the baby's entire nutritional requirement. But even those women can supplement their babies at the breast, much like an adoptive breastfeeding mother does.

It is important to remember that breastfeeding is much more than nutrition. By breastfeeding our babies, we fulfill a wide range of their emotional needs. When we understand success in this way, we are aware of the power we have to make breastfeeding possible and to be wholly satisfied with whatever unique direction our breastfeeding relationship may take. It is this empowerment that gives us strength in vulnerable moments and keeps the knowledge uppermost in our minds that we alone determine what success will mean for us. This book has been written to provide critical information and support so that any woman who has had a breast reduction and wants to breastfeed can do so.

What Is BFAR?

As the techniques of breast reduction surgery evolved over the past several decades, the viability of breastfeeding correspondingly increased. The earliest techniques were so injurious to the ducts and glands of the mammary system that breastfeeding was patently impossible. Surgeons steadfastly warned prospective surgical patients that it would not be possible for them to breastfeed. Increasingly, however, surgical advances were made that better preserved the mammary system so that by the late 1980s, surgeons were able to tell prospective patients that breastfeeding after the surgery may be possible. Only a few very confident and optimistic surgeons asserted that breastfeeding would be completely unaffected by the surgery.

These assessments of the future viability of breastfeeding, however, no matter how guarded, frequently gave unrealistic and inaccurate expectations to women who often had little knowledge of the importance of breastfeeding or how they would feel about it when they became mothers. In the late 1980s, when lactation professionals began seeing women who had had breast reduction surgery attempt to breastfeed, they found that their clients experienced varying degrees of success and, frustratingly, they had little information with which to help them.

Indeed, few resources exist for the many women who have had breast reductions and are now attempting to breastfeed. As most other BFAR mothers have done, I began my journey into the breastfeeding world by looking for any information at all on breastfeeding after breast reduction surgery. Other than scant paragraphs here and there, basically advising that one would only know if lactation was possible by putting the baby to the breast and seeing how it went, I could find nothing that addressed the many issues that surrounded my unique situation. My doctor, midwives, pediatrician, and lactation consultant were also inexperienced with this particular realm of breastfeeding.

I became very fortunate in January of 1996 when I met four other women who had had breast reductions on the Internet through bulletin boards and email lists–Carol Maranta, Lara Cowan-Vesper, Colleen Dunhill Jones, and Christine Gilmore Eubanks. We were amazed to find each other and decided to begin a private correspondence through email, so that we could compare our experiences and learn from each other. Eventually, other women wanted to join us so we began an automated email list. The list has grown to average two hundred active subscribers as of the writing of this book.

By combining and comparing our information we learned what worked and what didn't. The wealth of information that the members of the email list were able to collect from their experiences was tremendous. We passed along this information to new members and provided a forum of wholehearted support for the unique challenges we were facing; the email list became a tremendous resource.

All email lists need a descriptive and memorable name, and we decided to call ours BFAR, pronounced "bee-far," which is an acronym derived from BreastFeeding After Reduction. Over time, the term BFAR came to mean not only the email list, but we also began to use it as a part of our vocabulary as we discussed the issues surrounding our various experiences. Colloquially, the term BFAR is used on the email list as an actual word that can be conjugated to noun and verb forms. In this book, however, the use of the term BFAR will be restricted to that of an acronym without conjugations, so that the words for which it stands—Breastfeeding After Reduction—are inferred when it is used. The term does not infer any membership or association with the BFAR email list.

Aside from the prerequisite of having had breast reduction surgery, BFAR is defined most simply as feeding a baby at the breast with or without human milk, as well as feeding a baby your own milk with an artificial feeding device, such as a cup, syringe, or bottle. This definition is very broad because it encompasses many combinations of feeding methods. The important point is that while any amount of lactation qualifies as BFAR, a woman need not lactate to be a BFAR mother as long as she is feeding her baby at the breast.

For Whom This Book Is Written

This book has been written first and foremost for you, the BFAR woman, to provide you with a composite of information about BFAR, as well as empathy and encourage-ment to help you through any BFAR issues you may encounter. Whether you are just beginning to consider the possibility of BFAR, or are pregnant for the first time and faced with critical choices, or contemplating BFAR your second, third, fourth, or even ninth baby, the prospect of BFAR can seem like a daunting challenge. But with this book in hand you are armed with an advantage that wasn't available to you before. You will see that BFAR is possible.

If you are dedicated to providing the benefits of human milk and breastfeeding for your child, this book will provide you with the information and support to make breastfeeding a reality for you. You'll find support through validation of your feelings about BFAR and encouragement of your efforts to make it work for you and your baby. You'll read about the experiences and feelings of many BFAR women who have generously shared their stories to illustrate the wide range of experiences that are possible.

In addition to providing encouragement and support, this book is a concentrated compilation of the information collected through the research and experience of many dedicated lactation specialists over the past decade. I have reviewed the available information about BFAR, applied logic and common sense, and then observed the personal trial and error of many BFAR women to determine what is effective and what is not.

Of course, it must be said that no two BFAR experiences are alike, even for the same woman. Each woman and each birth has a different combination of factors that comprise her BFAR challenge. Some of these factors are physiological, some are psychological, and some are environmental. It is no more possible to address every situation that a BFAR mother might face than it is to promise that every BFAR mother will be able to avoid supplementation. Both would be unrealistic. What this book can do, however, is speak to the common denominators that we have all seemed to encounter, and address as many of the issues that a typical BFAR mother might face as possible. Readers are always encouraged to contact their local La Leche League Groups for further information.

Because each woman and each set of BFAR circumstances is unique, this book cannot provide a definitive recipe for BFAR success. The techniques that work for another BFAR mother are not always the best solution for you. You will not find any promises that if you do "X," "Y," and "Z" you will have a certain outcome. Breastfeeding is an art, not a rigid mechanical method; it must be adapted to the special needs and temperaments of each mother and her baby.

While the BFAR woman is this book's primary focus, it has also been written to assist health care professionals—including physicians, midwives, maternity and pediatric nurses, lactation consultants, WIC counselors, and La Leche League Leaders—in helping the BFAR woman achieve a satisfying breastfeeding experience. In the past, these professionals have been at a disadvantage, having no resources and scant research from which to draw information to help their BFAR clients. It has been very difficult for them to advise BFAR women at all. Conventional wisdom, common sense, and knowledge of the principles of lactation have been their only tools. This book, therefore, is intended to become the resource previously unavailable to the professional. While many chapters, such as those discussing basic anatomy and reduction surgeries, will be elementary to professionals, other chapters will provide practical information that can be utilized to assist the BFAR client. This book is intentionally comprehensive in scope so that the many aspects of lactation can be presented and considered from the BFAR perspective.

Finally, you may notice that all babies are referred to in the masculine gender. This has been done only for the sake of simplicity and it is hoped that all the sweet little girl babies will be forgiving.

What This Book Will Cover

Wonderful books, such as La Leche League International's THE WOMANLY ART OF BREASTFEEDING, as well as *The Nursing Mothers' Guide to Weaning,* by Kathleen Huggins and Linda Ziedrich, *Nursing Your Baby* by Karen Pryor and Gale Pryor, *Bestfeeding* by Mary Renfrew, Chloe Fisher, and Suzanne Arms, and *The Ultimate Breastfeeding Book of Answers* by Dr. Jack Newman, have been written to address normal breastfeeding issues and concerns. This book complements these comprehensive resources by further addressing the unique circumstances of BFAR. BFAR women are encouraged to obtain a copy of at least one of the books listed above in addition to this book so that you may have a thorough understanding of normal breastfeeding.

Where this book differs, though, is in its approach to each aspect of breastfeeding from the BFAR perspective. The experiences of hundreds of BFAR women have been examined so that it will be possible to discuss the issues common to all of us, as well as those encountered by only a small segment of the BFAR population.

This book has been divided into four sections. The first, Part I, is "Before Birth: Contemplating Breastfeeding after Breast Reduction Surgery." In these five chapters, the issues and information that provide the framework for considering the viability of BFAR are discussed.

Part II, "Baby Is Born: Maximizing Your Milk Supply and Developing Your Breastfeeding Relationship," explores the unique issues BFAR women confront when they begin breastfeeding and the specific methods of BFAR that maximize the milk supply while enabling the new mother and baby to bond at the breast.

"Beyond BFAR: Evolving Your BFAR Relationship," addresses BFAR after the first three months, explores common BFAR emotional issues, and facilitates an assessment of factors that help and hinder the BFAR effort.

The final section, Part IV, "Assisting the BFAR Woman from the Professional Perspective," addresses the professional caregiver, providing specific information according to professional specialty to those who assist the BFAR patient.

The Appendices include additional charts, checklists, and resources.

Following each chapter, you will read the stories of women who were able to breastfeed following breast reduction surgery, in their own words. They generously shared their stories so that you can gain insights into this experience and learn how they weathered challenges that you may also face. These first BFAR mothers were courageous pioneers—women who defied convention and the discouraging advice of so many professionals to give their own milk to their babies—and it is they who have provided the body of knowledge that makes the success of today's women possible.

As you read these stories, keep in mind that no two BFAR situations are alike. The physiological capabilities, the circumstances, prior knowledge, even the personality of the mother and baby, greatly influence the BFAR experience. Most importantly, these mothers were attempting to breastfeed in a time when very little was known about it and so their efforts were greatly trial-and-error. They had no real way to prepare for BFAR and they did not have accurate information upon which to base their decisions. Although you may have much in common with several of the experiences described here, with this book in hand you will have much better information to help you prepare for BFAR so that you will maximize your lactation potential and avoid much of the emotional trauma that these valiant BFAR pioneers endured.

Define Your BFAR Success!

From my own experience and from having known many other BFAR women, I am aware that many women who have never been exposed to breastfeeding before may be completely overwhelmed at the prospect of BFAR. These women need support and at least one comprehensive resource for information in order to address this unique experience that can seem to isolate them from the rest of the breastfeeding world.

Ultimately, it is the objective of this book that each person who reads it is left with a conviction that a BFAR mother can breastfeed her baby. With this understanding, every BFAR mother can then define her own success, no longer thinking of breastfeeding in terms of "all or nothing," but rather knowing that any amount of human milk given to a child is valuable beyond measure and worth any effort it may take to produce it.

This book carries one message on every page: Whether you are the professional or the BFAR woman herself, no matter what the physiological capability, you can make the difference . . . you can make it happen . . . you can give a baby the precious gift of a breastfeeding relationship.

DIANA'S STORY

I decided to have my breast reduction surgery for the reasons most women do; I was uncomfortable with my body, both physically and emotionally, and there was something I could do about it, so I did. Once I made the decision to have a breast reduction, I was surprised at how easy it was to get from the idea of it to making it a reality. And I was very lucky; my insurance covered the whole procedure as a medical necessity and my family and friends were wholly supportive of it.

I poignantly remember sitting in the plastic surgeon's office discussing the ramifications of the inferior pedicle technique with him, when he brought up the issue of breastfeeding. I recall that he looked me squarely in the eye and gently said, "You do know that you probably will not be able to breastfeed." Certain of my decision and probably wary of anything that could threaten it, I brushed off his warning with the casual reassurance, "That's fine. It doesn't really matter to me and besides, formula is just as good." As you can imagine, that statement haunts me now because, of course, I have since learned just how inadequate formula is and how very much breastfeeding does matter to me. But at that time, I did not have a serious boyfriend and children were a far-off dream. Being supportive, my mother did not contradict me, having faith that my decision was thoroughly considered. I wish she had, however, because she breastfed her children and must have known how valuable and rewarding an experience it would be.

As luck would have it, only a year after my surgery, I met and married my future husband, Brad. I became pregnant with our first son, Alex, two years later and began to read of the advantages of breastfeeding, leaving little room for any belief that formula was an equivalent substitute for human milk. I deliberately skipped descriptions of how to breastfeed, not wanting to set myself up for guilt and disappointment. I decided, though, that I would "try" to breastfeed, because I might just have milk after all. One night during my eighth month, I was reading a pregnancy book and tentatively ventured into a description of hand expression. On a whim, I tried it and, to my astonishment, managed to express several drops of colostrum from each breast. It was as if tension had been building within me and had suddenly been released. I remember feeling proud of my breasts—as if maybe they weren't going to let me down after all. Strangely, I hadn't been aware that I felt that way until then.

When Alex was born, I immediately put him to my breast and felt a sense of deep satisfaction. Because I had had a difficult delivery, the maternity nurses at the hospital wanted to "let me rest" and cup feed Alex formula. I hesitated, but finally agreed, thinking that at least they were savvy enough not to give him a bottle that could interfere with nursing. What I didn't anticipate was that I would not be able to drift off into a peaceful slumber. After about two hours, I awoke missing my baby so much that I tiptoed down to the nursery, where they brought me Alex, thankful that I had come because he was very fussy. I sat in their rocking chair and nursed him for almost an hour, feeling a bliss that I had never known before.

We only stayed for one more day, and I nursed him fairly often throughout it, not knowing if he was "getting much," but assured that there was plenty of formula in the world if he wasn't. Still, a nagging uncertainty persisted. Once home, I devoured THE WOMANLY ART OF BREASTFEEDING, and The Nursing Mother's Companion. It was as if I had finally earned the right to read about breastfeeding.

On the fourth day we began to think I might not have enough milk because Alex was strongly favoring the left breast over the right, and he never seemed satisfied after nursing. The pediatrician said that we should supplement with formula. We fed him a bottle and almost immediately, Alex seemed to forget how to nurse. Brad printed out a description of nipple confusion from the Internet and how to avoid it by feeding formula by spoon instead of bottle. We did this laboriously for a week and it was one of the hardest weeks we'd ever known. He seemed to fuss all the time, day and night, and nothing made him happy.

Finally, alarmed about Alex's slow weight gain, our pediatrician gave us the number of a lactation consultant, who, after hearing about my reduction surgery, rejected any idea of pumping to increase my supply. Instead, she showed me how to use an SNS (Supplemental Nursing System) so that I could nurse and supplement simultaneously. The SNS seemed to be heaven-sent. After three days, he had gained ten ounces and we were vastly relieved. By having me keep a record of three days' intake of formula, the lactation consultant calculated that I was providing one-third of his nutritional intake with my milk.

Although still a fussy baby, he now seemed much more contented and settled down to a routine. When he was four weeks old, I decided to try pumping to increase my milk supply and rented a Medela™ Lactina Select™. I soon discovered why Alex had shown a preference for my left breast over my right; it produced twice as much milk as the right breast did.

For the next two months, I pumped after feedings, even at night, filling the SNS with what I had pumped and formula. Unfortunately, we were told that we should begin introducing the bottle at around six weeks, because by then "he would be past any danger of nipple confusion." At first, we did this only when we were in a hurry. But by the third month, we used the bottle more and more and Alex began to show a strong preference for it.

I vividly remember the last time I breastfed him. While his bottle heated, I nursed him, enjoying the freedom of doing so without the SNS, but feeling as though I was depriving him because my milk couldn't possibly be as nutritious as the formula was. When the bottle was ready, I took him off the breast, gave him the bottle, and he eagerly sucked it down. That was the last time I ever nursed my Alex. From that point on, he screamed whenever I would try to latch him on. I thought to myself that he probably knew best and I gave in to bottle-feeding.

Because I knew about the antibodies and immunities in human milk, I didn't give up completely, though. I pumped three times a day, averaging about four ounces each pumping, and bottle-fed Alex the pumped milk combined with formula until he was fourteen months old. As I pumped I read breastfeeding bulletin boards and email lists on my computer. This was the turning point in my breastfeeding education. I learned so much about human milk and breastfeeding that I felt as though a whole new world had opened up to me. I "talked" to women all over the world about nursing babies. Even though I was bottle-feeding Alex, I still thought of myself as a breastfeeding mother because I was lactating and encouraged others to enlarge their concept of nursing mothers. I met four other women who were breastfeeding after reduction surgery and we formed the BFAR email list.

I had seen La Leche League's praises sung all over the Internet, but it wasn't until Alex was six months old that I attended my first meeting. I was so nervous knowing that he might need a bottle during the meeting. Fortunately, the Leaders and other mothers were supportive and encouraged me to nurture Alex in any way that was best for us. They were impressed and touched by my story and soon became my support network, as well as a fountain of information to quench my expanding thirst for knowledge about breastfeeding. They also helped me understand that I was grieving for the loss of the intimacy of the breastfeeding relationship I had had with Alex. Many nights I had lain awake yearning to feed him at my breast and reconnect with him in that special way. I resolved then that I would make every effort within my power to breastfeed our next child. I would take the information and support that I now had, and work diligently to expand them so I would have every resource to make that dream a reality.

When Alex was a year old, I became pregnant with Ben and read and reread every text I could find about breastfeeding. Brad and I took Bradley Method childbirth classes to maximize our potential for a drug-free birth to facilitate a good start to breastfeeding. Five days past my due date, Ben was born without drugs at a birthing center and put to my breast with the cord still attached. We went home a few hours later and began our breastfeeding relationship. He nursed almost continuously for the next few days, sucking for both comfort and nutrition. He was never fussy, but rather seemed very contented and often alert. My milk came in thirty-six hours after his birth and I had serious engorgement, which subsided after a day. Ben was so pleased with his new milk meals that he gained an average of two ounces a day (one ounce is normal for most babies in the first months) and soon grew into a chubby breastfed baby.

I never had to supplement Ben at all. This is not to say that there weren't moments when I doubted myself and was only a hair's breadth away from mixing formula. Like many babies, Ben had a fussy period in the early evening when he would latch on and off and cry inconsolably. Naturally, as a BFAR mother, I doubted my milk supply, but it was just a normal baby growth stage. What kept me from supplementing at those times was the daily weighings at home on our rented electronic scale that enabled me to remind myself over and over that a baby who was gaining two ounces a day was not starving.

Ben and I shared that breastfeeding relationship I had dreamed about, making me so thankful that I had the information and support to be able to breastfeed the second time. While my milk ducts clearly recanalized as a result of that year of pumping, I am *convinced that it was my understanding of BFAR, combined with the support of my family, my fellow BFAR mothers, and my friends in La Leche League, that maximized my potential and gave me the strength to persevere to the rewarding stages of breastfeeding.*

I was pregnant with our third son, Quinn, during most of the writing of this book. He was due to be born about the same time of the book's first printing, so although I don't know yet what our breastfeeding experience will be, I anticipate that I will continue to have a complete milk supply and will again enjoy the special bliss of being a nursing couple with my baby.

BEFORE BIRTH: CONTEMPLATING BREASTFEEDING AFTER BREAST REDUCTION SURGERY

WHY WOMEN HAVE BREAST REDUCTION SURGERY

In a society that values the female breast not for the functional purpose of producing milk, but rather as a highly desirable sexual attribute, with attractiveness directly correlated to large breast size, it might be difficult to understand why some women choose to surgically reduce the size of their breasts.

They do, though. In the US alone, 90,000 women underwent breast reduction surgery in 1999.[1] Although this is an elective procedure, it is not a surgery that is entered into lightly. Most women pursue it only after a great deal of consideration and consultation. They have been coping with the physical and psychological issues of being large breasted for a long time and have come to see breast reduction surgery as the only viable option to resolve these issues.

There are many factors that can contribute to a large-breasted woman's decision to have breast reduction surgery. A woman's reasons are often highly personal and individual, and usually a combination of physical and psychological issues. If you had a breast reduction and now find it difficult to remember exactly why it seemed so necessary to have at the time, perhaps this discussion of common reasons will revalidate your decision. If you haven't personally had the surgery, but are reading this in order to help mothers who did have this surgery, understanding the reasons that compel women to have a breast reduction can lend a quality of empathy to your efforts.

Physical Reasons

The most commonly cited physical issues that can result from large breasts are:

- Back and neck pain
- Difficulty breathing
- Poor posture
- Headaches
- Nerve damage
- Shoulder grooves
- Rounded shoulders
- Clothes fitting poorly

- Inability to exercise comfortably
- Inability to lie on stomach
- Prematurely sagging and pendulous breasts
- Frequent yeast infections under the breast
- Unequal breast size

Back and neck pain resulting from carrying the load of disproportionately large breasts can be severe. A study by the American Society of Plastic Surgeons (ASPS) revealed that large breasted women can suffer more pain than cancer and arthritis patients.[2] The added weight of breasts that weigh as much as six pounds, when the normal weight is about one pound, can place tremendous stress upon the vertebrae and the disks in between them. This weight is concentrated in an area that lacks a muscular system to support it. Disintegrated vertebrae and herniated disks are not uncommon among large-breasted women. Often, women experience the strain as a constant ache in the mid and lower back.

Many large-breasted women find that breathing is difficult when they are lying on their backs because the chest wall is required to lift the weight of the breasts for breathing.

The weight of the breasts can make proper posture difficult to maintain. Without continued, concentrated effort, it is easy to begin slumping forward. Many large-breasted women also hunch forward in a semi-conscious effort to hide their breasts. Improper posture can have painful repercussions throughout the muscular/skeletal system. It can contribute significantly to shoulder pain, back muscle pain, and foot pain from an improper distribution of body weight.

Headaches are another common side effect of having large breasts. Although the relationship is unclear, it is thought that the muscle strain of the upper back and neck be the cause of in frequent, severe headaches. Such headaches can be disruptive to everyday living, reducing one's ability to concentrate and be productive.

Nerve damage has been substantiated as an occasional consequence of large breasts. Women have experienced fainting spells and severe shooting pains in the breasts that were eventually diagnosed as damage to nerves from the weight of their breasts.

Many women find that over time the weight of their breasts causes permanent grooves to become imprinted in their shoulders from bra straps. This grooving effect is a testament to the force of the weight of large breasts. It is these grooves that are most often photographed as documentation of the severity of the effect of large breasts for the surgical candidate. One woman recalled, "Once, while getting undressed for the shower before sports, a team member saw my deep, red grooves and asked if I had been carrying something heavy on my shoulders. I told her that yes, I certainly had."

Rounded shoulders are also a common physical characteristic of the large-breasted woman. This is a combined result of poor posture and increased shoulder and neck muscles that have developed over time to carry the load of the heavy breasts. In many societies, rounded shoulders are not considered to be attractive for women. So in addition to having to cope with disproportionately large breasts, women must also suffer from the disfiguration of rounded shoulders and the resulting feelings of unattractiveness.

As a result of poor posture, rounded shoulders, and the large breasts themselves, finding clothes that fit well, hang properly, and are flattering is almost an impossibility for large-breasted women. Often, a partial solution is achieved by purchasing a top in one size and the corresponding skirt, shorts, or pants separately. This is not always possible, however, and even when it is, the top is usually too large in the arms and waist.

Exercising can be very difficult for the large-breasted woman. There are no bras that contain and support large breasts well enough to make aerobic activity comfortable. The added weight and physical presence of large breasts can make lifting and resistance exercises difficult to achieve. Many forms of controlled dance, such as ballet, are impractical with large breasts. Exercising with the added strain of large breasts can cause women to tire more easily, ending the exercise session prematurely. This impediment may be enough to discourage exercise for many women, which can compromise their overall physical health.

Large breasts make lying on one's stomach nearly impossible. While this position is not essential to satisfactory rest, many people find that stomach lying is a very comfortable position that rests the back and shoulders and is somehow soothing. It is also a desirable position for tanning, massages, and relaxation exercises, but one that is unavailable to the large-breasted woman.

Most women with large breasts find that over time the sheer weight causes the breasts to lose their tone and begin sagging. Having pendulous breasts can be embarrassing and unsightly, particularly for young women. Large, low-hanging breasts can also make a woman seem far heavier than she really is.

As a result of sagging breasts, many women are plagued with frequent, irritating yeast infections underneath their breasts. The area between the breasts and upper torso stays moist and warm, creating the perfect breeding ground for yeast. While there are many effective remedies for yeast infections, their recurrence can be a chronic problem for some women.

The least common physical reason for undergoing breast reduction surgery is having unequal breast sizes. Although most women's breasts are not precisely even in size and shape, most are close enough to seem equal to the casual observer. Some women, however, have breasts that are noticeably disproportionate often as a result of a glandular dysfunction, such as Poland's syndrome. A reduction of the larger breast is often recommended to cosmetically correct the effect of the dysfunction. For women with this syndrome, however, normal breast function is almost always compromised, not so much by the reduction surgery as by the lack of a well-formed, mature lactation infrastructure in both breasts. Not realizing this, plastic surgeons may tell a woman that she will be able to breastfeed on the breast that has not been reduced, and then compound the problem by not feeling compelled to preserve lactation tissue in the breast undergoing the surgery.

There are physical reasons for having reduction mammoplasty surgery beyond those discussed here, such as in the prevention or treatment of breast cancer.[3] When the cause of the physical problem is having large breasts, though, reduction surgery is viewed by most women to be a straightforward solution that has greatly enhanced their quality of life. The permanent relief of their physical problems usually more than compensates for the temporary discomfort of recuperating from the surgery.

Psychological Reasons

The psychological reasons women have for undergoing breast reduction surgery are individual and diverse. Many of these issues are experienced more prevalently by women in Western cultures where breasts are primarily equated with sexuality. Some of the most common psychological reasons for breast reduction surgery are:

- Peer pressure to fit in,
- Discomfort with unwanted attention,
- Pressure from family members,
- Sexual harassment,
- Poor self-image.

The pressure to belong to a group of one's peers without seeming different from them can be tremendous, especially for young women. To stand out physically can sometimes preclude inclusion in social groups, which can seriously affect self-esteem. Not being able to wear fashionable, attractive clothes can also prevent many young women from being welcome among their peers. The psychological pain of social ostracism can have lifelong repercussions. One woman shared her painful experience:

> "'I grew up on a small island in Alaska. Sexual harassment brought nothing but terror to me as a youth. I started developing in third grade and boys thought it was a great game to "accidentally" bump into me. At first I just tried to ignore them, but when bumping into me turned into falling on me hands first, I started complaining loudly to the teachers. It didn't do a whole lot of good, though. My parents were frustrated and encouraged me to just "turn the other cheek." I think the thing that baffled me the most was that being large breasted meant (to the eager boys and jealous girls) that I was promiscuous, a slut, even though I flatly refused to get involved with any boy on that island." The sexual harassment I had to endure made a serious negative impact on my ability to have intimate relationships.'"

Sexual harassment is a tragically common occurrence in schools and workplaces in many societies. In her article in Ladies' Home Journal ("My Life in a D Cup," June 1998), Holly Robinson describes her early school experience:

> "Junior high was a gauntlet of breast-seeking boys who would sneak up behind you at the water fountain to cop a quick feel, or pluck at your bra like a harp string as you huddled over an algebra book .... Never mind that I got excellent grades and was a responsible baby-sitter. None of this was visible. And so my breasts overshadowed my other accomplishments."

Another woman wrote about her experience:

> *"I loved to play basketball in my teens, and it was impossible to find a bra which not only fit, but was comfortable. Yet the physical problems were not the worst ones. Once, during a game, many people were on the side watching. I was 16 years old, and wore a uniform with the number 17 on the back. I was running fast to catch the ball and there was a shout from the audience, "Hey, Number 17, let them wiggle! Wow, what breasts!" Following this shout, everyone started laughing. I missed the pass, of course. My team members and the other team stopped playing immediately. Our center went up to the guy and started shouting at him. The guy was removed, but you can imagine how I felt. This kind of thing happened many times. Not always so loud, but I saw guys watching and talking about me many times when I came near the side of the court. Usually they kept their voices down, but I was able to hear it."*

This kind of harassment can severely traumatize a young girl with tender self-esteem. Having large breasts is interpreted as a signal of promiscuity to many boys and some men. Such beliefs often lead to unwanted, demeaning, and even frightening sexual advances and harassment toward some girls and women.

It can be equally painful and humiliating to a grown woman in the workplace. Many women have told us that they feel that they are not valued for their skills and abilities, but rather for their perceived sexuality. They are aware that other women with smaller breasts are respected and taken seriously, while it is often nearly impossible for them to command the same courteous regard. This can affect their potential for advancement and, ultimately, their livelihood.

The family members of large-breasted women have been known to put considerable pressure on them to have breast reductions. They may feel that they are acting in the large-breasted family member's best interests by helping her to achieve a body that will be more accepted by society and less subject to ridicule and misuse. Mothers, fathers, and even siblings and grandparents have been known to subtly and not-so-subtly push women toward an appointment with a plastic surgeon. This is not to say that the women have breast reductions against their will, but sometimes they feel pressured to do so by the influence of their families. This can be a positive or negative influence, depending upon the dynamics of the individual family situation.

One of the most powerful reasons for cosmetic surgery is a poor self-image resulting from a perceived physical abnormality. Aside from the physical problems of being large-breasted, being compared very negatively to a society's ideal of physical perfection can lead to such feelings of dislike of one's self that the body and the person are not differentiated. These feelings of negativity toward one's self can be so overwhelming that all facets of the woman's personality are affected. Her image of herself may be so painful to her that she becomes self-conscious and introverted. Her quality of life may be significantly diminished.

Making the Decision to Have Breast Reduction Surgery

From the moment when a large-breasted women first learns of the possibility of breast reduction surgery to actually implementing the process to accomplish it, there is often a long interval full of doubts, questions, perseverance, and determination. Some women inquire about the procedure but decide not to follow up on it. Others are unable to have the surgery for a myriad of reasons, financial and practical. Fortunately, it is often deemed "medically necessary" by health insurance companies in many countries so that the costs are covered completely.

For most women, it takes a great deal of courage to go through the process of committing to the surgery. Typically, after making the initial decision to inquire about the possibility of a breast reduction, a woman must visit at least two plastic surgeons in order to select a surgeon and corroborate the necessity for the procedure. During this interviewing and assessment process, it is necessary for her to bare her chest to many strangers. She must usually also be photographed for pre- and post-operative reports. For women who are already uncomfortable with their bodies, this process can feel intrusive and humiliating.

The physical aspects of recuperation are dictated by the type of surgery performed, the woman's physical fitness, her age, her perception of pain, her rate of healing, her activity level, her personal circumstances, and the quality of care she is given.

Adjusting to one's body after the surgery means encountering new feelings that are as varied as the feelings one can have beforehand. It is often a blend of doubt, shock, crisis of identity, adjustment of self-image, excitement about the repercussions of the positive change, discomfort with discussing the surgery with others, and fending off morbid interest. However, in the end, most women report feelings of liberation and comfort with their bodies.

Ultimately, after a time of recuperation, most women who have had breast reductions are very satisfied with the results and go on to enjoy a much-improved quality of life, both physically and psychologically. They are free from the pain that has haunted them for years, their shoulders return to a more natural shape, posture is improved, they are no longer targets of harassment or differentiation, and they simply feel better about themselves as women.

It is usually not until these women become pregnant with their first child after having the reduction that they must face the fact that their ability to breastfeed may have been diminished by the breast reduction surgery. Then having had the surgery takes on a whole new dimension.

REFERENCES

1. American Society for Aesthetic Plastic Surgery (ASAPS). 1999 Plastic Surgery Procedural Statistics. Arlington Heights, IL: National Clearinghouse of Plastic Surgery Statistics; 1999.

2. Kerrigan, C., E. Collins, T. Kneeland, et al. Measuring health state preferences in women with breast hypertrophy. *Plast Reconstr Surg* Aug 2000; Aug 106(2):280-88.

3. Brown, M., M. Weinberg, N. Chong, et al. A cohort study of breast cancer risk in breast reduction patients. *Plast Reconstr Surg* May 1999; 103(6): 1674-81.

LOUISE'S STORY

*While pregnant with my son, I had contemplated attempting to breastfeed.
Six years earlier, I had managed to nurse my newborn daughter for about two days before giving up. I had no information, no support, and what felt like no milk. Given this experience, I chose to formula-feed my son, thereby avoiding any frustration and disappointment with nursing. I felt comfortable with my decision, as I knew that having had the breast reduction surgery nine years ago was one of the best things I had ever done for myself.*

This decision changed, however, seven days after Nathan was born. While getting out of the shower, I noticed that both breasts were leaking milk! I'll never forget the look on my husband's face when I came running out of the bathroom, proclaiming, "I've got milk! Wake up the baby!" Since I had decided not to breastfeed, I didn't know a thing about it, including how to hold the baby while nursing. So I just did what came naturally. Nathan latched on and started sucking!

After receiving several supportive emails from the women on the BFAR email list, I decided to commit myself to breastfeeding Nathan. The first three months were very difficult. Nursing consumed every ounce of my physical and emotional energy. I had trouble with a poor latch-on, blanched nipples, plugged ducts, and exhaustion. I was getting extremely discouraged and ended up taking it one feeding session at a time. I had little confidence in my ability to actually produce milk and nourish my child.

Renting a double pump from the hospital was a real confidence booster for me. I felt so exhilarated the first time I pumped and actually saw my milk. I must have stared at those two ounces of liquid gold for 15 minutes! I later confessed to my lactation consultant that the main reason I wanted to start pumping was to convince myself that I really did have milk. Looking back, once I got into a routine of nursing/supplementing/ pumping, I felt much more comfortable about my milk supply. I may not have been able to produce all the milk Nathan needed, but I was able to provide close to half of his daily nourishment.

The beginning of the fourth month was like magic for us. Nathan finally started opening up his mouth wide enough to properly latch on, the blanching pain subsided, my nipples were no longer ultra-sensitive, and we were starting to get more rest by nursing in bed. I had even learned how to nurse comfortably in public. That special bond that other nursing mothers spoke of had finally become a reality for me and my baby. We were on our way to a wonderful year of breastfeeding!

BEFORE AND AFTER: THE EFFECT OF REDUCTION SURGERY ON THE ANATOMY AND PHYSIOLOGY OF THE BREAST

The human breast is a strikingly complex gland of the female human body that plays a dramatic role in the propagation and, in some cultures, the sexuality of our species. Surgery on the breast transforms the composition of a normal breast so that both the form and function—the anatomy and physiology—are altered.

While it is beyond the scope of this book to describe all of the anatomical and physiological aspects of the human breast, it is nonetheless important to have a basic understanding of them in order to comprehend how the reduction surgery you received may have affected your mammary system. Therefore, in this chapter, a basic explanation of the anatomy and physiology of the lactating breast is presented, followed by a discussion of the general anatomical differences of post-surgical breasts. The major reduction mammoplasty surgical techniques are then described, followed by a discussion of each surgery's effect upon lactation capability.

At this point, you may not know which techniques were used in your surgery; learning more about your surgery is recommended as part of your preparation for breastfeeding after reduction surgery. When you read this section, you may be able to determine the technique by your scar pattern, but many different techniques result in similar scars, so you may not know for certain until you have access to your surgical report.

If you do not have a scientific background, you may feel that a discussion of surgical techniques could be too technical to be easily understood. Actually, you probably already have a good understanding of most of the anatomy and lactation processes of the breast. There may be gaps in your knowledge, but chances are that you will be pleasantly surprised to find that you already know much of the material in this chapter. This chapter will help you understand the effect your surgery will have on lactation, so that you will be able to define your lactation expectations as realistically as possible.

The anatomical and physiological information presented in this section is descriptive of a female breast that has experienced no surgical trauma. Contemplating a breast with full lactation potential can be emotionally painful for some mothers who have had surgery on their breasts. Yet, having an understanding of unaltered anatomy and physiology gives us the greatest opportunity to manipulate the post-surgical mammary system to achieve our maximum lactation potential.

Anatomy of the Lactating Breast

Development Between Birth and Pregnancy

The female breast is an organ quite unlike any other organ of the human body. It is not fully developed at birth. All humans are born with breast tissue, however, the female breast begins to develop a mammary system in response to estrogen and progesterone produced by the ovaries at puberty. Fat deposits also begin to accumulate at puberty, enlarging the breasts to the adult size and providing space for lactation tissues to reside. The greatest portion of breast development is complete by the end of the teen years, but the mammary system does not become fully mature until pregnancy occurs. In anticipation of that event, breast development continues during each menstruation when hormones are released that enable further expansion of the mammary infrastructure, until around age 35. When a woman becomes pregnant and progresses past the 16th week, the mammary system becomes fully mature.[1]

Pregnancy Preparations for Lactation

In addition to growing and sustaining the fetus in the uterus during pregnancy, the body is simultaneously preparing to grow and sustain the baby after his birth by developing the mammary system. The existing lactation infrastructure of ducts, lobes, and glands that are described below is expanded and further developed, enabling it to produce milk when the baby needs it. The mammary system begins this expansion in response to increased levels of estrogen and progesterone, as well as the introduction of prolactin. By the 16th week of pregnancy, the mammary system is able to produce colostrum.

After Lactation

When weaning occurs, the mammary system must undergo a transformation in order to cease producing milk. As the milk accumulates in the glands in response to decreased nursing, the glands become distended, interfering with the blood supply to them so that no more milk can be produced. The existing accumulated milk is reabsorbed by the glands' alveoli (described below), which then collapse or rupture. A small portion of the mammary system remains in the lactational state for up to twelve months after weaning has occurred, which is the reason some women are still able to express small amounts of milk for several months.

External Anatomy

Structure

The nipple, areola, and general skin comprise the external structure of the breast. The nipple, also known as the *papilla mammary*, is a knob of very elastic skin and contains minute muscles surrounding 15-25 openings of the ducts that lead to the milk-producing glands. These minute muscles are interwoven in three distinct orientations: surrounding the circumference of the nipple, across the top of the nipple, and laterally on the sides of the nipple. Contraction of these muscles in response to cold, emotional, or lactational stimuli results in the erectile function that facilitates proper latching when the baby begins suckling the breast. These muscles also serve to control the ebb and flow of milk from the ducts, rendering them responsible for the extraneous leaking that some women experience when the muscles have a less constrictive inclination. Nipples are typically pink, red, brown, or black depending on general skin pigmentation, as a result of the generous blood supply they receive.

The *areola mammary*, usually known as simply the areola, is a highly sensitive area of the breast. It is a circular area surrounding the nipple that is much darker in pigmentation than the remainder of the breast. The depth of the pigmentation depends upon the woman's coloring and can vary greatly. The striking contrast of the areola is very helpful to infants in guiding them to the nutritional source, perhaps even encouraging them to grasp more of the areola-nipple complex in order to properly suckle the breast. Doing so is essential for effective extraction of milk because the action of the baby's mouth compresses the pooling areas in the ducts that reside directly underneath the areola. These pooling areas are called the *lactiferous sinuses*. It is this action, rather than suction, that compels the delivery and production of milk. This is why we say that the baby "suckles" the breast, rather than "sucks" it. The only suction is that which enables the baby's mouth to stay sealed to the areola so that milk does not leak from the baby's mouth. This is also the reason that a baby is far more effective at extracting milk and inducing milk production than a breast pump.

Most women have pronounced bumps on their areolae that appear in late pregnancy and may seep small amounts of a quasi-oily substance and milk throughout lactation. These are actually small sebaceous glands (glands that produce fatty substances called sebum), known as *Montgomery glands*, or *Montgomery's tubercles*. There is some question as to the purpose of the substance that the Montgomery glands produce, however, it is generally believed that it serves to lubricate the areolar skin and control bacterial growth.

Most women also have some hair around the outside of their areolae. In women who have had breast reduction surgery, these hair follicles are sometimes transported during the surgery and may be now located along the lower scar line.

Shape

The shape of the breast, the areola, and the nipple is determined by heredity, body fat ratio, racial factors, age, and the presence or absence of lactation. These change dramatically over the course of a lifetime. With the exception of glandular dysfunction, such as Poland's syndrome, or surgical alteration, all breasts will develop somewh symmetrically, enlarge during pregnancy, enlarge further during lactation, dim a prelactational state after weaning has occurred, and then atrophy at m significant number of women report that their left breasts are slightl right breasts. Moderate differences between the two breasts in s capacity are very normal. In fact, 80 percent of women difference in breast size. The composition of the brea younger women tend to have more glandular tis more fatty deposits.

Internal Anatomy

Components of the Breast

Each normal adult breast comprises two major components: the parenchyma, the elements of the mammary system, and the stroma, tissue that provides a formative structure to the breast.

Parenchyma

Lobes The mammary system of the mature lactating breast is comprised of between 15 to 25 sections, called *lobes*. These lobes are irregular in size, and radiate in each direction from the nipple. They are separated and cushioned by adipose (fatty) and connective tissues.

The structure of the lobes is similar to that of a tree: the ducts that lead from the nipple are like a tree trunk; at the top of the ducts, smaller ducts called *ductules* branch off; clustered like leaves on the ductules (actually resembling grape bunches) are the *alveoli*, which are individually called *alveolus*. The clusters of alveoli are called *lobuli*.

Many women who have had breast reduction surgery wonder if the number of openings in the nipple they see corresponds to the number of viable lobes that remain after the surgery. The answer is no: The number of ducts that express milk does not exactly correspond to the number of lobes because some ducts join just below the nipple surface and not all lobes produce milk at the same time. Different ways of positioning a baby at the breast can affect the stimulation of different lobes. And the spray that you see may be a combination of more than one duct. So lactational capacity cannot be evaluated by the number of openings that are visible on the nipple.

Alveoli The basic component of the mammary system is the alveolus, which contains secretory cells that extract and collect appropriate elements from the surrounding

Basic anatomy of a human breast

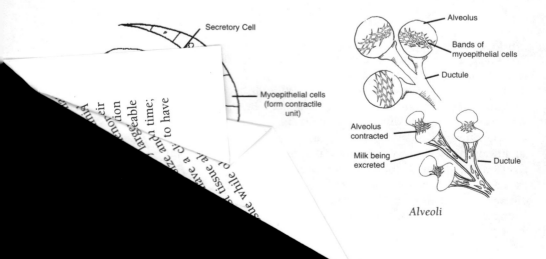

Alveoli

blood supply; the result of which is "milk." Each alveolus is surrounded by a band of *myoepithelial cells* that are like muscles in that they squeeze the secretory cells, forcing the milk into the ductule. The myoepithelial cells contract in response to the let-down reflex (described below).

Ductules and Ducts The ductules receive the milk that is squeezed into them from the alveoli and serve as a pathway to the main ducts, where all ductules terminate like tributaries to a river. As the ducts near the nipple, they widen to form a small pooling area, called the *lactiferous sinuses* or *ampullae*. The lactiferous sinuses are located beneath the areola. Compression of the baby's mouth during suckling forces the milk that is pooled in them out of the nipple, stimulating the production of more milk and triggering the let-down response.

Stroma

The elements of the breast that are not glandular tissue serve to provide structure and sustenance to the mammary gland, supporting and feeding it. These elements include adipose and connective tissue, blood vessels, nerves, and components of the lymphatic system.

Apidose Tissue One-third of the entire breast is comprised of fatty tissue, known as *adipose cells*. Unlike the fat in other parts of the body, the fatty tissue in the breast serves a very critical function for the lobes of the mammary system, which are seated directly in the adipose tissues, in order to protect and divide them. Therefore, in reduction surgery, it is nearly impossible for a surgeon to extricate the glandular tissue from the adipose tissue, especially when lactation is not present, as is never the case at the time of reduction surgery.

Connective Tissue Connective tissue is the "glue" of the human body, and as such gives the breast support, form, and cushion. Most connective tissue is collagen, which is the primary component of tendons and cartilage. The connective tissue also provides a mesh infrastructure that allows layering of the nerves, blood, and lymph vessels that serve the breast.

A type of connective tissue that figures prominently in the support structure of the breast are the *Cooper's ligaments*. These are minute ligaments that run vertically throughout the breast, originating from the covering of the muscles of the chest wall, supporting the lobes, and attaching to the inner layer of the breast skin. The ligaments are not elastic and, once stretched from accumulated body fat, pregancy, or lactation, never return to their shorter state. The inevitable result of stretched Cooper's ligaments is breast sagging, which can only be corrected by plastic surgery.

Blood Supply The blood supply to the breast is quite abundant—there are many blood vessels within the breast. Many surgeons suggest autologous (self) blood donation prior to reduction surgery in preparation for the possibility that a transfusion may be required. Sixty percent of blood in the mammary system is supplied by the internal mammary artery and thirty percent originates from the *lateral thoracic* artery. The remaining ten percent is from minor arterial branches of the *axillary* and *subclavian* arteries. Blood is carried away from the breast by the veins that run parallel to the arterial system.

Lymph Nodes The lymphatic system is prolific throughout the breast and has been studied extensively in the context of oncological (cancer) research. The lymphatic system is comprised of many small lymph glands, which are also known as *lymph nodes*, that are located in an interconnected sequence throughout the body. They have three primary functions: keeping body fluids in balance, filtering and eradicating toxic substances, and combating invading organisms that endanger body tissue by creating and distributing antibodies. Each lymph node contains a fluid that is slightly yellow, which is comprised of white blood cells (lymphocytes), some red blood cells, and other fluids, such as dissolved fat, that are collected from tissues in the body. When an infection is present and overwhelms the lymph nodes' ability to destroy the invading organisms, they become swollen and inflamed.

The lymphatics of the breast originate in the lymph capillaries of the mammary connective tissue, which surrounds the mammary structures, and drain through the deep substance of the breast. The majority of the lymph nodes follow the lactiferous ductal pathways, combining in a network (plexus) beneath the areola called the *subareolar plexus*.

Nerve Supply The nerve supply of the breast consists primarily of nerves that pass through the spaces between the ribs, which are called the intercostal spaces. The three major nerves of the breast pass through in the fourth, fifth, and sixth intercostal spaces and are therefore known as the fourth, fifth, and sixth intercostal nerves. The most critical nerve for lactation is the fourth intercostal nerve, which is located in the lower right quadrant of the right breast and the lower left quadrant of the left breast. This nerve supplies sensation to the nipple and areola and is therefore essential to lactation. Like the branches of a tree, the main stem of the fourth intercostal nerve divides into five branches called *fasciculi*; two above, one central, and one below. These branches then subdivide and subdivide again until the nerves extend throughout the breast.

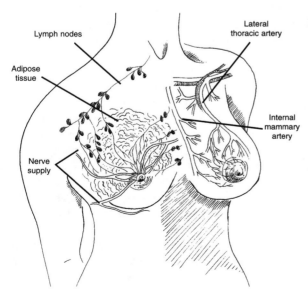

Compared to the nipple and areola, the main portion of the interior of the breast contains far fewer nerves. The greatest portion of nerves in the deeper regions of the breast surround and serve the arteries. There are no nerves near the alveoli. This is actually quite significant because it demonstrates that the process of lactation does not occur from direct stimulation of the fourth intercostal nerve, but rather that the stimulated nerves induce the release of hormones (oxytocin and prolactin, described below), which then affect the myoepithelial cells, prompting the let-down reflex. For mothers who want to breastfeed after breast reduction surgery, this is especially useful information, because galactagogues that stimulate the production of oxytocin and prolactin can imitate or enhance the action of nerves that may have been compromised by the surgery.

Exterior Anatomical Differences of the Breast after Reduction Surgery

Appearance of the Surgically Reduced Breast

Women who have undergone breast reduction surgery have a smaller areola circumference and, of course, smaller breast size. Scars differ widely according to the technique that was used, but in general can include a scar around the areola, a scar in a vertical line from the areola to the *intermammary fold* (the base of the breast where it meets the chest wall), a very small half-inch horizontal scar at the base of the breast, a short horizontal scar of about two inches somewhat above the intermammary fold, or a long horizontal scar along the intermammary fold. Some scars resemble an inverted T and others are broader like an anchor.

Changes in the Surgically Reduced Breast Over Time

By the time a woman who has had a breast reduction is considering breastfeeding, most post-surgical areolas and breasts are no longer as perfect as they were after they healed from the surgery. Weight gain, gravity, and especially pregnancy can all cause our areolae to stretch and our breasts to enlarge and sag. Many post-surgical women find that their areolae stay in the new position, but the majority of their breast tissue drops to the pendulous, sagging portion of the breast.

With these dramatic changes, scars can be also altered. Many vertical and horizontal scars spread and dramatically lighten. Areolar scars tend to remain the same or lighten to become almost unnoticeable, although some women report that this areolar tissue becomes a shade of pink unlike the normal breast skin or the areolar skin. Scar tissue on the interior of the breast can feel distinctly thick.

Fair-skinned women often find that pregnancy brings many more prominent blue veins to the surface. Most fair-skinned women experience this phenomenon during and after pregnancy. Women who have had breast surgery may be more aware of it, however, as we tend to notice breast changes more readily.

Some mothers find that a portion of the darker pigmented, previously areolar, skin is now located in the lower scar line. It may not have been noticeable before pregnancy, however the hormones that darken the areola also darken this areolar skin so that it becomes more pronounced during pregnancy. The reason extraneous areolar skin remains is that during the reduction surgery, when the areolar pedicle is cut, the skin blanches, making it difficult to differentiate the areola boundaries. The tissue remains blanched when it is being sutured, so that it cannot be identified.

Of course, time can be kind, as well. Most scars lighten considerably over the years and nerves regenerate so that we regain sensation in all regions of the breast. Sometimes the sensation that develops is more acute than it was previously when the breasts were so large.

Some women who have had breast reductions find that they have developed "dog ears" as their breasts changed since the surgery. A "dog ear" is the term describing the phenomenon of the horizontal scar that extends from under the breast that spreads at the outer edge under the arm, folding onto itself, with a pucker at the base, resembling a dog's ear. Most plastic surgeons can easily modify the scar during an office visit. As it is a common occurrence, it may also be included in your post-surgical care.

Occasionally, some women who have had breast reduction surgery find that small "holes" exist in the scar tissue. These may originate from poor healing around sutures. Such holes can be troublesome, however, as they tend to collect dirt, oil, and debris, and can sometimes become infected. If they become troublesome, it might be best to bring them to the attention of your plastic surgeon who will probably remove them.

Regaining or Exceeding Original Breast Size

Many mothers who have had breast reduction surgery lament the fact that during pregnancy their breasts are once again the size they were before the surgery (or even bigger). It is important to remember, though, that we had the surgery because we had a tendency to grow large breasts. This breast expansion that occurs as a result of weight gain and pregnancy would most likely have occurred anyway. However, had we not had the surgery, it would have occurred in addition to our then-existing breast size, rather than from our reduced size.

Vigilance for Breast Cancer in the Post-Surgical Breast

There is recent research from the Karolinska Institute in Stockholm University of Toronto demonstrating that breast reduction surgery may reduce the incidence of cancer.[2] It does not, however, reduce eliminate the risk by 100 percent, so there is still the possibility that cancer can manifest. It is therefore imperative that you remain vigilant for detection of suspicious growths in your breasts. This can be done by self-examinations, examinations by a health care professional, or mammograms.

Unfortunately, many women who received breast reductions, especially women who have or are lactating, experience great difficulty performing breast self-exams on their breasts. It can be very difficult to differentiate breast tissue from scar tissue from lactational tissue from suspicious lumps. Many health care professionals are also unable to differentiate problem areas in the lactating breast.

For this reason, it may be wise to have mammograms performed on a more regular basis than is normally suggested for women who have not had breast surgery. A compounding problem, though, is that because of the decreased presence of fatty tissue and increased density as a result of breast reduction surgery, mammogram interpretation can be difficult. It is important to find a skilled, experienced radiologist to interpret the mammographic films because the dense lactation tissue can somewhat obscure suspicious masses.

Physiology of the Lactating Breast
Hormonal Influences on Lactation
Prolactin

Prolactin is the primary hormone responsible for lactation. In fact, it has been called the "mothering hormone" because it induces an emotional response in the mother of tranquility, nurturing, and affection. It is secreted by the pituitary gland beginning at eight weeks of pregnancy and reaches its highest level at birth. By the end of the first week after birth, prolactin is fifty percent above the normal level. By the fourth month, it has returned to normal, pre-pregnancy levels, with the exception of bursts of prolactin released when the baby nurses.

Prolactin plays a significant role during pregnancy by causing the lobes of the mammary gland to develop to mature lactational capability. Milk is not produced at this time, however, because progesterone secreted by the placenta prohibits the secretory cells in the alveoli from absorbing milk elements from the blood. When the placenta has been delivered and it is no longer able to secrete progesterone and estrogen, the sudden elevation of prolactin, in combination with the removal of the progesterone influence, initiates the production of mature milk.

Oxytocin

Oxytocin is the partner hormone to prolactin, playing a key role in the delivery of milk that has been produced in response to alveoli stimulation by prolactin. In a sense, these two hormones work together; prolactin develops the mammary system and prompts the production of milk, while oxytocin causes the myoepithelial cells to contract and release the milk that has been produced. Stimulation of the nipple/areola complex prompts production of oxytocin. Unlike prolactin, oxytocin is not produced until tactile or psychological stimulation prompts its production.

Secondary Hormonal Influences

While prolactin and oxytocin are the primary driving hormones for lactation, other secondary hormones support the lactational function. These secondary hormones are *insulin, cortisol, thyroxine, parathormone,* and *somototrophin.* Insulin is a secretion of the pancreas that synthesizes sugar and carbohydrates. Cortisol makes fatty acids available for metabolic use. Thyroxine is secreted by the thyroid gland and regulates the growth of the body by increasing the rate of carbohydrate metabolism and protein synthesis. Parathormone is the hormone secreted by the parathyroid that regulates the metabolism of calcium and phosphate. Somototrophine is a growth hormone secreted by the pituitary gland that is necessary for normal skeletal growth. These are all hormones that act upon the mother's lactation system.

Compositional Qualities of Milk

The first milk produced by the body is *colostrum.* It is thick, clear or slightly opaque, and of a yellow/orange hue. The mammary system is capable of producing colostrum at 16 weeks of pregnancy. It is not actually required, however, until the baby is born. If the baby is born prematurely, the colostrum that is produced will have special compositional properties particularly suited to the needs of the preterm baby. The amount of colostrum that is produced is significantly less than that of mature milk. It can be measured in teaspoons rather than ounces, but this is entirely appropriate for the hydration and nutritional needs of the newborn. In response to the baby's suckling, colostrum is produced in increasing quantities over the first three days, followed by a dramatic increase in milk production when the milk begins transitioning to mature milk. For the next two weeks, the colostrum will be gradually displaced by the mature milk, transforming from a yellow/orange color to a bluish-white, depending upon the mother's diet and other contributing factors.

The milk that is produced at each feeding varies in composition from the beginning of the feeding to the end. The milk the baby receives when he begins suckling is called *foremilk*. It is fairly thin and can appear bluish. This is the milk that has accumulated since the last nursing. It has a higher protein but lower fat content than *hindmilk*, the milk actively produced during the feeding after most of the foremilk has been taken. Hindmilk is much higher in fat, which results in a thicker, whiter appearance. It is important for a baby to nurse long enough, at least on one breast, to receive the higher fat hindmilk, which is essential for proper brain growth and weight gain. The longer the duration of active feeding, the more hindmilk the baby is likely to receive. And he will benefit even more from the higher-calorie hindmilk when feedings are frequent because foremilk has had less opportunity to accumulate in the ducts and sinuses.[1]

The Manufacture and Delivery of Milk
The Endocrine and Autocrine Mechanisms
The manufacture and delivery of human milk is dependent upon the physiological processes that create and maintain it. The two processes that provide these functions are the *endocrine* and *autocrine* mechanisms. The endocrine mechanism is hormonally sponsored, while the autocrine mechanism is self-perpetuating.

The endocrine system of the body is comprised of certain organs and body tissues that produce, store, and secrete hormones, which are chemicals that contain instructions for tissue growth and function. The mammary system is most affected by the endocrine system immediately after delivery, when lactation is initiated by the sudden decrease in blood levels of the hormones estrogen and progesterone that had been secreted by the placenta during pregnancy, and which had been suppressing the milk-producing effect of prolactin. Removal of the suppressing hormones enables prolactin to rapidly initiate lactation.

Over the following three months, as levels of prolactin decrease, this endocrine-driven stimulation for lactation gradually converts to the autocrine mechanism that relies upon the response of the mammary system to the baby's demand of it. It's actually an elegantly simple system: when milk is removed, a corresponding amount of milk is created to replace it. If less is removed, less is made at the next feeding; if more is removed, more is made at the next feeding. It used to be thought that it took several days for the supply to catch up to the demand. Newer research, however, shows that the mammary system actually responds much more quickly, sometimes almost immediately.[3]

The Prolactin Receptor Theory

A very intriguing theory that has evolved from recent research is the hypothesis of finite prolactin receptor sites. Because the nature of hormones requires them to be synthesized directly by the tissue they seek to affect, researchers believe there are specific structural "receptor sites" for prolactin in the breast. These sites would be shaped precisely to receive the prolactin molecule, however there is a finite number of receptor sites that can be created. Researchers have concluded that milk production is affected primarily by the quantity of these prolactin receptors rather than by the levels of prolactin in the blood.[1] Breastfeeding in the first hour postpartum seems to have the most profound effect on establishing receptor sites, but receptor sites continue to be created through the first three months postpartum. The key to maximizing them is frequent feedings in the first few weeks. [1]

In addition to any post-surgical considerations, the amount of milk produced also depends upon the number of prolactin receptor sites that were established during the first few weeks. Nursing in the first hour after birth, as well as frequently thereafter, is the best way to ensure that as many prolactin receptor sites as possible are established. This can go a long way toward offsetting the surgical impact.

Research by Dr. Peter Hartmann and his colleagues in Australia demonstrates that on average, only 80 percent of the available milk is removed from the breasts at any given feeding, with 20 percent remaining. When more than 80 percent is taken, the breasts increase production to regain the 80:20 ratio. We also now know the rate that milk is replenished is in direct correlation to the amount of milk that is present in the milk ducts. Breasts that are emptier will "refill" more quickly than breasts that are full.[4,5]

Storage Capacity of the Breast

Most lactating women have had the experience of feeling that their breasts are "empty," as well as having times when they feel "full." It can be confusing to read, as so often stated, that "the breast is not a container that fills and then is emptied," because, of course, this is often exactly what it feels like.

The breasts are not containers that fill with a finite amount of milk. The process is actually more complex. The lobes of a lactating woman are always producing milk, although at varied rates. In between feedings, the milk simply accumulates in the ducts. When too much milk has accumulated because of a missed feeding, the mother can feel discomfort and milk may leak from her nipples. When the baby nurses, he takes the accumulated milk, which is the foremilk, first. After it has all been removed from the breast, the lobes then convert milk synthesis to production of higher-fat milk, commonly known as hindmilk. This process is why the breast never truly empties and cannot be compared to a container.

The amount of milk that is actually capable of accumulating in a mother's ducts is, however, determined by the storage capacity of her breast. In this regard, the breasts are indeed similar to storage containers. Each woman has a unique storage capacity for each breast, which is unrelated to her breast size but directly related to the functional levels of the working tissues and hormones within the breast.

When the storage capacity is smaller, most women will tend to breastfeed more frequently because they feel full sooner, but will ultimately produce the same amount of milk over a 24-hour period as women with larger storage capacities. The fat content of the milk, however, will be higher in the milk of women whose storage capacity is less, because hindmilk is produced for a larger portion of the feeding.[4]

For mothers who have had breast reduction surgery, the research findings about variable milk storage capacities contribute an added dimension to the question of lactational capability and explain an anecdotal finding. We have observed that mothers who have had breast reduction surgery tend to produce higher fat milk. It is also a logical conclusion that most of them will have a smaller storage capacity as a result of having fewer functional lobes. It is additionally known that frequent feeding is recommended for all breastfeeding women as a means of increasing the fat content and caloric density of milk. Further, we know that women with smaller storage capacities

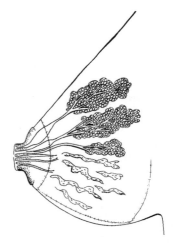

Surgically reduced breast showing severed lactiferous ducts and non-functioning, atrophied lobes.

tend to feed more frequently because they feel full sooner. Therefore, since mothers who have had breast reduction surgery have lower storage capacities and thus feed more frequently, their milk has a higher fat content, validating our anecdotal finding.

Engorgement

A normal event at the start of lactation is *engorgement*, when the mature milk begins to be produced during the first few days after birth and swelling occurs in the breasts. This is caused by the sudden decrease of estrogen and progesterone levels in the blood, which inhibited the existing high prolactin levels from producing milk before the baby's birth. The swelling that results is not all milk, however. The blood supply to the breast has been suddenly increased, and blood is congested in the tissues surrounding the alveoli cells. The cells rapidly produce milk in response to the tremendous availability of blood, but are unable to deliver the milk as quickly as it is produced because the baby is not yet nursing at an equal rate. A significant level of edema (fluid swelling) then develops around the lobes, which contributes to the fullness felt in the breasts.[6]

Many mothers think that stimulation of the breasts at this time will only result in the production of more milk, compounding the problem. This is not accurate, however. Removal of the milk is essential for resolving the engorgement and is critical for the prevention of permanent damage to and loss of alveolar tissue. This is best accomplished by allowing the baby to nurse without restriction. If this is not possible, pumping with a fully automatic electric breast pump is the next best solution to engorgement. Once the milk begins draining, the blood and edematous fluids will begin to dissipate.

Engorgement is not always experienced in such a profound way that the breasts become distended and rock-hard. In fact, if the baby is suckling effectively it rarely progresses to that degree. Instead, most women merely experience significant fullness and a sense of heaviness. If you do not experience any fullness at all, this can indicate that your prolactin levels are too low or the prolactin has not been able to affect milk production. Or, because you have had breast reduction surgery, it may mean that you do not have many viable, intact lobes to produce milk. Occasionally, some mothers experience unequal engorgement between their breasts, again indicating that the viable lactation tissue is present in greater quantities in one breast than the other. Less frequently, some mothers find that they have engorgement only on portions of one or both breasts, but that other areas of the breast remain soft. This is further evidence that little or no viable lactation tissue exists in the non-engorged areas.

The Let-Down Reflex

The *let-down reflex*, which is also known as the *milk ejection reflex* (MER), is the process whereby the alveoli are stimulated to release milk into the pooling areas, lactiferous sinuses, beneath the areolar region of the breast. Most babies begin swallowing more frequently during the let-down as the volume of milk increases. As we know from research about the let-down process and the storage capacity of the breast, the milk that is expelled during the let-down is milk that has already been produced by the glandular lobes; it is not a sudden increase in milk production.

The let-down occurs when the nerves in the nipple and areola are stimulated so that oxytocin and prolactin are produced by the pituitary gland. The let-down can also occur as a physiological reaction to thinking about your baby or hearing a baby (perhaps not even your own) cry. The let-down reflex can be inhibited by physical discomfort, particularly cold and pain, as well as feelings of stress and anxiety.[6] Aside from difficulties associated with surgical trauma, the let-down occurs most easily when you are comfortable, rested, well fed, happy, and secure.

Oxytocin released during the let-down causes the myoepithelial cells that surround the alveoli to contract, squeezing the milk from the alveoli cells into the ductules, where they are carried to the ducts and out the nipple. Prolactin increases the rate of milk production to replenish the milk that is expelled during the let-down. It also usually simultaneously produces a very pleasant sensation of relaxation and a desire to nurture.

The let-down reflex is a process that can often, although not always, be felt by the nursing mother. Some women describe the sensation as warm heat across their shoulder blades; others say that they feel a sensation like "pins and needles" inside their breasts. In the first few weeks after birth, most mothers feel uterine cramping and increased blood flow during the let-down.[7] Some mothers feel extreme thirst during the let-down. Other mothers feel absolutely nothing. Sensations associated with the let-down reflex diminish over time and are rarely felt after six months. The most reliable way to know that the let-down reflex is happening at any time during your nursing relationship is to simply watch your baby. Rapid, deep swallowing, which is often accompanied by slight wiggling of the earlobes and a noticible pause in jaw movement, is the most important indication that the let-down has occurred.

The let-down reflex usually occurs several times at each feeding, although it can take a few minutes to happen once the feeding has begun. This interval from the beginning of the feeding to the first let-down is often longer in the first few days after the mature milk has come in than it will be later when the let-down reflex is better conditioned.

In mothers who have had breast reduction surgery, initiation of the let-down reflex is more dependent upon the state of the neural pathways than it is upon the capacity of the mammary gland itself. Of course, even with an excellent let-down reflex, the ducts that are not connected will express no milk and will eventually atrophy. If the nerves of the nipple and areola have been completely severed, particularly the fourth intercostal nerve, assuming reinnervation (reconnection of nerve tissue) has not occurred, then let-down cannot happen, except as a psychological response or as a result of ingestion or inhalation of synthetic oxytocin. This is rarely the case, however, and most mothers who have had breast reduction surgery do not have difficulty with the let-down, except in response to stress and anxiety caused by worries about having enough milk for their babies. Your work in preparing to breastfeed by becoming educated about the process will give you a tremendous advantage, relieving much of the worry that uninformed mothers often feel.

Effects of Reduction Mammoplasty Surgical Techniques on Lactation

This section of the chapter provides an overview of the different reduction mammoplasty surgical techniques commonly performed by plastic surgeons in North America, Europe, and other parts of the world. This is also where you'll learn about the type of surgery you may have had and that surgery's probable impact upon lactation.

When I was researching this topic, I learned to my amazement that the first breast reduction was performed in 625 AD on a man with *gynecomastia* (male breast growth). It was not until 1897 that the first breast reduction was performed on a woman. Although it was not clear what surgical technique was used on the patient in 1897, it was certainly a primitive technique compared to the very sophisticated reduction mammoplasty techniques performed today.

The techniques in use today vary according to the surgeons' and the patients' outcome goals. Some surgeons and patients seek minimal scarring at the expense of shape, some prefer a better shape with moderate scars, others prefer more scarring with better preservation of nerve, blood, and lactational tissue.

Unfortunately, you can not know exactly which surgical technique you had just by judging the shape of your scars because several scar patterns are identical even though the surgical techniques are different and result in diverse lactational capabilities. The only way to know for sure which surgical technique was used is to obtain your surgical record from your surgeon or the hospital where the surgery was performed.

One question many women have is whether there is a relationship between the amount of tissue removed and the post-surgical lactational capability. It is unfortunate that this question has no answer at this time. There seem to be no clear patterns. It is certainly a question for future research.

The description and analysis of the reduction mammoplasty surgical techniques that follow are presented in a subjective ranking in order of least to most impact upon lactation capability. Those women whose surgery involved the techniques presented first will most likely yield the greatest milk supplies.

Please note, however, that speculation about the impact of the following surgeries upon lactation is not at all based on research, but merely on logic. The actual anatomical and physiological outcome will depend upon the surgeon's skill and motivation to preserve lactation tissue, the woman's original breast size, her unique anatomy, and the interval between the surgery and lactation. These estimates of lactation probability are only broad generalizations offered to help you form your own carefully considered expectations.

Most importantly, these estimates of lactation capability apply only to the first lactation experience. Subsequent lactation experiences will almost always benefit from the effects of *recanalization* and *reinnervation* (the body's ability to reconnect severed ducts and nerves, respectively, through certain hormonal and physical stimuli), which will result in a greater milk supply than the first experience.

Breast Reduction Exclusively by Liposuction

One surgical technique favored by some surgeons for a small subset of women who require only minimal reduction and who do not have significant sagging is breast reduction by liposuction alone. This process is attractive in that it leaves minimal scarring and nerve damage. Further, in the appropriate surgical candidate, the nipple-areola complex need not be surgically moved to a higher, proportional level, because the removal of the weight of fat from the breasts naturally causes the nipple-areola complex to rise to a proportional level. The areola will also naturally decrease in size when the breast is reduced in volume and tension on the areola decreases.[8] For these reasons, however, it is usually suggested that this technique be used only for reductions of two or fewer cup sizes.

Surgical Technique

The usual incision is a cut of only about a half inch directly under the inframammary fold underneath the breast, close to the rib cage. Occasionally, an incision is made on the edge of the areola to reach the upper breast tissue. Other small incisions can also be made elsewhere on the breast to access fat deposits.[8] A suction tube, called a *cannula*, is inserted through the incision(s) and removes fat tissue from the breast. The same suction machine used in liposuction of other body parts is used in this surgery. This technique can also be improved with the use of ultrasonic equipment, which may permit the surgeon to avoid the mammary lobes. [8]

This technique is occasionally used in conjunction with traditional reduction mammoplasty procedures as a means of removing only fat tissue from the breast, while leaving the maximum amount of parenchyma (lactational tissue) and stroma (supportive infrastructure) intact.

Implications for Lactation

It is possible for the cannula to remove lactation tissue, especially when a sharper instrument is used.[8] If an incision is required in the areola in order to reach the upper breast tissue, damage to the nerves of the areola is also possible. Therefore, it cannot be assumed that this surgery is guaranteed to preserve the patient's complete lactational capability. However, when lactation is known to be a priority so that a blunt cannula is

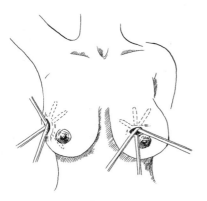

Incisions for liposuction

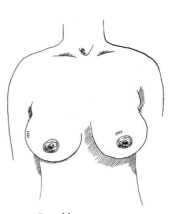

Possible scar patterns

used and no incision is made near the areola, full lactation capability is far more probable with this reduction mammoplasty surgery than with any other. It should be noted, though, that the use of this surgical technique seems to be somewhat rare.

This surgical technique may be ideal for women who have had previous reduction mammoplasty by other techniques, but who have experienced repeated breast growth and wish to again reduce breast volume, while minimizing the risk of further vascular or nerve damage to the nipple and areola.[8]

Anchor-Shaped Scar Breast Reduction— Inferior Pedicle Technique

The Inferior Pedicle surgical technique, often called the McKissock technique, is the most popular reduction mammoplasty technique performed in North America today. It is a highly versatile technique, being well suited for most types of breasts. A hallmark of this surgery is that the reduction is accomplished without compromising the nerve or blood supply to the nipple-areolar complex, which, although moved, remain attached to a portion of tissue (pedicle) containing the nerves, blood supply, and ductal tissue. The majority of tissue removed is from the perimeter of the breast, which ensures that the greatest proportion of lactation tissue remains.

Surgical Technique

The skin around the outside circumference of the areola that is not desired is removed, along with other breast skin inside the incision lines. The new area for the nipple and areola (above the previous location) is prepared by removing all skin layers inside the incision lines.

The areola-nipple complex is then separated from the underlying adipose (fatty) tissue and lifted into the new location, remaining attached to a mound (pedicle) of tissue containing the blood and nerve supplies, as well as lactiferous ducts, that extend down to the level of the new intermammary fold.

For the Inferior Pedicle Technique tissue is removed from the shaded area and the nipple is moved upward into its new position.

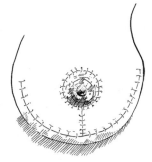

The wedges of tissue inside the lower incision lines on either side of the lower portion of the nipple-areola pedicle are then cut away and removed. The incision edges are brought together and sutured, as is the nipple-areola complex, where it resides in its new position. Finally, the bottom of the flaps are sutured to the skin at the chest wall, creating the new intermammary fold.

Implications for Lactation

Anchor-shaped scar pattern resulting from Inferior Pedicle Technique.

The Inferior Pedicle technique is renowned for being among the kindest reduction mammoplasty techniques for preservation of lactation tissue. It accomplishes this goal by removing tissue on the outermost parts of the breast, which allow more of the ducts and lobes to remain, while at the same time leaving the critical nipple-areola complex attached to the nerve, blood, and ductal supplies. Almost inevitably, some of the lobes and ducts will be cut; however, this surgery respects the lactiferous infrastructure and therefore preserves the ability of the breast to produce milk, often to a significant degree.

Periareolar Breast Reduction—"The Round Block"

"The Round Block" surgical technique was first introduced in Europe in 1983. It is the reduction technique with the least amount of visible scarring. The only incision is made around the areola. The outer portions of the areola are frequently removed, however, to provide an areola that is more symmetrical and proportional to the new breast size. Because the areola is not moved in order to preserve a natural appearance, this technique is only appropriate for women with slight to moderate breast enlargement.[8] From an aesthetic perspective, this surgical technique results in only a barely noticeable scar, but a breast shape that may not be ideal.

Surgical Technique

An incision is made around the areola and any undesired portion of the areola is cut away. The skin that surrounded the areola is retracted while the areola remains attached to the breast and is not moved. The breast tissue is removed in a similar

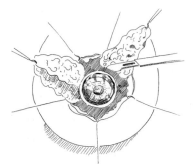

Incisions and removal of breast tissue using the "Round Block" Technique.

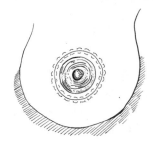

"Round Block" scar pattern.

fashion to the inverted T technique that characterizes the inferior pedicle technique, with the exception that the breast skin is not cut. The breast sections are removed in sections through the areolar opening. The decision as to what breast tissue is removed is determined by the future desired shape of the breast, rather than by differentiation of glandular tissue from fatty tissue.[8]

An important facet to this surgery is the use of a special suturing technique wherein the areola is reattached with stitches that begin and end at the top of the areola in a sort of "purse string," as the surgeons describe it. This special suture does not produce tension on the areolar scar, preventing enlargement of the future areola or areola scar, as well as flattening of the areolar mound.[8]

Implications for Lactation
This is the only surgical technique in which the areola remains attached and unmoved, although the circumference may be reduced by removing the outer portion. Because the areola is not moved, the possibility of nerve and blood supply damage is greatly reduced. However, reducing the size of the areola may still impact the critical fourth intercostal nerve. Also, because significant wedges of tissue are removed from the breast without regard to avoiding the glands and ducts (which admittedly are difficult to identify in the non-lactating woman), and because the ideal candidate for this surgery is the woman who only has moderately large breasts, which contain less fat than larger breasts, a significant amount of the lactiferous lobes may be removed or damaged.

The ability to lactate to some degree is most certainly preserved with this surgical technique.[8] However, because of the possibility of damage to the fourth intercostal nerve, as well as the removal of significant amounts of lactation tissue, it must be expected that this surgery would not yield a full milk supply for the first episode of lactation. Over time, recanilization and reneurotization may compensate for any deficits, yielding a more copious milk supply for subsequent children.

Central Mound Breast Reduction Technique
The Central Mound technique was developed to correct the "bottoming out," flat breast profile that is a problem commonly found with breasts altered by the inferior pedicle technique. Like the Inferior Pedicle technique, it preserves the nipple-areola blood, nerve, and ductal connections. It differs significantly, however, in that it greatly disrupts regions of the breast where the lobes and ducts are most likely to be seated. Because there are several variations to this technique, the degree of disruption of the lactation tissue varies.

Surgical Technique
Incisions are made in outline of the new parameters of the breast, cutting around the circumference of the areola, removing portions of the areola that are not desired. The skin inside of the incision lines is removed. The skin covering the breast is separated from the breast tissue, which is then lifted by traction off the chest wall. Tissue is then shaped and resected until the desired shape is achieved. The skin flaps are replaced and temporarily sutured at the vertical line beneath the areola, which is temporarily under

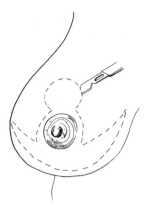

*Incisions for Central Mound Technique
marked by dotted line*

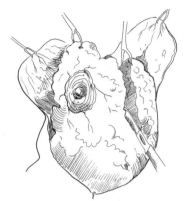

*The skin is separated from the breast and
pulled away as breast tissue is removed
and reshaped.*

the skin. The folded flaps that result are cut away so that the new intermammary fold appears. The sutures are then cut and the new area for the nipple-areola complex is prepared. When the nipple-areola complex has been properly positioned, it is sutured in place. The vertical incision lines are then permanently sutured, as is the intermammary fold.

Implications for Lactation

This technique is kind to the nipple and areola, but completely disrespectful of the delicate arrangement of the lactational infrastructure. The shaping and resecting of the interior breast tissue are potentially quite destructive to the lobes and ducts. Fortunately, the odds are that at least some will survive intact and, for those that do, the nipple-areola will be in a very excellent condition to receive them. Therefore, it seems that while lactation tissue is greatly disrupted by this technique, it may nonetheless have a good lactational outcome.'

Periareolar Breast Reduction with Mesh Support— The "Double Skin" Technique

The "Double Skin" technique was first introduced and popularized in Brazil in the 1980s. The addition of a mesh component was added in 1990 to improve the shape of the reduced breast, which is a problem with the Round Block technique. It is also the objective of the Double Skin technique to reduce the possibility of future sagging. Like the Round Block surgery, this technique involves an incision only around the areola, but may include reduction of the areolar circumference.[8]

Surgical Technique

The basic method of this technique is similar to that of the Round Block technique wherein the removal of breast tissue occurs only through the incision around the areola. The greatest portion of the tissue that is removed is taken from the top of the breast. A wedge from the bottom is taken only occasionally. The skin is separated from

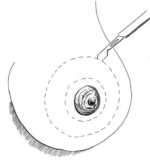

Incisions for the "Double Skin" technique marked by dotted lines

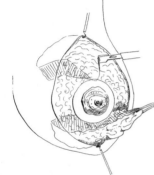

During the "Double Skin" technique he greatest portion of tissue is taken from the upper part of the breast. Occasionally a wedge of tissue is also taken from the bottom, as shown here.

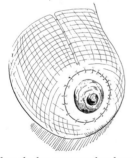

When the breast tissue has been removed, the skin is separated from the breast and mesh is applied between the breast tissue and the skin to shape the breast. The resulting scar pattern from the "Double Skin" technique is also shown here.

the breast tissue and mesh is applied beneath the skin to the entire outer area of the breast in order to provide lasting structure and optimal form. [8]

Implications for Lactation

One interesting facet of this method is that a much larger wedge of breast tissue is removed from the top of the breast than from the lower portion. This is positive for lactation because a somewhat greater proportion of glandular tissue is located in the lower portion of the breast than in the upper. Still, as with the Round Block technique, the incisions around the areola, including reduction of the areola circumference, increase the likelihood that the critical fourth intercostal nerve will be damaged, even though the areola is not moved. Also, the likelihood of removal of glandular tissue is increased because this surgery is only appropriate for women who have moderately large breasts, which contain less fat than larger breasts. Therefore, less fat is available to remove, making removal of lactation tissue more likely.

It can be expected that lactation will be impacted somewhat, however, it is possible that only minimal supplementation may be necessary. The impact of recanilization and reneurotization may further eliminate the need for supplementation for subsequent children.

Vertical Scar Breast Reduction (Superior Pedicle Technique) with and without Undermining

The Vertical Scar (superior-based pedicle) surgical technique was first performed in the early 1960s by Drs. Lassus and Lejour in France. The primary goal of this surgery is minimizing vascular damage to the areola-nipple complex so as to reduce the risk of infection and nipple loss. This surgical technique also seeks to minimize visible scarring by allowing only a scar around the areola, in addition to a vertical scar from the bottom of the areola to the intermammary fold. There is no horizontal scar along the intermammary fold. The nipple and areola are moved, to a new, higher position, but not severed.

In the "Without Undermining" version of the technique, the only tissue that is removed is from the area between the two edges of the incision. This technique prevents the gaps in breast tissue (dead space) that can

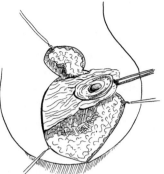

*Vertcal Scar Superior Pedicle technique
surgical process.*

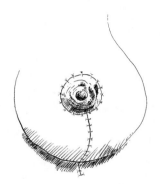

*Verticle scar pattern resulting from the
Vertcal Scar Superior Pedicle technique.*

occur when breast tissue is removed from skin or muscle. Such gaps can lead to postoperative hematomas (swelling by pooling of blood), which can damage breast tissue.[8] There is almost no risk of tissue necrosis (death).

In the "With Undermining" version of the technique, breast tissue is separated and removed from under skin.[8]

Surgical Technique

A football-shaped incision, with a rounded top to create the space for the new nipple-areola position, is made from the base of the breast to the new nipple-areola position. This surgery is a superior-based pedicle technique because the nipple-areola complex remains attached to the breast by a flap of breast tissue above the areola as it is moved into the new position. The size of the areola is reduced to a proportional circumference by cutting away the outer portion of the areola. The nipple-areolar connection to the fourth intercostal nerve is preserved. When the nipple-areola is relocated, a wedge of breast tissue between the open edges of the incision is removed in the "Without Undermining" technique,[8] and tissue is removed beyond the edges of the incision in the "With Undermining" technique.[8] The edges of the incision are then brought together and sutured. Once the initial suturing has been performed, the resulting breast shape is evaluated. If it is not in the desired form, the sutures are then separated and remedial excisions of tissue is performed. This process is repeated until the desired shape is achieved.

Implications for Lactation

Although this technique does not sever the nipple-areola complex from the breast and does not impact the blood supply to the breast, it does greatly impact the nerves and ducts connected to the areola and nipple, and indiscriminately removes a significant amount of breast tissue in the area most likely to contain lactational tissue. It is amazing that lactation is at all possible with this technique, although it has been known to occur to a limited degree. Nonetheless, if lactation does occur, a high proportion of supplementation will almost invariably be necessary for women who have received this technique.

Vertical and Short Horizontal Scar (Superior Pedicle) Breast Reduction

The Vertical and Short Horizontal Scar reduction procedure was first performed in 1977 in France and is characterized by a scar around the perimeter of the areola, in addition to a vertical scar radiating from the base of the areola to a space above intermammary fold, where it connects to a short horizontal scar. The technique is performed in a similar manner to the Vertical Scar technique, however, with the allowance of a short horizontal scar, this technique yields an attractive result without the necessity for repeated suturing.

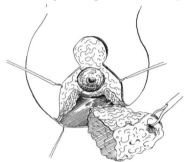

Verticle and Short Horizontal Scar Superior Pedicle technique surgical process.

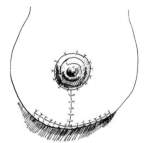

Verticle and Short Horizontal scar pattern resulting from Superior Pedicle technique.

Implications for Lactation

Because this technique yields a similar result to the Vertical Scar superior-pedicle technique, the lactation prognosis is the same. A great deal of critical lactational tissue is removed, which necessarily results in loss of lactational tissue. Nonetheless, some lactation is certainly possible.

Free Nipple Graft Breast Reduction

The Free Nipple Graft reduction mammoplasty technique is an appropriate surgery only for women who are not likely to bear children and who do not value nipple sensation. This technique is accomplished by complete removal of the nipple from the breast, followed by grafting it to a new location on the breast. As a result, extensive damage is done to the lactation tissue.

Surgical Technique

The Free Nipple Graft technique is begun by determining the new location of the areola-nipple complex using numerical and subjective estimates. The areola and nipple are excised, removed from the breast, and placed in a moist saline sponge. The new location for the areola-nipple complex is prepared by removing the skin. Incisions are made vertically from this point to the site of the new intermammary fold. A horizontal incision is made along the line of the new intermammary fold. Skin and tissue inside of the vertical and horizontal incision lines is removed. The nipple-areola complex is grafted onto the new site and sutured in place. The remaining incisions are sutured.

The scars are identical to the superior and inferior pedicle techniques.[8]

Implications for Lactation

This surgical technique yields the least lactation potential because the nerves and ducts of the nipple and areola complex are severed. Although recanalization and reinnervation are certainly possible, even moderate lactation is not likely. It is also likely that significant damage was done to the interior lobes of the mammary system, so that even if recanalization and reinnervation occur to any degree, the available lactation tissue will still be largely insufficient.

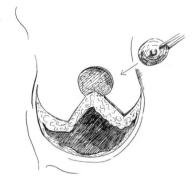

Free Nipple Graft Surgical process.

Conclusion

Although it is not easy to read a technically oriented chapter such as this one, taking the time to become thoroughly familiar with lactation anatomy and physiology, as well as understanding your surgical technique in order to form reasonable lactation expectations, is one of the most important and empowering steps you can take toward becoming prepared for your BFAR experience. An understanding of lactation is a solid foundation upon which to build a successful and fulfilling BFAR experience.

In the next chapter, the benefits of breastfeeding and human milk are explored to provide a rich understanding of the reasons that BFAR is well worth your efforts.

How much did you have removed?

In your surgical report, you will see that a certain volume of breast tissue was removed from each breast during your surgery. These figures are often recorded in metric numbers. The chart below will help you convert those numbers into more meaningful figures.

Grams	Pounds	Grams	Pounds
100	0.22	2200	4.84
200	0.44	2270	5
300	0.66	2400	5.28
400	0.88	2600	5.73
454	1	2724	6
500	1.10	2800	6.17
600	1.32	3000	6.61
700	1.54	3178	7
800	1.76	3200	7.05
900	1.98	3400	7.49
908	2	3600	7.93
1000	2.20	3632	8
1200	2.64	3800	8.37
1362	3	4000	8.81
1400	3.08	4086	9
1600	3.52	4200	9.25
1800	3.96	4400	9.69
1816	4	4540	10
2000	4.40		

Courtesy Carol Maranta

REFERENCES:

1. Riordan, J. and K. Auerbach. *Breastfeeding and Human Lactation*, 2nd edition. Sudbury, MA: Jones and Bartlett Publishers, 1999; 94, 128, 124, 101, 88.

2. Brown, M., M. Weinberg, N. Chong, et al. A cohort study of breast cancer risk in breast reduction patients. *Plast Reconstr Surg* May 1999; 103(6): 1674-81.

3. Daly, S., J. Kent, D. Huynh, et al. The Determination of Short-Term Breast Volume Changes and the Rate of Synthesis of Human Milk Using Computerized Breast Measurement. *Experimental Physiology* 1992; 77(1): 79-87.

4. Daly, S. and P. Hartmann. Infant Demand and Milk Supply. Part 1: Infant Demand and Milk Production in Lactating Women. *Journal of Human Lactation* 1995; 11(1): 21- 26, 27-37.

5. Cox, D., R. Owens, P. Hartmann. Blood and milk prolactin and the rate of milk synthesis in women. *Experimental Physiology* 1996; 81:1007-1020.

6. Lawrence, R. and R. Lawrence. Breastfeeding: A Guide for the Medical Profession, 5th edition. St. Louis, Missouri: Mosby, 1999, 255, 268.

7. Mohrbacher, N. and J. Stock THE BREASTFEEDING ANSWER BOOK, Schaumburg, IL: LLLI, 1997; 32.

8. Spear, S., ed. Surgeries of the Breast: Principles and Art. Philadelphia, PA: Lippincott-Raven, 1998; 709, 712, 685, 687, 686, 697, 699, 717, 738, 813.

VICKI'S STORY

I wasn't planning on breastfeeding for more than a day or so after the birth of our daughter. I figured I would see how things went and just play it by ear. Looking back, I'm surprised that I've lasted so long, given my half-hearted commitment. Makenna latched on like a champ, but was a bit sleepy, and I had trouble getting her to suck for more than a few minutes without falling asleep. By the end of the first day she hadn't urinated, and the nurse on duty said she needed a bottle of formula. I was relieved, actually, because, as a pediatric nurse, I was worried about her becoming dehydrated and needing IV fluids. Nipple confusion was the last thing on my mind. Within the hour she soaked her diaper, and we were discharged to go home.

I was so impressed with how well she latched on that I decided I would keep trying to nurse for a while. I worried a lot the first couple of days. At her two-day checkup, Makenna had dropped 10 percent of her birth weight, but I still wanted to try nursing her and the lactation consultant (LC) was very encouraging. I told the LC that I was trying to nurse Makenna at least 15 minutes on each side, every session. I had to wake her for feedings, though, every three hours at the LC's recommendation, because of her newborn sleepiness. In retrospect, this wasn't enough. I gave her a supplemental bottle three times a day—about half an ounce of formula each time. I didn't know there was such a thing as an SNS. She continued to be sleepy over the next two weeks, and I had trouble keeping her awake for feedings. The use of a supplemental bottle did cause nipple confusion, but I was becoming more determined to stick with breastfeeding and just kept relatching Makenna in the correct way if she tried sucking like she did on a bottle nipple. She really had a high sucking need and liked to nurse for comfort, so maybe this is why she didn't reject me altogether. We just kept trying to nurse.

When my milk came in, I never was engorged, though I did get lumps and tried to work them out, hoping those ducts could be productive. My nipples became sore and cracked, and each session was very painful, but I would repeat to myself that the pain was worth it. I would just latch Makenna on and say her name about ten times in a row really fast until the area became numb (about one minute). I also have a flat nipple on the right side, although I didn't figure this out until about six weeks into nursing. It always puzzled me why my right hurt so much more than the left, to the point where I dreaded using the right side. I eventually discovered that if I "worked" the nipple with my thumb and finger a second or two before Makenna fed, the process went a lot smoother.

I did a lot of early nursing in a wooden rocking chair that we had sanded and finished ourselves. It sat in front of a sliding closet door with a huge mirror in Makenna's bedroom that I used to frequently check Makenna's position and latch-on, body angle, and even my own posture as I wanted to do everything right. I would often gaze in the reflection of the mirror at my tiny, helpless child nibbling contentedly at my breast and making soft cooing noises. It would bring tears to my eyes. I knew this was the most natural and beautiful gift to my baby. It really affirmed my resolve to stick with breastfeeding no matter how difficult it was. I was also starting to realize that a lot of the rules and suggestions helpful for a mother who hadn't had breast reduction surgery didn't work for me and began to experiment with what worked and what didn't. There was very little relevant information that I could find, and I desperately searched for any scrap of information I thought would help.

Toward the end of the second week, I had made up my mind that I wanted to keep nursing. I tried to cut down on the bottles and breastfeed with as little formula as possible. My trial period lasted two days. Makenna's wet and soiled diapers were few. She didn't regain her birth weight by her doctor's appointment, and this, coupled with the lack of bowel movements and sleepiness, necessitated formula. I felt guilty for not giving her 100 percent of the milk she needed and even more guilty for trying to breastfeed without formula supplements. I was trying not to cry in front of the doctor!

I immediately went back to the LC and we determined that I was producing about half of what Makenna needed. I bought a double pump and started pumping between feeding sessions, about six to eight times a day. I diligently nursed Makenna at least 20 minutes (usually longer) on each side, every two-and-a-half to three hours. Then I gave a bottle of formula until she didn't want any more. After that I pumped for 20-25 minutes. This I did around the clock, though less at night. I took brewer's yeast, fenugreek, and whatever other herb remotely promised an increased milk supply. I drank lots of water and tried to eat regular meals. I used warm compresses and massages to aid in the let-down. I tried everything I knew to do.

This was very exhausting and for the next two months, I vacillated between wanting to quit and wanting to continue. Breastfeeding brought my daughter such comfort, and made me feel I was giving her a precious gift no one else could give her. I eventually came to a resolve to stop most of the pumping and just try to nurse. I was pleasantly surprised that Makenna really was nursing quite well, and I didn't dry up like I had imagined I would. She still liked to nurse just for nursing's sake, and I took advantage of this and lay down with her for a lot of feedings. Breastfeeding became so much more enjoyable after this.

Now at nine months we just take things as they happen. I still take an afternoon nap with Makenna nursing before the hustle of the evening sets in. I enjoy what we have and am so glad I stuck it out. I don't think I'll ever fully know why I kept breastfeeding in the light of all the difficulties, knowing the odds were against me. Maybe it was all the prayers for strength to continue to do what I know is best! I just keep looking at my precious daughter every time we sit down to nurse and gaze at her beautiful face relaxed and calm. Then all the problems seem to melt away. I don't have any regrets at all.

WHY BREASTFEEDING IS WORTH THE EFFORT

You have probably read about the superiority of human milk over formula, which is a synthetic substitute. You may also know that beyond the nutritional benefits of breastfeeding, there are tremendous emotional benefits for both you and your child. In fact, you may have read and been told so much about the excellence of human milk that, as a result of your breast reduction surgery, you are beginning to have feelings of anxiety or guilt because of the possibility that you may have to supplement with formula. But the beauty of breastfeeding is that every drop of human milk is precious. Even a small amount of colostrum given to your child after birth will benefit him immensely. And the more you can give, the more he will benefit. No matter how much milk you are actually able to provide, all that you really need to breastfeed is one breast with a nipple because you will be able to supplement as your child nurses from your breast. So even though you may need to supplement your baby's nutritional requirements with formula, you will almost always be able to provide him with some human milk. At the very least, you will be able to feed him at your breast even if you must supplement almost all of his nutrition. No matter what your situation, you can rest assured that if you are willing there is no reason that your baby cannot benefit in some way from the priceless gift of breastfeeding.

In this chapter, we will explore the nutritional and emotional benefits of breastfeeding. As you read this, it is important that you not burden yourself with feelings of anxiety or guilt because of your awareness that you may not have a full milk supply; instead, think of human milk as the precious gift that you will give your child in whatever quantity you are able to, and breastfeeding as the way that you will develop the intimate emotional bond that will enrich you both, regardless of whether your child is fed human milk or formula at your breast.

You may also notice that unlike most breastfeeding texts, this book does not actively compare human milk to formula or breastfeeding to bottle-feeding, although some comparisons are inevitable. This is because many mothers who must supplement as a result of their breast reduction surgery will choose to do so with formula and some mothers will give the supplement with bottles.

When presenting the benefits of human milk and breastfeeding, however, it is unavoidable that some comparisons will be implied and must occasionally be stated specifically. It is impossible not to point out the advantages of human milk and breastfeeding by stating that without it certain benefits are not available or some diseases are more prevalent, which inevitably implies a comparison to formula and bottle-feeding.

The intention of this chapter, though, is simply to make the point that human milk and breastfeeding are optimal for infant development. While formula is not the living, perfect food that human milk is, it is nonetheless a food that provides adequate nutrition for a baby. Today's commercial formulas are superior to those manufactured in previous decades. And many, although not all, of the artificial nipples marketed today are better for facial development than their predecessors.

It is the hope of this book that, in keeping with the "breast is half full" perspective, you will appreciate the ability to supplement with a nutritionally adequate human milk substitute, while at the same time be motivated by the optimal value of human milk and breastfeeding to maximize your child's access to them.

The Wonders of Human Milk

Human milk has been revered in many cultures for its seemingly miraculous properties. Indeed, it never ceases to amaze even the most cynical scientists with the extent of its protective, curative, and nutritive properties for both the nursing baby and his mother. Discoveries about its properties are ongoing, but at this time, it is known to contain over 100 components that are not found in infant formula.[1]

While greater knowledge about human milk has helped scientists improve infant formula, John D. Benson, PhD and Mark L. Masor, PhD wrote in the March 1994 issue of the journal *Endocrine Regulations* that it has become increasingly apparent that infant formula can never duplicate human milk. Human milk contains living cells, hormones, active enzymes, immunoglobulins, and compounds with unique structures that cannot be replicated in infant formula.[2]

Human milk is a perfect, complete food. It contains every nutrient necessary for optimal human health and growth. In fact, the American Academy of Pediatrics has stated that:

> "Human milk is uniquely superior for infant feeding and is species-specific; all substitute feeding options differ markedly from it. The breastfed infant is the reference or normative model against which all alternative feeding methods must be measured with regard to growth, health, development, and all other short and long-term benefits."[3]

As you review the biochemical overview of human milk that follows, it is important to bear in mind that while human milk is remarkably consistent within our human species, it does vary to a small degree from woman to woman, depending on her diet, nutritional status, and any medications she has ingested. Because the process of lactation places it at a higher physiological priority than the mother's own nourishment, the nutrients in her body will go first into her milk. Therefore, while it is almost certain that your milk will deliver the appropriate nutrients, each mother must eat a healthy diet to ensure that her own nutritional needs are met. Don't fear that an occasional meal of less than healthy food will reduce the quality of your milk. The nutritional stores in your body will compensate. In the event of true nutritional deprivation (starvation), the milk supply will substantially diminish in quantity before becoming nutritionally unbalanced.[4-7]

A Uniquely Perfect Food

The nutrients contained in human milk are in proportions precisely appropriate for the developmental stage of the nursing child, changing even from feeding to feeding to adapt to his needs. Human milk is the only substance that is perfectly formulated for the optimal development of the human brain and body. Human milk is more easily and completely digested in the baby's body than formula or milk from other animals. This is because only human milk contains lipase, a particular enzyme required by humans that completes digestion. Since digestion of human milk results in the formation of softer curds than those formed from formula or milk from other animals, it is assimilated into the baby's body much more quickly so that it is available for energy and growth. Of course, for this reason, breastfed babies require more frequent feedings.

Human milk offers the best nutrition to a sick baby. Supplements of an artificial electrolyte solution are unnecessary for the exclusively breastfed baby because human milk is perfectly balanced with electrolytes. The fact that human milk is so quickly broken down and utilized by the baby's digestive system makes it particularly advantageous during bouts of vomiting and diarrhea. Also, should a baby require surgery under general anesthesia, a breastfed child requires shorter periods of fasting before and after surgery.

It is particularly well suited for the premature baby because the milk produced by a mother of a pre-term baby is comprised of nutrient portions that are appropriate to that state of development. In fact, for the first month after a pre-term birth, the human body is so wise that it will slow the maturation of the milk, keeping it closer to the composition of colostrum, which includes higher levels of calories, protein, calcium, phosphorus, nitrogen, long-chain and medium-chain fatty acids, sodium, chloride, magnesium, iron, and antibodies exactly appropriate to the needs of the premature baby.[8] Even if you are not able to provide copious amounts of colostrum or milk for your baby, any colostrum or milk that you can give your baby will be beneficial.

Most importantly, however, human milk contains antibodies to combat the bacteria and viruses that the mother and baby have been exposed to. Even as a baby nurses, the bacteria and viruses in his mouth immediately prompt his mother's breast to produce and deliver antibodies to the contagion. And nursing comforts a sick baby like nothing else can.

The Experts Agree

In 1997, as a result of overwhelming research proving the superiority of human milk and breastfeeding, and as a reflection of the evolution of the philosophy of the pediatric medical establishment, the American Academy of Pediatrics issued a landmark policy statement that unequivocally endorsed breastfeeding:

"Human milk is the preferred feeding for all infants, including premature and sick newborns.... It is recommended that breastfeeding continue for at least the first twelve months, and thereafter for as long as mutually desired." [3]

The World Health Organization and UNICEF have also publicly recommended breastfeeding, stating that:

"Breastfeeding is an unequalled way of providing ideal food for the healthy growth and development of infants; ... it forms a unique biological and emotional basis for the health of both mother and child; ...the anti-infective properties of human milk help to protect infants against disease; and ... there is an important relationship between breastfeeding and child spacing." [9]

These prominent associations have issued such frank statements because current research in lactation (both human milk and breastfeeding) has proven beyond a shadow of a doubt that human milk and breastfeeding have no equals. There was a time when some physicians and the public thought that formula was a close substitute for human milk. The overwhelming evidence, however, has demonstrated conclusively that human milk is not only superior to man-made formula, it is, in fact, far superior. It contains living cells and nutrients that can never be duplicated and packaged.

The following section provides an overview of the biochemical makeup of human milk in order to give you some insight into the complex components of this phenomenal substance. The more you know about the amazing properties of human milk, the more you will feel motivated to give it to your child. Knowing that it contains so many unparalleled nutrients and immunological qualities might very well make the difference one night when you are exhausted and wondering if it is really worth all the effort.

Breastfeeding is more than biochemistry and nutrition, however, so following the biochemical description of human milk, you will read about some of the more practical benefits of human milk and breastfeeding. When you finish this chapter, you'll know for certain that there is nothing better you can give your child than all the milk you are capable of producing, even if it is only a few drops, especially when it is given to him at your breast.

The Living Biochemistry of Human Milk

Human milk is understood scientifically to be a living substance. This is because, like blood, it contains living cells that exist to combat bacterial and viral contagions, while at the same time fostering an ideal environment in the infant gut for the proliferation of beneficial bacteria that prevent the growth of harmful intestinal organisms. Human milk conveyed directly by breastfeeding or even left at room temperature for a few hours is unlikely to be contaminated by detrimental bacteria because of these inherent anti-infective properties.[10-12] The living cells in human milk are actually white blood cells that are especially important for bolstering a baby's immune system, which is immature at birth.

Colostrum

The first fluid produced by the breasts after birth is called *colostrum*. It is quite different from mature milk in composition and function. Rather than the opaque and white nature of mature milk, colostrum is almost clear and distinctly yellowish as a result of the vitamin A (*beta-carotene*) it contains. It is produced in very little volume in the first days after birth; only around an average total of 7.9 teaspoons (37 ml), consisting of between 1.5 teaspoons (7 ml) to 3 teaspoons (14 ml) per feeding. [13, 14] It contains very little fat, but higher concentrations of sodium, potassium, chloride, protein, vitamins, and other minerals than mature milk. Electrolyte-balanced, it provides the newborn with all the hydration and nutrition he needs for the first few days of life. The highest value of colostrum, though, is that it contains a wealth of immunological factors, primarily in the form of *immunoglobulins*, especially *secretory immunoglobulin A* (sIgA), that convey anti-infective properties to protect the vulnerable infant from bacteria, viruses, and fungi. It also lines the infant's intestine to protect it from absorbing hostile organisms and harmful proteins into the bloodstream, as well as fostering a hospitable environment for the growth of *lactobacillus bifidus*, a highly beneficial intestinal bacteria.[15]

Colostrum also has a laxative effect, helping the newborn to flush out the black, tarry meconium that has accumulated in his lower intestines before birth. Meconium contains high levels of *bilirubin*, which is the principal pigment of bile and a byproduct of the liver, and is accumulated in high levels immediately after birth because of the rapid synthesis of red blood cells. If bilirubin is not eliminated effectively through stooling, it may harm developing cells, particularly in the brain. Colostrum, and to a lesser degree mature milk, performs the necessary laxative function more effectively than formula or water. Water, even sugar water, given to a newborn will not "flush" bilirubin from his system because water merely results in urination, which eliminates only two percent of bilirubin, compared to ninety-eight percent that is eliminated in the stool. Water supplements can even decrease bowel movements because fewer nutrients exist to push the meconium through the colon.[16]

Transition Milk

Colostrum begins transitioning into the more opaque mature milk on average between the second to the fifth day after birth. For up to two weeks, it may appear yellowish from diminishing quantities of vitamin A (beta-carotene) as the transition is completed. During this time, it is commonly called *transition milk*.

Mature Milk

White Blood Cells

When the transformation is complete, the milk is then known as *mature milk*. With the vast quantities of substances in human milk that are described below, one might be

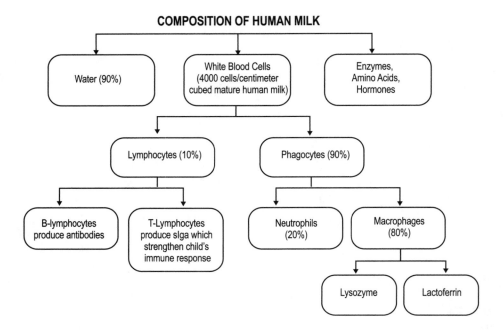

COMPOSITION OF HUMAN MILK

- Water (90%)
- White Blood Cells (4000 cells/centimeter cubed mature human milk)
  - Lymphocytes (10%)
    - B-lymphocytes produce antibodies
    - T-Lymphocytes produce sIga which strengthen child's immune response
  - Phagocytes (90%)
    - Neutrophils (20%)
    - Macrophages (80%)
      - Lysozyme
      - Lactoferrin
- Enzymes, Amino Acids, Hormones

very surprised to discover that milk is actually comprised of over 90 percent water. Nonetheless, it is teeming with living white blood cells, at a density of around 4,000 cells per centimeter cubed of mature human milk.[17] Ninety percent of these white blood cells are called phagocytes. There are two types of phagocytes: *macrophages* and *neutrophils*.

Macrophages comprise eighty percent of the phagocyte cells in human milk and primarily kill bacteria, fungi, and viruses by producing the enzyme *lysozyme*, which destroys alien cells by dissolving their cell walls. Unlike other protective cells in human milk that gradually decline in quantity over the course of lactation, macrophages actually increase, beginning around six months postpartum, which coincides well with the average child's readiness for solid food.[18, 19] In addition to human milk, lysozyme is also found in saliva and tears. It is very soothing to human tissue and reduces inflammation and redness. Human milk contains 300 times more lysozyme per milliliter than cow's milk.

Macrophages also produce *lactoferrin*, which is a powerful protein that binds to iron, preventing harmful organisms such as *Staphylococci*, *E. coli*, and *Candida Albicans* (the yeast that most commonly causes thrush) from having access to iron, the primary mineral they require to subsist. Because of the unique proportions of vitamin C, lactose, calcium, phosphorus, and protein contained in human milk, the iron in human milk is readily absorbed at the rate of fifty percent. The iron in commercial infant formula, on the other hand, is poorly absorbed at the rate of ten percent, and the iron in infant cereal is very poorly absorbed at four percent. Since iron in infant formula and infant cereal is not well absorbed, the manufacturers simply add more to ensure that adequate amounts will be absorbed. Unfortunately, an influx of iron from formula, cereal, or even iron supplements into the baby's system will overwhelm the lactoferrin so that it can no longer bind to all the iron, which then becomes available to feed the bacteria.

The remaining twenty percent of phagocyte cells, the neutrophils, act upon invading pathogens by overwhelming and consuming them.

The final ten percent of the white blood cells in human milk are called *lymphocytes*. There are two types of lymphocytes: *B-lymphocytes* and *T-lymphocytes*. B-lymphocytes facilitate the production of antibodies that target specific microbes to which it has been exposed. T-lymphocytes destroy infected cells directly or excrete chemical directions to initiate other systemic defenses, such as secretory IgA, to strengthen the child's immune response.

Secretory immunoglobulin A (sIgA), a product of T-lymphocytes found in greatest quantities in colostrum, but also significantly present in mature milk, acts as a physical barrier in the infant's mucus membranes of the throat, lungs, and intestines, where harmful bacteria, viruses, fungi, and proteins attempt to enter the infant's bloodstream. Conveyed to the infant in human milk, sIgA also stimulates the baby's own immune system to produce sIgA, the benefits of which far outlast digestion of the milk. One particular benefit to some BFAR mothers is that levels of sIgA are higher in human milk that is extracted less frequently from the breast.[20]

Additional Bacterial Deterrents

Other non-antibody factors in human milk that inhibit the viability of infectious bacteria are the *bifidus factor*, the enzyme *lactoperoxidase*, and the carbohydrate *oligosaccharides*. The bifidus factor promotes a low stool pH acidity of between five to six, creating an inhospitable environment for harmful bacteria such as *Salmonella* and *E. coli*, which prefer a less acid environment. Cow's milk contains virtually no bifidus factor. Lactoperoxidase is an enzyme that, in conjunction with sIgA, is particularly effective in killing *streptococci*. Oligosaccharides are carbohydrates that deter harmful bacteria such as *Pneumococcus* (which causes pneumonia) and *E. coli* by aiding the bifidus factor and preventing microbial adhesion to intestinal tissues. Oligosaccharides are ten times more prevalent in human milk than in cow's milk.[17]

Enzymes

The enzymes most critical to human digestion are *lysozyme,* which was discussed earlier in conjunction with macrophages, *lipase, amylase*, and *biotinidase*. Lipase is an enzyme found only in human milk and the milk of mountain gorillas[17] that, when combined with bile salt, serves to aid in the digestion of fat, which is critical to brain and body growth. The mechanism enabled by lipase for efficiently digesting fat is one of the reasons that the breastfed baby's stool is relatively inoffensive. Lipase has also been shown to rapidly kill protozoa such as *Giardia lamblia.* [21] Amylase, an enzyme present in human milk that is necessary for the digestion of starch, is not found in the milk of cows, goats, or pigs.[17] Because of this enzyme, breastfed babies are able to digest starches far more efficiently, resulting in less intestinal irritation. The role of biotinidase, which is found in high levels in colostrum and lower levels in mature milk, is not fully understood, however it is thought to aid in the digestion of biotin, a vitamin present in human milk, the absence or malabsorption of which is known to cause dermatitis. It may be this enzyme, in combination with essential fatty acids, that is responsible for the phenomenon of the breastfed baby's uniquely silky skin.

Amino Acids

Lactation researchers have discovered the presence of *polypeptides* (combinations of amino acids) in human milk that are not well understood, but seem to play a role in promoting human tissue growth. Known as *growth modulators*, the most readily identified of these polypeptides are the *epidermal growth factor* (EGF)[22] and *human growth factors I, II, and III.*[23] EGF stimulates the production of *mucosa* and *epithelium*, the cellular tissue that lines the interior surfaces of the body. Mucosa and epithelium serve to prevent the inappropriate internal transfer of microorganisms. While we do not yet have a good understanding of the role of human growth factor I and II in human milk, we do know that human growth factor III is known to stimulate DNA synthesis and cell growth, possibly also on the epidermal level.[17]

Another amino acid present in human milk is *taurine*, the role of which has only recently been made clear. Taurine is naturally present only in human milk and serves the critical role of a neurotransmitter, stimulating human brain cellular growth and interlacement, as well as development of the retina.[17, 24]

Hormones

Human milk contains hormones—*insulinlike growth factor, thyroxine, cortisol, cholecystokinin* (CCK), and *prostaglandins*. Believed to promote cell growth, insulinlike growth factor is found in high concentrations in colostrum and in moderate levels in mature milk.[25] Thyroxine is not well understood, but is thought to play a role in intestinal maturation.[26] The purpose of cortisol remains to be established, but seems to be related to maternal stress levels.[20] CCK is a hormone present in the gastrointestinal system that aids in digestion, simultaneously conveying a sensation of satiation, drowsiness, and well-being.[17] Finally, prostaglandins are a type of lipid (fatty acid) that play myriad roles in human physiology. Its presence in human milk is thought to convey anti-inflammatory properties.[27]

The Nutrition of Human Milk

Human milk is well established scientifically as the perfect food for human babies. As such, it has become possible to determine exactly which nutrients human babies require for optimal growth by identifying the nutritional properties of human milk. The resulting analysis demonstrates that the following fats, lactose, proteins, vitamins, micronutrients, and minerals are present in human milk and thereby exclusively appropriate to infant maturation.

Fats

Fat is a primary source of energy in human milk, conveying one half of available calories. Human milk contains two types of beneficial fats: *triglycerides* and *lipids*. Triglycerides make up the greatest proportion of fat contained in human milk. Although present in far lesser quantities, lipids are essential fatty acids that are critical for brain growth. *Docosahexanoic acid* (DHA) and *arachidonic acid* (AA) are long-chain polyunsaturated fatty acids derived from linoleic and linolenic acid that are abundantly present in human milk, and until only recently were distinctly lacking in infant formula. DHA is essential to retinal development and is necessary for formation of *myelin*, the membrane covering the critical nerve fibers in the brain.[28] The other type of lipids are known as short-chain fatty acids, which combat bacteria, viruses, and fungi.[29, 30]

Carbohydrates

The primary carbohydrate in human milk is *lactose*. It has often been noted that human milk is very sweet. This is true because it contains thirty percent more lactose, a type of sugar, than the milk of any other mammal; far more than cow or goat milk. (Analyses of the milk of many mammals has shown that lactose is present in direct correlation to the brain size of the mammal, with the highest concentrations in human milk.)[31] Apart from providing energy for living, this unique natural sugar serves many functions in the human body, not the least of which is fostering brain growth. This is accomplished in combination with the enzyme *lactase* to produce *galactose* and *glucose*, which are critical to human brain growth. Lactose is also beneficial to calcium absorption, promoting bone growth. Additionally, lactose promotes the growth of the beneficial intestinal bacteria *lactobacillus bifidus*.

Nucleotides

Nucleotides, including *deoxyribonucleic acid* (DNA) and *ribonucleic acid* (RNA), serve many critical functions in the human body, such as supplying chemical energy, combining with other phosphate groups to form enzymes, and signaling between and within cells. DNA and RNA are made from five different nucleotides: *guanine*, *adenine*, *cytosine*, *thymine*, and *uridine*. Each cell in our bodies contains DNA, which is read in order to secrete or requisition the proteins the cells need. Alveolar cells in the breast read DNA like a recipe to make the proteins present in human milk.

Nucleotides also serve to reinforce the strength of tissue cells in conjunction with the protein *actin*, while prompting the growth of intestinal *villi*, the miniscule projections that attract and absorb nutrients from passing food. Additionally, they are a component of the immune system, facilitating its defense against bacteria, viruses, parasites, and malignancies.[32]

Proteins

Proteins are created from combinations of the 20 amino acids. Human milk is rich in proteins, comprising nine percent of the total volume. Proteins are critical in maintaining and building body tissue, therefore they are very important to infant development. Proteins are differentiated by two types: *casein* (40%) and *whey* (60%). In addition to having nutritional benefits, digestion of casein results in beta-casomorphins, which are short peptides that have behavioral effects, such as lowering response to pain and elevating mood.[33] Casein also prevents attachment of the harmful bacteria *Helicobacter pylori* to intestinal mucosa.[34] Whey is the protein that results in the cottage-cheese type curds found in the typical breastfed baby's stool. It allows efficient processing of nutrients. It also contains critical immunological elements.[17]

Vitamins

The vitamins contained in human milk have a high bioavailability, meaning they are well absorbed into the infant's system, with very little waste. Only whole unprocessed foods (appropriate only for infants over six months old) are able to provide close to this level of high bioavailability. Dietary supplements and infant formula have much lower bioavailability.

The vitamins in human milk include vitamin A (ß -carotene), vitamin B1 (thiamin), vitamin B2 (riboflavin), vitamin B3 (niacin/nicotinamide), vitamin B5 (pantothenic acid), vitamin B6 (pyridoxine), biotin, vitamin B8 (folic acid), vitamin B12 (cobalamin), vitamin C (ascorbic acid), vitamin D (calciferol), vitamin E (tocopherol), and vitamin K (phylloquinone).

Vitamin	Function
Vitamin A (ß–carotene)	Essential for maintaining cell membranes, including skin and eyes, and necessary for the proper formation of bone, proteins, and growth hormone. It also has an immunological function by preventing invasion of pathogenic microorganisms.
Vitamin B1 (thiamin)	Required for metabolism of carbohydrates, fats, and proteins. Thiamin is required by each living cell to form adenosine triphosphate (ATP), which is the actual fuel required by our bodies on a cellular level. Thiamin is also required by nerve cells and heart muscle to function appropriately.
Vitamin B2 (riboflavin)	Also needed by the body to convert carbohydrates into ATP. Additionally, it aids in the metabolization of amino acids and fats, activates vitamin B6 (pyridoxine) and vitamin B8 (folic acid), and can act as an antioxidant, scavenging harmful free radicals from the body.
Vitamin B3 (niacin)	Required by the body to convert carbohydrates into fat, thereby releasing the carbohydrate's energy into a usable form. It aids in digestion, as well as regulating cholesterol, and promoting circulation and skin development.
Vitamin B5 (pantothenic acid)	Metabolizes energy from fats and synthesizes cholesterol for metabolism of vitamin D and hormone synthesis. It is also required for production of the neurotransmitter acetylcholine and proper functioning of the adrenal glands.

Vitamin	Function
Vitamin B6 (pyridoxine)	An essential nutrient in many bodily functions, it is the primary vitamin necessary for processing amino acids, production of digestive acids and protein and fat absorption, balancing of sodium and potassium levels, and red blood cell creation. Because it is a critical component of seratonin, melatonin, and dopamine, as well as many neurotransmitters, it is considered to be very necessary to proper mental function, as well as emotional balance. It is required for the synthesis of RNA and DNA, the absorption of B12, and antibody production. It also inhibits production of homocysteine, a chemical that is damaging to the heart and facilitates arterial cholesterol plaque deposits. Biotin serves the function of an enzyme catalyst for metabolism of carbohydrates, protein, and fats.
Vitamin B8 (folic acid)	Essential for the proper formation of DNA and thereby critical for the appropriate development of human tissue. It is required in energy production, protein metabolism, and critical to red and white blood cell formation.
Vitamin B12 (cobalamin)	A co-enzyme that is necessary for proper enzyme functioning. It also \transports and stores folic acid in cells and is thereby necessary to proper DNA replication. It plays a role in the metabolism of proteins, fats, and carbohydrates, aiding in the absorption of vitamin A and iron.
Vitamin C (ascorbic acid)	A powerful antioxidant that serves to increase absorption of iron, which is necessary to collagen synthesis. It aids in tissue regeneration and is an antihistamine. It is a component in the formation of liver bile and aids the immune system in combating viruses. It also improves nitric oxide function, which serves to dilate and regenerate blood vessels, improving circulation.
Vitamin D (calciferol)	Regulates calcium and phosphorus in the body, increasing its absorption and preventing its loss in urine, and is thereby necessary for formation of bones and teeth. It also plays a significant role in blood cell formation, as well as modulating insulin levels and processing sugars.
Vitamin E (tocopherol)	A powerful antioxidant that protects cell membranes by inhibiting oxidation of lipids and creation of free radicals. It promotes normal blood clotting and tissue repair, and strengthens capillary walls.
Vitamin K (Phylloquinone)	Transports calcium and is thereby critical for bone formation by facilitating creation of the bone tissue protein osteocalcin. It is also essential for production of prothrombin, which clots blood.[35]

Minerals

The minerals found in human milk include calcium, chloride, chromium, copper, fluoride, iodine, iron, magnesium, manganese, phosphorus, potassium, selenium, sodium, and zinc.

Mineral	Function
Calcium	Crucial for the formation of bones and teeth, as well as clotting blood and aiding in muscle contraction. It also serves as a neurotransmitter and binds fats and cholesterol as a component of digestion.
Chloride	Necessary for the creation of hydrochloric acid, which aids in digestion. It also aids in the absorption of vitamin B12.
Chromium	Necessary for maintenance of sugar levels in the blood and aids in digestion of cholesterol, fats, and proteins.
Copper	Necessary for synthesizing iron and the production of ATP, as well as several hormones, collagen, and enzymes.
Fluoride	Present in all living tissue, especially organs, teeth, and bones. It also regulates enzymes.
Iodine	A component of hormones produced by the thyroid, it is critical for cellular metabolism.
Iron	A component of hemoglobin in the blood, it transports oxygen to cells. It is also a component of myoglobin, which stores oxygen in the muscles. It is necessary for the processing of ATP and maintenance of the immune system.
Magnesium	Required for creation of bones, protein, fatty acids, and new cells. It activates B vitamins, aids in clotting blood, aids in insulin production, prevents muscle spasm, and plays a role in the formation of ATP.
Manganese	Crucial for formation of skin, bone, and cartilage, as well as facilitation of some enzymes.
Phosphorus	A highly essential mineral found primarily in the bones and teeth, as well as the DNA of every living cell. It facilitates the functioning of most enzymes and B vitamins and is critical for the metabolism of proteins, fats, and carbohydrates.
Potassium	Regulates systemic water and acidity balance, blood pressure, and neuromuscular function. It is also a component of carbohydrate and protein synthesis.
Selenium	Facilitates the antioxidant enzyme glutathione peroxidase, immunological functioning, and the generation of thyroid hormones.
Sodium	An electrolyte integral to the regulation of the cell fluids, the generation of nerve impulses, the metabolization of proteins and carbohydrates, and regulation of cellular acidity.
Zinc	A critical ingredient of most enzymes needed to regenerate tissues, metabolize protein, replicate cells. It also acts as an anti-oxidant.[35]

Although some minerals appear to be present in higher levels in cow's milk or formula, these minerals are not as bioavailable to the infant and are, in fact, less beneficial than the lesser amounts found in human milk. For instance, calcium is found in lesser quantities in human milk, however, it is present in a form that is highly absorbable by human infants and so is precisely appropriate to the human infant's needs.[28]

Protection Against Disease

As one becomes educated about the immunological and nutritional properties of human milk, it might not be surprising to learn that research has actually established that babies who receive any human milk on a regular basis are healthier than those fed only with human milk substitutes. As a result, babies fed human milk require far fewer medical interventions. [36]

Research has established that the breastfed child is better protected against:
- Urinary tract infections,[36]
- Crohn's disease, [37, 38]
- Diarrheal infections, [39, 43]
- Bacterial meningitis/Haemophilus influenza B (HiB),[44, 46]
- Respiratory infections,[47, 49]
- Childhood cancer, including Hodgkins Disease, [50, 51]
- Ulcerative colitis, [38, 52, 53]
- Necrotizing enterocolitis, [54, 55]
- Eczema, [56, 57]
- Gastrointestinal reflux, [58]
- Inguinal hernia, [59]
- Breast cancer (in later life), [60]
- Juvenile, insulin-dependent (Type I) diabetes, [61, 62]
- Certain childhood lymphomas, [66, 67]
- Multiple sclerosis, [68]
- Asthma, [69]
- Night blindness, [70, 71]
- Allergies, [72, 73]
- Otitis media, [74, 75]
- Adult obesity. [76]

This list is not exhaustive. New findings continue to be published that present new information about the role of human milk and breastfeeding against disease

The Functional Benefits of Breastfeeding

Human milk is indeed an amazing substance. But it only reaches its complete potential when it is fed to a baby at the breast. The benefits of the combination of breastfeeding and human milk are priceless.

As Dr. Jack Newman has written, "Breastfeeding is a life affirming act of love." [77] It is a way of feeding your baby that goes far beyond mere feeding. It is cuddling and touching and connecting. While bottle-feeding can most certainly be performed with love, the intimate contact of the baby suckling from his mother's breast cannot be equaled. It has far-reaching benefits. This is one of the primary reasons that, should supplementation be necessary, it is preferable for the baby to be supplemented at the breast than with a bottle.

Because human milk received directly from the breast is always the perfect temperature, there is no chance of scalding as can happen with improperly heated milk fed from a bottle. An excellent benefit of supplementing at the breast, rather than with a bottle, is that the milk or formula contained in an at-breast supplementer such as the Lact-Aid or Medela SNS need not be heated because the supplement warms as it travels through the tubes that are lying against your body.

There are many specific benefits to the infant when he is fed at the breast, such as the development of greater hand-to-eye coordination, especially when fed from both sides.[78] Breastfeeding also facilitates proper dental, jaw, and facial development. One research study concluded that, "Suckling at the breast is good for a baby's tooth and jaw development. ...As [the babies' jaw] muscles are strenuously exercised in suckling, their constant pulling encourages the growth of well-formed jaws and straight, healthy teeth." [79] Another study found, "Among breastfed infants, the longer the duration of nursing the lower the incidence of malocclusion." [80] As a result of the optimal dental, jaw, and facial development, children who receive no artificial nipples also tend to have better speech development. Children who have been bottle-fed often develop tongue thrust difficulties because they learned to slow the flow of formula from the artificial nipple by pushing their tongues forward against it. Research has shown that this habit can result in speech difficulties, as well as mouth breathing, lip biting, and gum disease.[79]

One very important benefit of breastfeeding is protection against cardiopulmonary (breathing) disturbances, including prolonged airway closure, obstructed respiratory breaths, and oxygen saturation levels below ninety percent that are occasionally experienced by infants who are bottle fed. These breathing difficulties can occur because bottle-feeding involves a less efficient suck/swallow technique than breastfeeding, which results in overly frequent swallowing and decreased breathing efficiency. [81, 82]

Research has shown that breastfeeding fosters better social development. One study found, "The psychomotor and social development of breastfed babies clearly differs from that of bottle-fed ones and leads at the age of twelve months to significant advantages of the psychomotor and social capabilities." [78] Although it is not precisely understood why this is so, it is speculated that the profound intimacy and increased interactions of the breastfeeding couple increase self-esteem, empathy, and social skills.

The cuddling posture of breastfeeding is certainly soothing, but breastfeeding has powers beyond mere comfort. As discussed earlier in the context of nutrition, human milk contains a hormone called *cholecystokinin* (CCK) that induces a feeling of well-being, thereby suppressing the sensation of pain. Of course, the mere act of suckling at the breast conveys a remarkable degree of comfort for the infant or child. Many mothers find that a child who has been upset by a minor injury can be instantly soothed by drawing the child to the breast to nurse. CCK also helps calm and sedate overtired or overstimulated babies. Mothers through the ages have been amazed at the transformation in mood of a baby after only a few minutes at the breast. Countless tantrums have been averted in just this way.

The Maternal Benefits of Breastfeeding

Even as beneficial as human milk and breastfeeding are for the child who receives them, breastfeeding is also advantageous for the nursing mother.

Uterine Protection

The first benefit the nursing mother experiences when she is able to nurse immediately after the birth of the baby is the release of the hormone oxytocin into her system, which stimulates uterine contractions, preventing hemorrhage and greatly reducing bleeding, while returning the uterus more quickly to the non-pregnant state.[79] Women who do not breastfeed forgo this benefit; they often must be given shots of oxytocin to prevent hemorrhage. Further, their uteruses never shrink back to the pre-pregnant state, but instead remain slightly enlarged. [82]

Mood Enhancement

When the mother nurses, another hormone, prolactin, is released. Prolactin has an auxiliary benefit of fostering positive maternal feelings toward the nursing child, promoting bonding and mutual satisfaction. It is also wonderfully relaxing for the mother and can often soothe away many of her feelings of stress and being overwhelmed. When a nursing mother and her baby have been separated for a period of time, nursing offers them the chance to refocus on each other and reconnect on a very basic level.

Decreased Cancer Risk

Breastfeeding decreases the nursing mother's risk of developing ovarian cancer.[83, 84] It has also been shown to stabilize the progression of maternal endometriosis and reduce her chances of developing endometrial cancer.[85] Additionally, breastfeeding decreases a mother's risk of breast cancer. One study by Newcomb et al. concluded:

> *"If all women who do not breastfeed or who breastfeed for less than three months were to do so for four to twelve months, breast cancer among parous pre-menopausal women could be reduced by eleven percent (11%), judging from current rates. If all women with children lactated for twenty-four months or longer, however, then the incidence might be reduced by nearly twenty-five percent (25%). This reduction would be even greater among women who first lactate at an early age."* [86]

Increases Insulin Production

Diabetic nursing mothers require lower insulin doses than mothers who formula-feed.[87] This may be because breastfeeding has a hormonal ability to relax a mother, increase her feelings of health, well-being, and normalcy, and reduce her stress, all of which have a positive influence upon diabetes. Breastfeeding during the postpartum period results in a more gradual return to the non-pregnant state, which allows a more stable metabolic transition.[88]

Unless the blood glucose levels are kept under strict control, however, the transition from colostrum to mature milk may be delayed by two to three days for some diabetic mothers, necessitating earlier supplementation than might otherwise have been necessary for BFAR.[88]

BFAR mothers with diabetes are encouraged to read LLLI's pamphlet *The Diabetic Mother and Breastfeeding* for a thorough discussion of breastfeeding with diabetes.

Reduces Osteoporosis

Osteoporosis, which is deterioration of the bones and a concern of many post-menopausal women, is less likely to afflict those women who have breastfed at least one infant. In fact, one study found that women who bottle-feed are four times more likely to develop osteoporosis than women who breastfeed. [89-92]

Facilitates Weight Loss

Losing weight after the baby is born is less of a concern for breastfeeding mothers because breastfeeding requires an average of 500 extra calories per day.[93] Studies have shown dramatic differences between mothers who breastfeed and mothers who bottle-feed at one month postpartum. Nursing mothers lost significantly more weight.[94] Of course, if you are supplementing a significant portion of the baby's nutrition, you will not require as many calories to produce the milk you are making, so your weight loss will not be quite as dramatic.

Affects Fertility

In general, breastfeeding confers natural contraception when a mother is exclusively breastfeeding by preventing ovulation and the return of her period. This is especially true when the baby regularly nurses at night. [95-97] A mother who does not fully lactate, even if she supplements at the breast rather than using bottles, may not enjoy this benefit, however. In addition to possible contraceptive benefits, the suspension of periods also protects mothers against anemia by not depleting maternal iron stores by menstruation.

For more information on breastfeeding's effects on fertility, see LLLI's THE WOMANLY ART OF BREASTFEEDING or *Breastfeeding and Natural Child Spacing* by Sheila Kippley. Understanding how this process works will help you evaluate how your fertility may be affected.

Fights Infections

The antiviral, antibiotic, and anti-inflammatory properties of human milk render it an excellent fluid for treating conjunctivitis (eye infections), flushing wounds, and treating cracked nipples.[98] Many nursing mothers find that this readily available fluid is at least as effective as topical antibiotic solutions and ointments.

More and Better Sleep

Breastfeeding at night often results in more and better sleep for both the mother and the father. This may be even more true if the baby sleeps with them. Many BFAR mothers who must supplement find they do not need to do so at night and are able to simply nurse the baby when the baby wakes and quickly return to sleep. Burping, especially at night, is rarely necessary for breastfed babies.

Because prolactin levels in the blood are highest when the mother is sleeping, allowing the baby to nurse frequently at night will raise the average baseline prolactin level which can affect the maximum amount of milk you will be able to produce. For this reason, many mothers have found that co-sleeping with the baby is a convenient, restful way to increase their milk supplies. Of course, it is also this principle that makes it detrimental to the mother's milk supply to forgo nighttime nursings. It may be tempting to have another caregiver give the baby a bottle so that you can get more sleep, but you should consider that skipping nighttime feedings will have a negative impact upon your baseline prolactin levels, and hence your milk supply.

Fewer Sick Days

Most mothers of breastfed babies who work outside the home find that they must spend fewer days away from work to care for sick children than do their colleagues whose children were bottle fed. The tremendous health benefits and protective qualities of human milk virtually guarantees that a breastfed child is a great deal less prone to developing illness and helps him to more quickly overcome any illness he does contract.

Sweet Smelling

Finally, although it is subjective, many mothers will say that one of the nicest benefits of feeding human milk to your child is the smell of the top of his head or the back of his neck. It is sweeter than a bouquet of flowers and more appealing than the smell of baking bread. This uniquely wonderful smell is often present even when a large portion of his nutrition is supplemented with formula.

A Mother's Pride

The most profound benefit of breastfeeding, though, is that incredible feeling we each ultimately feel when we realize that the health and vitality of this darling child is a direct result of what our own body has given to him.

REFERENCES:

1. Williams, R. and I. Stehlin. Breast milk or formula: Making the right choice for your baby. *FDA Consumer* 1998.

2. Benson, J. and M. Masor. Infant formula development: past, present and future. *Endocr Regul* Mar 1994; 28(1): 9-16.

3. American Academy of Pediatrics. Breastfeeding and the use of human milk (RE9729). *Pediatr* 1997; 100(6):1035-1039.

4. Brown, K., et al. Lactational capacity of marginally nourished mothers: relationships between maternal nutritional status and quantity and proximate composition of milk. *Pediatr* 1986; 78:909-19.

5. Forman, M. et al. Undernutrition among Bedouin Arab infants: The bedouin infant feeding study. *Am J Clin Nutr* 1990; 51:339-43.

6. Neville, M. and J. Oliva-Rasbach. Is maternal milk production limiting for infant growth during the first year of life in breast-fed infants? In: Goldman, A., S. Atkinson, L. Hanson, eds. *Human Lactation 3: The Effects of Human Milk on the Recipient Infant*. New York: Plenum, 1987; 123-33.

7. Van Steenbergen, W., et al. Energy supplementation in the last trimester of pregnancy in East Java, Indonesia: effect on breast-milk output. *Am J Clin Nutr* 1989; 50:274-79.

8. Hamosh, M. Breast-feeding: Unraveling the mysteries of mother's milk. *Medscape Women's Health* 1996; 1(9).

9. World Health Organization, United Nations Children's Fund. *International Code of Marketing of Breastmilk Substitutes*. 1981.

10. Pardou, A. et al. Human milk banking: Influence of storage processes and of bacterial contamination on some milk constituents. *Biol Neonate* 1994; 65:302-09.

11. Barger, J. and P. Bull. A comparison of the bacterial composition of breast milk stored at room temperature and stored in the refrigerator. *Int J Childbirth Ed* 1987; 2:29-30.

12. Sosa, R. and L. Barness. Bacterial growth in refrigerated human milk. *Am J Dis Child* 1987; 141:111-12.

13. Hartmann, P. Lactation and reproduction in Western Australian women. *J Reprod Med* 1987; 32: 543-47.

14. Hartmann, P. and C. Prosser. Physiological basis of longitudinal changes in human milk yield and composition. *Fed Proc* 1984; 43:2448-53.

15. Houston, M., P. Howie, A. McNeilly. Factors affecting the duration of breast feeding: 1. Measurement of breast milk intake in the first week of life. *Early Hum Dev* 1983; 8:49-54.

16. Nicoll, A., R. Ginsburg, J. Tripp. Supplementary feeding and jaundiced newborns. *Acta Paediatr Scand* 1982; 71:759.

17. Riordan, J. and K. Auerbach. *Breastfeeding and Human Lactation*, 2nd edition. Sudbury, MA: Jones and Bartlett Publishers, 1999; 140, 141, 145, 146, 147, 129, 133.

18. Goldman, A. et al. Immunologic factors in human milk during the first year of lactation. *J Pediatr* 1982; 100:563-67.

19. Prentice, A. et al. Breast-milk antimicrobial factors of rural Gambian mothers. *Acta Paediatr Scand* 1984; 73:796-812.

20. Groer, M., S. Humenick, P. Hill. Characterizations and psychoneuroimmunolgic implications of secretory immunoglobulin A and cortisol in preterm and term breast milk. *J Perinat Neon N* 1994; 7:42-51.

21. Blackberg, L. et al. The bile salt stimulated lipase in human milk is an evolutionary newcoming derived from a non-milk protein. FEBS Lett 1980; 112:51.

22. Carpenter, G. Epidermal growth factor is a major growth-promoting agent in human milk. *Science* 1980; 210:198-99.

23. Shing Y. and M. Klagsburn. Human and bovine milk contain different sets of growth factors. *Endocr* 1984; 115:273.

24. THE WOMANLY ART OF BREASTFEEDING, 6th edition. Schaumburg, IL: LLLI, 1997; 338.

25. Read, L. Changes in the growth-promoting activity of human milk during lactation. *Pediatr Res* 1984; 18:133-38.

26. Morriss, F. Method for investigating the presence and physiologic role of growth factors in milk. In: Jensen, R. and M. Neville, eds. *Human Lactation: Milk Components and Methodologies*. New York: Plenum, 1985; 193-200.

27. Reid, B., H. Smith, Z. Friedman. Prostaglandins in human milk. *Pediatr* 1980; 66:870-72.

28. Lawrence, A. and R. Lawrence. *Breastfeeding: A Guide for the Medical Profession*, 5th edition. St. Louis, Missouri: Mosby, 1999; 112-13, 129-31.

29. Garza, C. et al. Special properties of human milk. *Clin Perinatol* 1987; 14:11-31.

30. Siigur, U., A. Ormission, A. Tamm. Fecal short-chain fatty acids in breast-fed and bottle-fed infants. *Acta Paediatr* 1993; 82:536-38.

31. Kretchmer, N. Lactose and lactase. *Sci Am* 1972; 227:73.

32. Barness, L. and J. Carver. Nucleotides and immune function. *Semin Gastroenterol Nutr* 1991; 2:11.

33. Hamosh, M., M. Hong, P. Hamosh. beta-Casomorphins: Milk-beta-casein derived opioid peptides. In Lebenthal, E. ed. *Textbook of Gastroenterology and Nutrition in Infancy*, 2nd edition. New York, NY: Raven Press, 1989; 143-50.

34. Stromquist, M., P. Folk, S. Bergstrom, et al. Human milk k-casein and inhibition of Helicobacter pylori adhesion to human gastric mucosa. *J Pediatr Gastroenterol Nutr* 1995; 21: 288-96.

35. Balch, J. and P. Balch. *Prescription for Nutritional Healing*, 2nd edition. Garden City Park, NY: Avery Publishing Group, 1997; 13-21, 22-29.

36. Kaiser Permanente Health Maintenance Organization. *Internal research to determine benefits of sponsoring an official lactation program*. North Carolina; 1995.

37. Koletzko, S., P. Sherman, M. Corey, et al. Role of infant feeding practices in development of Crohn's disease in childhood. *Br Med J* 1989; 298:1617-18.

38. Rigas, A., B. Rigas, M. Blassman, et al. Breast-feeding and maternal smoking in the etiology of Crohn's disease and ulcerative colitis in childhood. *Ann Epidemiol* 1993; 3387-92.

39. Kovar, M., M. Serdula, J. Marks, et al. Review of the epidemiologic evidence for an association between infant feeding and infant health. *Pediatr* 1984; 74:S615-38.

40. Dewey, K., M. Heinig, L. Nommsen-Rivers. Differences in morbidity between breast-fed infants. *Pediatr* 1995; 126:696-702.

41. Howie, P., J. Forsyth, S. Ogston, et al. Protective effect of breast feeding against infection. *Br Med J* 1990; 300:11-16.

42. Popkin, B., L. Adair, J. Akin, et al. Breast-feeding and diarrheal morbidity. *Pediatr* 1990; 86:874-82.

43. Beaudry, M., R. Dufour, S. Marcoux. Relation between infant feeding and infections during the first six months of life. *J Pediatr* 1995; 126:191-97.

44. Cochi, S., D. Fleming, A. Hightower, et al. Primary invasive Haemophilus influenzae type b disease: a population-based assessment of risk factors. *J Pediatr* 1986; 108:997-96.

45. Istre, G., J. Conner, C. Broome, et al. Risk factors for primary invasive Haemophilus influenzae disease: increased risk from day care attendance and school-aged household members. *J Pediatr* 1985; 106: 190-98.

46. Takala A., J. Eskola, J. Palmgren, et al. Risk factors of invasive *Haemophilus influenzae type b* disease among children in Finland. *J Pediatr* 1980; 115:695-701.

47. Frank, A., L. Taber, W. Glezen, et al. Breast-feeding and respiratory virus infection. *Pediatr* 1982; 70:239-45.

48. Wright, A., D. Holberg, F. Martinez, et al. Breast feeding and lower respiratory tract illness in the first year of life. *Br Med J* 1989; 299:935-49.

49. Wright, A., C. Holberg, L. Taussig, et al. Relationship of infant feeding to recurrent wheezing at age 6 years. *Arch Pediatr Adolesc Med* 1995; 149:758-63.

50. Davis, M. Review of the evidence for an association between infant feeding and childhood cancer. *Int J Cancer Suppl* 1998; 11:29-33.

51. Davis, M., D. Savitz, B. Graubard. Infant feeding and childhood cancer. *Lancet* Aug 1988; 2(8607): 365-68.

52. Chong, S., A. Blackshaw, B. Morson, et al. Prospective study of colitis in infancy and early childhood. *J Pediatr Gastroenterol Nutr* May-Jun 1986; 5(3):352-58.

53. Meeuwisse, G. Immunological considerations on breast vs. formula feeding. *Klin Padiatr* 197:322-25.

54. Lucas, A. and T. Cole. Breast milk and neonatal necrotizing enterocolitis. *Lancet* 1990; 336:1519-23 .

55. Convert, R., N. Barman, R. Comanico, et al. Prior enteral nutrition with human milk protects against intestinal perforation in infants who develop necrotizing enterocolitis. *Pediatr Res* 1995; 37:305A.

56. Saarinen, U. and M. Kajossari. Breastfeeding as prophylaxis against atopic disease: prospective follow-up study until 17 years old. *Lancet* 1995; 346:1065-69.

57. Chandra, R. Influence of Maternal Diet During Lactation and the Use of Formula Feed and Development of Atopic Eczema in the High Risk Infants. *Br Med J* 1989; 299(6693):228-30.

58. Heacock, H. Influence of breast vs formula milk in physiologic gastroesophageal reflux in healthy newborn infants. *Jour Pediatr Gastroenterol Nutr* Jan 1992; 14(1):41-46.

59. Pisacane, A. Breast-feeding and inguinal hernia. *J Pediatr* 1995; 127(1):109-11.

60. Freudenheim, J., et al. Exposure to breast milk in infancy and the risk of breast cancer. *Epidemiology* 1994; 5:324-31.

61. Virtanen, S., et al: Diet, Cow's milk protein antibodies and the risk of IDDM in Finnish children. Childhood Diabetes in Finland Study Group. *Diabetologia* Apr 1994; 37(4):381-87.

62. Mayer, E., R. Hamman, E. Gay, et al. Reduced risk of IDDM among breast-fed children. *Diabetes* 1988; 37:1625-32.

63. Virtanen, S., L. Rasanen, A. Aro, et al. Infant feeding in Finnish children <7 yr of age with newly diagnosed IDDM. *Diabetes Care* 1991; 14:415-17.

64. Gerstein, H. Cow's milk exposure and type 1 diabetes mellitus. *Diabetes Care* 1994; 17:13-19.

65. Borch-Johnson, K., et al. Relation between breastfeeding and incidence of insulin-dependent diabetes mellitus. *Lancet* 1984; 2:1083-86.

66. Davis, M., D. Savitz, B. Graubard. Infant feeding and childhood cancer. *Lancet* 1988; 2:365-68.

67. Shu, X., H. Clemens, W. Zheng, et al. Infant breastfeeding and the risk of childhood lymphoma and leukaemia. *Int J Epidemiol* 1995; 24:27-32.

68. Dick, G. The Etiology of multiple sclerosis. *Proc Roy Soc Med* 1989; 69:611-15.

69. Breastfed babies have lower risk for developing recurrent wheezing when they are older (age 6 or more). *Archives of Pediatric and Adolescent Med* July 1995.

70. Birch, E., et al. Breastfeeding and optimal visual development. *J Pediatr Ophthalmol Strabismus* 1993; 30:33-38.

71. Bloem, M., et al. The role of universal distribution of vitamin A capsules in combating vitamin A deficiency in Bangladesh. *Am J Epidemiol* 1995; 142(8):843-55.

72. Lucas, A., O. Brooke, R. Morley, et al. Early diet of preterm infants and development of allergic ar atopic disease: randomized prospective study. *Br Med J* 1990; 300:837-40.

73. Halken, S., A. Host, L. Hansen, et al. Effect of an allergy prevention programme on incidence of atopic symptoms in infancy. *Ann Allergy* 1992; 47:545-53.

74. Aniansson, G., B. Alm, B. Andersson, et al. A prospective cohort study on breast-feeding and otitis media in Swedish infants. *Pediatr Infect Dis J* 1994; 13:183-88.

75. Saarinen, U. Prolonged breast feeding as prophylaxis for recurrent otitis media. *Acta Paediatr Scand* 1982; 71:567-71.

76. Kramer, M. Do breastfeeding and delayed introduction of solid foods protect against subsequent obesity? *J Pediatr* 1981; 98:883-87.

77. Newman, J. *Toddler Nursing*. Handout #21: Jan 2000.

78. Baumgartner, C. Psychomotor and social development of breast fed and bottle fed babies during their first year of life. *Acta Paediatrica Hungarica* 1984.

79. Eiger, M. and S. Olds. *The Complete Book Of Breastfeeding*, 3rd edition. New York, New York: Bantam Books, 1999.

80. Labbok, M. Does Breastfeeding Protect against Malocclusion? An Analysis of the 1981 Child Health Supplement to the National Health Interview Survey. *Am J Prev Med*1987.

81. Koenig, H., A. Davies, B. Thach. Coordination of breathing, sucking and swallowing during bottle feedings in human infants. *J Appl Physiol* 1990; 69:1623-29.

82. Chua, S., S. Arulkumaran, I. Lim, et al. Influence of breastfeeding and nipple stimulation on postpartum uterine activity. *Br J Obstet Gynaecol* 1994; 101:804-5.

83. Rosenblatt, K. and D. Thomas. WHO Collaborative study of neoplasia and steroid contraceptives. *Int J Epidemiol* 1993; 22:192-97.

84. Schneider, A. Risk factor for ovarian cancer. *N Engl J Med* 1987; 317(8):508-9.

85. Petterson, B., et al. Menstruation span- a time limited risk factor for endometrial carcinoma. *Acta Obstst Gyneocol Scand* 1986; 65:247-55.

86. Newcomb, P., B. Storer, M. Longnecker, et al. Lactation and a reduced risk of premenopausal breast cancer. *N Engl J Med* 1994; 330:81-87.

87. Davies, H. Insulin requirements of diabetic women who breast feed. *Br Med J* 1989; 298(6684): 1357-58.

88. *The Diabetic Mother and Breastfeeding*. LLLI, Dec 1998. Publication No. 17a.

89. Blaauw, R., et al. Risk factors for development of osteoporosis in a South African population. *SAMJ* 1994; 84:328-32.

90. Fewtrell, M., A. Prentice, S. Jones, et al. Bone mineralization and turnover in preterm infants at 8-12 years of age: The effect of early diet. *J Bone Miner Res* May 1999; 14(5):810-20.

91. Melton, L., S. Bryant, H. Wahner, et al. Influence of breastfeeding and other reproductive factors on bone mass later in life. *Osteoporos Int* 1993; 22:684-91.

92. Cumming, R. and R. Klineberg. Breastfeeding and other reproductive factors and the risk of hip fractures in elderly woman. *Int J Epidemiol* 1993; 22:684-91.

93. Dewey, K., M. Heinig, L. Nommwen. Maternal weight-loss patterns during prolonged lactation. *Am J Clin Nutr* 1993; 58:162-66.

94. Kramer, F. Breastfeeding reduces maternal lower body fat. *J Am Diet Assoc* 1993; 93(4):429-33.

95. Kennedy, K. and C. Visness. Contraceptive efficacy of lactational amenorrhoea. *Lancet* 1992; 339: 227-30.

96. Gray, R., O. Campbell, R. Apelo, et al. Risk of ovulation during lactation. *Lancet* 1990; 335:25-29.

97. Labbock, M. and C. Colie. Puerperium and breast-feeding. *Curr Opin Obstet Gynecol* 1992; 4:818-25.

SARAH'S STORY

I had a breast reduction when I was 22 years old. I was an E-cup and went down to a C-cup. As my mother was a La Leche League (LLL) Leader and my sister exclusively nursed her children, I was very pro-breastfeeding. I did discuss it with my surgeon and she assured me that there would be no problems with breastfeeding. So, I went for it because I had always been large breasted and very self-conscious. My bra straps dug into my shoulders and I had a difficult time finding clothes that fit. My husband supported me completely. After the surgery my breasts did look a lot better, but I hadn't expected the level of scarring that I had.

During my pregnancy with our first child, Kate, my small C-cup breasts blossomed to a DD cup, despite my having lost almost 50 pounds since my surgery. After a long labor, we delivered a healthy, beautiful baby without any drugs. I was very proud of myself. We nursed right away and she took to it like a champ. At four days, she had lost more than ten percent of her birth weight and my doctor recommended supplementing, but I was in complete denial. She was having wet diapers and was nursing well and the surgeon had said I would have no problems. My family also discouraged supplementing. So we just did our own thing until at three months I took her for her checkup. Well, she had only gained one pound over her birth weight. I was devastated.

We started supplementing and were referred to a lactation consultant to get an SNS. Kate hated it and refused to nurse with it. So we gave her bottles after nursing sessions several times a day. I hated them. I tried every other way I could to get formula into her. Eye dropper, syringe, cup, you name it. But she did gain one pound in a week. We went every two weeks to the pediatrician and she continued a steady gain, although slower than the average. She is still slim now at five years old.

I couldn't understand, though, how she could not be getting enough of my milk when at night I leaked all over. Fortunately, she did sleep with us and so was able to nurse frequently during the night.

At four months, I started solids because I didn't like using bottles. The pediatrician approved it because Kate liked solids a lot better than the formula. I used high quality foods like avocado and banana. I would mix her supplement into sweet potato. I always thought that I would wait to introduce solids, but I did what I felt I had to. I was desperate to maintain our nursing relationship.

During this time, I started to gather information about building up my milk supply. I had become an LLL member and was reading everything I could find, which was little. I had found information on the Internet, though, about the herbal galactagogue fenugreek and how it could increase a mother's milk supply. When Kate was three, I became an LLL Leader and was really enjoying helping other mothers. Kate continued to nurse until she was three-and-a-half years old.

58

When we had our second daughter, Hannah, I was much better informed. She, like Kate, had lost a little more than the ten percent of her birth weight at three days, but after my milk came in on day four, she gained one-and-a-half ounces in a day. But then she gained nothing the next week. So, I went to the health food store and bought some fenugreek and at the next weight check she had gained another one-and-a-half ounces.

I then doubled my intake of the fenugreek and she gained nine ounces the next week. So, it was working miracles for me. We nursed exclusively until five-and-a-half months when she wanted to start solids. I was going for weight checks regularly during the first several months.

It was a real shock to me, though, when at eight months she had gained only one ounce since her six-month checkup. I was devastated again. But she was old enough to just increase her solids to three meals a day and snacks. I worked with a health nurse, who is an LC, and my family doctor. She gained one pound in two weeks after our increased solids plan. I also started the fenugreek again, which I had stopped around six months.

I encouraged nursing before all meals and whenever she wanted. Hannah is now 23 months old, still nursing, and has continued to grow steadily, although she is also slim like her sister.

I encourage anyone who is starting the BFAR journey to find someone they really trust to work with. I was not in a proper state with my first daughter to decide whether supplementing was necessary or not. Frequent weight checks at the beginning are also very important. Learn all you can about the herbs and drugs to boost supply, breastfeeding management, and nursing supplementary systems. Find a support system like the BFAR online discussion group made up of women who have "been there, done that." I was not prepared for the emotional toll that my struggles with breastfeeding would have on me. The support has really made all the difference.

WHAT TO EXPECT

This chapter addresses the concerns of women who are not yet breastfeeding, but soon will be. Many mothers who read this book may already be breastfeeding and may not need the information in this chapter. But if you are pregnant and considering breast-feeding for the first time, this chapter may seem vitally important to you right now. You are trying to understand what breastfeeding after breast reduction surgery is going to be like and how much milk you will be able to give to your baby. If you have tried to breastfeed after breast reduction surgery before (or breastfed before your reduction surgery), you may want to know how this experience will be different. You may even be coming from a different perspective altogether.

You are not alone. Almost every woman who has decided to breastfeed after breast reduction surgery has worried about what her body will be able to do. Although at times it may be difficult to learn all that you can and prepare yourself for breastfeeding when you have fears and concerns, rest assured that because of your efforts now, you are ensuring your chances of having the most satisfying experience possible for you and your child.

So What Will Your BFAR Experience Be Like?

Breastfeeding after breast reduction surgery would be so much simpler if it were pos-sible to clearly spell out each woman's abilities by saying that if she had "type A" sur-gery, and does "B," she will have "C" result. The truth is that there are so many vari-ables that few experiences are the same. In fact, the range of BFAR experiences is extremely diverse and dependent upon myriad factors, including the type of surgery you had, your state of mind, your attitude, your environment, your support structure, and what you are able to do to prepare.

In order to be clear about your lactation probability, it is important for you to understand that because you had breast reduction surgery, your lactation capabilities will almost certainly be impacted, especially with your first child after the surgery. This does not mean, however, that you will not be able to breastfeed your child. What it does mean is that you very well may need to supplement with donated human milk, formula, or an alternate human milk substitute.

Learning that supplementation is likely may be somewhat disappointing to BFAR mothers who are hopeful that they will have a full milk supply. And nothing is set in stone—perhaps you will have a full milk supply. It is highly likely, though, especially with your first child, that you will not. The purpose in preparing you for this probability is not to discourage you or disappoint you. Rather, it is to allow you to become as informed and prepared as possible before your baby's birth so that you will be able to cope with the challenges you may face.

It is also important to transform your thinking about your lactation capability from viewing it in "the glass is half empty" perspective to understanding it as "the glass is half full." Thinking about your lactation capacity in these positive terms makes it so much easier for you to appreciate every drop of milk your body is able to produce, rather than resenting each ounce of supplementation. It is actually helpful for you to appreciate the supplementation. Yes, we know and appreciate the many benefits of human milk. But how wonderful it is that there are viable substitutes for human milk when it is not possible for us to produce a complete milk supply. I firmly believe that one of the key factors to developing a deeply satisfying breastfeeding relationship is to be optimistic and positive about your experience. You will have negative feelings. These are normal and natural and you must accept them as valid when they occur. However, it is important to maintain an overall loving, positive perspective. It will make all the difference to your perception of your experience and your ability to enjoy it with your baby.

This chapter will help to prepare you by outlining the range of possible BFAR experiences and describing what those different experiences can be like. The factors that will determine your lactation potential will then be discussed so that you can ascertain your own range of possibilities and begin your preparations for breastfeeding your baby.

The Range of BFAR Experiences

BFAR experiences are comprised of combinations of variables of two factors: lactation capability and feeding method. Your lactation capability will fall somewhere on a continuum of possible experiences: you will have either a full milk supply, a partial milk supply, or no milk supply at all. Your feeding method options will encompass feeding at the breast, feeding at the breast with an at-breast supplementer, and feeding with artificial feeding devices. The method by which you choose to feed your baby will depend upon your milk supply, the feeding method most appealing to you in terms of comfort and convenience, and your baby's preferences.

Determining Your Lactation Potential

When consulting with a plastic surgeon prior to breast reduction surgery, women are usually advised that the surgery will affect their lactation capability to some degree. Depending on the surgery, doctors commonly describe the potential capability by stating that there is either no possibility that she will be able to lactate, a "50/50" chance, or that it will not affect her lactation capability at all. What the surgeons perceive as the answer to the question of lactation capability, however, and what women really need to know can be quite different. A surgeon's projections of lactation capability is often based on the assumption that any lactation is full lactation. It is not often quali-fied by how much of a milk supply the mother will have. In fact, the "50/50" chance so often quoted refers to having a 50 percent chance that she can lactate at all. The crit-ical information to a future mother, however, is not whether she will be able to lactate at all, but rather *how much* she will be able to lactate.

It may be that the reason plastic surgeons tend to predict post-surgical lactation capabilities in terms of "all" or "nothing" is because the process of lactation is not well understood by many physicians, especially those outside of the obstetrical/ gynecolog-ical and pediatric specialties. In fact, as illustrated in the discussion of the anatomy and physiology of the breast, the mammary system is comprised of many co-operative, redundant networks of glands and ducts. It is possible that some portion of the original number of gland/duct networks will remain intact after the surgery. It is even possible that some of the gland/duct networks that are damaged by the surgery will reconnect, which is known as "recanalization." Our bodies are remarkably resilient; almost all women who have breast reduction surgery will be able to lactate to some degree. But if a significant portion of the lactation system was impaired by the surgery, then the milk supply will not be enough to meet a baby's entire nutritional requirement.

Plastic surgeons' statements about post-surgical lactation capabilities tend to stick very firmly in the minds of women when they consider breastfeeding. Most BFAR mothers can tell you exactly what their surgeons said to them about it and those words can haunt them in the early days of their BFAR experiences. Some misinformed lactation consultants and physicians will even reinforce the perception of lactation absolutes by telling women incorrectly that if they have any milk at all, they will be able to exclusively breastfeed; or that if they have no milk, they will not be able to breastfeed at all. Thus, because their probable lactation capability was described in absolute terms of having or not having the capacity to lactate, many mothers mistakenly think that if they are able to express any colostrum or milk, then they will produce a full milk supply. Conversely, if they cannot express colostrum during pregnancy or they don't see any milk in the first few days postpartum, they may think they are completely unable to lactate. The process of lactation, however, especially after breast reduction surgery, is more complex than these basic assumptions.

Research Findings

Unfortunately, few studies have been conducted to investigate the effects of breast reduction surgery on lactation. Nonetheless, it is helpful to examine the latest research on lactation after breast reduction surgery as a fairly objective way to understand the probability of doing so.

One often referenced study by Harris et al. collected information by sending a standardized questionnaire to women who had had inferior-based pedicle breast reduction surgery. Seventy-three patients were contacted. Of the 68 who responded, 20 patients had become pregnant after reduction mammoplasty. All 20 women lactated. Seven of these women (35 percent) went on to breastfeed successfully. Thirteen (65 percent) decided not to breastfeed or discontinued breastfeeding for personal reasons.[1] This study does not actually provide a great deal of information beyond indicating that the women studied were able to lactate.

A study published in early 2000 specifically investigated the impact of the inferior pedicle reduction technique upon lactation. Brzozowski et al. sent a standardized questionnaire to 334 women who had had this type of surgery between 1984 and 1994, ranging in age from 15 to 35 years at the time of surgery. In the questionnaire, they defined successful breastfeeding as the ability to feed at the breast for at least two weeks.

> *"Seventy-eight patients had children after their breast reduction surgery. Fifteen of the 78 patients (19.2 percent) breastfed exclusively, 8 (10.3 percent) breastfed with formula supplementation, 14 (17.9 percent) had an unsuccessful breastfeeding attempt, and 41 (52.6 percent) did not attempt breastfeeding. Of the 41 patients not attempting to breastfeed, 9 patients did so as a direct consequence of discouragement by a health care professional. Of the 78 women who had children postoperatively, a total of 27 were discouraged from breastfeeding by medical profes-sionals with only 8 of the 27 (29.6 percent) subsequently attempting to breastfeed, despite this recommendation. In comparison, 26 patients were encouraged to breastfeed; nineteen (73.1 percent) of them did subsequently attempt breastfeeding. Postpartum breast engorgement and lactation were experienced by 31 of the 41 patients not attempting to breastfeed. Of these 31 patients, 19 believed that they would have been able to breastfeed due to the extent of breast engorgement and lactation experienced."* [2]

This study concluded that:

> *"Given the use of an inferior flap mammaplasty technique and patient encouragement, the possibility for breastfeeding after reduction mammaplasty exists. This prevalence falls near the breastfeeding rate found in the population not having undergone breast surgery, according to an article in the* Canadian Journal of Public Health.*"* [2]

Another study also published in early 2000 by Ahmed and Kolhe compared the nipple and areolar sensation after breast reductions that used the free nipple and inferior pedicle surgical techniques. They found some degree of recovery of nipple and areolar sensation in all patients, with areolar sensation being similar in the two groups, but nipple sensation being superior in the inferior pedicle group. [3] This was particularly interesting because it had always been widely believed that the free nipple technique resulted in a complete loss of nipple and areola sensation. This would have a severe impact upon lactation since milk production depends a great deal on responding to nerve stimulation during breastfeeding. This study gives new hope to those who had the free-nipple surgical technique, especially those for whom considerable time has elapsed, for reasons that shall be explored later in this chapter.

Finally, a study by Sandsmark et al. in 1999 compared the effects of the superior and inferior pedicle techniques. The 292 patients studied had received surgery between 1984 and 1990. Two hundred and thirty-three received the superior pedicle technique,

36 received the inferior pedicle technique, and 23 had other types of reduction surgery. Not surprisingly, the authors found that the inferior pedicle technique yielded better results in terms of increased sensitivity, particularly of the nipple-areola complex, and better lactation.[4]

The information in texts, both clinical reference books and more popular consumer-oriented books, differs greatly in the opinions presented on the possibility of breastfeeding after breast reduction surgery. Drs. Riordan and Auerbach present the most accurate information in their book, *Breastfeeding and Human Lactation*, in which they state that "Full breastfeeding may be possible with the pedicle technique, but it is rarely possible with the free-nipple technique, because blood supply of the nipple-areola is completely severed."[5] Of course, they refer to lactation rather than this book's definition of breastfeeding, which is defined as feeding at the breast, and which can include full supplementation. But, nonetheless, this conclusion is quite accurate; the free-nipple technique yields a significantly diminished probability of lactation.

Some popular books include misleading information about breastfeeding after reduction surgery that puts the blame for lactation failure on the mother's lack of a positive perspective. One example is Dr. Christiane Northup's book *Women's Bodies, Women's Wisdom* in which she states that:

> "*Dr. Janet Hurley, a family physician and breastfeeding advocate in Calgary, Alberta, told me that in her practice, women can often nurse successfully following reduction mammoplasty, as long as they feel good about their choice to breastfeed and have no difficulty appreciating their breasts' normal function.*"[6]

In *So That's What They're for–Breastfeeding Basics*, Janet Tamaro relates that:

> "*Carolyn had breast reduction surgery more than ten years ago, before surgeons had really perfected the art of keeping breasts functioning to breastfeed at a later date. Your milk glands and all of the necessary bio-logical equipment in your breasts is kind of like a tree with branches. If during surgery, the tree gets robbed of all of its branches and roots, you will probably not be able to breastfeed.*"[7]

This incorrectly implies that surgeons have now perfected the preservation of lactation capabilities in breast reduction surgeries. Certainly advances have been made in some techniques, but any surgery will impact lactation. However, this does not preclude the option of supplementing at the breast to preserve the breastfeeding relationship.

Certainly, the research available on breastfeeding after breast reduction surgery needs to be expanded. In *Surgery of the Breast, Principles and Art*, edited by Scott Spear, it is stated that "Lactation after breast reduction remains an unresolved question. Normal lactation after reduction certainly occurs frequently but may be impaired in some patients. The precise percentage or number of patients with impairment of lactation after breast reduction remains to be documented in future studies."[8] With the increased prevalence of women who want to breastfeed following breast reduction surgery, it is likely that more research into this field will occur, resulting in even better developments in reduction mammoplasty surgical techniques to preserve the lactation function.

Baseline Lactation Capability

As the research and anecdotal evidence demonstrates, the question is not whether you will have milk, because you almost certainly will. The true question is how much milk you will have. In order to project what your likely lactation potential will be, you must first consider several critical factors that define the state of your present mammary system. These factors do not determine your lactation capability, however. They are merely an indication of your baseline lactation capability because your efforts and the information and techniques presented in this book will have a significant impact upon your yield.

Type of Surgery

The starting place to determine your baseline lactation capability is to know what type of breast reduction surgery you experienced. This information is important because some surgical techniques preserve more lactation tissue than others. A review of the breast reduction surgical techniques in Chapter 2 may help you narrow down the type of surgery you have had. The shape of your scars will also give an indication. However, the only way to know for certain is to place a call to your plastic surgeon's office or to the hospital where your surgery was performed. Ask for a copy of your surgical record. Each surgeon dictates an account of every surgery that he performs. A copy of this record will be filed both with the surgeon's and the hospital's patient records. The surgeon's office or the hospital should be willing to give you a copy of this record. There may be a photocopying charge, however.

Once you have a copy, you'll need to analyze it to determine the type of surgery that was performed, how much breast tissue was removed, any unusual occurrences during the surgery, and any comments the surgeon may have recorded about the state of the mammary system. Many terms may be unfamiliar to you. Look up any words or phrases that you do not understand in an unabridged or medical dictionary (found in most libraries), locate more information online by performing a browser search, or ask a doctor who is willing to help you. An understanding of the type and extent of your surgery will allow you to refine your understanding of the impact the surgery had upon your mammary system.

Although the type of reduction surgery you experienced will have a significant impact on your future lactation capability, the aspect of the breast reduction surgery that is most likely to affect lactation is the surgical treatment of the areola and nipple, which can vary even among similar surgical techniques according to the individual woman's anatomy and the surgeon's skill. The surgeries that have resulted in the greatest lactation capability are those in which the areolas and nipples were not completely severed, even though they may have been moved. Many women believe their areolas and nipples were severed because they have a scar around the outside of the areola. They may also know that the areola and nipple were moved, and therefore assume they must have been severed to do so. With surgical techniques performed since 1990, this is unlikely to be the case. Most current breast reduction surgical techniques involve moving the areola and nipple attached to a wedge of tissue, called a pedicle, which contains the lactiferous sinuses. The pedicle remains attached to the ducts that connect to the lactiferous sinuses, as well as the primary nerves. If damage to the lactation system occurs in these types of surgeries, it is more likely to be a result of cuts deeper in the breast tissue, where glands were removed along with fatty tissue and ducts were severed.

The types of surgeries that utilize the inferior pedicle technique have consistently yielded the greatest lactation results. However, in his book, *Everything You Wanted to Know about Cosmetic Surgery But Couldn't Afford to Ask*, Dr. Alan Gaynor states "There are slightly different methods of doing the same technique. The inverted T is most widely used. Several techniques use this approach because it is possible to maintain the integrity and function of the breast. The internal treatment of the gland can vary a lot according to the surgeon."[9]

There are, of course, breast reduction surgical techniques that do completely sever the areola and nipple from the breast. These techniques were commonly performed in the 1970s and 1980s before the more advanced pedicle techniques were developed. They are also occasionally performed on women who, according to the judgment of the surgeon, have such large breasts that the pedicle technique would not provide satisfactory results.

When the areola and nipple have been completely severed, lactation will be far less likely. However, although it is not common with non-pedicle surgery, some possibility of lactation remains because of the miraculous process of recanalization. On occasion, women who have had their areolas and nipples completely removed have been known to be able to easily express colostrum during pregnancy. While this was certainly a good sign and proved that some ducts had recanalized, they later found that they were able to produce very little milk. This is usually because the severed nerves prevent the lactation system from producing milk in response to nerve stimulation at the nipple and areola. Colostrum is produced easily because it is hormonally driven and not dependent upon nipple/areolar stimulation. Only very rarely have women with completely severed areolas and nipples produced a significant milk supply, and usually this is a result of the use of substantial amounts of galactagogues. Of course, the amount of the milk supply does not at all preclude any woman from having a deeply satisfying breastfeeding relationship because she can supplement at the breast with a specially designed at-breast supplementer.

Length of Time between Surgery and Subsequent Pregnancy

The next important consideration that influences your milk supply is the length of time between your surgery and your next pregnancy. The anecdotal experience has been that, despite the type of surgery, a woman seems to have a better milk supply when her surgery occurred five or more years before her pregnancy. This could be the result of three separate physiological processes, each of which contributes to repairing and developing the mammary system.

The first two of these processes, recanalization and reinnervation (regrowth of ductule and neural pathways, respectively), are described in greater detail below. However, they are pertinent to mention in this context because both healing processes are more probable when the interval between the surgery and the pregnancy is greater. Both processes are also directly responsible for increases in the milk supply. Although recanalization seems to result more from the demands of actual lactation, it is still probable that some recanalization, like reinnervation, would occur as a normal healing process of the body.

The third beneficial process is the normal, progressive linear development of the mammary system, wherein hormonal influences result in further mammary system development with each menstrual cycle experienced until the event of the first pregnancy, when the mammary system normally becomes fully mature. A longer length of time between the surgery and the pregnancy enables this process to redevelop mammary tissue.

Breast Changes during Pregnancy

Consider whether you have experienced any enlargement, including a feeling of heaviness, of your breasts during your pregnancy. Also, have you had any soreness or tenderness? Changes such as these during pregnancy will not tell you how much of your mammary system is functioning or if your ducts are connected to the nipples, but they do indicate that the breast tissue is responding appropriately to hormonal influences and that at least some of your mammary system is intact. If you had been pregnant before your surgery, these changes will be less pronounced during this pregnancy than during previous pregnancies, but they should still be present to some degree.

Wondering if they have any lactation capability, many BFAR mothers attempt to express colostrum in the last few months of pregnancy. This practice can be somewhat reassuring. Expressing a few drops of colostrum indicates definitely that at least one duct is connected. However, not being able to express colostrum is not an indication that no ducts are connected. Many mothers cannot express colostrum during pregnancy. It is not a true indication of your lactation capability.

Some BFAR mothers find that when they are able to express colostrum, they can differentiate the number of functional openings in the nipple and wonder if that means that those are the number of connected ducts. It does not. It merely means that colostrum was readily expressed from those particular openings. Other ducts may also be connected to openings, but were not capable of producing colostrum at that point, for any of number of reasons. Also, some ducts merge together just below the surface of the nipple.

Recanalization and Reinnervation

Recanalization is a very exciting physiological phenomenon for BFAR women. It is the process wherein breast tissue actually regrows, reconnecting previously severed ducts. On occasion, completely new pathways that permit transportation of the milk from the glands to the nipple may be formed. The most profound instances of recanalization seem to occur in direct response to lactational demand. This means that any efforts to lactate encourage the mammary system to reestablish the mammary ductule system. Of course, at this time, the process of recanalization is not well enough understood to be able to predict the extent to which recanalization will (or can) occur. Because it seems to be directly correlated with the duration and degree of lactation, a mother whose previous lactation efforts resulted in an incomplete supply may find that future attempts result in a much greater yield. In some mothers, recanalization has resulted in a complete milk supply for subsequent children. As a general rule, the longer the lactation experience, the greater the extent of recanalization will be.

Reinnervation, on the other hand, seems to occur in response to the passage of time and the body's normal regenerative process, rather than as a result of previous lactation events. Reinnervation is the process whereby the nerves that serve the nipple and areola that were damaged by the surgery are regenerated. The nerves of the nipple and areola are critical to the process of lactation, so regeneration of such nerves would be a key component of increased lactation capability. Many BFAR women wonder if the sensitivity currently present in their nipples and areolas is indicative of the state of the lactational nerve connections. The answer is that if they are once again responding normally to touch and temperature, it may indicate that the nerve infrastructure is functioning well and would therefore conduct the appropriate sensations to the pituitary gland for production of prolactin and oxytocin. Of course, the ability of the mammary system to fulfill the demand is dependent upon the state of the glands and ducts. Nonetheless, the longer the length of time since the surgery, the greater the chances that the nerves critical to lactation have regenerated, which is an important factor for lactation.

Inherent Yield

Each woman is capable of an inherent lactation capability that existed before her surgery according to her own unique physiology and anatomy. Some women tend to have copious milk supplies, perhaps even to the point that it presents a problem. A certain percentage of BFAR women would have had this "problem" had they not had the surgery. What this means for them, though, is that their lactation system will compensate very well for surgical damage and they will have better milk supplies because of their greater inherent yield. Of course, unless you lactated before your surgery, you have no way of knowing if you have an inherently copious milk supply. It is simply one factor that accounts for the different yields experienced by BFAR mothers when all other factors are the same.

Many surgeons have told prospective breast surgery patients that because their breasts were so large, they would never have been able to successfully breastfeed anyway. This is patently untrue and unjustly shifts the responsibility for lactation insufficiency from the surgery to the woman's inherent physiology. The truth is that the size of a woman's breasts does not bear any impact upon her ability to lactate. An incomplete milk supply following breast reduction surgery is almost invariably a direct result of that surgery. It is not a result of the woman's natural breast size.

As explained in Chapter 2, there is a natural fluctuation to a woman's milk supply over the course of breastfeeding that is unrelated to the surgery, but is rather a normal process for all lactating women. Contrary to common belief, mothers do not initially produce eight ounces of milk at a feeding, nor do newborns need such a large amount of food. Instead, their bodies begin producing milk in much smaller quantities that are perfectly suited to the needs of our babies at the particular age they may be. For instance, even in women who have not had reduction surgery, colostrum is produced in mere teaspoons during the first few days after birth. When the milk matures over the next few weeks, it is normal and appropriate for a mother to only produce a few ounces per feeding. As the baby progresses through the standard growth spurts at about three weeks, six weeks, three months, and six months, the milk supply is correspondingly increased by the baby's increased demand so that a mother begins lactating in greater quantities. After the baby begins solids and begins nursing less, the milk supply decreases to produce only as much as the baby requires. This process continues in diminishing quantities until the baby no longer takes any milk and weaning has occurred.

Manipulated Yield

Many BFAR mothers increase their inherent milk supplies by manipulating them with herbal and prescription galactagogues (milk-inducing substances), special massage techniques, and pumping. These actions can be effective and can increase milk supply. Taking galactagogues in particular is a very common component of the average BFAR experience. A discussion of increasing your milk supply is presented in Chapter 9.

Birth Order

As mentioned in the discussion of recanalization, most BFAR mothers find that they have a greater milk supply with each subsequent baby. Although recanalization and reinnervation certainly play a significant role in this, so does the increased experience, information, and support that she may have with subsequent babies. Each of these factors contribute to a woman's perspective about her BFAR experience.

Combinations of Feeding Methods

Because there are so many variables to consider, it is unrealistic to attempt to portray a "typical" BFAR experience. Yet reviewing the options, benefits, and challenges of various types of BFAR experiences can help you see a clear illustration in your mind's eye of what each scenario may entail. This will help you to be prepared for a wide range of possible outcomes, as well as helping you to avoid solutions that may not be comfortable for you. And you may find that you will want to use different techniques as your milk supply fluctuates and your needs or priorities change.

When a Baby Requires Full Supplementation

When a woman has no (or nearly no) milk supply, but still desires to breastfeed, she has several options:

1) Feed baby exclusively at the breast with an at-breast supplementer;
2) Feed baby at the breast with at-breast supplementer plus use artificial feeding devices;
3) Nurse at the breast for comfort plus use artificial feeding devices.

Feeding the baby at the breast with an at-breast supplementer, such as the Lact-Aid or Medela's Supplemental Nursing System (SNS), confers the greatest benefit to the baby, as well as the mother. This type of supplementer involves using a plastic bag or bottle that hangs around the neck by a cord. Extending from the bag or bottle is a tube that is placed alongside the nipple. As the baby nurses from the breast, supplement is delivered through the tube. Adoptive mothers often use these at-breast supplementers to breastfeed their babies.

Supplementing a baby's complete nutritional requirement at the breast requires more effort in some ways than bottle-feeding, but it is much more rewarding. Of course, if the mother has no milk at all, the baby does not receive the benefits of human milk, however, he does receive the advantage of better oral and facial development as a result of the suckling motions unique to breastfeeding, as well as better hand-eye coordination as a result of switching from side to side during feedings. Most importantly, though, the baby who is supplemented completely at the breast is able to enjoy all the benefits of the intimate, deeply satisfying emotional bond that a breastfeeding couple have. And even though little or no milk is present, these babies are usually willing to nurse without the supplementer for comfort.

If the mother is feeding her baby exclusively at the breast, for the most part, she will be the only one who can feed the baby, both day and night. Most mothers do not find this is a restrictive role, however, and come to enjoy the special relationship they and their babies develop through nursing.

Some BFAR mothers find that a combination of feeding methods works best for them. Although they wish to feed their babies at the breast as much as possible, it is not always practical for them to do so. They are able to work out a routine so that baby is fed at the breast using an at-breast-supplementer for a certain number of feedings each day while other feedings are given with an artificial feeding device, such as a cup or bottle.

The use of a cup for feedings avoids any risk of nipple preference or confusion. Switching from breast to bottle is only possible when the baby is able to easily manage both kinds of nipples. Some babies cannot go back and forth and come to strongly prefer either the breast or the bottle.

Many mothers who use an at-breast supplementer in conjunction with bottles find it more comfortable to feed the baby at the breast when they are at home and feed the baby with a bottle when out in public.

Mothers who have little or no milk supply, but find that their babies have no trouble switching between a human and artificial nipple, sometimes give up on using the at-breast supplementer and discover that they can develop a comforting nursing relationship by nursing the child at the breast for comfort and feeding him his nutritional requirements by bottle. When both the mother and the baby are comfortable with this arrangement, it can work well.

Lactation plus Supplementation

Mothers who are able to lactate, but still need to provide part of their baby's nutritional requirements with a supplement, have several choices:

1) Feed baby exclusively at the breast combining active lactation with at-breast supplementing;
2) Feed baby at the breast with at-breast supplementer, combined with active lactation, plus use artificial feeding devices;
3) Feed baby at the breast plus use artificial feeding devices;
4) Pump milk supply and feed baby with artificial feeding devices.

Most BFAR mothers are able to lactate to some degree, and may choose to supplement exclusively at the breast in order to maintain the maximum sucking stimulation and enhance milk production. Feeding the baby exclusively at the breast provides both mother and baby with the harmonious quality of breastfeeding. Of course, using any type of supplement means more work is involved in feeding the baby. The at-breast supplementer must be cleaned, prepared, and filled before each feeding. It is sometimes more difficult to use the at-breast supplementer at night, although many mothers find they do not need to supplement at night because their milk supplies are higher then.

A mother who is producing a portion of the baby's nutritional needs with her milk may find that there are times when using a bottle or cup is more convenient for her than using the at-breast supplementer. She may choose to use the at-breast supplementer at home, but use a bottle away from home. As long as the baby is adept at using both the human and the artificial nipple, this combined feeding method can work well.

Some BFAR mothers who have a partial milk supply find that they are not comfortable using the at-breast supplementer. They may have tried it and not liked it, or they may never have used it at all. Instead of supplementing at the breast, these mothers nurse their babies at the breast, but then supplement the remainder of the feeding with a bottle or cup. Alternately, they may simply bottle-feed during some feedings in place of breastfeeding. Again, as long as the baby is able to go back and forth between the human and artificial nipple, this system can work well.

Occasionally, a BFAR mother may have so many difficulties breastfeeding her baby, or her baby may have such severe nipple confusion or nipple preference, that she is no longer able to breastfeed at all, even though she is still lactating. This leaves her with the options of stopping lactation completely or giving her baby her pumped milk in bottles. Many mothers who face this decision realize that giving their babies their milk in bottles is still a precious gift since human milk contains tremendous benefits.

While the baby no longer receives the benefits of feeding at the breast, the mother continues to receive the full benefits of lactation even when she is pumping her milk. Most importantly, she encourages recanalization and reinnervation, which may enable her to have a more satisfying breastfeeding relationship with her next baby, should she have one.

There has been some question about the ability of the lactation system to be sustained by pumping alone. There are many women who have exclusively pumped for a year or more. It most certainly can be done. Diminishing lactation during exclusive pumping may be more a result of less extensive or less frequent pumping than failure of the mammary system. Pumping is indeed a learned art and must be practiced regularly and faithfully. A thorough discussion of pumping, including extended pumping, is provided in Chapter 9.

Full Lactation

Even a mother who is producing a full milk supply has certain options as to how she will feed her milk to her baby. Some of these options may be influenced by the BFAR experience; others are choices available to all lactating mothers.

1) Feed baby exclusively at the breast;
2) Feed the baby at the breast and also pump and feed with an artificial feeding device;
3) Pump and feed with artificial feeding device.

Exclusively feeding the baby at the breast and avoiding the use of artificial nipples is the most beneficial choice. It avoids any risk of the baby becoming nipple confused or developing a preference for an artificial nipple. It ensures that the breasts are stimulated frequently and effectively so the mother's milk supply is enhanced. Both mother and baby fully experience the joys and benefits of breastfeeding. However, mothers who work outside the home, or mothers who are separated from their babies for other reasons may find it necessary to pump their milk and use artificial feeding methods. If at all possible, cup-feeding should be used on these occasions in order to avoid artificial nipples. If bottles and artificial nipples are used, the mother should be alert to any signs of nipple confusion or preference that her baby is exhibiting if she wants to ensure that breastfeeding can continue.

In some rare cases, however, even when a BFAR mother has a full milk supply, perhaps because of early difficulties resulting from structural complications from the breast surgery, or because of other early difficulties that were not resolved soon enough, feeding at the breast may not be successful. Rather than weaning to formula, however, many mothers choose to continue pumping their milk to give to their babies in bottles. As discussed above, this can be a difficult course to follow, but the benefits are many.

The Effort and Rewards of BFAR

Many new mothers wonder whether or not they want to face the challenges involved in breastfeeding after breast reduction surgery. It can be said with reasonable certainty that breastfeeding will entail more work and probably more worry for a mother who has had breast reduction. If supplementation is necessary, the efforts can sometimes seem very arduous and time consuming. Pumping and managing galactagogue intake can also be a lot of work. And, as you may already know, it is certainly time consuming to learn about BFAR in order to be able to do it as well as possible. But the efforts expended in supplementing are usually no more than that expended by other bottle-feeding or partially breastfeeding mothers. And after the initial learning curve when you and the baby are working out your optimal system, things can run very smoothly.

If you are able to maintain breastfeeding, you will always have that special breastfeeding bond as a foundation of your relationship. You and your child will enjoy the health and developmental benefits discussed in Chapter 3. You will be able to nurse for comfort and soothe your child. There are many sweet rewards for all your efforts.

If you supplement completely at the breast without lactating at all, you will be rewarded by your intimate breastfeeding relationship, as well as many of the structural benefits of breastfeeding, like better facial development. And if it turns out that you can't have the breastfeeding relationship, but still go to the effort to give your child your milk in a bottle, you will always have the satisfaction of knowing that your body provided a priceless gift to your child at each and every feeding.

No matter how things turn out, as long as you can continue to give your child any human milk at all, it will be well worth the effort. Every drop of human milk is a precious, enduring treasure for your child. And feeding him at your breast even if you have no milk at all will be deeply satisfying for you both.

Keep in mind, though, that even when you've prepared in every way possible, your baby is likely to have a mind of his own. He may have very different ideas about how he wants to go about things. After all, you are entering into a relationship; compromise is necessary. You'll work it out, though, and find the best system for you and your baby.

The most important thing to keep in mind when preparing for BFAR is that while it is certainly very important to learn all you can and be as fully prepared as you can be, the reality will probably be much more intense than you can possibly imagine before it happens. This is not because of your having had breast reduction surgery. It's because you are having a baby and babies tend to turn your world upside down in an amazing way.

R E F E R E N C E S :

1. Harris L., Morris SF; Freiberg A. Is breast feeding possible after reduction mammaplasty? *Plast Reconstr Surg* May 1992; 89(5): 826-29.

2. Brzozowski, D., M. Niessen, H. Evans, et al. Breast-feeding after inferior pedicle reduction mammaplasty. *Plast Reconstr Surg* 2000 Feb; 105(2):530-34.

3. Ahmed, O. and P. Kolhe. Comparison of nipple and areolar sensation after breast reduction by free nipple graft and inferior pedicle techniques. *Br J Plast Surg* Mar 2000; 53(2):126-29.

4. Sandsmark, M., P. Amland, F. Abyholm, et al. Reduction mammaplasty. A comparative study of the Orlando and Robbins methods in 292 patients. *Plast Reconstr Surg* Mar 1999; 103(3):890-902.

5. Riordan, J. and K. Auerbach. *Breastfeeding and Human Lactation*, 2nd edition. Sudbury, Massachusetts: Jones and Bartlett Publishers, 1999; 494.

6. Northrup, C. *Women's Bodies, Women's Wisdom*. New York, New York: Bantam Books, 1998; 376.

7. Tamaro, J. *So That's What They're For: Breastfeeding Basics*, 2nd edition. Holbrook, Massachusetts: Adams Media Corporation; 1998.

8. Spear, S, ed. *Surgery of the Breast, Principles and Art*. Philadelphia, Pennsylvania: Lippincott-Raven, 1998; 673.

9. Gaynor, A. *Everything You Wanted To Know About Cosmetic Surgery But Couldn't Afford To Ask*. New York Broadway Books, 1988.

PATTI'S STORY

I had my breast reduction surgery when I was 21. The surgeon warned me that it might mean I couldn't breastfeed, but at the time I didn't care. I was a freewheeling university student with an abiding dislike of other people's children. I wanted to travel, be a writer, and have adventures. Babies were not on my agenda at all. I also reasoned that I had been bottle-fed and turned out just fine.

So I went ahead with the surgery, and I had no complaints for more than ten childless years. I ran, cycled, swam, played volleyball, lolled around on beaches, and traveled extensively. I became a writer. I did most of the things I had hoped to do back in university. But then I went and did one extra thing that hadn't been part of my grand plan: I got pregnant. And the more I read about breastfeeding, the more determined I became to do it despite the odds.

Chloe arrived after an ordinary vaginal delivery, and the midwife placed her directly on my chest. She opened her dark blue eyes and gazed at me with all the wide-eyed trust in the universe. I knew then that I would do anything for her. And that was when the trouble began.

Chloe was a breastfeeding pro. She latched right on with a strong, enthusiastic suck and stayed there for more than 20 minutes. We put her on the other side, where she repeated her untiring performance. By the time I was out of the delivery room and into the maternity ward, my nipples felt as if they'd been scoured with sandpaper.

We went home early the next morning, and I continued to breastfeed her on cue, every hour or two. My nipples got worse. The midwife arrived for a home visit and asked how many wet and soiled diapers she'd produced. So far, we had only seen one barely wet one, and it had been streaked with pinkish-orange crystals—which is often a sign of dehydration.

We had planned to use cloth diapers after the chaos of the first month had subsided, but we switched to cloth on day two so that we could more easily tell when the diaper was wet. We continued to fall short of the healthy minimum of wet and soiled diapers. We'd been told to look for bowel movements that looked like curry, or mustard, with little seeds. We saw nothing of the kind.

Somehow, by the end of day three, Chloe had lost less than ten percent of her birth weight despite the inadequate showing of wet diapers. She was holding her own. But by the end of day four, she still had not gained anything back. My milk had finally started to come in, though, so we decided to give it another day before starting supplements.

We grasped at every positive sign—one nipple leaked milk when I fed on the other side, and the afterpains I felt must mean that breastfeeding was causing my body to produce the necessary oxytocin. Maybe the "make more milk" message was getting through to my brain somehow. Maybe it would work out after all. Except that she still wasn't gaining.

On day five we rented a double electric hospital-grade breast pump from a lactation consultant, who told me to use it for twenty minutes after each feeding, for a total of 160 minutes a day. The idea was to trick my body into thinking it had to feed triplets. We were to keep a careful tally of minutes spent pumping, minutes spent nursing, milliliters of breast milk produced by the pump, ounces of supplemental formula given to Chloe, numbers of wet and dirty diapers. The lactation consultant provided us with charts. My husband was impressed with the scientific nature of it all. He was happy to have a plan.

I started taking fenugreek, blessed thistle, and alfalfa leaf. I also started taking domperidone.

During the first week, I hated using that pump. It hurt my already painful nipples even more, and deprived me of much-needed rest. But at least my husband was home to hold Chloe while I pumped. The second week, with my husband back at work, was hellish by comparison. Chloe would lay on the floor at my feet, sobbing and eating her little fists while I held the pumps to my breasts and desperately watched the clock, counting down every terrible minute and cursing my circumstances.

After it became obvious that she would need some formula, we tried cup-feeding, syringe feeding, finger feeding, and tube feeding to avoid nipple confusion. We were miserly with the amounts we gave her. We wanted her to be hungry enough to breastfeed as much as possible. She cried and cried, and since we thought we'd fed her enough, we didn't know what was wrong. We walked her and bounced her and rocked her and cuddled her, and still she screamed and screamed.

At three weeks, she saw a pediatrician for the first time—her introductory visit. He weighed her and found that she was still an ounce below her birth weight. He chastised me with grim tales of failure-to-thrive babies hospitalized and hooked up to tubes and machines. He ordered me to take her home and let her drink as much formula as she wanted to, from a bottle, and bring her back the next day for another weigh-in.

I did as he'd said. She gained 12 ounces overnight. The doctor and his staff could hardly believe it. Apparently, we'd been starving her.

When it became obvious that Chloe would need to be supplemented with formula at every feeding, I bought the Lact-Aid. It needed to be meticulously cleaned with a syringe after each use, and sterilized every 24 hours.

Breastfeeding in those early weeks became a source of anger, guilt, and anxiety for me. The pain in my nipples took seven weeks to resolve. Nobody could find anything wrong with our latch; I saw three midwives, two lactation consultants, and two public health nurses about it. Everybody said our latch was just fine. I was just one of these unusual, unfortunate women whose nipples are not very "stretchy." The last lactation consultant I spoke to, during the sixth week, diagnosed me with what she called "unresolved negative pressure." In other words, too much sucking when nothing was coming out. She advised me to stop pumping.

Aside from the physical pain, I grew resentful of being treated with skepticism by other mothers who didn't know my situation. I would explain to moms I met in the park that I couldn't go for coffee with them because I had to take my baby home to feed her—that I couldn't just breastfeed her on the spot, because I had to supplement her with formula, since I didn't produce enough milk.

"Did you try pumping?" was always the first question. Nobody believed, without a lengthy explanation, that I really just didn't produce enough milk. I grew tired of being judged, of reading attachment parenting magazines that made me feel as though I was poisoning my baby with formula, tired of rinsing and sterilizing the Lact-Aid, tired of relying on tubes and plastic to feed my daughter. I felt cheated out of a natural breastfeeding experience.

The experience did get better, though. In the end, we used the Lact-Aid for seven months. During that time, I took domperidone each day, as well as various herbs. I monitored my water intake. I worried about eating too little or exercising too much. I continued to pump from time to time. It was a full-time, all-consuming occupation. I determined that I was able to provide Chloe with roughly half of what she needed, so most of the time it seemed worth the effort.

I developed a love-hate relationship with my Lact-Aid. I loved the fact that it allowed me to breastfeed Chloe. I hated the mess, the fuss, the cleaning and sterilizing, the fact that more often than not, it would leak all over me. I hated feeling that I had to choose between never breastfeeding Chloe in public (which meant never leaving my house), or feeling compelled to explain my medical history to all curious onlookers. Despite all the determination I could muster, I never did get the hang of nursing discreetly with the Lact-Aid, although I know that other women do.

At seven mnths of age, Chloe developed a trick. Instead of latching onto my nipple, she would try to get the Lact-Aid tube into her mouth without my nipple, and suck on it as though it was a straw. Then she would cry and refuse to breastfeed when I removed the tube from her mouth and tried to latch her back on to the nipple. Breastfeeding became an ongoing battle, and one day in a fit of frustration I decided to abandon the Lact-Aid. What kind of bonding experience between mother and infant, I wondered, included the baby crying hard, arching her back, and fighting the entire process?

I started supplementing with bottles instead. I would nurse Chloe first, then top her up with a few additional ounces from a bottle at each feeding. This worked perfectly for about a month and a half, but then Chloe began to launch nursing strikes. At first it was just once every two weeks, then once a week, then several times a week, always at unpredictable times. She would refuse to latch on, arching her back, screaming and struggling to get out of my arms. She wanted her bottle. I knew the bottles were causing my problems, but I couldn't bring myself to go back to the Lact-Aid.

For a long, long time, I pumped every time she refused to feed, in order to keep my meager supply going so that at least I could still breastfeed at night if she needed it.

Then I started to cut back on the domperidone. I had been on it for seven months. After I had gradually eliminated the domperidone and the Lact-Aid entirely, my milk supply plummeted dramatically. Chloe began to get more and more frustrated at the breast. The one feeding we both had always enjoyed, and which she'd never refused, was the early morning one. I had always found that after a full night's sleep, I had enough milk first thing in the morning for a full serving. It was my single, glorious, daily taste of what breastfeeding must be like for most "normal" mothers. It was the joy and highlight of my day.

Chloe increasingly lost interest in breastfeeding. Eventually she began to refuse all of her feedings except the morning one, and I finally gave up pumping. By the time she was nine months old, even the single morning feeding needed to be followed by a six-ounce bottle. One day I wondered dismally if all the herbs I was taking were helping at all, and in a fit of resentment I threw them all down the toilet. Two weeks later, Chloe refused her morning nursing session for the first time ever, clamoring instead for her bottle. She was weaned. I was crushed. She never breastfed again.

I kept hoping she would have a series of restless nights and want to breastfeed at night again, as she had before—but as luck would have it, she spent the next two weeks sleeping soundly for ten or more hours at a stretch at night. I thought about waking her up, but that seemed crazy. We let her sleep while my milk dried up.

In retrospect, I still can't see that I could have done very much differently. I might have persisted with the Lact-Aid, and maybe she would have learned to accept it, instead of trying to suck on it like a straw. I could have taken the domperidone for a full year or longer, but that wasn't likely.

I know that I ought to be pleased that I produced at least half of what she needed for so long under the circumstances. But when she wakes up at midnight upset by a bad dream, or distressed by a scratchy throat or an earache, and she has to wait to be comforted while I run downstairs to make a bottle, the fact that I knocked myself out trying doesn't always cut it. I will always wonder if I could have somehow tried even harder. On the other hand, she has always been a very independent little soul who was never all that passionate about breastfeeding. She doesn't seem to miss it at all.

Nowadays when I show her a breast just to see her reaction, she playfully bites the nipple, grins at me and toddles off in the direction of a favorite book or toy. It's only been a few months, and already she seems to have no recollection of her breastfeeding days. Weaning her has been a source of both relief and regret. Twelve years ago when I reasoned that bottle-feeding would be just fine for me, I had no idea how special a breastfeeding relationship could be. Now that I know, I treasure every memory I have of it, and I know I would go through all the same efforts again for a second child.

PREPARING TO BREASTFEED AFTER BREAST REDUCTION SURGERY

Now that you have decided to breastfeed and have a reasonable idea of what your breastfeeding experience may be like, you will need to begin actively preparing. Many of the general breastfeeding books you may have read that mentioned breastfeeding after reduction surgery state that you will only know if you can "successfully breast-feed" by trying to breastfeed after the baby is born. This is far from accurate. There is much you can do beforehand that will positively influence your BFAR experience.

Information and support are important predictors of your chances of developing a satisfying breastfeeding relationship. But what information and what kind of support do you need? This chapter represents the experience of hundreds of BFAR mothers and shares what they learned were the most critical factors that made a difference in their BFAR experiences.

What You Can Do before the Baby Is Born

Learn What to Expect

One of the factors to consider when determining your reasonable BFAR expectations is the type of surgery you had. Because this is such an important predictor of your lactation capability, it is important that you learn about your particular surgery by obtaining and reading your post-surgical report. Your doctor's office or the medical records department of the hospital will be able to provide you with a copy. If necessary, do not hesitate to ask for help in translating unfamiliar medical terms.

Learn Relaxation Techniques

Learn deep relaxation techniques and practice them frequently so that they will be second nature when you need them after the baby is born. Your state of mind can have a profound influence on lactation, especially the let-down reflex, so learning how to cope with the inevitable postpartum stress and fatigue will enhance your lactation potential. Deep relaxation can also be beneficial while you are still pregnant, and will help you cope during labor.

Most proponents of relaxation methods believe that our modern, stressful lives do not allow our bodies to ever fully relax, which is necessary for maintaining a healthy physiology. Certainly relaxation provides a pleasant, refreshed feeling, which makes problems seem less overwhelming.

Deep relaxation can be achieved in different ways, through physical and psychological relaxation techniques. Good examples of both types of relaxation techniques are provided in Appendix 4.

The physical relaxation techniques are most effective when you are able to peacefully concentrate on consciously relaxing all muscles in your body. Examples of physical relaxation techniques are progressive muscular relaxation, yoga, and massage. The deep muscular relaxation you will achieve from these techniques will also serve to calm and soothe your mind from the concerns, worries, and aggravations that led to the stress you were experiencing.

Psychological relaxation focuses first on the mind, allowing the physical relaxation to naturally follow. Visual imagery is a common, psychological relaxation method that relies on a moderately well-developed imagination. Another method is actively remembering a pleasant experience in which you concentrate on a specific, pleasant memory in order to relive the pleasure that you experienced then. Visualization is also an effective psychological relaxation technique, especially for BFAR mothers. Picturing a successful future breastfeeding moment in elaborate detail gives you a specific goal and may even help you keep on track in moments of doubt. Additionally, prayer and meditation can be highly effective relaxation methods.

The method of relaxation you choose is less important than finding one that feels comfortable to you. Then practice it on a regular basis so that it will become second nature to you when you need it.

Learn about Normal Breastfeeding

Learn all you can about breastfeeding from every possible source. There are many reliable resources for breastfeeding information on the Internet; books such as La Leche League's THE WOMANLY ART OF BREASTFEEDING; support groups like La Leche League; classes offered by health care providers in your area; and you can receive support from the experienced breastfeeding mothers among your own friends and family. Becoming knowledgeable about the "normal" breastfeeding process and issues will help you in your BFAR experience. You should have a thorough understanding of proper positioning and latch-on techniques, including different ways to position your baby at the breast. You will find that some positions work better for you than others and knowing about the different methods beforehand will make the going easier when you are in the trenches. Chapter 6 provides an overview of proper breastfeeding mechanics.

Attend Breastfeeding Support Group Meetings

Join or develop a network of supportive nursing mothers to provide emotional bolstering and an avenue for finding additional breastfeeding resources. It is helpful to attend meetings while you are pregnant so that you will know women who can help you later, in either a supportive or informational capacity.

One great place to find friendly breastfeeding mothers is La Leche League, an international organization that was founded to provide information and support to breastfeeding mothers, many of whom have experienced difficult breastfeeding situations. La Leche League has nearly a fifty year history of helping mothers and their babies. Look for an LLL Group in your local area where you can attend monthly meetings and continue to develop friendships outside of the Group meetings. There are also other breastfeeding support groups in the US and elsewhere in the world, and you are encouraged to contact them if La Leche League is not available in your area. Information on finding a breastfeeding support group in your area is located in Appendix 1.

The following excerpt from THE WOMANLY ART OF BREASTFEEDING explains what you can expect to gain from attending a La Leche League meeting:

> "*Today, La Leche League gatherings are held monthly in all parts of the world. The information is divided into topics for a four-meeting series. As no two Series Meetings are exactly alike, many mothers continue to attend for many months beyond the first series and even for many years.*
>
> *LLL meetings are sometimes held in the home of a La Leche League member or in a convenient public meeting place. All members are encouraged to bring along their nursing babies. The meetings are conducted by an experienced breastfeeding mother who has been qualified to represent La Leche League. She presents a somewhat structured outline of information at each meeting, but these meetings are not classes; they are open, informative discussions. At the LLL Group meetings in your area, you will learn about much more than the basics of breastfeeding.*
>
> *The first meeting of the series is usually about the advantages of breastfeeding. You will discover benefits of breastfeeding that may never have occurred to you—results of research on the value of human milk and mothers' own stories of breastfeeding advantages. Many mothers have remarked after this meeting, 'I knew that breastfeeding was good for my baby and good for me, but I didn't know how good it was. This information makes me more confident than ever in my decision to nurse, and it makes me feel proud to know that I am doing something so wonderful for my baby.'*
>
> *At the next meeting, the discussion usually centers on the family and the breastfed baby. Mothers share tips on how to get off to a good start in the hospital and at home with the new baby. Knowing what to expect in the way of procedures and routines at local area hospitals or birthing centers can be helpful to a new mother. Easing the emotional adjustment of all family members, lightening the work load, establishing a good milk supply, and preventing problems from ever beginning are all topics of discussion.*

Another meeting covers basic breastfeeding techniques and prob-lem-solving. You can receive specific advice from the best breastfeeding experts in the world: experienced nursing mothers. The overall message is that no matter what problem may arise, there is almost always a solution that does not require weaning the baby.

At another meeting, the proper diet for lactating and pregnant women is discussed, as well as starting the baby on solid foods and when and how to wean the baby. Often discipline of toddlers is also explored at this meeting.

Almost all La Leche League Groups have an extensive lending library available to their members. Current titles on breastfeeding, childbirth, parenting, and nutrition that may not be widely available can be found at LLL meetings. Most Groups also have books, booklets, and breastfeeding-aid products that LLL members can purchase.

All mothers who have an interest in breastfeeding are invited to attend La Leche League meetings. All mothers are accepted with open arms at La Leche League meetings: mothers of all races and religions, single mothers, working mothers, and mothers whose philosophy on various aspects of infant care and childrearing may differ from La Leche League's. Each mother is encouraged to take from La Leche League's philosophy what seems sensible and helpful to her. The ideal time to begin attending is during pregnancy, because the information received in advance may prove to be vital to a mother when her baby arrives."[1]

One thing many BFAR mothers worry about is that they will feel uncomfortable among mothers in a breastfeeding support group, especially if they need to supplement their babies with bottles during the meeting. Actually, most groups go to great effort to make all mothers feel comfortable, no matter what their situations or circumstances. Bottle-feeding mothers are welcome to attend La Leche League meetings because La Leche League Leaders know that every mother is doing the best she can with the resources and support available to her. Group members know that sometimes breastfeeding is not possible for an individual mother, and learning more about breastfeeding and developing a breastfeeding support network are the best ways to make the next experience turn out differently. La Leche League celebrates each drop of human milk that is given to a baby, even when it must be given in a bottle. If you should attend a La Leche League meeting and find that you do not feel comfortable, it may help to speak to a Leader after the meeting and explain your circumstances and directly ask for her support. She may not have realized that comments made during the meeting had made you uncomfortable and she will then make an effort to encourage the Group's acceptance of your unique situation.

Evaluate Your Nipples for Flatness or Inversion

Something that you can do during pregnancy to prepare for lactation is to evaluate your nipples for flatness or inversion. Despite (or possibly even because of) your surgery, you may have flat or inverted nipples. These are not necessarily small nipples, which may be tiny but are otherwise quite adequate for functional nursing. Flat nipples are those in which the nipple does not protrude very much, if at all, making the baby's latch-on a bit more troublesome. Inverted nipples actually draw inward when the areola is compressed, making latch-on more difficult. If positioning and latch-on are correct, however, most babies are able to nurse effectively from even flat or inverted nipples. Identifying these conditions early, though, gives you the opportunity to evaluate the use of specially designed devices or exercises to correct them.

To check your nipples for inversion, simply place your thumb and your index finger at the base of your nipple, with the thumb on top and the index finger underneath. Very gently, bring your fingers together. If your nipple retracts into your breast, you have an inverted nipple.

If you think you might have inverted or flat nipples, consultation with a La Leche League Leader or a lactation consultant before the baby is born is the best way to learn how to correct such nipple structural issues. If you determine that you have flat or inverted nipples, you can perform special exercises to draw out your nipples or use breast shells during pregnancy or after the baby comes.

For BFAR mothers, performing exercises or using breast shells may cause slight pain because some flatness or inversions can be complicated by interior adhesions that result from the surgery. Such adhesions tend to stretch and cease to cause problems after you have been breastfeeding for a period of time. But initially, lengthening them by using breast shells or by letting the baby's active nursing stretch them out can cause discomfort.

One recommendation that many mothers with flat or inverted nipples find particularly helpful is to pump the breast for a minute or so before feeding in order to draw out the nipple. You should also pay careful attention to latch-on and proper positioning, so that you can minimize the difficulty and ensure that the baby can nurse effectively. If you find flatness or inversion to be a problem, you can be consoled by the knowledge that breastfeeding subsequent children is likely to be easier because breastfeeding tends to elongate nipple ligaments.

There is no need for you to prepare your nipples for breastfeeding by roughening them. In fact, this could lead to sore nipples after the baby is born because the skin of the nipples may be dry. Instead, the only preparation your nipples need before the baby is born is to be well-hydrated. Avoid soap. Any cream or moisturizer can be used for this purpose, however, many mothers find that Lansinoh® Brand Lanolin for Breastfeeding Mothers, which is hypoallergenic, purified lanolin, works very well.

Employ Breastfeeding Friendly and Breastfeeding Knowledgeable Health Care Professionals

It is important that you identify and employ breastfeeding friendly and knowledgeable professionals before you need them. Make some calls or ask your breastfeeding friends for names of lactation consultants, obstetricians, midwives, and pediatricians. You will want to work with professionals who have a sound knowledge-base of and experience in lactation. Professionals who believe that formula is "just as good" as human milk and breastfeeding may not help you to work through the issues you may face as a BFAR mother, and can actually undermine your efforts with incorrect advice. On the other hand, as a BFAR mother you must be open to the possibility of supplementation and the professionals you consult must be able to determine when this is truly necessary.

One suggestion some mothers have for determining whether a physician is supportive of breastfeeding is to not tell them of your convictions, but rather ask the following question, "I'm trying to decide whether to breastfeed. Can you tell me what you think of it so that I can make my decision?" This way, the doctor will tell you what he or she really believes, and not what he or she thinks you want to hear.

Finding a knowledgeable support person is also very important. In most cases, your best source of information and support will be your local LLL Leader. While she may not have personal experience or knowledge about BFAR, she has a resource network that can give her the technical information she may need to help you. In addition, an LLL Leader has a complete and thorough understanding of normal breastfeeding management and can offer support throughout your breastfeeding experience. Also, LLL Leaders are volunteers who do not charge for their help. If there is no LLL Leader nearby, you may need to work with a lactation consultant. Lactation consultants charge for their services. One who is board-certified will use the initials IBCLC as her credential. This means she has fulfilled the background and training requirements for board certification and passed a certification exam. Even so, not all lactation consultants have had background or experience working with mothers who have had breast reduction surgery. However, she will have the technical expertise to help you with your breastfeeding efforts, working with any latch-on or positioning problems and helping you to maximize your milk supply.

While you are investigating the best health professionals to employ in your area, you may wish to check with your health insurance carrier to determine if the services of a lactation consultant, rental of a breast pump, or purchase of supplemental nursing devices may be covered expenses. Some insurance companies require a prescription from your health care provider in order to pay for the services or supplies. Others will reimburse you for the cost. It never hurts to ask. Some mothers have even been able to convince insurance companies to cover expenses when it was against their usual policy because of their special BFAR circumstances. When all else fails, write a letter appealing the decision. All they can say is no. But you may be pleasantly surprised. Most insurance companies know that it is cost effective in the long run for you to breastfeed your child, especially when your child is also one of their insured patients.

Use a Breastfeeding Friendly and Breastfeeding Knowledgeable Health Care Facility

Finding a breastfeeding-friendly hospital or birthing center is also critically important to breastfeeding success. The length of your stay in the hospital or birthing center should be as short as possible so that you can minimize separations from your baby, as well as unnecessary interventions. Although you may feel that you need to rest and recuperate from the birth, it is crucial that you keep your baby with you so that you can nurse frequently and on demand and prevent the use of artificial nipples or pacifiers, which can interfere with the development of your baby's sucking skills. Rooming-in can actually result in better rest for both you and the baby by reducing your stress level and encouraging harmonious nursing patterns. But truly, being home is probably going to be the most comfortable and restful place for both you and your baby and the sooner you get there, the better.

Learn about Birthing Methods that Minimize Interventions

Many studies have shown that medications, including epidurals, especially epidurals containing bupivacaine,[1,2] during childbirth can significantly inhibit the sucking abilities of newborns by causing the baby to be sleepy and somewhat uncoordinated for a significant period after birth. This very period after birth, however is a critical window of time to begin breastfeeding which, of course, cannot begin until baby is alert and able to latch on properly. This is not to say that there are never circumstances that warrant the use of drugs during birth, but rather that whenever possible, avoiding or minimizing their use will maximize the baby's initial sucking abilities, which are so important for establishing the milk supply. Of course, if an epidural is used during labor, it certainly will not make breastfeeding impossible, but will only mean that it may be necessary to pay closer attention to any latching problems that come up and seek help from a lactation specialist to remedy them.

Preparing for the birth by attending classes in birthing methods that focus on avoiding the use of medications during labor can enhance your chances of having a drug-free birth. The Bradley Method is a particularly good method for achieving this goal.

Learn about At-Breast Supplementers

Learn about the various methods of supplementation other than bottle-feeding so that if supplementation becomes necessary, you will already be prepared with the most breastfeeding-compatible methods. There are many devices to provide supplementary nutrition (which can be human milk or formula) that are more effective in preserving the nursing relationship than bottles. It is recommended that you purchase an at-breast supplementer before the baby is born so that you will not need to go to any effort to get one when you have less ability to do so. If you do not need the supplementer, you can always return or resell it if it has not been opened.

An at-breast supplementer allows a mother to breastfeed, while at the same time supplementing the baby's nutrition with donated human milk, formula, or another nutritional supplement. Supplementing at the breast gives the baby all the emotional benefits of breastfeeding while ensuring that the baby's nutritional requirements are fulfilled.

Ideally, an at-breast supplementer supplies supplementation in direct proportion to the available milk delivered from the mother's breast. So when there is less milk, more supplement is delivered, and when there is more milk, less is given.

There are four models of at-breast supplementers on the market today. Two of these, the Medela SNS (and SNS Starter) and the Lact-Aid are available worldwide. The Supply Line is marketed in Australia by the Nursing Mothers Association of Australia and the Axicare Nursing Aid is available in the United Kingdom from Colgate Medical

Ltd. Contact information is provided in Appendix 1. All of these supplementers consist of a container that hangs from a cord around the mother's neck. One or two plastic tubes run from the container (a disposable bag or a rectangular plastic bottle) to the nipple(s). Depending on the supplementer model, alternate tubing in different sizes may also be included.

For information on at-breast supplementers, please see Chapter 8. You will also find purchasing information in Appendix 1.

Learn the Signs of Dehydration

In order to assess your baby's status in the first few weeks after birth, it will be important for you to know and be aware of the signs of dehydration. You will have a general sense of whether your baby is acquiring adequate fluids by making a point of noticing his general activity level and responsiveness to the surrounding environment. Your baby should be alert, demonstrate clear hunger signals, and even be a little fussy at times. Most importantly, he should act satisfied after feedings. Conversely, a baby who hasn't had enough fluid is either very fussy or uninterested and listless. A dehydrated baby will simply not look well and may act sick.

Some objective signs of dehydration are:

- A weak, high-pitched cry. This is characterized by a lack of any energy and will not be very loud;

- A depressed or sunken "soft spot" (anterior fontanel) on the head. Be sure to assess this when the baby is lying down and not when held in an upright position, which can give an inaccurate presentation;

- A dry mouth. Periodically put your freshly washed (dry) finger in the baby's mouth and feel the amount of saliva. Adequate hydration is present when you can move your finger across the tongue or cheeks easily without sticking;

- Insufficient and infrequent wet diapers. At first, before your mature milk comes in, a newborn will only wet one or two diapers a day. When your colostrum turns to milk, around the third day, you should then expect your baby to wet six to eight (6-8) cloth diapers or four to six (4-6) disposable diapers, and have two to five (2-5) bowel movements each day. Later, after about four weeks, the frequency of bowel movements usually slows down to once a day or once every few days. Keep track of the wet and soiled diapers in whatever way is easiest for you, either by keeping notes or collecting them all in one location each day;

- Hands and feet or fingers and toes that are cool and clammy to your touch. Gauging this can be a bit subjective, but keep it in mind as something to check in conjunction with the other signs of adequate hydration;

- A fast pulse and very low blood pressure. You probably won't be able to assess this at home, but be sure your baby's health care giver is carefully monitoring these criteria;

- Absence of tears in infants older than three months. (Before a baby is three months old, he usually will not have the capacity to produce tears); and

- When gently pinched, failure of the skin to quickly return (spring back) to normal surface. [3]

If you notice any of these signs, you will need to take your baby to a health care professional or facility as soon as possible. These signs do not all need to be evident for dehydration to be indicated. They are danger signs and must be taken very seriously.

One of the most important signs of dehydration in the first month is a lack of sufficient wet diapers. Many new parents, however, do find it difficult to know whether a diaper is "wet," especially when using disposable diapers. For this reason, it may be better to use cloth diapers in the first few weeks. It is sometimes easier to detect wetness on a cotton diaper than on a disposable diaper.

If you do choose to use disposable diapers, in order to know what a wet diaper really feels like, try pouring 2-3 tablespoons of water into a fresh diaper. Feeling the weight of this wet disposable diaper can help you judge the wetness of your baby's diaper.

Prepare an Assessment Checklist

Some BFAR mothers find that they are best able to assess the status of their babies' hydration, growth, and development in the early weeks by tracking objective criteria on a chart. For this purpose, a sample chart has been provided in Appendix 3. You may wish to photocopy several pages and put them on a clipboard that you keep by your bedside, your favorite rocker, or above the baby's changing table. This chart can then be taken with you to doctors' appointments to add a detailed record of your efforts and your baby's progress.

Learn about Galactagogues

Learn about galactagogues, which are substances that have the effect of increasing the milk supply, usually by affecting the production of prolactin, which prompts the mammary system to increase milk production. As with all drugs, especially those taken during lactation, galactagogues have a physiological effect and should be taken with care and complete understanding of the substance to be ingested. Many BFAR mothers find galactagogues to be critical to increasing their milk supplies. However, taking galactagogues is a decision each mother must make for herself, in conjunction with her partner and health care professional. Chapter 9 provides a discussion of herbal and prescription galactagogues that addresses the concerns and questions you may have about them.

If you think galactagogues might be something you would want to try to maximize or increase your milk supply, you will need to have an understanding of which ones will be effective for you and how to use them before you actually need them. You may not have the time or mental energy to learn about them after the baby is born. If you have a good understanding of galactagogues you will be better able to explain them to your lactation professionals and family, who may be skeptical. Once you have learned the basics, you may want to purchase an initial supply of the galactagogues that you think might benefit you so that you have them on hand and can begin using them as soon as the baby is born.

Some of the most popular herbal galactagogues are fenugreek, blessed thistle, goat's rue, brewer's yeast, aniseed, and fennel. Fenugreek and blessed thistle, especially, have well-established reputations as highly effective galactagogues with no serious side effects.

The most effective prescription galactagogues are domperidone (brand name Motilium) and metoclopramide (brand name Reglan). Both of these drugs have well-documented galactagogic properties. Domperidone, however, does not cross the blood-brain barrier and so has fewer side effects and can be taken for longer periods of time. Metoclopramide, which does cross the blood-brain barrier, can only be taken for two-week time periods, and has been known to cause headaches and depression. Many BFAR mothers who use domperidone report increases in milk production. Anecdotally, metoclopromide's galactagogic effect seems to be less significant. While domperidone is not available in the US, it can be obtained from Canada, Mexico, or New Zealand (contact information can be found in Appendix 1).

Many BFAR mothers wonder when they should begin taking galactagogues if they choose to do so. They should be taken only when a low milk supply has demonstrated, such as by signs of dehydration, and no sooner than the mother's milk begins transforming from colostrum into mature milk. This is the beginning of the transfer from the endocrine-driven mammary system to the supply-and-demand-driven (autocrine) mammary system, which relies upon prolactin for milk production. Tricking the system into thinking that more prolactin has been "demanded" by chemicals that induce prolactin production is the key to having an increased milk supply.

Learn How to Express Your Milk

Learn how to effectively express your milk by practicing any of the several manual expression techniques. There are times when manual expression is a better option than using a breast pump because it is completely free, portable, and requires no energy source (other than you). Sometimes you may just want to express milk to reassure yourself that it is there. Becoming familiar with manual expression will also help you to learn how to massage and compress your breasts during breastfeeding in order to encourage better let-downs and increase your milk supply.

During pregnancy, you will want to avoid overstimulation of your breasts or nipples. Stop stimulating your nipples if you feel a dramatic increase in cramps, backache, or contractions (even painless Braxton-Hicks); you've practiced enough. And if they don't diminish in intensity or frequency, call your health care provider immediately.

Despite the technique used, one problem BFAR mothers have is differentiating the glands and other lactation tissues inside the breast when other scar tissue is present. This is also the reason that self-examinations are more difficult for BFAR women. Of course, one way to know that you have compressed a gland is when milk is ejected from the nipple. But aside from this tell-tale sign, it may simply be a matter of exploring your breast tissue through massage and compression to learn the feel of different types of breast tissue. Lactating glands are usually large and can be firm. They can be located anywhere in the breast area, including as far up as under the arm and as close as just behind the areola. When you find what seem to be milk glands, these will be the areas you will concentrate on when you begin manual expression.

The two manual expression methods that work most successfully for mothers are the Chest Compression Technique and the Marmet Technique. Both of these methods take some practice to develop proficiency—there is no technique that will feel completely normal at first. But with time, you should be able to develop your skill to the point that you can express your milk when you need to without much trouble. Before attempting to express your milk, of course, you will need to wash your hands thoroughly.

The Chest Compression Technique is described in La Leche League's WOMANLY ART OF BREASTFEEDING:

> *"Place your fingers on your breast with your thumb above and fingers below so they form a "C." Push back toward your chest wall while squeezing your thumb and fingers together rhythmically just behind the areola. In the case of a very large areola, fingers should be positioned about one to one-and-a-half inches (two-and-one-half to four cm.) behind the nipple.*
>
> *Do not slide your fingers along the skin. Rotate your hand around the breast in order to reach all the milk ducts. Do this for three to five minutes on one breast; then switch to the other breast. Switching back and forth at least twice helps to increase the flow of milk.*
>
> *You may find it more comfortable to use your right hand, but it's better to alternate, using both hands on each breast in order to reach more of the milk ducts.*
>
> *Have a clean container ready to collect the milk."*[1]

The Marmet Technique is provided in Appendix 6 and was developed by Chele Marmet, who is a La Leche League Leader and lactation consultant, as well as the Director of the Lactation Institute in Encino, California. This method may be more effective for BFAR mothers because it seems to induce the let-down very effectively.

Learn about Breast Pumps and Pumping

Pumping is occasionally an effective means of increasing a BFAR mother's milk supply and may be recommended by some lactation specialists for this purpose, especially for first-time mothers. The most appropriate circumstances and methods for pumping are discussed in detail in Chapter 9. However, because it is possible that you may need or want to pump, it may be helpful for you to be prepared for the possibility of pumping so that you will understand your options when the baby arrives.

Of course, there are advantages and disadvantages to renting a pump before the baby is born. On the one hand, it might be wonderful to have it handy if you need it to help increase your milk supply. But on the other hand, if you have it, you may feel you need to use it to justify the rental expense, when doing so would actually be less effective than simply letting the baby nurse frequently. There are times when using a pump is an effective way to maximize a BFAR mother's lactation capability. But many mothers find that pumping can be stressful and time-consuming, which is actually detrimental to their milk supply. Whether or not to pump is a decision you will need to make with your lactation specialist, but just keep in mind the possibility that renting a pump before the baby is born may be counterproductive as you may tend to depend on it or begin using it before allowing enough time to establish a breastfeeding relationship.

When considering pumps, it is important to know that there are many models of breast pumps on the market, and some are more effective than others. Hospital-grade automatic cycling electric rental pumps are a much better choice for BFAR mothers as they are more effective and efficient. Less effective battery-operated pumps are not a good choice for a mother who is trying to establish or increase her milk supply. There are other automatic electric pumps including the Medela Pump-In-Style™, the White River Concepts Model 9600, and the Ameda® Purely Yours™, which are excellent choices for any mother, including a BFAR mother, who is pumping to collect milk while she is away from her baby. However, these have not been found to be as effective as a rental pump when a BFAR mother is pumping to increase her milk supply.

To find vendors of hospital-grade, automatic-cycling pumps in your area, see Appendix 1.

Rent a Scale

Monitoring weight gain is a critical factor in evaluating your baby's health and development, especially in the first two months, and renting an electronic baby scale to use at home is the best way to do this effectively. The experience of BFAR mothers has been that having an electronic baby scale can be crucial in preventing unnecessary supplementation. Scales used in doctors' offices are often calibrated differently, leading to incorrect measurements that can unnecessarily frighten or falsely reassure parents of their baby's weight gain. Even a slight difference in calibration between two scales in the same doctor's office can make a difference in evaluating a baby's weight gain. Regularly using your own electronic scale will give you a more consistent means of assessing your baby's weight gain.

Some BFAR mothers have said that in the wee hours of the night, when their babies were fussy and crying and they were feeling most vulnerable, they began wondering if the baby was hungry and if maybe they just did not have enough milk. It was only because they knew definitively by the information charted from their baby scales that showed their babies were gaining adequately that they were reassured that "a baby who is gaining well is not starving" and they were able to resist the temptation to supplement. Of course, if you find that your baby does not gain appropriately, a scale may give you the first indication that supplementation is indeed necessary. Either way, you will retain more control over the information you need to make necessary decisions in consultation with your baby's health care givers.

Most exclusively breastfed babies gain an average of one-half ounce (16.2 g) to 1 ounce (28.4 g) per day (4 ounces [113.4 g] to 8 ounces [226.8 g] per week) in the first three months.[4] If baby is not gaining at this rate, it could be an indication that the baby needs to be assessed for frequency of nursing, proper positioning, and sucking technique. If these are ruled out, the issue of milk supply and the possible need for supplementation need to be addressed. Some babies grow in length and head circumference without gaining as much weight.

If you choose to rent an electronic scale, it is important not to weigh the baby too frequently. Frequent weighings can lead to so much anxiety that your let-down may be inhibited, which affects your milk supply and leads to less weight gain, which fuels more anxiety. Instead, it is recommended that you weigh your baby at the same time once a day so that you will know exactly how much your baby is gaining each day. Keeping a simple chart that you have handy near the scale, such as the Assessment Chart in Appendix 3, will make it easier to track.

Like breast pumps, not all scales are alike. Many baby products catalogs and stores carry "baby scales." These spring-type scales are merely able to estimate a range of weight. Only electronic scales such as the Medela BabyWeigh or BabyChecker are designed to accurately measure the precise degrees of weight gain that may concern a BFAR mother. The Medela BabyChecker scale is accurate to one ounce (28 grams) for babies under 20 pounds. The BabyWeigh is accurate to two grams. Medela scales can usually be rented from the same rental stations that rent breast pumps. Additional sources are listed in Appendix 1.

Purchase Breastfeeding Accessories

Breastfeeding itself does not require any special equipment. There are, however, a few accessories that can make your life much easier. Many breastfeeding mothers find that night and daytime clothing with special nursing openings make nursing sessions easier. A low, inclined nursing stool can be very pleasant as it elevates your legs to a comfortable height, making it easier to position the baby correctly. Lansinoh® Brand Lanolin for Breastfeeding Mothers, which is purified, hypoallergenic lanolin sold at many retail outlets and also available from La Leche League International, can help prevent and ease soreness in the first few days.

If you choose to wear a bra, having a good nursing bra will make breastfeeding easier. Look for a bra that allows you to easily lower the flap with only one hand because most often you will have the baby in the other arm. It is also best to purchase a bra that does not put pressure on any part of the breast, which can lead to plugged ducts and mastitis. It should be supportive, but not confining. For this reason, underwire bras are not a good choice during lactation because the wires tend to put pressure on breast tissue. Sports-type minimizing bras can also constrict circulation in the breasts, which may negatively impact lactation, as evidenced in many traditional societies when breasts are bound to cease lactation.

You might find it helpful to have some breast pads on hand in the event you experience leakage problems. But do keep in mind that leaking is not at all an indication of your milk-producing capabilities. It is only a gauge of the strength of the miniature nipple muscles that restrain the milk from leaking out of the ducts.

Additionally, many mothers find that having a sling-type carrier is an indispensable tool for mothering. Babies have been held snugly in their mothers' uteruses for the majority of their lives and most find that being in a snug position up close to their mothers, where they can hear her heartbeat and be in constant contact with her, is comforting. It also frees mothers to comfort their babies and have hands free to do other things at the same time. A sling can be used in many different positions, depending on your and your baby's preference.

There are so many ways mothers have found to use slings. A sling is versatile, transforming from a baby carrier to a diaper changing pad to a car seat blanket with ease. One of the best features is that a sling is compact and can be easily stuffed into a diaper bag when not in use. Many fathers find they like to use slings, too. Slings come in many colors and designs, as well as different lengths for different body builds. Best of all, some babies are soothed by the snugness of the sling—if you find you have a hard time soothing your baby, just put on your sling, place the baby in a straight-up-and-down, tummy to tummy position, and go for a walk. Most babies are sound asleep in moments. For more information about sling wearing and positioning, refer to the descriptions and pictures in Dr. William Sears' *The Baby Book*.

Create a Nursing Station

Take the time to set up a "nursing station" with a comfortable chair next to a sturdy table. Later, when you begin breastfeeding, you can put all the convenience items you may want to have near you on the table. This nursing station will be a place of comfort and refuge for you where you will have everything you need at arm's reach to be completely comfortable and worry-free. When you have such a place to go to, nursing can become a refuge, allowing you to thoroughly enjoy your special time with your baby.

Arrange for Postpartum Help

When the baby is born and you begin your BFAR experience, you will probably have very little energy to cook, clean, care for the home, other children, your partner, or even yourself. You will need help in the form of a nurturing, understanding, non-intrusive helper. Historically, such a person has been called a doula, which means "mother's helper." Today, the term commonly includes helping the mother cope with labor, especially when an unmedicated labor and birth are planned. Many doulas also help the mother during the postpartum time by cooking meals, doing laundry, caring for other children, and keeping the home tidy because it is well known that a mother tends to her baby best when she has no other responsibilities to worry her. Of course, a doula need not be hired help—it can be your partner, a mother or mother-in-law, a grandmother, an aunt, a sister (or even a grandfather, an uncle, or a brother), a friend, or someone from your religious community or La Leche League group. But if you do decide to hire a doula, you will find them listed in most yellow pages or your midwife or childbirth instructor may have recommendations.

One factor to be cautious about when selecting your doula will be finding a person who will not sabotage your BFAR efforts by expressing doubts or concerns, even subtly or in the context of kindness. This point should gently be made clear before the doula service begins.

Educate Your Partner

Finally, take the time to involve and thoroughly educate your partner about the BFAR issues that you will be facing. You are learning a great deal and will be making many decisions based upon what you have come to understand. You will need compassionate support during this time. Your partner will only be able to give you complete support by having knowledge of the challenges you will be facing as a BFAR mother and the techniques you will use to overcome them. You will then be able to embark on the BFAR journey together, committed to developing a successful nursing relationship with your new baby.

R E S O U R C E S :

1. THE WOMANLY ART OF BREASTFEEDING Sixth Revised Edition. Schaumburg, Illinois: LLLI, 1997; 34-36, 19, 121-22.

2. Lawrence, R. and R. Lawrence. *Breastfeeding: A Guide for the Medical Profession*, 5th edition. St. Louis, Missouri: Mosby, 1999, 241.

3. Riordan J. and Auerbach K., *Breastfeeding and Human Lactation*, 2nd Edition. Sudbury, Massachuetts: Jones and Bartlett, 1999; 313, 638.

4. Mohrbacher, N. and J. Stock. THE BREASTFEEDING ANSWER BOOK, Schaumburg, Illinois: LLLI, 1997; 27.

CAROL'S STORY

To be perfectly honest, my reason for having a breast reduction wasn't physical. It was because I was so painfully shy that I couldn't even look people in the face. After all, they were never looking me in the face either. Not surprisingly, my first appointment with the plastic surgeon was humiliating. He didn't seem to realize how embarrassed I was as I stood there naked from the waist up. After getting dressed again, we discussed the surgery. He said, "You should be able to breastfeed, but I can't guarantee it." "Who cares?" I replied. "I was raised on formula and I turned out just fine." Little did I realize how that comment would haunt me years later. I left his office with an appointment for my surgery.

Eight years after my surgery, married and pregnant for the first time, I started wondering about breastfeeding. I asked my doctor, but all he said was we would have to wait and see. When I was eight months pregnant, I discovered I was leaking colostrum. I was surprised and happy and decided I would try to breastfeed.

My husband will always remember the look of shock and pain on my face the first time I latched Heather on forty-five minutes after she was born. My baby girl was a little barracuda and that bad latch wasn't helping things. A couple of days later I had a very unsatisfied baby and badly cracked and bleeding nipples. I found that the nursery was supplementing her with formula at night. They said they were only trying to help a new mother get some sleep. None of us had any idea what these feedings could do to my milk supply or even that my breast reduction would have an effect.

I did meet one very pro-breastfeeding nurse who loaned me her copy of THE WOMANLY ART OF BREASTFEEDING. I read as much as I could. I did have engorgement, especially on the outsides and under my arms. I had grown back to my pre-surgical size! I was so sore from the cracked nipples that each and every latching on would hurt worse than any pain I had felt during labor.

Over the next few days Heather got more and more unsettled. I was getting more and more upset myself and started to slip into a depression. At around two weeks my cracked nipples finally healed and breastfeeding stopped hurting, but Heather was still not gaining weight. The nurse came out to visit a few days later and it looked as though Heather had lost a whole pound in a week. We panicked. I was told to feed her every two hours during the day whether or not she acted hungry and every three hours at night. I was to supplement with formula after every feeding.

Soon after this, I switched doctors, looking for one with up-to-date information on breastfeeding. I could not find anyone who had any experience with a woman breastfeeding after reduction surgery. The public health nurse even brought my case up at a local breastfeeding conference. Still no information. My new doctor didn't believe that my breasts were unable to accommodate my baby. She had me stop all supplementing for a weekend. She felt that Heather would be fine for at least that long. We weighed her on Friday and then again the following Monday. She gained four ounces! We thought we were home free. I was so happy.

Another bit of advice I was given was to drink one beer a day. Brian went on a three week trip out of town when Heather was four-and-a-half weeks old. I was left with my baby girl and a case of beer. Within a week I was on the verge of a breakdown. Heather cried from morning to night. I knew my milk wasn't enough for my baby. I started supplementing again. The only reason Heather didn't cry at night was because I had given up entirely trying to get her settled into her cradle. We slept together with her latched on almost all night long. However, I couldn't take the daytime crying. I finally called my husband and started to cry. I spent about four hours on the phone with him, but I don't think we said more than ten words the whole time. After we got off the phone he went to his boss and they sent him home to me. I was definitely dealing with postpartum depression.

A few months later we discovered that Heather was sensitive to barley and we were causing her distress by my drinking that beer each day. I later learned that beer acts as a diuretic and probably decreased my milk supply. Brewer's yeast is the ingredient I wanted and it is available in health food stores without the alcohol or barley.

At my milk supply's best, Heather was four months old and taking one or two six to eight ounce bottles of formula a day. I continued supplementing after feedings. I even tried pumping. I didn't really give it much effort though since I collected very little milk for my time. I didn't realize this was normal after my baby had taken all my easily accessible milk and that the pumping was for the extra stimulation.

My second daughter was born one month early. We were a team. She was such a good little breastfeeder and I had the patience I didn't have the first time. She was so contented. She slept for two to three hours and then breastfed for forty-five minutes or so. I thought that this time it was going to work. Within thirty-six hours I checked us out of the hospital. I hadn't spent a night away from Heather until I had Lisa and I missed my family terribly.

Lisa stayed contented. She slept well. She fed well. She only woke me up two to three times a night. Then I started to have to wake her up. When she was three days old, I noticed she had a yellow nose. We had a doctor's appointment the next day so I didn't worry about it. When I got her under the fluorescent lights at the office she was yellow all over! We were sent straight to the local children's hospital, where she was admitted and spent the next several days under the bili-lights.

I tried to keep up with the breastfeeding. I was only allowed to take her out from under the lights for thirty minutes every three hours. Soon enough we knew she needed more liquid to flush out the bilirubin. I was told to supplement with formula. She would barely get the recommended two ounces of formula in her before the thirty minutes were up. Breastfeeding was put on hold. I borrowed a hospital-grade pump and pumped every three hours. I could only pump 10 to 15 ml. I was so disappointed that I gave up on pumping. I didn't realize that four days after birth a mother doesn't produce several ounces of milk per feeding.

Soon enough we realized that the two ounces of formula wasn't enough. An IV had to be put in. Finally, several days later, we were cleared to go home. I was sent home with a bag full of two-ounce formula bottles and disposable nipples. My initial engorgement that had started on day three disappeared overnight. By the time Lisa was three weeks old, I was convinced I had no milk for her. The only reason I continued to breastfeed her was because she had picked up a cold and I wanted to get as many antibodies to her as possible. By the time she was six weeks old, we had our last breastfeeding session. She never seemed to notice or care. I never felt engorged, even though I had quit cold turkey.

When Lisa was fifteen months old, I became pregnant with my third baby. I immediately began searching the Internet newsgroups for information. One of my searches was in a newsgroup where I found the topic "Breastfeeding after reduction surgery." I wrote to the original author and through that post met four other post-surgical women either breastfeeding or soon to be breastfeeding. We each told our stories and agreed that it felt so good to find out we were not alone. I set up an email list for us, which we named BFAR and opened it up to other BFAR mothers.

It was wonderful to have so many experiences to learn from. I started keeping a list of all the "what worked for me" and "what didn't work for me" points. I felt so ready to have my baby and this time I was going to exclusively breastfeed him or her. At 38 weeks, Kira was born and we started breastfeeding within five minutes of her birth. She really wanted to. Unfortunately, she couldn't breathe properly and was suctioned several times. We tried to breastfeed again, but it still wasn't working. About an hour later Kira was taken to the special care nursery. Her blood was tested about three times a day due to my gestational diabetes. We breastfed as often as I was awake or she was. I decided that this time I would not tell anyone about my breast reduction. I felt confident that I would recognize if my baby needed more than I could give before she was in any danger. Everything seemed to be going well. The nurses were absolutely wonderful. They told me in advance that if Kira's blood glucose levels came back too low they would call me to nurse her before allowing anyone to give her formula. Unfortunately, we soon discovered that all that suctioning during her first hour after birth caused an inflammation in her sinuses. Kira was very uncomfortable out of the humidity of the isolette.

Finally, we were able to be together and we nursed as often as she wanted. One of the nurses noticed my scars, though, and asked about them. The next morning the pediatrician told me that Kira had lost ten percent of her birth weight and he was worried that she was not getting enough. He used some scare tactics to get me to stay in the hospital with my baby another night. Those scare tactics also got me feeding formula to my baby. The pediatrician told me that he wouldn't let Kira go home unless she had gained by the next day. Trying to avoid the very real possibility of nipple confusion with such a young baby, I cup fed Kira half of an ounce about three times that evening. The next day she had lost again, but it had slowed down. The pediatrician said to me, "Well, maybe she was about to turn around anyway." I was furious! I knew that the only reason we were singled out was because that nurse had noticed my scars. Unfortunately, the seeds of doubt had been planted.

When Kira was seven days old, I found myself writing to the BFAR email list. I felt that Kira was getting too much formula and wanted to know if I should cut back. She was sleeping for up to five hours after receiving her supplement. My concerns were that she wasn't stimulating my breasts to produce milk since she was sleeping from the formula. Another fear was caused by the fact that at seven days old she was still passing brown stools and not as frequently as the charts said she should have been. I was already sick of pumping and felt as though I was ignoring the rest of my family.

My writing to the BFAR email list saved our breastfeeding relationship. The wonderful women on the list supported me through my fears. I started to think of breastfeeding as one day at a time, even one feeding at a time. I made the decision to spend less time pumping, thereby giving up a potentially greater supply in favor of spending more time with my family and keeping my sanity. My goal became to continue my breastfeeding relationship with my daughter for as long as was mutually needed and enjoyable. I would just have to work at other ways to increase my supply. I know that if Kira had been my first baby, and if I had the information that I have now, I would have produced more milk for her. However, I chose what worked best for us at that time, and that included giving up the pumping.

When Kira was twelve days old, I started to notice a problem with nipple confusion. She couldn't figure out how to latch on to me or the bottle. I think a big reason we did not lose our relationship to nipple confusion was because I didn't give up trying to get her latched on to me when she was having problems. It took a couple of weeks to get good at switching from breast to bottle again, but we did it. By the time Kira was four weeks old, I produced enough milk at night to exclusively breastfeed her then.

Through the use of galactagogues, and by offering to breastfeed as often as every hour, I was able to increase my supply, so that by three to four months old, Kira was getting over 60 percent of her nutritional needs from me. The best part was that she was getting 100 percent of non-nutritional needs from our breastfeeding relationship. We had a closeness that is hard to explain.

As I write this, she is three-and-a-half years old. She weaned on her own at two-and-a-half and sometimes still pats my breast when we cuddle in the mornings. She remembers. I will always remember the tiny baby I held to my breast in her first days as she looked up at me as if to say, "Who are you?" I remember her in the later weeks when she would latch on with such vigor, needing to reconnect with mommy, and I look at her now, so much bigger, and such a wonderful, loving, independent little girl.

I may not have exclusively breastfed my babies, but by redefining my ideas of what breastfeeding means, from exclusive feeding of my milk alone to a relationship that benefited us all, I realize I was having successful breastfeeding relationships. Breastfeeding is so much more than nutrition.

BABY IS BORN: MAXIMIZING YOUR MILK SUPPLY AND DEVELOPING YOUR BREASTFEEDING RELATIONSHIP

BIRTH AND BFAR MECHANICS

Like most new mothers, you may find it helpful to turn to general books about breastfeeding in order to learn the basic mechanics of lactation. Having a good knowledge of breastfeeding basics will help you to understand the ways in which the process may differ for a mother who has had breast reduction surgery. This chapter is not meant to replace books like THE WOMANLY ART OF BREASTFEEDING, *The Nursing Mother's Companion, Bestfeeding: Getting Breastfeeding Right for You*, or *The Ultimate Breastfeeding Book of Answers*. These books and others like them provide an excellent overview of normal breastfeeding. This chapter will provide an overview of the special concerns and issues that are not addressed in general breastfeeding books.

During your initial breastfeeding efforts, you may also find you need gentle guidance from experienced mothers or health care professionals. Having competent help is vital in the early days because no matter how much you have learned, you will still need objective observations and personal guidance. There are a few hazards, though, that you should be wary about when seeking breastfeeding help. First, you may receive advice from every person you speak to in the early postpartum days, which can leave you feeling overwhelmed. You are likely to be confused by conflicting information. When this happens, it may help to consider the background of the person giving the advice. Not everyone is an expert and too often people simply relate what worked for them, which may be more personal opinion than objective information. A La Leche League Leader or an International Board Certified Lactation Consultant (IBCLC) will usually have the best information. But even the trained lactation experts do not necessarily have information about BFAR, which can differ in many ways. The surgically altered breast is anatomically and physiologically different and will not perform or respond in exactly the way a normal breast would. A lack of understanding about these differences can lead to breastfeeding mismanagement, which can jeopardize the early days of breastfeeding when the milk supply is most sensitive.

It is therefore important for you to have an understanding of BFAR breastfeeding mechanics in addition to normal breastfeeding mechanics in order to be successful. Naturally, much of what happens is common to both BFAR and normal breastfeeding experience, but there are also significant differences. This chapter will discuss those differences so that you will be well-prepared to initiate BFAR.

Ensuring a Good Start

Nursing in the First Hour Postpartum

Ideally, breastfeeding should begin as soon after birth as the baby is ready to nurse. There is a sensitive one-hour window of time right after birth when the baby is in a quiet, alert stage, and very receptive to learning to breastfeed correctly. Research has shown that when most newly born infants are placed immediately on the abdomen of their mothers, they will find her breast and initiate suckling in less than fifty minutes. This same study, however, demonstrated that because most infants will become drowsy after the first hour following birth, separating the infant from his mother during this crucial time missed this window, resulting in more difficulty in learning to breastfeed.[1]

This finding is very important to BFAR mothers because the greatest proportion of prolactin receptors can be established during this same small window of time. As explained in Chapter 2, prolactin receptors are special sites in the human breast that receive the hormone prolactin, which promotes and maintains the production of milk. While prolactin receptors are most impressionable during the first six weeks after the baby's birth, they are considerably more impressionable during the first hour after birth. Therefore, ensuring that the baby has every opportunity to suckle during this time will be one of the best things that you can do.[2]

Another reason to nurse in the first hour is because a full-term healthy newborn's sucking reflex is usually strongest about twenty to thirty minutes after birth, if he is not drowsy from drugs or anesthesia given to his mother during labor and delivery. If this "window of opportunity" is missed, you may find that the baby's sucking reflex will be diminished for about 36 hours, which can adversely affect the programming of the prolactin receptors.

Because of factors associated with either the labor, the mother's health, or the baby's health, however, immediate nursing may not always be possible. These factors may include significant levels of anesthesia, postpartum complications, a premature infant, an infant who aspirated meconium, or an infant with a five-minute Apgar score of less than six.[1]

Infants born before 38 weeks gestation may have sucking difficulties and, depending on the amount of care that is needed, may be unable to nurse for some period of time. In order to adequately stimulate the lactation system, mothers of premature infants who cannot nurse should begin pumping their breasts regularly with a hospital-grade automatic electric pump. This is especially important for BFAR mothers. Do not worry about how much milk you are able to collect in this way. The milk obtained from a pump is not at all indicative of how much milk is present in the breast or how much it is capable of producing. Any milk that is collected, though, can be given to the baby. This milk will be very valuable because it is specially tailored by your body to meet the nutritional and immunological needs of your preterm baby.

Mothers who have cesarean births (c-sections) may find that nursing immediately after the baby is born is not possible. Even if the mother receives an epidural and not general anesthesia, abdominal suturing occupies a majority of that first-hour window of time, which may make breastfeeding impractical. In addition, the infant may be more sleepy and less receptive to nursing. Some studies also suggest that cesarean births result in delayed milk production, which could be due to blood loss.[1] This could have implications for BFAR since there may be lower initial prolactin and oxytocin levels and fewer prolactin receptor sites established. However, frequent nursing afterward will go a long way toward minimizing these obstacles if they do exist. It may also help to know that many BFAR mothers have had cesarean births and gone on to have very satisfying, successful breastfeeding relationships.

Even when nursing is possible, some babies do not seem to be able to latch on well immediately after delivery. This can be the result of epidural anesthesia given to the mother during labor. Epidural anesthesias, particularly those containing bupivacaine, have been shown to diminish the initial sucking behavior of infants. Infants of mothers who received bupivacaine epidurals during labor have also been found to have less ability to orient to their environment over the first month of life.[1] This effect continues to impact BFAR because having an alert baby is important to establishing successful breastfeeding. If an epidural is necessary, it may be worth the effort to ensure that bupivacaine anesthesia is not used.

It is important to understand that not being able to nurse the baby right after birth certainly does not preclude breastfeeding. It only means that it may be necessary to pay closer attention to any latching problems that come up and seek help from a lactation specialist to remedy them. In addition, it will be beneficial to encourage frequent nursing to establish as many prolactin receptors as possible.

If nursing soon after birth is not possible, the next best alternative is to use a hospital-grade automatic electric pump for ten to twenty minutes every two hours until the baby begins nursing. This will maximize prolactin receptors and minimize the impact of delayed nursing upon your mammary system. If you are giving birth in a hospital or birthing center, a hospital-grade pump should be readily available, although you may need to specifically request one. Your nurse or midwife should be able to show you how to operate it.

For those babies who are willing and able to nurse immediately after birth, it is important to delay application of prophylactic eye drops. Once applied, the drops can cause temporary blindness in the newborn, which can interfere with nursing and with bonding. Only those babies with a known gonorrhea risk factor need to receive eye drops immediately. [1]

Most examinations of the baby and mother can be performed with the baby on the mother's abdomen or in her arms. Research has shown that a blanket placed over both the mother and the baby when both are in skin-to-skin contact will maintain the baby's body temperature.[3]

The most important factor during the time immediately after the birth is being surrounded by a pleasant, tranquil, and comforting environment so that you can meet and bond with your new baby. Feeling supported, encouraged, and peaceful goes a long way toward enabling you to calmly manage the challenges you will face.

The Tremendous Value of Colostrum

It can be very helpful for BFAR mothers to understand and appreciate the incredible value of colostrum, the translucent, yellow "pre-milk" that you will produce in the first few weeks. As explained in Chapter 3, colostrum is low in fat and carbohydrates and high in protein, which is precisely what the baby requires in the first days. It is easy to digest and is comprised of living cells that serve to protect the newborn against bacteria, viruses, and allergens. Colostrum actually coats the intestinal lining and prevents the absorption of substances that trigger allergies. The immune factors (IgG and IgA) are more concentrated in colostrum than in mature milk, continuing the role of the placenta in protecting the baby from threatening bacteria and viruses. These factors also serve to stimulate and enhance the baby's own immune system, which will benefit him throughout his entire life. Further, colostrum acts as an effective laxative, flushing meconium from the intestines, and thereby reducing the factors that can cause elevated levels of bilirubin. And colostrum does not suddenly disappear when the mature milk comes in; rather it is gradually replaced by mature milk over the first two weeks. That is why any milk you express during this time will appear yellowish.

Some mothers have not seen or been able to express colostrum prior to the baby's birth. When BFAR mothers still do not see any colostrum when the baby nurses and cannot manually express any in the first few postpartum days, it is natural for them to worry that this means that they are unable to produce milk because all their ducts were severed. In fact, not seeing colostrum when the baby nurses does not mean that it is not there. It is produced in very small quantities and is immediately swallowed by the baby. It is also somewhat clear and can look like saliva, so that it may not be easy to identify. Expressing colostrum or milk can be especially difficult in the first days postpartum because the breast tissue may be swollen from edema. It is also a skill that takes some practice. You may wish to refer to the expression methods described in Chapter 5 and in Appendix 6 as you practice your technique.

Remember, too, that colostrum is not produced in copious amounts even in women who have not had reduction surgery; only around an average total of 7.4 teaspoons (36.23 ml) per day, consisting of between 1.4 to 2.8 teaspoons (6.86 to 13.72 ml) per feeding.[4-6] Regardless of how much colostrum you are or are not able to produce, it is so valuable that just the tiniest bit that you are able to give to your baby will be a priceless gift to him, even if breastfeeding doesn't work out. It truly will be worth any effort you can make to give your baby colostrum.

Beginning to Breastfeed

The most important factors for breastfeeding are good positioning and an effective suckling technique, which are usually achieved when baby is latched on well. Most supply and soreness problems can be solved by correcting the baby's positioning and latch-on. For BFAR mothers, using effective positioning and latch-on techniques as early as possible will establish a solid foundation for BFAR and play a significant role in ensuring that the milk supply is fully stimulated.

Learning proper positioning and latch-on techniques can be especially important for BFAR mothers who have decreased or absent areola and nipple sensitivity. It is natural to rely on how a position or latch-on feels to determine correctness, but a mother who does not have this type of sensory feedback can sustain damage to her nipples and decreased stimulation of the milk supply. Scar tissue on the nipple and areola will only compound this problem and may even affect the baby's ability to position and latch-on well. If you find this to be the case, it will be necessary to work with a lactation specialist who will be able to show you ways to overcome the structural obstacles that you are facing.

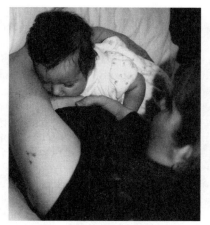

Making sure that baby's mouth is open wide, center your nipple in his mouth above his tongue and pull him toward you. Baby's lips should be flanged outward and his gums should be well past the nipple in order to properly compress the milk sinuses.

Baby should be lying on his side with his whole body facing you. Baby's ear, shoulder, and hip should be in a straight line.

Once you have learned several of the positions for breastfeeding your baby, it will be good to begin using all of them as often as possible. This is because the direction from which the baby approaches the breast determines which ducts and lobes are stimulated and emptied. For BFAR mothers, it is important to stimulate and empty as many lobes as possible to ensure that every possible lobe is working to your advantage. In addition to the positions you may see described in breastfeeding books, you might also experiment with other positions that work well for you and your baby. This will be more difficult with a newborn, but as he grows older, finding new positions will be much easier.

Latching on to the Surgically Reduced Breast

Because the nipple-areola complex may have been altered in your reduction surgery, the mound upon which it rests may not be as plump and protruding as in a breast that has not been surgically altered. This can make latching on difficult. If this is the case for you, compressing the areola tissue with your hand underneath and supporting your breast, with a finger on one side and a thumb on the other, could make an easier target for your baby and stimulate a stronger suckling reflex. If you cup your breast with your thumb on top and fingers below, you could inadvertently cause the nipple to tip upward, which can result in nipple abrasions from the nipple rubbing the top of

Supporting your breast from underneath with thumb on one side and fingers on the other is commonly known as the U-hold.

your baby's mouth. Ideally, the nipple should always be centered in the baby's mouth, between the tongue and roof of mouth and pointed toward the back of the mouth so that abrasions are avoided.

Many BFAR mothers find that their breasts have enlarged significantly since the surgery as a result of weight gain and the changes of pregnancy. Temporary engorgement can also cause breasts to become heavy. This added breast dimension and weight can make maintaining a good latch-on position difficult for your baby because he must hold the weight of your breast in his mouth. For a newborn, especially, this can be difficult and can cause him to slide off the areola onto the nipple, where nipple abrasions become likely and the breast cannot be adequately stimulated. A solution to this problem is to support your breast with either your hand (from underneath) or a rolled-up washcloth, small towel, burp cloth, or cloth diaper tucked under your breast.

If your baby has difficulty latching on in the early days, take heart. While you should most certainly seek immediate help to correct the problem, it will not always seem this difficult. Babies grow quickly and both you and he will become much more skilled in no time at all. What can seem overwhelmingly difficult one morning may be "old hat" a few days later. In some babies, this increased skill may actually be the result of having all the labor medication passed from their systems.

The Let-Down Reflex

The let-down or milk ejection reflex occurs as a response to stimulation of the nipple and areola and compression of the lactiferous sinuses beneath the areola. When these areas are stimulated, the tiny muscles around the alveoli buds squeeze the milk they have produced through the ducts down to the openings at the nipple. This process occurs repeatedly during every nursing session and can be felt in widely varying degrees. Some women experience this sensation as a warmth across the back of their shoulders. Others feel a tingling in their breasts or cramping in their uteruses. It is common to feel sleepy or thirsty during let-down. Some women do not feel any sensation at all. Occasionally, the let-down can occur in between feedings, as well. Some mothers, especially first-time mothers, do not feel the let-down in the beginning weeks, and most women cease to feel it by about the sixth month postpartum. But this does not at all mean that the let-down is not occurring. Sensations that accompany the let-down are the least reliable way to know that it is happening. A much more reliable indicator is to watch your baby. During the let-down, he will begin swallowing more rapidly and more deeply. This deep swallowing is often apparent when you may notice that it causes your baby's ears to wiggle.

Although the let-down is experienced as an increased milk flow, sometimes with leaking or spraying, and is an efficient way to deliver a large quantity of milk to the infant, it is not an indication that milk is being produced at that moment. The let-down is only the process of squeezing milk that has already been made through the ducts. Milk is always being produced in the milk glands. Of course, ridding the glands of the stored milk will induce them to make more, so the more let-downs that occur, the more milk that will be produced.

The process of let-downs may be problematic for some BFAR mothers who have compromised nerve function in the nipple and areola region. If these areas are not stimulated, it is more difficult for a let-down to occur. It is not, however, impossible.

The let-down can be induced by biofeedback techniques wherein the mother trains herself to "let down" to thoughts of her baby. This may actually happen without any conscious action on your part, especially when you hear your baby crying. The let-down can also be aided by the use of galactagogues that seem to specifically target the let-down process. These biofeedback techniques and galactagogues are discussed in Chapter 9.

It is very important, though, for BFAR mothers not to assume that the let-down reflex is not happening if they do not feel it. The let-down sensation is an unreliable indicator of the let-down and is sometimes not recognized by first-time mothers. This is true for all mothers, but because a BFAR mother is already more anxious about her milk supply, it is natural for her to assume the worst when she doesn't feel the let-down sensation when she expects to. While increasing the number of let-downs is an important component of a strategy to increase the BFAR milk supply, not much stock can be put into sensing when it has or has not occurred. Instead, we must look to more definitive indicators, such as softening of the breast during the feeding, deep swallowing during nursing, adequate wet and soiled diapers, and an alert, satisfied baby. When these factors are present, adequate let-downs have occurred whether the mother recognizes them or not.

Falling Asleep at the Breast

When a BFAR mother who is not supplementing at the breast is concerned that her baby is not receiving adequate nutrition, it is natural for her to be worried when her baby falls asleep at the breast. She may wonder if her baby has simply tired himself out from the effort of nursing when he can't extract enough nutrition. She may also know, though, that a baby who has received an adequate and satisfactory nursing may simply fall asleep at the breast in complete satiation. But she may not know which of these situations has caused her child to fall asleep during nursing, especially because she is very aware that she may have a less-than-adequate milk supply. A sleepy baby can be very confusing to a BFAR mother.

There are actually three situations in which babies fall asleep at the breast. They fall asleep when they are completely full and satisfied; they fall asleep when they do not have enough energy to continue nursing; and they fall asleep when they are already very sleepy and nutritionally satisfied and were only nursing for comfort. In fact, human milk efficiently facilitates sleep because it contains tryptophan, a substance that is known to induce adults to sleep.[3] For this reason, you will not be able to use sleepiness at the breast as an indication that your milk supply is insufficient. You must look to all the other factors that comprise the complete picture of your baby's nutritional and hydration status presented in the next chapter. When your baby is gaining well and is well hydrated by these criteria, you will know that when he falls asleep at the breast, it is merely a compliment to your good milk.

Non-Nutritive Nursing

Like falling asleep at the breast, nursing for reasons other than nutrition can be worrisome to the BFAR mother, causing her to doubt her milk supply. Non-nutritive nursing, though, is not an indication that the milk supply is lacking. All babies nurse when they are not hungry because nursing conveys emotional comfort. Being born is a very frightening time for an infant. A nursing baby quickly discovers that there is great comfort to be found when he nurses at his mother's breast. Part of this, of course, is because he is satisfying his need to suck, which is a powerful and necessary need of newborns. But even more importantly, he is able to nuzzle close to her body, smell her familiar smells, and be held in her loving arms. He can also look into her face and see her love and caring. This loving nurturance is the closest he can come to the bliss he felt in the womb.

Babies nurse for many other reasons, as well. They may be cold or hot or wet and not know how to tell you, but they know that nursing makes them feel better. They may be overstimulated and not know how to calm down. They may be in a strange place and feel insecure. Babies feel many of the same emotions that we do, but have few ways to work through the emotions. They simply know that nursing in mother's arms makes everything seem okay. Babies also nurse during growth spurts to increase the milk supply. This is a natural process and is explained in Chapter 7.

Nursing for comfort is advantageous to BFAR because it provides the added stimulation that you'll need to increase your milk supply. Many lactation consultants recommend that mothers pump regularly after feedings to increase the milk supply. While this can be helpful, a baby who desires to nurse for comfort is a far more efficient stimulator of the supply than a pump. It will really help your milk supply to let your baby nurse for comfort.

Of course, sometimes you may be tired and simply do not want him to nurse so much. This is a normal feeling and BFAR mothers may be especially prone to feeling this way because they are already expending so much effort in trying various ways to get their baby to nurse effectively and do not look upon feedings as a relaxing experience. If you feel this way, it may be tempting to give your baby a pacifier to soothe him. While you will need to make your own decision on this issue, you need to understand that artificial nipples of all kinds, and this includes pacifiers, can be detrimental to the breastfeeding relationship. Babies can easily become confused by the different sucking style that is induced by artificial nipples.

Engorgement as Your Milk Comes In

Almost all normal lactating breasts experience some degree of engorgement around the third to sixth day postpartum. As explained in Chapter 2, engorgement is the process whereby the mature milk appears and swelling occurs in the breasts. The breast is mostly congested with blood and fluid surrounding the milk glands, however, rather than milk itself, as is commonly believed. For BFAR mothers, engorgement can be actually reassuring because it indicates that milk is present. Although it shows that milk glands may be functional, it does not indicate how much milk can be expressed because the ducts that lead from the milk glands may have been severed so that the milk cannot reach the nipple.

Some BFAR mothers find that they do not experience any fullness at all. This can indicate either that prolactin levels are too low or that prolactin has not been able to affect a significant level of milk production because there are too few viable, intact lobes to produce milk. Should you find that you have unequal engorgement between your breasts, it would be safe to conclude that there is more lactation tissue in the fuller breast than the softer one. Less frequently, engorgement occurs only in portions of the breasts, so that some areas of the breasts remain soft. This indicates that little or no viable lactation tissue exists in the non-engorged areas.

Many BFAR women worry that engorgement in non-connected lobes will lead to mastitis (an infection of the breast). Anecdotally, this has not been the case, probably because non-connected lobes do not have exposure to bacteria, as connected lobes do (through openings in the nipple).

As explained in Chapter 2, the best way to reduce engorgement is to remove the milk from the breasts. This is done most efficiently by allowing your baby to nurse without restriction (as much as he is willing to do so). If your baby can't or won't nurse frequently enough, however, you may need to use a hospital-grade automatic electric pump to extract the milk. You'll find that once the milk begins draining, the swelling will rapidly diminish, usually within 24 hours, with the exception of those ducts that were severed, which will take a bit longer to resolve. Eventually, milk that is collecting in severed ducts will be harmlessly reabsorbed into the body and the lobes delivering milk to those ducts will cease production.

Aside from draining the milk, reducing the edema by other means is very helpful in treating engorgement. Many mothers find that applying bags of frozen peas to the covered breasts for a few minutes every 20 minutes is very helpful in reducing the edema. Hot therapies, such as heating pads, on the other hand, can increase edema, which is counterproductive. Cabbage leaves are recommended in many breastfeeding resources as an effective treatment for engorgement, however, their use is probably not a good treatment choice for BFAR mothers. The active chemicals in cabbage that reduce edema may negatively affect the mammary system, especially with prolonged use.[8] BFAR mothers cannot afford any unnecessary loss of lactation function. Instead, engorgement is better treated in the BFAR woman by nursing or pumping. Discomfort can be minimized with over-the-counter pain medications.

Engorgement can be experienced differently after subsequent pregnancies due to differing amounts of lactation tissue and stimulation. As explained in Chapter 2, with each BFAR experience, recanilization reestablishes portions of the mammary system so that a mother will have a greater lactation capacity. Stimulation plays a key role, as well, because the more the lactation system is stimulated, the more milk is produced in the short run and the more recanilization occurs in the long run.

Establishing Your Milk Supply

From the first moment of nursing through at least the beginning six weeks, your milk supply will be working to establish an equilibrium of supply to meet the demands that are placed upon it. This is why it is critical to place a heavy demand upon it during this time so that the most copious milk supply possible can be created. After the first six weeks, the milk supply is, for the most part, "established." This means that while natural increases to meet the baby's growing needs occur, and while increases can be artificially prompted, there is a set baseline from which all increases occur. The goal of BFAR is to force this baseline to be as high as possible. The remainder of this chapter discusses the key factors to maximizing your baseline milk supply.

BFAR Supply and Demand

All the best breastfeeding reference books discuss the principle of breastfeeding "supply and demand." This principle states that the milk supply will increase to meet the demands placed upon it. When a baby begins nursing more, such as during a growth spurt, the milk supply will increase to meet that demand. When the baby nurses less, the milk supply will correspondingly diminish.

Many health care professionals have assumed that this principle also applies to BFAR and have assured BFAR women that if they just place enough demand on their milk supply, it will increase accordingly. Unfortunately, the BFAR lactation system simply cannot respond to demand in the same way because it is not whole. Some portions of most BFAR mammary systems have been damaged, rendering them unable to produce milk. It is not just that the remaining lobes cannot compensate to create a full milk supply. For many BFAR mothers, the nerve system has also been damaged, making it impossible for viable lobes to receive the proper stimulation.

So if the principle of supply and demand does not apply when the lactation system is impaired, as it is for most BFAR mothers, how does the BFAR milk supply respond to the demands placed upon it? Quite simply, it responds to its highest capacity, depending upon the capacity of the lobes, the nerves, and the hormones, and their interrelationship. If the capacity of any of these factors can be enhanced through the techniques discussed throughout his book, then the supply will correspondingly increase.

One Breast or Two at Each Feeding?

In general, breastfeeding mothers are told that the baby should feed from both breasts during each feeding in the early weeks in order to allow maximum stimulation to each breast. Mothers are also told to alternate which breast is used to start each feeding.

These recommendations do not apply precisely to BFAR mothers, however, because many have one breast that produces a significantly greater quantity of milk than the other; occasionally the difference has been reported by some mothers to be as much as 75 percent. Both breasts cannot be relied upon to deliver adequate quantities of milk so that they could be interchangeably the primary breast at alternate feedings.

A sensible approach for BFAR mothers would be to begin feeding at both breasts, alternating the breast offered first, as is normally recommended in the first month, until you have an idea of the lactation capability of each breast. Although this may not be immediately apparent, most babies will eventually fuss when put to a breast that produces a significantly lesser amount of milk. This is not the only reason for fussing at the breast, though. Positioning and other subtle differences can prompt preference for one breast over another. If you find that your baby begins showing a definite preference for one side over the other, it may be helpful to try pumping on both sides to see if you truly do have a significant difference in yield. Of course, even pumping is not a definitive test, but it may give you validation of what you already suspect.

If you do determine that you have a significant difference in the yield of one breast over another, it will be most effective for you to begin each nursing on the higher-yield breast. Nurse until the baby seems mostly satisfied, give him a gentle burping, and then top off the feeding with the lower-yield breast. Of course, if you are supplementing, you will need to adjust this technique so that it works optimally for you and your baby depending on your method of supplementation. The point is that by giving the higher-yield breast first and allowing the baby to nurse there until he is mostly satisfied, the baby is more likely to get a greater quantity of the higher-calorie hindmilk.

Breastfeeding Frequency

When your baby is first born, especially during the first week, nursing sessions can sometimes seem to last so long that you barely have any time to get anything done before the next session begins. This is normal and not necessarily related to BFAR. Because human milk is so easily and rapidly digested, frequent feedings are normal—and for BFAR mothers they are essential. It is important to feed frequently in order to stimulate as many prolactin receptors as possible, increase the amount of hindmilk the baby receives, and ensure production of the greatest milk supply possible.

Scheduled vs. Demand Feedings

Some breastfeeding resources and experienced breastfeeding mothers tell women that they should only let the baby nurse for 10 to 20 minutes on one breast. They recommend scheduled feedings as a means to achieve an ordered routine. This is not wise, especially for BFAR mothers, because even the least-impaired surgically reduced breast may not be able to deliver sufficient milk in this timeframe. Moreover, a surgically reduced breast requires as much stimulation as possible to reach its maximum lactational capacity. Allowing the baby to nurse for as long and as frequently as he desires is best for your milk supply. He should have complete access to the breast so that you will only need to watch his early hunger cues (rooting, fussing, etc.) to know when to feed him. This is called "demand feeding" or "cue feeding."

It may be reassuring to know that frequent feedings are actually better for producing a higher fat milk supply than are more widely spaced feedings. Since BFAR mothers have a smaller milk storage capacity as a result of having fewer functional lobes, frequent feedings cause them to produce less foremilk, which stimulates the body to produce more higher calorie hindmilk.

Minimum Feeding Timeframes

Of course, even though you will be feeding your baby according to his demands, you will need to make sure that feedings occur in a certain minimum timeframe. At times, you may have to suggest feedings by offering the breast if too much time has elapsed. In the first month, feedings at least every two hours during the daytime are necessary in order to maximize the milk supply. Feedings are timed from the beginning of one feeding to the beginning of the next feeding, so that if the feeding lasts 40 minutes, you would start the next feeding at most 1 hour and 20 minutes later.

At night you can go a little longer between feedings, but it should still be no longer than three hours from the start of one feeding to the start of the next. One of the benefits of night feeding is that when mother is sleepy she tends to be more relaxed and the let-down seems to occur more readily. She also produces more higher-fat milk when rested. While you are in the hospital, if you are not rooming in with your baby, it is very important that the nursery staff bring your baby to you when he awakens during the night so that you can take advantage of these benefits.

At home, you may find that sleeping with your baby next to you allows both you and the baby to get more sleep and permits the baby greater access to your milk. More and more health care professionals are becoming supportive of co-sleeping because it is now well known that mothers and babies who sleep together tend to sleep in the same rhythms. The baby and the mother wake together naturally for feedings.

Do not believe any comments that feeding your baby formula or cereal at night will help him sleep longer. Research has consistently proven this claim to be a myth.[8]

Switch Nursing

For some breastfeeding problems, "switch nursing," in which the baby is allowed to feed for only a short, set time on each breast, switching back and forth, is suggested as a means to increase the baby's total intake. This feeding method, however, does not work well for BFAR mothers because it does not allow the baby to obtain the greatest proportion of hindmilk. Even if total volume were increased, the caloric value of the milk would be less. Prolactin levels are not increased by this feeding technique and would therefore not be beneficial for BFAR mothers.[5]

Although the technique of switch nursing for short, set periods of time at each breast is not beneficial for increasing the milk supply in BFAR mothers, there is a variation of this technique that is quite beneficial in increasing both milk volume and hindmilk content. Simply allow your baby to feed from the first side until the frequency of let-downs diminishes, without regard to the length of time that it may take. Then, move him to the other side to feed until the let-downs diminish on that side. Repeat the process by returning to the first side and even moving again to the second side if possible, until your baby indicates that the feeding is complete. This better method of switch nursing is an excellent way to maximize let-downs and ensure that the highest quantity of hindmilk is conveyed to your baby. It also tends to keep sleepy babies awake at the breast longer and feeding more efficiently, which encourages longer and more effective nursing sessions.

Milk Production and Severed Ducts

It is common for BFAR mothers to be concerned that maximizing the milk production will cause lobes with severed ducts to back up with undelivered milk. They are worried that such impacted lobes could result in severely plugged ducts or lead to mastitis. This does not tend to happen, however, because the lobes with severed ducts simply stop producing milk when the milk is not removed from them. Eventually, the milk is reabsorbed, the lobes atrophy and become non-functional.

Leaking

Leaking milk is common to all breastfeeding mothers. Not leaking is also normal for all mothers. In fact, leaking is not at all an indication of a mother's milk-producing capability, but only shows that she is lactating. Many nursing mothers do not leak at all. It is not any kind of reflection on the quantity of their milk supplies.

Leaking occurs because the minute muscles in the nipple (not the areola) control the flow of milk from the nipple. The strength of these muscles is genetically determined. When they are loose, leaking occurs. When they are firm, no milk escapes. Of course, a buildup of milk in the ducts can create pressure so that leaking is more prone to occur (especially in the early days when the lactation system is hormonally driven). But there is nothing that can be done to improve the tone of these muscles. It is simply important that BFAR women never try to judge the amount of their milk supplies by whether or not they experience leaking.

The First Three Days

As a BFAR mother, it is natural for you to be concerned that your baby might not be receiving adequate nutrition and hydration. You can put this concern aside for the first three days, however, because most full-term babies are born with sufficient fat reserves to allow them to cope very well without food or water for at least three days. Ideally, during this time, you will be giving your baby colostrum and allowing him to learn to nurse on a soft breast before your milk comes in. But while colostrum provides carbohydrates, it is not his only source of energy.

Unless unusual circumstances occur, you do not need to supplement, even at the breast, during this time. As explained earlier in this chapter, allowing him to feed frequently at the breast is the best way to bring in the greatest milk supply possible. Determining when supplementation might become necessary is discussed in the next chapter.

Should supplementation be absolutely necessary for a medical reason during the first three days, however, it is very important to give this supplement at the breast using an at-breast supplementer in order to stimulate the critical prolactin receptors and avoid nipple confusion. At this point, artificial nipples should be completely avoided if at all possible. Even cup feeding and syringe feeding (away from the breast) will limit the stimulation of the prolactin receptors. Of course, if you must supplement away from the breast during the first three days for a medical reason, this does not preclude successful BFAR; it means that you will need to ensure that the baby stimulates the breast as much as possible when he returns to it.

The Dangers of Artificial Nipples

"Nipple confusion" is a term that is often discussed by lactation specialists. It refers to the phenomenon whereby a baby has been fed both at the breast and from a bottle and learns different ways to suck from each so that he is unsure of which technique to use with which feeding source. Most lactation specialists agree that nipple confusion can occur in most babies when artificial nipples are introduced and that it can negatively impact breastfeeding, sometimes to a devastating degree.

"Nipple preference" is a term that refers to the phenomenon when babies come to prefer another feeding method, usually a fast-flow bottle, over the breast. Nipple preference, rather than nipple confusion, is usually responsible for a baby's refusal of the breast in preference for the bottle. Some lactation specialists refer to this as "flow preference" because they have learned that it is often less a factor of the shape of the nipple than the flow rate of the milk that the babies prefer. Although nursing provides a great deal of pleasurable, tactile stimulation, it is natural for some babies to prefer a feeding method that delivers the milk rapidly, providing immediate gratification of their hunger. Some babies simply like the feel of an artificial nipple in their mouths.

Giving an artificial nipple to a baby, even though it may only be a pacifier, introduces the very real risk that nipple confusion or nipple preference can occur. When it does, breastfeeding is in serious jeopardy and it can take a great deal of hard work to overcome. Sucking from an artificial nipple requires a different mouth and tongue action from the baby than nursing at the breast does, almost a reverse technique. And rather than using the action of his jaw to control the flow of the milk at the breast, a bottle-fed baby uses the tip of his tongue to control the flow of milk from the tip of the artificial nipple. Using this same technique at the breast pushes the human nipple out of his mouth against his intentions, which can be very frustrating to him and painful for his mother.[6]

Some babies do seem to be able to easily switch back and forth between a bottle and the breast. Yet, even though it may appear that a baby has no trouble switching back and forth, it is very likely that the baby has developed a nursing technique that allows him to extract milk from both sources, but which does not extract milk from the breast very effectively. As a result, the milk supply will diminish and his mother is likely to experience soreness.

Some lactation specialists believe that there is a timeframe in which babies are more likely to develop nipple confusion or preference. They believe that after this time period, babies are better able to use an artificial nipple without detriment to the nursing relationship. Most lactation specialists, however, have seen many mothers with babies at all ages who are nipple confused. The theory of a specific timeframe has not proven to be true—babies can and do become nipple confused at all ages.

Having said this, however, it is also true that the importance of avoiding artificial nipples is greater in the early months than it is later on. For some BFAR mothers, using bottles is necessary for a variety of reasons. While it may not be the optimal method of supplementation, it has been used effectively by many BFAR mothers. Although artificial nipples should be avoided whenever possible, each BFAR mother must determine the best supplementation method for her and her baby.

There is an exception to this warning to avoid artificial nipples: If the baby is not able to nurse at the breast and is being fed by cup, syringe, or spoon, so that the baby is not sucking at all to receive his nourishment, the baby should be given an opportunity to suck. Offering a clean, well-trimmed finger to your baby is a good way to help him satisfy this need without risking the development of an artificial nipple preference. Sucking is a strong emotional need for babies and they can become depressed if deprived of the ability to do so. They should not be totally denied sucking opportunities. The baby's emotional needs are every bit as important as his nutritional needs.

BFAR with One Breast

BFAR mothers who have only one breast with a nipple-areola complex will have additional challenges. For this special BFAR circumstance, it is especially important to ensure effective positioning and latch-on techniques because if the only existing nipple becomes sore or traumatized, there will be no alternative breast/nipple to use while the sore nipple heals. A sore nipple when there is only one may significantly impact the milk supply and the breastfeeding relationship. Taking care to ensure that the positioning and latch-on are correct will avoid this problem.

Interestingly, BFAR mothers who have had only one functional breast report they do not usually experience soreness from nursing on only one side. The increased time spent on the one breast seems to have no greater tendency to cause soreness than two-sided nursing. This reinforces the fact that nipple pain results from trauma caused from incorrect positioning, latch-on, or suckling techniques, rather than frequency or length of feedings.

In order to maximize the milk production of the one breast, it is necessary to vary positions as much as possible from feeding to feeding so as to stimulate all viable lobes.

It is also important to avoid the use of artificial nipples, such as bottles and pacifiers, in order to ensure that all suckling occurs at the breast so that the glands are stimulated as much as possible. While this is true for all BFAR mothers, it is especially true for those who have only one functional breast.

Nighttime nursings with only one breast, particularly for mothers who co-sleep with their babies, can present a unique challenge. Nursing in one position for a period of time can become uncomfortable. But because there is only one breast, there is not the luxury of switching to the other breast. One solution some BFAR mothers have found is to move the baby to the other side and simply roll toward him, lowering the breast to his level. Keeping your arm under your baby's head will also help him reach the breast. Approaching the breast from this new position will also allow him to empty it more completely.

BFAR with Multiples

BFAR with more than one baby can be a significant, but rewarding, challenge. There is no question that providing the benefits of breastfeeding and human milk to your babies will be advantageous for them. Logistically, though, and depending upon your milk supply, BFAR with multiples may require a great deal of determination and perseverance.

Many of the principles for breastfeeding twins and multiples applies directly to BFAR with twins and multiples. La Leche League International's MOTHERING MULTIPLES has many helpful suggestions. You will need to track the progress of each child independently, keeping close track of all the data. Watching for signs of dehydration, including wet and soiled diapers, as explained in Chapter 7, will be logistically more challenging. Using a good assessment chart, such as the one provided in Appendix 3, may be very helpful.

If you are supplementing, you will need to prepare and coordinate supplementation multiplied by the number of babies who must be fed. It will also be necessary to ensure that each baby is receiving the proper amount of supplementation because it cannot be assumed that each child's nutritional needs and intake are identical.

Many mothers of twins find that it is convenient to "assign" a breast to each child from which he always nurses. This is not advisable for BFAR mothers of twins because each breast is more likely to produce differing amounts of milk. A better approach would be to have each child take a different breast at each feeding.

The Influence of the Hospital and Health Care Professionals

If you've been fortunate enough to choose your health care professional team so as to be surrounded by professionals who are supportive of BFAR, your birth experience and postpartum care will be greatly enhanced. The LLL Leaders and lactation consultants in particular will be most helpful to you during this time. Keep in mind, though, that not all LLL Leaders or all lactation consultants have the same level of expertise or diagnostic skills. If you don't feel that the La Leche League Leader or lactation consultant you are working with has helped you resolve any issues you may face to your satisfaction, seek out the help of another one, even at the risk of offending the first specialist. Sucking issues, especially, can be difficult to sort out and most lactation specialists will never be offended by your decision to seek additional help; they will want to have your problem solved using whatever resources are necessary to preserve your breastfeeding relationship.

Rooming-In

Many hospitals offer the option of having the baby stay with his mother in her room. This is often called rooming-in. Although central nurseries that kept babies in a separate location were common in hospitals a generation ago, research has shown that there is no medical reason for healthy mothers and babies to be separated, even temporarily. [7, 9, 10,] Being together is reassuring for both of you and will allow you to immediately begin nursing on demand, which is most beneficial to your milk supply.

Letting Health Care Professionals Know about Your Reduction

Making it known to your health care professionals that you had a breast reduction can be a delicate undertaking. Of course, you want them to be informed of your complete medical information, but there is a real risk that knowing about your surgery will result in unreasonable panic and fear for your baby's health. It is not unusual for BFAR mothers to be pressured into premature supplementing while still in the hospital simply because they informed their physicians that they had had a breast reduction. Little or no effort is usually made in these circumstances to determine whether an adequate milk supply exists. Of course, your experience may be completely different depending on your health care professionals.

In order to forestall unreasonable panic, it is best to be as fully informed as possible and to be prepared to assert your rights as your baby's mother. It is likely that you will be better informed about BFAR than many of the health care professionals who assist you and this will be an excellent opportunity to share your knowledge about this subject.

Testing Blood Glucose Levels

Knowing that you are at-risk for a diminished milk supply, some physicians may recommend that your baby's blood be tested for glucose levels in order to assure that he is receiving adequate nutrition and hydration. Unfortunately, research has shown that a blood glucose test for this purpose may not be a reliable indicator of milk intake.[11]

The method of administering a blood glucose test can impact the result. Research studies have established that blood obtained from a prick to the heel and applied to a Dextrostix or Chemstrip is not a reliable indicator of blood glucose levels.[12, 13] Furthermore, there is disagreement about the levels at which a newborn should be considered hypoglycemic.[11] Low serum glucose levels in a newborn have also been shown to be the result of a rebound effect caused by glucose given to the mother intravenously during labor.[14, 15]

Of course, if a baby is premature or the mother is gestationally diabetic, hypoglycemia may be a valid concern wholly apart from BFAR.

When Health Care Professionals Declare that BFAR Is Not Possible

BFAR is such a new field that many health care professionals do not believe that it can be possible. They may take the judgment of plastic surgeons at face value and flatly declare that BFAR simply cannot occur. After reading this book, you, of course, know that BFAR is indeed quite possible. This would be the time to respectfully share the highlights of your knowledge on the subject with them. Do not be surprised, though, if they do not immediately embrace the information. Nonetheless, your gentle confidence in the subject and your practical plans to BFAR will earn you respect and cooperation from most health care professionals.

R E F E R E N C E S :

1. Lawrence, R.A. and R.M. Lawrence. *Breastfeeding: A Guide for the Medical Profession*, 5th edition. St. Louis, Missouri: Mosby, 1999; 240, 249, 252, 241, 250, 286, 271, 254.

2. Riordan, J. and K. Auerbach. *Breastfeeding and Human Lactation*, 2nd edition. Sudbury, Massachusetts: Jones and Bartlett Publishers, 1999; 100-101.

3. Johanson, R. Effect of post-delivery care on neonatal body temperature. *Acta Paediatr* 1992; 81:859-62.

4. Hartmann, P. Lactation and reproduction in Western Australian women. *J Reprod Med* 1987; 32:543-47.

5. Hartmann P. and C. Prosser. Physiological basis of longitudinal changes in human milk yield and composition. *Fed Proc* 1984; 43:2448-53.

6. Houston, M., P. Howie, A. McNeilly. Factors affecting the duration of breast feeding: 1. Measurement of breast milk intake in the first week of life. *Early Hum Dev* 1983; 8:249-54.

7. Yamauchi Y. and I. Yamanouchi. The relationship between rooming-in/not rooming-in and breastfeeding variables. *Acta Paediatr Scand* Nov 1990; 79:1017-22.

8. Newman, J. and T. Pitman *Doctor Jack Newman's Guide to Breastfeeding*. Toronto, Canada: HarperCollins, 2000: 120.

9. Buranasin, B. The effects of rooming-in on the success of breastfeeding and the decline in abandonment of children. *Asia Pac J Public Health* 1991; 5(3):217-20.

10. Oslislo, A. and K. Kaminski. Rooming-in: A new standard in obstetrics and neonatology. *Ginekol Pol* Apr 2000; 71(4):202-7.

11. Heck, L. and A. Erenberg. Serum glucose levels in term neonates during the first 48 hours of life. *J Pediatr* 1987; 110:19.

12. Cornblath, M. Hypoglycemia in infancy: The need for a rational definition. *Pediatrics* 1990; 85:834-37.

13. Hawdon, J., M. Platt, A. Aynsley-Green. Prevention and management of neonatal hypoglycaemiaa. *Arch Dis Child* 1994; 70:F65-F70.

14. Keppler, A. The use of intravenous fluids during labor. *Birth* 1988; 15:75-79.

15. Newton N., M. Newton, J. Broach. Psychologic, physical, nutritional and technologic aspects of intravenous infusion during labor. *Birth* 1988; 15:67-72.

TRACY'S STORY

I had my breast reduction surgery for all the usual reasons—backache, discomfort, poor-fitting clothes, and, above all, extreme self-consciousness. I had been married for four years already and we had lost our first two babies to miscarriage in the previous year. I knew I wanted children and I knew I wanted to breastfeed them. But I wasn't ready to try again for a while. With an obsessive desire to be "normal," I went into the surgery without any doubts or second thoughts. I told the doctor that I wanted to be as small as possible, but that my first priority was to preserve my ability to breastfeed. As I recall, he warned me that there were no guarantees that I would be able to breastfeed, but I still felt confident that I would have no problems.

My surgery went smoothly without any complications and only very faint scarring. I had the inferior pedicle procedure. I was thrilled with the results. The surgery changed how I felt about nearly every aspect of my life. A little over a year later, I became pregnant for the third time.

During my pregnancy, I noticed none of the changes in my breasts that I had experienced in my first two pregnancies. There was only a very minimal tenderness in the beginning, which quickly disappeared, no enlargement, no change in pigmentation, no pronounced vein structure, or anything else to indicate that there was any preparation underway for breastfeeding. I didn't know whether to be worried about this lack of change or not. Finally, midway through my third trimester, I found I was able to express some colostrum from my nipples. I did try, several times, to get information from the doctors and LCs at the hospital about whether I could expect to be able to breastfeed, but no one really had any good information for me. They told me if my milk came in, I could breastfeed. If it didn't, I couldn't. I read about breastfeeding in my pregnancy and baby books and because I had seen my sister breastfeed her two children, I felt more or less prepared.

My labor was induced three weeks early to prevent developing preeclampsia and my baby was small for gestational age. Due to the drugs I had to take during labor because of my high blood pressure, my daughter was very sleepy after birth. She had little interest in latching on at the breast and promptly fell asleep every time I did manage to get her latched on. She was born at five pounds, 11 ounces, but dropped down to five pounds within a day. I had a great deal of water retention and I believe she did, too. I had very little help learning to breastfeed. I was visited a couple of times in the hospital by lactation consultants, but as my milk had not yet come in and my daughter was uninterested in nursing, there were no real problems to deal with at that point.

We left the hospital three days after her birth and during her first week, my daughter's bilirubin levels climbed and she continued to lose weight. I had been put on diuretics to get rid of the excess water I had been retaining and my milk did not come in until late on day five. Because her bilirubin levels were continuing to go up and she was continuing to lose weight and becoming dehydrated, I was told to give my daughter bottles of water or *formula after nursing. I did try to supplement with cup feedings but was warned not to by a health nurse who came to our house to check my daughter's bilirubin levels and weight. She told me that cup feeding newborns could cause them to choke (I have since learned that is completely untrue and many breastfeeding-friendly hospitals use this method when a baby needs supplementing). My baby was put on phototherapy for two days at home and the day she finished with that, I was rehospitalized with postpartum preeclampsia. I was so drugged up the first 24 hours that I was unable to nurse my daughter and my husband gave her bottles of formula. Five days later, I was released from the hospital again. By this time, my daughter was getting so many bottles I started to wonder if I would ever have enough milk for her.*

On the heels of all this came postpartum depression which was not diagnosed until my baby was six weeks old. I had lost a lot of confidence in my ability to mother my baby at all, let alone be able to breastfeed her and I would often reach for a bottle of formula straight away if her fussiness was not quickly quieted by the breast. I was too depressed to seek support from other mothers and it didn't even occur to me to try to find local LLL meetings for help. Breastfeeding was difficult and often painful and I had no help. The fact that we could not figure out how to nurse while lying down and that my broken tail bone was too sore to sit on made it that much worse. My baby's pediatrician told me that giving her a bottle was just fine if that's what I wanted. My own doctor told me that there were no proven benefits to breastfeeding beyond the fourth month, which is untrue. I tried a few times to call the lactation consultants at the hospital where I delivered, but I always got answering machines. I didn't really even know if they could help.

My only encouragement and support were my husband and my sister. My sister's example of never giving up on breastfeeding motivated me to stick with it. My husband did everything he could to help support my choice including going to my obstetrician while I was hospitalized with postpartum preeclampsia and asking that he write a prescription for a breast pump for me. Then, he made several phone calls until he determined how much insurance would pay, what was the best pump, and where he could get one. Everyone kept telling me "just give her a bottle" or "I was formula-fed and I turned out just fine." But, I knew if I quit, I would really regret it. So, I promised myself to stick it out for four months and then see how I felt.

By the time my baby was four months old, breastfeeding was going a lot better. I wasn't so sore and she didn't want to spend hours at a time at the breast. I was starting to enjoy it. But she was being supplemented with one or two bottles of formula a day and I felt uncomfortable with this.

By the time she was five months old, my daughter had developed a clear preference for the bottle and quit comfort nursing altogether. Shortly after, she started refusing to nurse in public and refused the breast at bedtime, only accepting a bottle. She was becoming what I termed a "business nurser"—she only wanted to nurse when there was plenty of milk. If the milk didn't come fast enough, she wanted a bottle.

During the early months, I tried to pump to supplement her bottles and I managed to put a small amount of my milk away in the freezer. But often, it would take a day's worth of pumping just to collect one or two ounces. I didn't pump regularly or frequently because it was discouraging. I started her on solids at four months, which she loved, and she nursed even less. Between solids and breastfeeding, I only needed to supplement her with four to eight ounces of formula a day, but I was uncomfortable with this. I couldn't understand why I wasn't producing enough milk to eliminate those formula feedings. I never thought it could be due to my surgery. After all, it was all or nothing, right? I could produce milk, therefore, I should be able to exclusively breastfeed. At least, that's what I thought.

While her interest in nursing continued to decrease over the second half of her first year, I did manage to keep my daughter breastfeeding until she weaned herself at 17 months. At that point, she was only nursing regularly in the mornings when she woke and occasionally she might nurse at other times of the day, though rarely, and only for a minute or two. When she did finally wean, nothing I did could get her to come back. She was finished and never looked back. I felt that I had been a huge failure at breastfeeding. I had not been able to exclusively breastfeed her, which made me feel as if I didn't have the right to say she was a breastfed baby. I had also fully expected to nurse her a minimum of two years. It never occurred to me that she wouldn't want to continue, at least our morning sessions, which she seemed to dearly love. I'll never forget that excited little giggle of hers when she was an infant and would see me pulling my shirt up, getting ready to nurse her. And, most wonderful of all, those sweet morning nursings when my husband would get her up, change her diaper and then bring her into our bed. She would snuggle into me and nurse for a good thirty minutes or more. There was no nicer way in the world to wake up than that!

Finding the BFAR email list, completely changed my perspective on my experience breastfeeding my daughter. I have come to feel a certain amount of satisfaction and even pride in the fact that we stuck it out for as long as we did. I don't know exactly why I had the problems with breastfeeding my daughter that I did. Maybe I had a low supply due to my surgery, maybe my supply decreased because of my low confidence, introducing bottles, and the circumstances surrounding the first days and weeks after my daughter's birth. Maybe it was a combination of everything; I don't know.

I learned so much about BFAR from that email list that I was able to have high hopes when I became pregnant again with my son. During my pregnancy, I had a vivid, recurring dream in which I had an abundance of milk. It was just flowing from my breasts. I can distinctly remember how this felt after I woke up. The strong feelings and images generated by these dreams helped me to visualize after the baby came. I also had an SNS on hand in preparation for my son's birth should supplementation be needed, in the hope of avoiding bottles altogether. And I learned about the different herbs and even prescription drugs that can help with supply as well.

My son was born after a fast and drug-free labor. I was able to latch him on within an hour after he was born. He took to it like a pro. Unlike my experience with my daughter, he had no drugs in his system and we were not separated at all after his birth. I kept him in my arms and in my bed from that moment on and nursed him whenever he showed even the slightest interest. This time, my milk came in on day two. I nursed even more frequently. I have no idea how many times a day he nursed since he nursed so often. I started wearing him in a sling and going about my day while he nursed and napped. At night, he slept snuggled up next to me (and still does). It appeared that my milk supply was meeting his needs in the early weeks, but I was concerned that it would not be able to keep up as he hit growth spurts. I pumped every chance I had and put the milk in the freezer so that, should I need to start supplementing, at least I would have some milk put aside before having to give him formula. We monitored his weight gain weekly. He was gaining at a rate of nearly three-quarters of a pound a week on my milk alone. He passed the six week mark and continued to gain steadily. He is now nearly four months old and has gained well over eight pounds since birth. He is all dimples and roly-poly! He has never had a bottle, never had a drop of supplement.

I don't know why I have been so fortunate this time to be able to exclusively breastfeed. So many things were different with my son than with my daughter. I had a drug-free birth, nursed within an hour of his birth, no separations, no bottles, no pacifiers, no PPD, and I nurse him night and day. But, I think the most significant difference this time around is the BFAR education and the support of the BFAR listserve, which I found almost a year after my daughter had weaned. I had a year to prepare for breastfeeding my next baby. But, most of all, I think I was just very fortunate and I am very grateful. I plan to nurse my son until he chooses to wean.

THE FIRST MONTH OF BFAR

Now that the initial excitement of the birth is over and your milk is coming in, you are about to begin the experience of BFAR. It's time to put into practice all the ways that you prepared.

The first few weeks are very important in establishing your milk supply. As a BFAR mother, there is much that you can do to ensure that you will be able to have the greatest milk supply that your mammary system is capable of producing. The methods that will be described in this chapter have proven to be effective by BFAR mothers themselves.

Because we want to give lactation every possible opportunity to be initiated at its greatest possible capacity, it is important not to supplement unnecessarily. Therefore, the first focus of this chapter will be about nurturing yourself so that you can be in the best physical and psychological condition. Next, we will discuss what you can do to track your baby's progress, followed by how to maximize your milk supply, and concluding with a discussion of how to evaluate your baby's progress to determine if supplementation is necessary.

During this time of learning and adjustment, it is important that you do not expect to become completely comfortable with breastfeeding right away. Breastfeeding is an art that a mother learns over weeks and months. Some feedings will seem more awkward and troublesome than others. Eventually, though, you and your baby will become experts and easily manage feedings in all kinds of circumstances. Remember, while almost all BFAR mothers can give their babies some milk, all mothers can offer their babies love and nurturance at the breast.

Nurturing Yourself

You may have just arrived home from the hospital or birthing center, or perhaps you gave birth at home. No matter where the baby was born, though, you now have a new family member to care for in your home, which takes some getting used to. Each new child introduces a new dynamic into the household that requires all family members to make adjustments. BFAR, though, adds an additional factor of uncertainty that can be stressful for you and your partner. For this reason, you need to ensure that all the other elements in your home environment are as comforting and supportive as possible. In fact, the most important element is for you, the new mother, to be well cared for so you are able to recuperate fully from giving birth, even as you care for your new baby.

Surround Yourself with Supportive People

This is a very sensitive time in your life. You are physically and emotionally vulnerable. The last thing you need as you begin BFAR is to be near anyone who would undermine your efforts by expressing doubts or criticism. Breastfeeding in and of itself is not a feeding method some people feel comfortable with and such persons are likely to feel even more critical of BFAR. This lack of ease with breastfeeding stems from a lack of understanding and sometimes a mistaken view of the breast as sexual. You deserve to have only positive support and encouragement now. You do not need any negativity that would undermine your confidence.

It can be difficult to distance yourself from unsupportive people during this otherwise exciting postpartum time, but remember that you have the right to structure your environment so that it is most conducive to successful BFAR, which is essential to the well-being of your baby. And ultimately the needs of your baby are far more important than the needs of others.

Suspend Feeling Obligated

One of the first things to do is suspend your normal feelings of obligation. Nurturing your child, breastfeeding, and caring for yourself will be your most important responsibilities during the first month. Nothing else matters nearly as much. If you have older children, you will certainly need to focus on them as much as you are able, but your new baby's needs and your own needs are paramount right now. Your partner or another caregiver will need to tend to your older children's basic needs as much as possible during this time.

Although it is natural for your friends and family to want to visit to see the new baby and congratulate you, entertaining them can be a drain on you, and you may not feel free to nurse your baby, especially with an at-breast supplementer, with visitors present. Try to gently and politely discourage as many visits as possible, but for those who insist on dropping by, the best way to limit their visits is for you to stay in your nightgown and robe, sending a clear signal that you are convalescing and need your rest. You may want to go even one step further and receive your visitors in bed. This will usually guarantee brief visits.

Stay in Bed

In fact, staying in bed for the first few days is actually one of the best things you can do to get BFAR off to a good start. You can bring books and magazines or even a television set into your room, have drinks and snacks near the bed, and get up only to go to the bathroom and bathe. Spending concentrated time snuggling and nursing your baby whenever he wants will ensure the greatest possible milk supply. Your let-down reflex will be better because you will be relaxed and the frequent nursing will stimulate creation of a greater number of prolactin receptors. Tell everyone it is "doctor's orders" if you feel you need justification; many doctors instruct their postpartum patients to do just this because even though you may feel fairly close to normal, your body has just completed a great physical exertion and it absolutely must recuperate. If you don't take the time to recuperate now, the next few months will be much harder for you, which could significantly impact your milk supply.

Meals and Housework

Among the obligations that you should not feel responsibility for are meals and housework. When your friends and family ask what they can do for you, request that they bring in dinner or lunch. Even if two friends bring a meal the same day, graciously accept both and freeze one. People like to feel helpful and a meal is much more valuable to a newly expanded family than another baby outfit.

Housework, especially if you have been gone a few days, can seem very compelling, and yet daunting. This is not the time to resume your household chores, no matter how much they need doing or how many visitors you're likely to have. Having a tidy and clean house simply doesn't matter a fraction as much as your critical need for rest. Resist the temptation to do bits of housework because it's easier than telling someone else how to do it. The truth is that the explanation requires far less of your limited energy than if you were to do it yourself. Remind yourself over and over again that for right now housework is not your responsibility. If it is not done, it does not reflect poorly on you at all. Only the most insensitive, unrealistic person could possibly think less of a new mother with a less-than-perfect house. One of the BFAR email list members hit the nail on the head when she said,

> *"Easier said than done, but—relax, ignore the house, and just nurse! Take it easy and just nurse! Forget about obligations and just nurse!*
>
> *I can say this because I didn't do it and I really regret it. You have the perfect excuse to take it easy and focus just on your new little bundle and everybody understands. It makes a tremendous difference in your long term nursing. I really wish I would have listened to this advice."*

It all boils down to this: Don't expend one ounce of unnecessary energy; save all of it for nursing your baby.

Doula Postpartum Care

Many new mothers are blessed with having a partner or family member who is wonderfully supportive and quite capable of performing all of the household tasks. Even so, there is more than taking care of the household that is necessary now. You are caring for your baby, but you need special nurturing care yourself. You may also be feeling a great deal of anxiety. Having a professional postpartum doula, a woman who cares for a new mother by helping around the home and giving support and encouragement, can make all the difference. Doulas mother the mother. Some doulas help during the actual birth, but most will also help at home during the postpartum time. She can do household chores, help with older children, or simply focus on nurturing you. It almost doesn't matter what she actually does; the presence of a mature, reassuring, and non-judgmental woman will help you build confidence while you focus on bonding with your new baby.

A doula may also have training in basic breastfeeding techniques, which could come in very handy. But since she probably won't have any formal knowledge about BFAR, it is important that your doula not sabotage your BFAR efforts by expressing doubts or concerns, even though they may be well-intentioned. Evaluation of your baby's health is a matter between you and your health care providers.

As a matter of fact, you may find that your physician also endorses having a doula help you at home because recent research has confirmed the value of doula care for a new mother.[1] This is a perfect use for the monetary gifts that you may have been given for the baby's birth. Getting proper care for yourself now is absolutely necessary for you to be able to give the best care to your baby.

Eating, Drinking, and Sleeping Well

In addition to saving your energy for nursing, you need to replenish your energy through nutritious meals, sufficient fluids, and a lot of sleep. Never skip a meal. In fact, try to have several nutritious snacks throughout the day in addition to regular meals. In general, the quantity and quality of your diet will have little or no effect on your milk, but it is important to eat well in order to maintain your energy and emotional reserves. Eating foods that you enjoy and are good for you will nourish both your body and your soul.

Drinking properly is every bit as important as eating properly. It is important to stay properly hydrated by drinking to thirst. Do not, however, drink large amounts of fluids with the idea of increasing your milk supply. It doesn't work and can actually reduce your supply.

Water is the best fluid, although non-caffeinated teas are a good choice for their soothing properties. Fruit and citrus juice are also beneficial, and can be nutritious, as well. But you need to read the labels to be sure the fruit juice you are drinking is pure. Some mothers have found that drinking excessive amounts of citrus juice can cause fussiness in their babies.

It is not necessary to drink cow's milk. Many babies are sensitive to the proteins in cow's milk that may be present in their mother's milk and it is not at all essential for adults to drink milk. In the early part of the last century, mothers were sometimes told that they must drink milk to make milk. We now know that this is untrue; milk is made from blood, not the milk of another species. Adult cows certainly don't drink milk and are able to lactate quite sufficiently.

You should make a point of limiting the amounts of caffeine and alcohol you drink. Depending on your caffeine tolerance, drinking more than two cups of caffeinated tea, soda, or coffee could make it difficult for you to sleep easily and deeply when you need to. Caffeine is also a diuretic (a substance that dehydrates the body) and so it could reduce your milk supply if ingested in significant quantities.

Alcohol should only be used in moderation while you are breastfeeding. An occasional glass of wine or beer will not make much difference, but alcohol appears in the milk in proportion to the amount that is ingested, peaking between 30 to 90 minutes afterward. In addition to being potentially harmful to the brain and nervous development of your baby, alcohol is an even stronger diuretic than caffeine. Depending on how much you drink, it can have a negative impact on your milk supply. You may have heard that a beer helps a nursing mother, either with her let-down or as a galactagogue. While it may help the let-down since it can encourage relaxation, because of its diuretic properties, alcohol is not a galactagogue—it is an anti-galactagogue.

Next to food and water, sleep is your most critical necessity. You need as much of it as you can get. Take at least one nap a day—preferably when the baby does. The baby will need to be up during portions of what would otherwise be your normal sleeping time, so you will need to make up your sleep. The best way to do this is to sleep when the baby does. When the baby falls asleep for a nap during the day, it may be tempting to use that time to catch up on thank-you notes, birth announcements, housework, and phone calls. But this is precious time that can be much better spent resting. Sometimes it's hard to simply drop off to sleep—you may be on edge wondering if the baby will suddenly wake up again. But it is important to learn not to worry about that and fall asleep as quickly as possible. If the baby wakes, you will, too. But if he doesn't, you'll get some valuable rest.

Retreat to Your Nursing Station

If you haven't already done so, take the time to create a nursing station—a place of comfort and refuge that has everything you could possibly need during a nursing session within easy reach. You might include:

- A comfortable chair;
- A table next to your chair large enough to hold other items on this list;
- Plenty of pillows for positioning the baby and supporting your arms and back;
- Wonderful books or magazines to read;
- A tube of Lansinoh® for moisturizing your nipples after feedings (a tiny amount is all you need);
- Your nursing stool;
- A burp cloth;
- Delicious, healthy snacks;
- Iced water or a mug of steaming tea;
- A telephone (cordless works well);
- A notepad and pen to jot messages or notes;
- A remote control assuming a television set is nearby;
- A radio/cassette/CD player;
- Tissues;
- Hand lotion;
- Medical-grade tape or Band-aids if you are using an at-breast supplementer;
- Pump and pumping supplies if you are pumping;
- Books for older children so that you can read to them while you nurse the new baby;
- Good light (which can be soft or bright depending on your preference);
- Anything else you need to be completely comfortable and worry-free.

When you have such a place to go to, nursing can become a refuge, allowing you to thoroughly enjoy your special time with your baby.

Dress Comfortably

This is the time to eliminate as much stress as possible in your life. Being uncomfortable because your clothes are binding or tight is particularly stressful. You can't possibly expect to be at your pre-pregnancy weight soon after giving birth, but you may not want to continue wearing your maternity clothes. Today's nursing fashions are a nice option. They are cut a bit more generously than normal sizing and can be very forgiving to the postpartum figure. Having nursing clothes will also help reinforce your identity as a breastfeeding mother.

Along the same comfort lines, but for a different reason, don't wear bras that are too tight. Your pre-pregnancy and maternity bras will be too small once your milk comes in. Having a properly fitting bra, even during this time of breast size fluctuation, is very important. It is essential that your bra not put pressure on any areas of breast tissue because this can reduce the blood supply to a functional lobe and impair lactation from that part of your breast. Underwire bras can be especially detrimental.

The Arrival of Mature Milk

For all breastfeeding women, the arrival of mature milk can sometimes take longer than three days, so that it is occasionally necessary to temporarily give your baby a supplement. This is a decision you will need to make with your baby's health care provider and will depend upon the baby's birth weight and other critical factors.

If it is decided that supplementation is necessary, though, this supplementation should be given at the breast with an at-breast supplementer to avoid any issues of nipple confusion and to continue stimulating the breasts as much as possible.

Nipple Soreness

If you experience nipple soreness after the third day (slight sensitivity at first is normal), enlist the aid of a La Leche League Leader or a lactation consultant. Nipple trauma and pain are a clear indication that something is not happening correctly—it may be a problem of positioning, latching-on, or anatomical issue of the baby's, such as having a short frenulum (the bit of skin that anchors the tongue to the bottom of the mouth). It can also be related to yeast. You do not have to suffer—breastfeeding should not cause you any pain. A lactation specialist will be able to help you correct the problem.

Deliberate Relaxation and Visualization

As you prepared for BFAR, it was recommended that you learn deep relaxation and visualization techniques so that you could use them as a coping mechanism during this challenging first month. Research has shown that a mother's state of mind can have an influence upon lactation, especially the let-down reflex. Most people who practice relaxation techniques report that they feel a very pleasant, refreshed feeling afterward, which makes problems seem much less overwhelming. Having such a respite from worry and anxiety can be very rejuvenating for BFAR mothers, and may help their milk supplies.

There are two types of relaxation techniques: physical relaxation and psychological relaxation. In physical relaxation, you concentrate in a peaceful setting on consciously relaxing all the muscles in your body. The deep muscular relaxation that can be gained from physical relaxation also seems to calm and soothe the mind of concern, worry, aggravation, and stress.

Psychological relaxation focuses first on the mind, allowing the physical relaxation to follow naturally. Visualization is an effective psychological relaxation technique, especially for BFAR mothers. You can visualize anything that gives you peace and a feeling of well-being, but it is most powerful to envision happily breastfeeding your baby, adding as much elaborate detail as you can imagine. This will not only give you pleasure in the thought of such a happy moment, but will impart a specific goal and may even help you keep on track in moments of doubt.

Another visualization that many BFAR mothers find helpful is to picture milk flowing in large streams from their breasts. Some mothers even think of this image every time they nurse, finding that it can help them with their let-down.

Take Time to Bond with Your New Baby

In all the effort of BFAR, it is easy to be distracted from the miracle of your new baby. Don't let this happen, though. Take the time to get to know your new son or daughter and fall in love with him or her. This baby is unlike any other baby in the world and will ultimately be among the most important people in your life.

Wear Your Baby to Maximize Rapport

Many BFAR mothers find that wearing their babies in a sling-type carrier is soothing to their babies and goes a long way to maximize their rapport. A baby who is in close contact with your body, hearing your heartbeat and smelling your smell, develops a very strong sense of personal security that helps him feel more tranquil and secure even when you are not holding him. Sometimes just a short time in the sling is all the baby needs to feel secure and tranquil for the rest of the day.

Slings also help mothers go about their days with two hands free but with the baby held close. You might think that carrying a baby in a sling might be very hard on your back, but a sling distributes the weight so evenly that it is actually much easier to carry a baby in a sling than in your arms. You never need to worry that your baby is safe or entertained when he is with you in the sling. He will be naturally interested in whatever you are doing.

Wearing a sling properly takes a bit of adjustment. It needs to be snug along the rails (the top portion that feeds through the rings). This can be accomplished by pulling the rails separately (the bottom rail separately from the top rail) through the rings. The portion that goes over your shoulder should not be bunched on top of your shoulder, but should be spread over it and the upper part of your arm so that the weight of the baby is distributed evenly.

There are many positions that work well for carrying babies in slings, depending upon the baby's age and personality. For a newborn baby, many mothers find that an upright position with the baby facing you (tummy to tummy) so that his head is against your chest and he can hear your heartbeat is very soothing. His legs can be folded up into the sling or hanging below it. Dr. Sears' book, *The Baby Book*, has many excellent illustrations of other positions, as well as "baby wearing" tips and techniques.

Tracking Your Baby's Progress

Because there is a strong possibility that your milk supply will not yield as much milk as your baby will need to meet his nutritional needs during the first few months, it will be necessary to carefully monitor his weight gain and hydration so that you can have accurate information from which to make decisions about supplementation. This section will discuss the tools and techniques you'll need for tracking your baby's progress.

Keep an Assessment Chart

Many BFAR mothers find that keeping an assessment chart that records feedings, feeding methods, supplementation, sleep, diapers, and baby's mood, is a very powerful tool for helping keep track of the babies' activities so that they can objectively assess the babies' progress. You may find it convenient to make several copies of the assessment chart included in Appendix 3 to put on a clipboard that you keep near your bedside, nursing station, or on a string above the baby's changing table.

You are likely to find that patterns and trends become obvious when displayed on a chart that were not clear before. Sometimes such a record can be very reassuring and can prove to you that when your baby is eating well and having sufficient wet and soiled diapers, his fussiness is for reasons other than hunger. At other times, an assessment chart can give you an early warning that things might not be going well. It is very helpful for physicians to have such a complete record to rely upon when trying to assess both babies who are doing well and those who are not.

Record Wet and Soiled Diapers

Keeping track of wet and soiled diapers in every twenty-four (24) hour period can sometimes be difficult, but it is essential. One easy way that some mothers have found to do this is to collect them all in one place. At the same time each day, count the number of wet and soiled diapers and record it in your chart. If you are using disposable diapers, it may help when tallying diapers if you have used a marker to write "X" on the outside of the soiled diapers. After you have recorded the number of diapers, you can then throw them away if they are disposable or put them in the laundry if they are cloth.

At first, before your mature milk comes in, a newborn will wet only one or two diapers a day. When your colostrum turns to milk, between the third day and the end of the first week, you should expect your baby to wet six to eight cloth diapers or four to six disposable diapers, and have two to five bowel movements each day. Later, after about four weeks, the frequency of wet diapers usually slows to five to six per day, but becomes heavier because the baby's bladder has grown. Bowel movements usually slow down to once or twice a day or once every few days. It is not unusual for a thriving breastfed baby to stool even less frequently, provided that he is otherwise healthy and growing well and that when the stool does occur, it is copious.

Many mothers find that using cloth diapers, at least in the early weeks, is very helpful in gauging when a diaper is wet. Cloth diapers have come a long way since the time our mothers used them. Pins have been replaced by Velcro® and snaps so that they are now every bit as convenient as disposable diapers, plus cloth diapers may be more comfortable for the baby, more aesthetically pleasing, kinder to the environment, less toxic, and less expensive than disposable diapers. To make them even more convenient, many families use a diaper service, at least for the first month or so, to minimize laundry. A great resource for learning all about today's new methods of cloth diapering is Theresa Farrisi Rodriquez' book, *Diaper Changes*.

Urination

Because they are designed to keep babies dry, it can be difficult to determine if urination has occurred in a disposable diaper. To learn what a "very wet" disposable diaper feels like, take a fresh diaper and pour two to four tablespoons of water into it and observe the weight change when the diaper is wet.

Be sure to check the front of the diaper if the baby is a boy and the back of the diaper if the baby is a girl. Many parents also find that putting a piece of tissue or toilet paper into the inside of the diaper helps conclusively show whether urination has occurred.

The urine that you see on the diaper should be light in color, free of strong smells, and absent of any substance, such as small grains that look like sugar crystals. If you notice any deep color or odor to the urine, or if crystals are present, make a note of when it occurred on your assessment chart and bring it directly to the attention of your pediatrician. These can be signs of dehydration and should be carefully monitored.

Stools

A newborn baby's first stools, which are called meconium, are black and tarry and somewhat difficult to clean. After the first few days, however, when your milk has come in, the meconium will begin to be replaced by thin, yellowish stools that contain curds like cottage cheese. When supplementation is introduced, the stools will change to be thicker brown, orange, or sometimes dark green (from the excess iron in the formula). It is also common for BFAR mothers to see combination stools that are first yellow and "curdy," and then brown, all in the same diaper. A stool that is green and full of foamy bubbles usually indicates that the baby is not getting enough hindmilk, which can be corrected by keeping the baby feeding on each breast longer.

Meconium should be completely passed by the fourth day after birth. If your baby is still passing meconium on the fifth day or later, this is an indication that he has not been getting enough milk and supplementation may be needed.

Stools are less frequent for formula-fed or supplemented babies. Do not think that less frequent stools after supplementation begins is an indication that baby needs even more food.

You may think that it is strange to pay so much attention to your baby's stools, trying to determine what was from human milk and what was from formula. Most BFAR mothers do this, because it is definitive "proof" of how much human milk our babies have received from us. It can be very reassuring to see this proof when we're concerned about our milk supplies.

Even when the baby is having sufficient wet diapers, it is possible that he could have too few soiled diapers, which would indicate either that he is not receiving enough nutrition or that he has an obstruction or anatomical problem. Insufficient stools are a very significant indication that there is a problem and should be promptly brought to the attention of your baby's pediatrician to rule out an obstruction or anatomical problem and to consider whether there is a need for supplementation.

Be Aware of the Signs of Dehydration

It is absolutely critical that you are aware of the signs of dehydration. As a reminder, the classic signs of dehydration are included at the bottom of the assessment chart in Appendix 3. Some objective signs of dehydration are:

- A weak, high-pitched cry. This is characterized by a lack of any energy and will not be very loud;
- A depressed or sunken "soft spot" (anterior fontanel) on the head. Be sure to assess this when the baby is lying down and not when he is held upright as this can give an inaccurate presentation;
- A dry mouth. Periodically put your freshly washed (dry) finger in the baby's mouth and feel the amount of saliva. Adequate hydration is present when you can move your finger across the tongue or cheeks easily without sticking;
- Insufficient and infrequent wet diapers. At first, before your mature milk comes in, a newborn will only wet one or two diapers a day. When your colostrum turns to milk, around the third day, you should then expect your baby to wet six to eight cloth diapers or four to six disposable diapers, and have two to five bowel movements each day;
- Hands and feet or fingers and toes that are cool and clammy to your touch. Gauging this can be a bit subjective, but keep it in mind as something to check in relation to the other signs of adequate hydration;
- A fast pulse and very low blood pressure. You probably won't be able to assess this at home, but be sure your baby's health care giver is carefully monitoring these criteria;
- Absence of tears in infants older than three months. (Before a baby is three months old, he usually will not have the capacity to produce tears);
- When pressed, skin that stays dented; when gently pinched, failure of the skin to quickly return (spring back) to normal; and
- Fever.[2,3]

Aside from these classic signs, you can get a general sense of whether your baby is getting adequate fluids by making a point of noticing his or her general activity level and responsiveness to the surrounding environment. Your baby should be alert, demonstrate clear hunger signals, and even be a little fussy at times. Most importantly, he should act satisfied after feedings. Conversely, a baby who isn't receiving enough to eat is uninterested and listless. A dehydrated baby will simply not look well and may act sick.

Feed the Baby Frequently

How often to breastfeed your baby was discussed in some depth in the previous chapter, so you know that allowing your baby to nurse for as long and as frequently as he desires (demand or cue feeding) is best for your milk supply. Keeping him near you at all times will help you to be aware of his early hunger cues (rooting, fussing, etc.) so that you can feed him without allowing him to work up into a hungry, stressful cry. Minimizing your baby's crying in this way will also be less stressful on you and the other members of your household.

As you know, you will need to nurse your baby as often as he is interested in feeding. At the very least, this should be every two hours during the day and every three hours at night for a total of ten to twelve feedings every 24 hours. Count feedings from the beginning of one feeding to the beginning of the next, but don't watch the clock during the feeding—it doesn't matter at all how long the feeding lasts. The first month is a learning time for your new baby. He is learning how to nurse efficiently to satiate his hunger and thirst. During this month, he will perfect his nursing skills so that near the end of it, he will need less time to consume the same amount of milk.[1] Many BFAR mothers worry that long feedings indicate a low milk supply. This is a very unreliable gauge of your milk supply and it is important that you not put much importance on the length of feedings. Other objective criteria (described below) are more indicative of the state of your milk supply.

If it should seem as though you are nursing more often than every two hours, remember that smaller, more frequent feedings are much higher in calories than larger, less frequent feedings. And even though it can seem like it at first, you will not always spend all your time nursing. Remember that you are recovering from giving birth now—you need to rest and nursing is nature's way of ensuring that you do so. These feedings will eventually stretch out and become more manageable. Your baby will establish a feeding pattern to some degree, which will make life more predictable. The patterns that he establishes, however, will be his patterns and will be appropriate to his unique emotional and physiological needs. And these patterns will change as he grows and matures. Keeping an assessment chart will help you see these patterns.

Take Advantage of Nighttime Feedings

Many BFAR mothers find that nighttime feedings are often the time when they are subject to moments of self-doubt and worry. Among the benefits of night feeding is that prolactin levels are higher at night so that the milk supply is greater. Many BFAR mothers find that even if they need to supplement during the day, they can forgo supplementation at night and just breastfeed the baby. Let-downs also occur more easily at night because mothers are more relaxed. And, of course, the more let-downs that occur, the higher in fat the milk will be.

Unfortunately, though, the early morning hours are usually when a mother can feel the most vulnerable and least sure of her convictions, especially about BFAR. If the baby has been crying a lot and you are exhausted and at the end of your emotional rope, it is easy to begin second-guessing your efforts to BFAR. Anything can seem more tragic and monumental at 3:00 in the morning. It's not the best time to make long-term decisions, though. Do what you need to do to get through the night, but in the morning, seek the help of an LLL Leader, a lactation consultant, or the baby's physician to help you find the best solution for the problem.

Sleep with Your Baby to Facilitate BFAR

Because nighttime feedings are so important for BFAR, many mothers find that sleeping with their babies next to them allows both of them to get more sleep and permits the babies greater access to their milk. They try to feed as often as possible during the night to take advantage of the increased supply and higher-fat milk. Many physicians are supportive of this practice because research has now shown that when mothers and babies sleep together, their sleep cycles become synchronized and they wake together naturally for feedings.[4,5] This is less disruptive for both the mother's and the baby's sleep needs, as well as the needs of the rest of the family.

Babies who co-sleep with their mothers also seem to be more secure and pleasant because they are reassured by the presence of their mothers. The deep attachment that they feel from this security has a positive effect on BFAR because happier babies tend to thrive more readily. And mothers, in turn, are reassured by the deep attachment they feel to their babies by having them with them during the tender, intimate hours of the night.

Obviously, no drugs or alcohol should ever be used by an adult who is co-sleeping with a child. But other than this caution, co-sleeping is considered by many experts and a great deal of research to be a safe way to care for one's baby at night (or even during the day). Some mothers worry that they or their partner will roll over on the baby. The truth is that we are naturally aware of our "boundaries" in bed; we don't roll off the edge of the bed, nor do we roll on top of our animals or partners. For mothers, co-sleeping with an infant makes them even more aware of protecting the baby's space so that no harm can come to him. We can also be better in tune with the baby's health by being next to him and right there if the baby should have any kind of problem.

There are many ways to co-sleep safely. Many mothers find that putting the mattress right on the floor prevents any worry about the baby rolling or falling off the bed. Another alternative is to put the bed up against the wall, with the baby next to the wall. A mesh crib rail is also a good solution, but it is important to make sure that it is installed correctly and that there are no gaps between the crib rail and the mattress. When co-sleeping, dress warmly so that you need only light blankets; do not overdress the baby or pile blankets on top of him. Use a pillow only for yourself and keep it away from the baby's head. An alternative is to put the baby's bed or crib up against your bed in a "side-car" arrangement. Again, be sure there are no gaps between the mattresses where baby could become trapped. This technique and other co-sleeping ideas and issues are discussed in wonderful detail in Tine Thevenin's book, *The Family Bed* and Nighttime Parenting by Dr. William Sears.

Of course, co-sleeping is not a practice that all families feel comfortable with or that all babies prefer. We have to find the sleeping arrangements that work best for the members of our families. This is especially true for BFAR mothers as they try to minimize stress and maximize rest.

Condition Your Let-Down Reflex

Many BFAR mothers find that because there is a psychological component to the let-down reflex, it can be conditioned to occur in response to certain stimulus that you can create through a routine. For example, you can try to nurse in the same comfortable place in the house (your nursing station), or always have a certain drink with you. Any routine that you can create to accompany your nursing session will help condition your let-down reflex so that it is likely to occur when you follow the routine.

Whenever possible, take advantage of let-downs that happen unexpectedly between feedings by stopping right then to feed the baby. Having let-downs in this way is a factor of your still-developing milk supply; it will not tend to happen after the first couple of months.

Pay Attention to Your Baby's Nursing Style

A baby suckles at the breast in a very specific way when he is accepting significant amounts of human milk. His suckling will be slowly rhythmic and he will pause for a slight moment when his jaw opens widest. In general, the longer the pause, the more milk he is receiving. A deep swallow will follow. You may even be able to see his earlobes wiggle as he swallows.

Some babies are loud nursers and others are not. Swallowing cannot always be heard. Many lactation consultants actually use a stethoscope to listen for swallowing, but you can detect it yourself simply by putting your free index finger under his chin, lightly against his throat.

Occasionally, when the baby relaxes his jaw and stops suckling, his lower jaw will quiver. This really has no relationship to nursing, but is rather an immature neurological response to the partially tensed jaw muscle.

Avoid Artificial Nipples

For reasons that have been explained in previous chapters, you will want to avoid using artificial nipples, including pacifiers. Aside from the risk of nipple confusion, every bit of sucking that the baby does that is not on the breast is a missed opportunity for critical stimulation of your milk supply in the early weeks.

Encourage Comfort Sucking

Comfort sucking has also been discussed in a previous chapter, so you won't need to be concerned whether your baby is nursing for nutrition or for comfort. It is ideal for BFAR babies to engage in a significant amount of comfort sucking in order to stimulate the milk supply as much as possible. Allow him full access to your breast and trust that his nutritional and emotional needs are being met through nursing. The additional stimulation that your lactation system receives from the extra sucking will serve to encourage a greater milk supply than any pump could.

Calculate Your Baby's Acceptable Weight Loss

Take the time in the first couple of days after your baby is born to calculate your baby's acceptable weight loss. For instance, if you have an eight-pound baby (3600 grams), and you know that your pediatrician is comfortable with up to an eight percent weight loss, you can determine that your baby can safely lose up to ten ounces (280 grams), so that your baby's weight could go as low as seven pounds, six ounces (3320 grams) without undue concern. Any loss beyond this would signal that a lactation specialist should be consulted to evaluate the baby's latch-on and positioning and determine which milk-increasing or supplementation measures may be appropriate. In addition, your baby may need medical attention. Knowing this figure up front will help you better understand the numbers as your baby is weighed in the first two weeks.

Weigh Your Baby Once a Day

A critical component of monitoring your baby's nutritional status is to know what his accurate weight is on a regular basis. Obtaining weight information depends upon two factors: accuracy and appropriate time intervals.

It is critical that the reading on the scale on which your baby is weighed be accurate. But the truth is that all scales are calibrated slightly differently and can differ from each other between five to eight ounces (155.5 to 248.8 grams). The scale your baby was weighed on in the hospital or birthing center will not give the exact reading that the scale in your doctor's office will. When only a few ounces can make the difference between supplementation and exclusive breastfeeding, having an accurate number is essential. With a small baby, even when he is weighed on the same scale, the weight reading can be also skewed by the presence of an impending bowel movement. If one weight is taken with a full bowel and the next weight is taken right after baby has had a large bowel movement, the differential between the two readings will be inaccurate.

The only way to get consistently accurate weights is to weigh your baby on the same scale, preferably a highly sensitive electronic scale, at optimal time intervals. The spring-loaded scales available in the baby superstores and catalogues are not adequate for the sensitive measurements of a BFAR baby. A high-quality, electronic scale can be rented for a very modest price on a weekly or monthly basis from the same places that rent hospital-grade breast pumps (resources are provided in Appendix 1). It is recommended that BFAR mothers rent an electronic scale for the first month when weight gain is so critical. An electronic scale can be very helpful after the first month, as well.

Having your own accurate scale at home gives you control over the information that is being relied upon to make decisions about your baby's health. It gives you an invaluable sense of reassurance when your baby is gaining well and you know it on a regular basis, and it allows you to know very quickly when a pattern of weight stagnation or loss begins.

The second component of the ability to obtain accurate weight information is to weigh the baby at appropriate time intervals. It is easy to become overly focused on weighing your baby, especially when you have your own electronic scale at home. This can cause anxiety and unnecessary worry, detracting from the bonding time with your child and almost certainly inhibiting your let-downs. In order to avoid over-focusing on the baby's weight, it is recommended that you weigh the baby only one time each day. It doesn't matter when, as long as you weigh the baby at the same time each day.

Ideally, the baby should be weighed naked, but the electronic scales provide a feature so you can weigh a fresh diaper first and it subtracts the weight of the diaper from the weight of the baby.

Finally, in order to maximize the accuracy of the reading, it is important to always weigh your baby with as close to the same amount of food in his stomach as possible. Since the amount obtained in feedings can vary, the best way to accomplish this is to weigh him right before a feeding, so that his stomach is empty.

Do Not Weigh Baby Before and After Feedings

A very common recommendation is to weigh a baby before and after a feeding in order to determine how much milk was ingested. This practice is controversial, however, because researchers have shown that pre- and post-feeding test weights are less than reliable.[6] More importantly, it could cause the mother to experience performance anxiety, which can inhibit her let-down reflex. BFAR mothers, who already have reason to suspect their milk supplies, are apt to feel even more anxiety. Moreover, it is not the amount consumed at each feeding that is important but the cumulative effect of the milk on the baby's growth, which is more accurately reflected in daily weight checks.

When You Need to Pump

Another common recommendation is telling mothers to pump for a specific period of time after feedings to increase their milk supplies. The premise is that the increased stimulation will result in a greater milk supply. This does not necessarily hold true for all BFAR mothers.

First, no pump can duplicate the suckling action of a baby's mouth, tongue, and jaws, and therefore it cannot signal the lactation system to make as much milk as a baby can. It relies on rhythmic suction and release and does not compress the lactiferous sinuses beneath the areola. Only your baby can do this. If your baby is already comfort sucking a significant amount of time, then you are getting more efficient stimulation of your milk supply than any pump could give.

Second, pumping can be exhausting, especially when you are already coping with the stresses associated with BFAR. Your time is better spent relaxing, recouping, and bonding with your baby than it is pumping. This is especially true for BFAR mothers who have older children. It isn't practical to feed a baby for half an hour or more and then pump for twenty minutes with only an hour left until it is time for the next feeding.

If the Baby Won't Nurse Often

Not all babies want to nurse for comfort, though. And some babies are unwilling to nurse every two to three hours. If you find that your baby will not nurse that often and has no interest in comfort sucking, then you may wish to consider taking proactive measures to maximize your milk supply during the sensitive time that prolactin receptors are created. In Chapter 9, many techniques are presented that can effectively increase your milk supply by providing additional stimulation and demand, thereby maximizing prolactin receptor creation.

Visit Your Pediatrician

Most pediatricians will want to see the baby within three days after birth and then when the baby is two weeks old. This allows them to calculate weight losses and gains and obtain an overall impression of the baby's progress. Knowing that you have had breast reduction surgery, your pediatrician may wish to see your baby more frequently. At each of your visits, take your assessment chart so that he will have as much information as possible in order to make informed recommendations.

Remember, though, that you are ultimately responsible for your baby's care. Only you can make decisions about his health. Not all physicians are well educated about breastfeeding management and few have specialized knowledge about BFAR. You may be more of an expert in this area than he or she is. Trust your instincts and remember that your doctor's recommendations are based on his or her expert opinion, but no physician has the authority to order you to do anything. Only you can make decisions about your child's care, using the information and opinions of the experts you consult as factors in your decision.

If you are using an electronic rental scale at home, take the weight readings taken at your pediatrician's office with a grain of salt. Remember that all scales are calibrated differently and you will most likely get a different reading from the doctor's scale than your own. The doctor's scale is not necessarily more accurate; in fact, it may be less so because it is used heavily and probably not checked frequently for precise accuracy.

Establish a Relationship with a La Leche League Leader or Lactation Consultant

It is very important to enlist the help of an LLL Leader or a board certified lactation consultant. It is not necessary that this person know much about BFAR, although it would certainly be advantageous if she did. Her role, though, is not so much to provide BFAR advice as to be an objective observer of your baby's progress and a resource for basic breastfeeding issues that may arise.

Seeing your baby hour after hour, day after day, can make it easy to miss a gradual deterioration in his health. This is especially true if this is your first baby. We can get very used to seeing a face we love so dearly and not notice that it has become gaunt and lacks proper tone. A lactation specialist who sees healthy babies on a regular basis and who is trained to look for the signs of dehydration can give an objective observation of your baby's appearance.

Occasionally, BFAR mothers become so focused on the mechanics of BFAR and increasing their milk supplies that they fail to realize that their problems are caused by latch-on or positioning problems. It is especially important to correct problems like this in the early days so that the creation of critical prolactin receptors is not missed.

Take Your Baby's Personality into Account

All babies have unique personalities and these personalities extend to their breastfeeding styles. Both LLLI's The Womanly Art of Breastfeeding and Dr. Sears' *The Baby Book* present an overview of the types of personalities breastfeeding babies commonly demonstrate. It is important to understand your baby's special personality type and take it into account as you evolve your BFAR techniques. Not all babies respond the same way to breastfeeding management or supplementation methods. Sensitivity to his unique needs is very important in order to ensure his psychological happiness and physical health.

Evaluating Your Baby's Progress to Determine If Supplementation Is Necessary

Using the previous guidelines, you will be able to accumulate the correct information in order to determine if supplementation will be necessary for this baby. Before you can make that decision, however, you will need to have a basic understanding of normal growth patterns so that you can know if your baby does not meet the minimum expectations.

Normal Growth Patterns

BFAR mothers usually spend a great deal of time paying attention to their baby's weight gain. This is very good to do, because it gives us a clear indication of the baby's progress. While all babies are different and all babies grow at different rates, there are weight growth ranges that indicate normal growth for breastfed babies. These rates are not the same as for formula-fed babies, and also depend upon genetic disposition, racial or ethnic differences, and geographical region.[3] In general, however, during the first three to four months, a breastfed baby should gain between four to seven ounces per week (113 to 227 grams), which works out to between a half ounce to one ounce (14 to 28 grams) per day.[2] When calculating weight gain, add the gained amount from the lowest the baby has weighed, rather than from the baby's birth weight.

It is also important to consider increases in your baby's body length, which should be a half inch (1.25 cm) per month on average, as well as his head circumference, which should be a quarter inch (.625 cm) per month on average, showing that his brain is developing appropriately.[3]

Regaining Birth Weight

In the first two to three weeks, pediatricians usually give significant attention to a baby regaining his birth weight. An acceptable overall loss is considered to be no more than seven to eight percent. In general, this is appropriate because it gives a definite early indication of developmental progress. There are subtle aspects to this common newborn requirement, however, that must be considered in the context of BFAR.

Research has demonstrated that breastfed babies are often slower to regain birth weight than are formula-fed babies.[3] Physiologically, breastfed babies are the norm against which artificially fed babies must be compared, so the rate at which breastfed babies regain their birth weight should be considered the biological standard. This means that if it takes three weeks for a breastfed baby to regain his birth weight, this may be perfectly normal and not a cause for concern.

The birth weight of any baby is artificially high because babies are born with a significant amount of meconium that has been accumulating in their bowels during gestation. When a baby is fed colostrum, which contains a natural laxative, he is likely to expel all the meconium very soon after birth, which makes it appear as if a sudden weight loss has occurred. Further, human milk is taken in lesser quantities than formula because it is more bioavailable which simply means that it is in a form that is more immediately, easily, and completely used by the body. But because it is more fully digested, there is little waste material and what there is, is quickly expelled, leaving little in the bowel to add to the body weight. Formula, on the other hand is not very bioavailable and the byproducts accumulate in significant quantities in the bowel, giving the appearance of weight gain.

Some babies' birth weights must be viewed in light of other health concerns. For example, babies who are born even a week or two early will have lower birth weights by as much as a half pound (224 grams) to a full pound (450 grams). Maternal gestational diabetes may also cause a baby to have extra fluid stores that will be quickly shed after birth.

Weight loss, then, is only one factor to consider in a broader context when evaluating the necessity of supplementation. By the end of three weeks, if all factors are standard and if no other primary signs of dehydration are present, supplementation may not be required at this point. However, if there are other health concerns and signs of dehydration are present, supplementation is warranted and should begin immediately, sometimes even earlier in the two or three week timeframe.

If there is any question about a baby not gaining enough, contact your La Leche League Leader or lactation consultant to work with you on latch-on, sucking, and positioning issues. It may be that that the problem is caused by those kinds of issues rather than by your surgery. Making sure that all is well with latch-on, sucking, and positioning will help you maximize your milk supply and ensure that you are able to give as much of it as possible to your baby.

Putting It all Together: Evaluating Your Baby's Nutritional Status

We have many criteria from which to evaluate our babies' nutritional status. You need to review each of these criteria and then consider them together in order to determine if supplementation will be necessary. If you've been keeping an assessment chart, you will have a complete record of your baby's statistics from which an overall picture will emerge.

Weight gain will be one of the most significant factors in determining your baby's nutritional status. You may even wish to take a few minutes to plot his weight gain on a chart so that you can visually see his weight gain or loss pattern.

- Has baby regained his birth weight? Did he lose more than eight percent of his birth weight?
- After the first four days, did he begin gaining a half ounce to one ounce (14 to 28 grams) a day?
- Does your baby have both wet and soiled diapers in sufficient amounts? Are you seeing typical (often described as yellow and curdy) human milk stools?

- Have you checked for signs of dehydration listed on page 132. Even the presence of only one of these signs is a red flag.
- Is your baby alert and active? Does he look well?

If any are deficient, supplementation may be necessary, at least for a short time. The most important priority is that the baby must be fed. For this reason, it is best to begin supplementing conservatively and then work to increase your milk supply. Remember that supplementing at the breast is always preferable to using bottles or other feeding devices because it continues to stimulate your milk supply and will not detract from your efforts to increase it. Supplementation is discussed in detail in the next chapter.

Special First Month Concerns

Growth Spurts

Babies do not grow at a constant rate. They have growth spurts that occur on a fairly predictable schedule of six days, fourteen days, three weeks, six weeks, three months, and six months. You may find that your baby begins nursing more during this time and may even become a bit fussy. Increasing his nursing demand is the natural way for him to increase your milk supply. During these times it can feel as though he nurses all the time and never seems satisfied, but your milk supply will actually increase within a couple of days and nursing will return to normal. Do not take this as an indication that your milk supply is suddenly insufficient. Milk supplies do not suddenly diminish. If your baby is demanding more, it is most likely because he needs more. As long as his hydration remains adequate, you do not need to increase his supplement. Simply continue to monitor for the signs of dehydration and count his wet and soiled diapers to reassure yourself that he is okay.

Early Evening Fussies

Many LLL Leaders receive calls from mothers who say their babies become very fussy and nurse often in the evenings, especially during the first three months. These babies nurse for just a few sucks, pull off, cry and fuss, and then latch on again, repeating this pattern over and over. This is not colic, which tends to occur for long stretches of time each day and is accompanied by other behaviors that indicate the baby is in pain. This pattern is actually a common one among breastfed babies and is not at all related to BFAR, although it can make BFAR mothers doubt their milk supplies, especially when well-meaning family members observing the obvious distress of the baby offer advice that implies the mother's milk is deficient. It is also natural for mothers to wonder if it was something they ate or if something is seriously wrong. In most cases, none of these reasons is causing the behavior.

For some babies, the early evening hours are a time when they are overstimulated and exhausted. They are not actually hungry and do not want food, but do want the comfort of nursing. As a matter of fact, they may have already nursed so much that their tummies are overfull and they are objecting to the milk they get when they try to comfort nurse.

I experienced early evening fussies with my second son, Ben. Even though I was a knowledgeable and experienced breastfeeding mother, I still doubted my milk supply. But I had been weighing Ben once a day on my rented electronic scale and knew for a fact that he was gaining two ounces a day. So I began to say this mantra to myself, "A baby who is gaining well does not need to be supplemented." It forced me to accept the truth that my baby was not starving, but was rather overstimulated or tired and simply needed to nurse to feel better.

It is important that you be reassured that your milk supply is not deficient because of early evening fussiness. Dr. Peter Hartmann has extensively studied mothers' milk supplies during this phenomenon and has demonstrated that the milk supply is not actually low at all.[7]

If you are not supplementing at this time, the best approach to this kind of fussiness is to permit the baby complete access to your breasts and not offer a supplement. Eventually, you may find other means of soothing the baby, which may require that another caregiver who does not smell of mother's milk take the baby for a little while. In many societies, this time of day is called "Grandma's Hour" for this very reason. Many mothers find that having the baby carried in a sling either by them or another caregiver is particularly soothing to babies at this time of day.

Other Reasons for a Low Milk Supply

Before concluding that the reason for a low milk supply is your reduction surgery, it is worth the effort to have your obstetrician or midwife rule out the possibility that there may be another contributing medical condition, such as a retained placenta, which can severely inhibit the milk supply. This and other causes for a low milk supply are explored in the next chapter.

BFAR and Fertility

Many mothers wonder how BFAR will affect fertility if they need to supplement, even though they may be providing a significant amount of milk to their babies. The answer is that only exclusive breastfeeding with no supplements, skipped feedings, or solids for the first six months is considered sufficient to inhibit ovulation. However, some prescription drugs, such as domperidone, which is often taken by BFAR women to increase their milk supplies, do prevent ovulation by inducing high levels of prolactin in the system. Questions about potential fertility should be discussed with a knowledgeable health care provider.

Feelings of Depression

It is important for you to know that almost all BFAR mothers go through some degree of depression in the first few weeks. There may be some moments, especially during the wee hours of the night, when you wonder why in the world you are going to all this effort and you feel sorely tempted to just quit and begin formula-feeding. This is a very natural feeling and it is commonly experienced by BFAR mothers. This is also the time when you need a support system, such as the BFAR email list, to reassure you and remind you of how well you're really doing. Your LLL Leader will also be a good resource to listen to your feelings and help you sort things out.

BFAR elicits a great deal of emotion and for this reason Chapter 12 discusses emotional issues. It would be good to review it when you are feeling low so that you can be reassured that your feelings are normal.

BFAR Perfectionism

Don't try to do everything "exactly right." Many BFAR mothers try to maximize their milk supply through achieving what they believe to be BFAR performance standards. Such standards, though, don't allow room for real life or human inconsistency. Just do the best you can and forgive yourself if you don't always live up to your expectations.

Conclusion

The first month of breastfeeding is very important in determining the course of your BFAR experience. No matter how much you prepared beforehand, until your baby was born, you had no way of knowing just what it was going to be like for you. Now, though, you have begun your BFAR journey with the techniques and tools to help maximize your success and quickly identify problems that indicate that supplementation may be required. Because supplementation is an issue that most BFAR women must address to some degree, the next chapter provides a detailed discussion of supplement issues and management, should it be necessary.

The actions that you take during this first important month have a direct impact upon your entire breastfeeding experience. Using the information, techniques, and tools as fully as possible, in combination with the support of your friends and family, will ensure that you and your baby will work out a BFAR system that meets your needs and gives you both the benefits of breastfeeding that you desire.

REFERENCES:

1. Lawrence, R. A. and R. M. Lawrence. *Breastfeeding: A Guide for the Medical Profession*, 5th edition. St. Louis, Missouri: Mosby, 1999; 258, 235.

2. Mohrbacher, N. and J. Stock. THE BREASTFEEDING ANSWER BOOK, Schaumburg, Illinois: LLLI, 1997; 115, 114.

3. Riordan, J. and K. Auerbach. *Breastfeeding and Human Lactation*, 2nd edition. Sudbury, MA: Jones and Bartlett Publishers, 1999; 313, 638, 604, 378.

4. McKenna, J., S. Mosko, C. Dungy, et al. Sleep and arousal patterns of co-sleeping human infant/mother pairs: A preliminary physiological study with implications for the study of sudden infant death syndrome (SIDS). *American Journal of Physical Anthropology* 1990; 83:331-47.

5. Mosko, S., J. McKenna, M. Dickel, et al. Parent-infant co-sleeping: The appropriate context for the study of infant sleep and implications for sudden infant death syndrome (SIDS) research. *Journal of Behavioral Medicine* 1993; 16(6):589-610.

6. Inch, S. and M. Renfrew. Common breastfeeding problems. In: Chalmers, I., M. Enkin, M. Keirse, eds. *Effective Care in Pregnancy and Childbirth*. Oxford, England: Oxford University Press, 1989: 1375-89.

7. Daly, S. and P. Hartmann. Infant demand and milk supply. Part 2: The short-term control of milk synthesis in lactating women. *Journal of Human Lactation* 1995; 11:27-37.

VANESSA'S STORY

I had my breast reduction surgery done when I was 21, back in the early 1980s. At the time, I was told that I would not be able to breastfeed, but then what 21-year-old college student is even thinking about it? I just accepted that breastfeeding would not be an option when I finally got around to having a child.

When I got pregnant, I started looking into it, and discovered that the type of reduction I had, where they leave the nipple attached, might make it possible to breastfeed. I looked high and low for information on the Internet. The only information I could find was that it depended on the type of surgery that you had, and on how much support you had, and that it was possible that support was the critical variable. I also found that the medical perspective was that supplementing was pretty much always necessary with a reduction.

So, I made up my mind to give it a try, figuring if it failed, I wouldn't be any worse off. I am a good researcher so I was persistent in trying to find some information on managing breastfeeding and supplementation, or trying to find anyone who had experience in helping someone with a breast reduction to establish breastfeeding. No luck. I made an appointment with the hospital lactation consultant. She was very nice, but pretty much inexperienced as far as dealing with breast reductions. She did suggest that if I couldn't produce any milk at all she could set me up with an SNS so I could have the "experience" of nursing, but that seemed silly to me at the time. The point of nursing was giving my milk to my baby as far as I was concerned.

Basically, all of the advice that I got seemed to emphasize that the breasts are magical organs that produce what you need. As my lactation consultant put it, plenty of women nurse twins, or nurse with just one breast, and the breasts just increase production to compensate. The gist of it was that I should stop thinking about supplementing and concentrate on breastfeeding exclusively.

Emma was induced at 38 weeks, because I suddenly developed pregnancy induced hypertension (PIH). We had two additional complications as far as breastfeeding goes, Emma was a very small baby (five pounds, 13 ounces), and my milk came in unusually late at six days postpartum. I was able to give Emma colostrum in the first days but my milk hadn't come in when we were sent home 36 hours postpartum. Because of her small size and my potential breastfeeding problems, the hospital checked her blood sugar before releasing her. It came out high enough that they okayed continuing to try to breastfeed for a few more days, as long as she had at least six wet diapers a day.

By the end of her third day, Emma was screaming, nursing constantly, and she just didn't look right. I wound up giving her a little formula in one of those desperate 2 AM moments, and she calmed right down and fell asleep. I felt like a failure, because there is so much pressure about not supplementing, that first bottle being the first step down the slippery slope to bottle-feeding. But something was clearly wrong, every nerve in my body said so. I talked to the lactation consultant later that morning, and she said that she had a lot of faith in "mother's instincts." She was very kind and nonjudgmental, and basically said that "Well, sometimes with a breast reduction it works and sometimes it doesn't, continue supplementing, but also continue giving the baby the breast first before pulling out the bottle for a few more days, and let's see what happens."

Six full days after Emma was born, my milk finally came in. I called the lactation consultant in jubilation, and basically went to bed with Emma for three days, doing nothing but sleeping and nursing, trying to get my supply up. We were still offering what Penelope Leach calls "complementary" bottles. I would nurse for an hour, and if Emma was still unsatisfied then we'd top her off with an ounce of formula.

After three days I rented a hospital breast pump, so that I was either feeding or pumping at least 10 to 12 times a day. We gradually decreased the formula supplements, and after a full week put Emma on the breast alone. Thirty-six hours later we had a fussy baby, and only four wet diapers. Not good.

So we went back to the "complementary bottles." I would always nurse Emma first, and then after a full hour of nursing, if she was still clearly unsatisfied, offer her a bottle. This tended to happen toward the evening feeds, and it pretty much worked out that she would take about two to four ounces of formula a day in addition to my milk. She was still fussy, but what two-week-old isn't? She produced about six to seven wet diapers a day, on average, but had infrequent bowel movements.

I took her to the pediatrician for her three-week checkup, and she had only gained three ounces in two weeks. Not good. The pediatrician asked us to bring her back for another weigh-in the next week. I had been being very tight with the bottles, trying to keep supplementation to a bare minimum in order to maximize the chances for my milk supply to grow. Now we increased the supplementation, and I started pumping between feedings a couple of times a day, so that we could give her expressed milk rather than formula for at least one of the bottles. Unfortunately, I was never able to pump more than an ounce or two at a time.

At the next weigh-in, she had gained enough weight to satisfy the pediatrician, and she asked us to bring her in again in two weeks. We kept up the same regimen, breastfeeding on demand, following with formula or expressed breast milk in a bottle if her nursing sessions went longer than an hour (1/2 hr per breast), with an average of four to six ounces of formula a day.

At the next weigh-in, Emma had only gained a couple of ounces in two weeks. The doctor ordered metabolic tests for Emma, and we all pretty much agreed that although it was good for Emma to get as much benefit as possible from human milk, she clearly needed more than I was able to provide. At that point the doctor ordered us to start giving her at least 22 ounces of formula a day (breast first, then formula), and bring her back in five days for a weight check.

It was like night and day. Emma suddenly became a different child. She filled out really quickly, she stopped having long fussy sessions in the evening, she slept more during the day, and she started having regular bowel movements. In five days she had put on eight ounces. She continued to gain quickly in both weight and height; basically she jumped in a month from being ninth percentile in both weight and height to being in about the 30th percentile.

Emma is now a happy, healthy, beautiful, and active seven-month-old girl, and has tripled her birth weight at six months. She's around the fiftieth to sixtieth percentile nowadays.

The downside is that once we started the heavy supplementation, breastfeeding quickly went into the inevitable spiral. I was still giving her the breast for fifteen minutes on each breast before giving her the bottle at every feeding, which meant that feedings were taking more than an hour out of every two. And as she increased in size my ability to generate more milk did not. Her bottles were getting bigger and bigger, and the amount of milk I was able to pump (with the Medela Lactina Select double-pump) remained constant at about one-and-a-half ounces. I'll be honest, it got harder and harder to justify that half-hour out of every two hours that it was taking to get an ounce of my milk into her. I gradually started letting it slide "just this once, because she's so hungry, or because I'm so tired..." and by the time she was nine weeks old I was basically just giving her the breast for comfort nursing. She was fully weaned by the time she was 12 weeks old.

We're planning to have one more child. I want to breastfeed again, but next time I want to do better at it. I guess the first thing is going to be to plug my ears when people start talking about the importance of "exclusive" breastfeeding. I'm thinking that using the SNS might be a good idea for the first month, right from the second or third day postpartum.

It's been wonderful knowing other BFAR mothers. They've really helped me put my experience with Emma into perspective. I thought our weight-gain problems were unique, and could never decide which made me feel guiltier: that the weight-gain problems might have been due to trying to breastfeed, or that the weight-gain problems might have had nothing to do with breastfeeding and that I allowed the doctor to push me into supplementing. Now I feel sure that we did the right thing for our circumstances.

SUPPLEMENTING

It is usually in the first few weeks that BFAR mothers determine whether or not supplementation will be necessary. Supplementation is not inevitable in BFAR; a significant number of BFAR mothers do not need to supplement at all. But for a great many others, it is a necessary component of BFAR. This chapter will help you determine when and how much to supplement, as well as the best ways to manage supplementation, so that you can maximize the benefits of your breastfeeding experience and minimize interruption of the harmonious breastfeeding relationship that you and your baby are developing.

Determining that your baby requires supplementary nutrition can often be a traumatic point in your BFAR experience. Every BFAR mother who has had to supplement can empathize with the mixed feelings you may be having. On the one hand, we want our babies to have the nutrition they need and we are thankful that there are alternatives to our own milk, but at the same time, we are disappointed that our bodies are not capable of producing enough milk to meet our babies' needs. Your feelings are natural and have been shared by thousands of BFAR mothers. If you find that you need to begin supplementing, it may help to read Chapter 12 about the unique emotions related to BFAR so that you can have the reassurance and validation you need as you go through this experience.

When to Begin Supplementation

Delay Supplementation for the First Few Days

Despite the common tendency of some hospital staff and new grandmothers to fret about a baby's hunger and thirst from almost the moment he is born, it is actually not necessary to give most full-term babies any fluid or nutrition for the first two to three days. This is because almost all full-term babies are born with sufficient fluid and fat reserves to forestall their need for significant additional hydration or nutrition for the first several days, until the mature milk comes in. For BFAR mothers, this can be a trying time. Friends, family, and health care givers may be aware of the possibility that you may have a sub-optimal milk supply. You certainly have this concern at the forefront of your mind. Despite all your best preparations for BFAR, you still won't know how breastfeeding will work for you until your milk comes in and you are able to see how your baby is doing. This is the time, though, to be as optimistic as you can be and to focus your thoughts and energies on nothing more than falling in love with your new baby as you begin your breastfeeding relationship.

Unless the ducts within your nipple/areola complex were completely severed during your reduction surgery, the chances are good that you will be able to produce at least some colostrum. Your baby should have the maximum opportunity to receive as much of this precious substance as possible. Nursing as often as you can will also allow your breasts to create as many prolactin receptors as possible, ensuring that your milk supply is maximized to its complete potential.

Determining When Supplementation Is Necessary after the First Few Days

After the first two to three days, it is important to begin assessing your baby's hydration level. Review the signs of dehydration and weight loss discussed in Chapter 7 and be aware of any changes that occur, for better or for worse. Begin recording any changes on your assessment chart so that you will be able to relate your baby's condition to his health care provider and see patterns as they develop.

Although it may be difficult to determine if supplementation is necessary, the guidelines provided in Chapter 7 will help you sort out the differences between your baby's actual condition and the fears that you and others concerned with your baby's health may be having. While concern for your baby's well-being is completely appropriate, it is important to make decisions about supplementation based on objective criteria. Having said this, however, it is also equally important to trust your motherly instincts and listen to that little voice if it whispers that something isn't right. You know your baby best and you are more in tune with him than anyone else. You may pick up on subtle clues that others might miss. Just try to be sure that any alarm signals are truly coming from your motherly instinct and not simply from fear.

Precisely when to begin supplementation depends upon the baby's degree of dehydration or weight loss. The greater the degree of dehydration or weight loss, the more critical it is to begin immediate supplementation. Conversely, the less the dehydration and weight loss, the more room one has to determine if, when, and how much supplementation may be necessary.

Should clear signs of dehydration or significant, rapid weight loss be present, immediate supplementation is warranted. Even though it is a complex emotional experience for a BFAR mother to begin supplementation, it is important to keep in mind that feeding and hydrating your baby must be your first priority, especially if he has demonstrated an early and immediate need for supplementation. The section "How Much to Supplement" will help you determine the appropriate quantity of supplementation to give your baby in order to have a minimal impact on your milk production.

Rule Out Other Causes of Inadequate Milk Production

Once your baby has had his immediate nutritional needs met, it is important to rule out mechanical breastfeeding problems as the cause of inadequate milk production. Apart from a little tenderness in the first few days, breastfeeding should never hurt. If it does, it means that there is a problem with the way the baby is positioned, latched-on, or how he suckles the breast. Even if it all seems right, take the time to have an expert give you an objective analysis anyway. Many mothers find they have a poor milk supply early on because of positioning, latch-on, or suckling problems. Your La Leche League Leader or lactation consultant can help identify and resolve any mechanical breastfeeding problems that you and your baby may be having.

Delaying Supplementation

If your baby isn't gaining weight well, but is not showing signs of dehydration, supplementation may not be necessary yet. In fact, it may not be necessary at all if you can increase your own milk supply. As long as he hasn't experienced significant weight loss and is well hydrated, you have an opportunity to increase your milk supply using the chemical and mechanical methods discussed in Chapter 9.

Determining whether or not to supplement while you work to increase your milk supply is a decision you will have to make carefully, taking the advice of your health care provider into consideration. Some BFAR mothers decide to go ahead and supplement small amounts, and this is sometimes a prudent course to take to ensure that your baby's needs are met. It is important to keep in mind, though, that every feeding that is supplemented away from the breast is a lost opportunity for stimulating the sensitive lactation system and could result in a corresponding decrease in the milk supply. This loss of stimulation has an even greater negative impact during the first few weeks when the prolactin receptors are being established. For this reason, it is important for BFAR mothers to supplement at the breast using an at-breast supplementer. This method of supplementation will ensure that your baby receives the nutrition and hydration that he needs, while also stimulating and maintaining the milk supply. Supplementation devices are discussed in greater detail later in this chapter.

False Indicators for Supplementation

Whether you are a first-time mother or an experienced mother of many children, it can be very difficult to interpret the behaviors your baby is showing you and whether or not they are indicators of hunger. Frequent feeding and general fussiness in particular can seem to be strong signals that your baby needs more to eat. But feeding frequently and fussiness are not true indicators of the need for supplementation, especially if your baby is showing these behaviors at about three weeks, six weeks, three months, or six months. These are the classic timeframes at which nearly all breastfed babies experience predictable growth spurts. Frequent feeding and general fussiness are normal behaviors at these times. As long as signs of dehydration are not present and your baby continues to gain adequately, he does not need supplementation.

When teething begins, some babies begin chewing on their fists, especially after feedings, which may seem to indicate that they are still hungry. Actually, they almost always are not hungry, they are just trying to soothe sore gums. Finding them something safe to chew on will help.

Most breastfed babies also begin experiencing regular fussy periods in the early evening hours at about six weeks of age and sometimes as soon as three weeks. Almost all breastfeeding mothers worry when this happens, but it is all that much easier for a

BFAR mother to attribute this fussiness to a low milk supply. If this happens to you, you will need to take the time to look objectively at both your criteria for adequate hydration and your baby's weight gain. Check your chart if you are keeping one and confirm that he is continuing to gain at an acceptable rate. If he is not demonstrating any signs of dehydration and he is gaining well, then remind yourself (and anyone else who is concerned) that "a baby who is gaining well is not starving." And a baby who is well hydrated, gaining well, and not starving does not need to be supplemented. This is normal behavior and will resolve itself very soon. Unnecessary supplementation will only serve to negatively impact your milk supply.

Separating normal behavior from cues that supplementation is necessary can be difficult for BFAR mothers who are already stressed, especially if your baby is simultaneously experiencing any colic or allergic reactions. It is important to separate your fears and empathy for your baby's distress from the objective information available to you. If your baby is gaining adequately and is well hydrated, then you can feel safe in holding off on the supplementation and waiting for him to settle down at about three months, as most breastfed babies do.

Late Supplementation

Some BFAR mothers find that their babies gain adequately and they are able to entirely avoid supplementation at first. After a time, though, their babies' rate of growth slows down and they need to reevaluate the necessity of supplementation. Should you find that your baby is definitely exhibiting signs of dehydration and is not gaining well, or is even losing weight, you will need to begin supplementing. This can seem traumatic when your milk supply has been adequate until that point. If your baby is not gaining weight, you'll need to begin supplementing immediately so that your baby's nutritional needs are met, and then afterward you can begin to sort out why supplementation became necessary and determine if there is anything you can do to increase your milk supply.

The first causes of a decreased milk supply that should be considered are the same for all mothers:

Were the weight checks performed on the same scale and with the same amount of clothing? Remember that all scales are calibrated differently and a significant weight loss can seem to have occurred when the true cause was really the difference between scale settings. It is best to weigh babies without any clothes at all (even a diaper) so as to ensure that the weight reading is most accurate. If a diaper must be used, however, weigh the diaper first and then subtract that weight from the baby's weight.

How often does your baby feed? For adequate nutritional intake, it is usually necessary for babies under four months old to feed at least every two hours during the day and at least every three hours at night. Some babies don't demand to feed this often, but if they are not gaining weight, they should be encouraged to do so.

Is your baby sleeping through the night? At night, especially, some babies will sleep right through feeding times and it is mighty tempting to let them do so. You're probably very tired and our culture places great value on babies sleeping long stretches at night. Unfortunately, though, a baby who is not gaining well is not physically able to go so long without a feeding, and so, difficult as it may be, you'll have to wake him to feed him at least once, but preferably twice, during the night.

How long do feedings last? Babies should be allowed to feed until they seem satisfied. Limiting the duration of feedings limits the amount of stimulation to the lactation system, as well as the amount of high-calorie hindmilk the baby receives, and may not allow sufficient time for let-downs to occur.

Have you decreased the number or length of feedings recently? Sometimes feedings become disrupted during vacations, holidays, or family visits. It's difficult to keep to the normal routine when you are in unfamiliar surroundings or when you feel uncomfortable about nursing around some people. It's also easy to be distracted and not want to let nursing sessions last for as long as you normally would because there are other, more interesting things to do.

Have you used artificial nipples? Artificial nipples can be detrimental to breastfeeding because babies will suck differently on an artificial nipple than from a human one. If you've begun using a bottle and are seeing a sudden decrease in your milk supply, it may be that the baby is not nursing as effectively at your breast because of the influence of the artificial nipple. If you've begun using a pacifier, this, too, can cause breastfeeding difficulties. As time goes on and your baby gets older, it can sometimes seem difficult to allow him to nurse on demand, especially if he seems to have a high need for comfort sucking. It can be very tempting to give such a baby a pacifier to soothe him between feedings. But pacifiers can teach poor sucking behaviors just as easily as artificial nipples on a bottle.

Is your baby sucking his thumb, fingers, or toes? Some babies prefer the independence of satisfying their sucking needs with their own appendages. They may not actually feel a sensation of hunger. But if they are not gaining adequate amounts of weight, they need to nurse more often and must be encouraged to satisfy their sucking desires more often at the breast.

Have you or your baby been ill? Slight infant weight loss during an illness is very common and not usually an indication of a lactation problem. During this time it is important to keep your baby nursing often so he receives as much of your milk as possible, especially if he is dehydrated from vomiting or diarrhea.

Do not worry that nursing when you are ill can make your baby ill. Your milk contains anti-infective properties that effectively combat the specific bacteria and viruses that you and your baby have been exposed to.[1]

When you become ill, though, your milk supply can become temporarily reduced. To minimize this effect, it is important to rest as much as you can and drink plenty of fluids to stay well-hydrated. Your milk supply will increase again as you recover.

Is your baby suddenly discovering the world around him and less interested in nursing? Many babies become fascinated with their environments during the middle of their first year. They don't want to sit still for nursing sessions. But they do still need the hydration and nutrition. Many mothers find that nursing in a darkened, quiet environment helps focus their babies' attention back to nursing.

Is your baby teething? When new teeth begin to break through sensitive gums, some babies find that nursing is a little painful, so they fuss when put to the breast in fear of pain. Some babies find relief by sucking or chewing on a cold wet washcloth or a cold teething toy and are then more willing to nurse.

Do you have any nipple or breast soreness? Soreness of any kind during nursing, especially in conjunction with dehydration and weight loss, is a strong indication that something is not right. Call your LLL Leader or lactation consultant right away to have your positioning, latch-on, and baby's sucking techniques evaluated.

Have you begun taking birth control pills or had a birth control shot? Some birth control drugs can have a very significant effect on milk supply.[4]

Are you having frequent let-downs? While it is very common for the sensation of let-downs to diminish after the first six weeks, they still occur in a normally functioning lactation system. So because you may not be able to rely on actually feeling them as a basis for knowing when they occur, you will have to look at the other tell-tale signs of let-down, such as frequent deep swallowing and earlobe wiggling. Decreased frequency of let-downs can be caused by many factors, including physical dysfunction relating to your surgery, a poor sucking technique, or environmental causes, such as stress and exhaustion.

Are you under a lot of stress? BFAR in and of itself can be stressful, but there are many other things in our lives that can cause stress, not the least of which is having a baby to care for. While you may not be able to reduce the stress in your life, you can find ways to cope with it that allow you to find some peace. Relaxation techniques are especially helpful in soothing away stress, but there are also many other ways to make the world seem a little better. Some women like reading and others like chocolate. Everyone has a favorite way to unwind and you need to be sure to take time to do pleasant things for yourself, even if only in small stolen moments.

Are you getting enough rest? Parents of small babies are known for being sleep-deprived. Waking every three hours or so for night feedings can be very taxing, especially if you find it difficult to go back to sleep. Knowing the baby is likely to cry again soon can keep you on edge and unable to fully relax. It's important that you train yourself to fall asleep quickly, though. Put your anxiety aside, being reassured that if the baby does wake, you will too. But if the baby doesn't, you'll get some sleep.

A breastfeeding mother often finds that having the baby sleep next to her bed in a bassinet or by her side in bed is an excellent way to combine night feedings with getting back to sleep easily. Because you don't have to get out of bed, you remain in a relaxed state and save a great deal of time. Babies who are fed quickly don't get as upset and are more easily soothed back to sleep. When your baby was small you may have heeded the suggestion to sleep when the baby sleeps during the daytime. However, as baby gets older, you may be expecting everything to return to "normal" and it doesn't seem very practical to nap when there is so much to do around the house. Still, it can make a big difference in your milk supply to take advantage of one or two short naps during the day instead of catching up on housework. You may find that you feel considerably better and that your milk supply improves.

Are you feeding from both breasts at each feeding? Because you are a BFAR mother, you may have a different milk supply in one breast than the other. It is, therefore, important that you make sure that your baby is getting enough access to both breasts, offering the lower-supply breast after he seems to have finished the first.

After you have ruled out or addressed all the usual causes of a decreased milk supply, you can then consider causes for a decreased milk supply that may be a result of your reduction surgery. In most cases, a need for late supplementation is caused by the transition from the endocrine-stimulated (hormone) lactation system to the autocrine-stimulated (supply and demand) lactation system over the first three months. A BFAR mother can have an initially adequate milk supply because her milk supply is being created more from the hormones her body is generating than from the demand that is placed upon it. When the body slowly stops creating hormones automatically, though, the lactation system becomes more and more dependent upon nerve stimulation. At this point, the milk supply can decrease if the stimulation is not adequate to sustain it. As a BFAR mother, the inadequate stimulation is usually not because you are not breastfeeding enough, but is rather because the nerves in your nipple/areola complex were damaged during your surgery and cannot relay the proper stimulation messages to the lactation system.

When this is the case, most BFAR mothers find that herbal and prescription galactagogues (milk-inducing substances) have a dramatic impact on the milk supply because they bridge the gap between the nerve stimulation and prolactin production. Some galactagogues also greatly facilitate let-downs. A discussion of galactagogues is presented in Chapter 9.

Supplementation after Six Months

It can be very helpful for BFAR mothers to keep in mind that supplementation may become much easier when the baby reaches the age of being able to eat solid foods and drink from a cup, which is usually around six months. After this age, your baby can ingest a significant portion of his nutrition from healthy prepared foods. Of course, when solid foods are given in place of supplementation, it is important to increase the amount of fluids so that adequate hydration is maintained. Once the baby is eating a good quantity at regular intervals, and provided you are able to produce at least 15 to 18 ounces (442 to 532 ml) of milk each day, nursing at the breast can become the supplement to your baby's regular meals. If you cannot produce at least this amount, then, depending upon how much solid food he is regularly eating, you may still need to provide additional supplementation through the end of his first year.

Human Milk Substitutes

Once it has been determined that supplementation must begin, the next consideration is what the supplement should consist of. Determining the appropriate substitute for your own milk is not an easy choice because there are many factors to consider. For this reason, it is important to consult with your baby's pediatrician or a nutritionist so that you will have as much information as possible from which to make your decision.

As you go about deciding what you will use to supplement, there are general guidelines and information for the feeding of human infants that may help you in your decision. These guidelines have been developed by the World Health Organization, a widely respected international health authority. (Clearly, because they do not specifically apply to BFAR, the first two feeding methods are not viable options in the context of supplementation.)

Appropriate Foods for Infant Feeding
(Listed in order of suitability for infant feeding.)

- Milk from baby's own mother fed at the breast
- Milk from baby's own mother expressed and fed with artificial feeding device
- Human milk from milk banks (pasteurized and screened for HIV and other diseases)
- Commercially prepared synthetic infant formula

Human Milk from Milk Banks

In 1980, the World Health Organization and UNICEF formed a joint resolution, stating that, "Where it is not possible for the biological mother to breastfeed, the first alternative, if available, should be the use of human milk from other sources. Human milk banks should be made available in appropriate situations."[2] In 1997, the American Academy of Pediatrics officially concurred by issuing a policy statement affirming that, "Human milk is the preferred feeding for all infants, including premature and sick newborns, with rare exceptions."[3] These landmark policies from the definitive international authorities on infant feeding are based on extensive research into the appropriate foods for infant feeding. Their mutual conclusion that donated human milk is the first and best alternative to a mother's own milk is momentous and in direct refutation of the formula industries' claim that their products are the second best option to a mother's own milk.

Although wet nursing and informally donated mother's milk are also ways of obtaining human milk, the risks of communicating serious diseases through untreated milk are too great to suggest these as viable options. Milk banks are presented as the preferred method of obtaining human milk because their facilities collect, process, and store human milk in a standardized manner.

Repositories of human milk, collected for the purpose of dissemination for the feeding of infants who do not have access to their own mothers' milk, have been in existence in the United States since 1911, when two physicians in Boston, Massachusetts, sought a means of providing suitable food to prevent frequent infant deaths from malnutrition in a local orphanage. Collection, sterilization, pasteurization, storage, and freezing protocols for human milk have been developed and refined since that time so that human milk banks are now a viable source of consistently safe human milk. As of this writing, seven milk banks were in operation in North America; five in the United States, one in Canada, and one in Mexico. Contact information for these banks is provided in Appendix 1.

In response to the growing need for a formal advocacy and liaison organization for independently run milk banks, the Human Milk Banking Association of North America (HMBANA) was established as a nonprofit organization in 1985. It is a unifying entity for the member milk banks and serves as the authority on the practical aspects of human milk banking.

As a BFAR woman, you have invested a great deal of time and energy into learning more about lactation and infant feeding than the average mother. In your self-education, you may be surprised to find that you are more knowledgeable on some points than the health care providers you consult. On the matter of human milk banks, this may be especially true. Due to their large marketing budgets and sophisticated marketing strategies, formula manufacturers present abundant amounts of information about infant formulas to physicians and health care providers. Human milk banks, on the other hand, are usually nonprofit organizations and are largely run on grants and donations. They do not have the resources to promote the availability of their services to health care providers and so, unfortunately, most physicians are not aware that banked human milk is a viable feeding option. They may be interested in the information that you can provide to them about obtaining donor human milk.

The milk available from human milk banks is considerably safer than milk that is informally shared by nursing mothers because it is obtained under standardized guidelines for cleanliness from healthy, non-smoking, unmedicated lactating women. The mothers are regularly screened for unacceptable health conditions.

Once it has been collected, the milk is pasteurized and frozen, which serves to kill pathogens, but still preserves most of the human milk's unique immunological and nutritional properties, such as immunoglobulins and long chain polyunsaturated fatty acids.

As you can see, milk collected, processed, and stored in this fashion is very safe for human infant consumption. As a result, there have been no documented cases of transmission of disease through milk received from a milk bank.

Obtaining donor human milk is not a difficult process. You will need a prescription from a physician and you will need to be under the care of this physician while giving the donor milk to your baby. The milk can be picked up directly from the milk bank if it is local or it can be safely shipped to you no matter where you live in North America. The cost for human milk currently ranges between $2.25 to $2.50 (US) per ounce, which covers only about sixty percent of the actual costs of processing the milk. Shipping fees, of course, are additional. Fortunately, many medical insurance policies cover a portion of your cost for donor human milk, as do most WIC programs, and, in most cases, but depending on the particular policies of each bank, no baby with a medical need for human milk is refused banked milk because his family is unable to pay.

Commercially Prepared Synthetic Infant Formula

When obtaining donor human milk from a milk bank is not possible, the next most suitable food for human infant feeding is commercially prepared synthetic infant formula, which is closely regulated in the United States by the Food and Drug Administration (FDA) as a food for special dietary use.

Formula Content and Quality

Using well-researched recommendations from the American Academy of Pediatrics (AAP) Committee on Nutrition, the FDA has developed specifications for infant formula that dictate precise nutritional requirements. The nutrients that must be provided in all infant formulas include: protein, fat, linoleic acid, vitamin A, vitamin D, vitamin E, vitamin K, thiamine (vitamin B1), riboflavin (vitamin B2), vitamin B6, vitamin B12, niacin, folic acid, pantothenic acid, vitamin C, calcium, phosphorus, magnesium, iron, zinc, manganese, copper, iodine, sodium, potassium, chloride. Further, choline and inositol must be added to those infant formulas that are not based upon cow's milk.

In addition to nutritional requirements, the FDA requires formula manufacturers to maintain strict quality control protocols, which necessitates testing of every batch of formula, periodic testing of the product for compositional stability, and inclusion of a printed code on each product container that provides manufacturing source information. Records of these quality control procedures must be available to FDA investigators at all times.

Formula Types

The type and brand of formula that you decide to use is a decision that should be carefully made with the advice of your baby's health care provider according to the unique nutritional requirements of your baby. The amount of milk you are able to produce may also have a bearing upon the type of formula that is best suited for him. Those mothers producing at least a sixty-percent milk supply may want to choose a low-iron formula so as to avoid introducing excessive iron that will bind with lactoferrin and interfere with its protective activity.[4]

All commercially prepared formulas in the US contain the same basic nutritional ingredients because each product is required by the FDA to adhere to the same stringent quality and nutritional requirements. For this reason, there is very little difference between brands, including store and generic brands, which are generally less expensive.

Formulas are almost exclusively based upon either cow's milk or soybean protein sources, with variations that are low-iron, high-iron, and lactose-free, and also are available in hydrolosate preparations, which are proteins that have been chemically dissolved so as to be potentially less allergenic.

Formula Forms

Commercially prepared formulas are available in ready-to-feed form, which is most expensive; liquid concentrate form, which is less expensive; and powdered form, which is least expensive. Physicians will only rarely express a preference for the form of formula that should be used. For the most part, it depends on what you determine to be convenient and economically appropriate. Some specialized formulas, however, such as the hydrolosate preparations, may only be available in certain forms.

Formula Preparation

When preparing formula for your baby, it is important that you prepare it carefully according to the manufacturer's instructions and that you refrigerate it properly when the prepared portions are not used immediately. Be sure to follow the exact measurements for mixing water with liquid concentrate and powdered formulas because using too little water can severely tax your baby's organs and digestive system, while using too much water will not provide adequate calories and nutrition, jeopardizing his growth and development.

It has been customary to warm the formula before it is given to a baby, but this is not always necessary. The temperature of the formula makes no difference in its nutritional qualities—it is merely a preference that some babies have or that they acquire. When milk is given in an at-breast supplementer, it is warmed to a certain degree by proximity to the mother's skin. Many bottle-fed babies are quite content to drink cold formula. If you do choose to heat the formula, though, do not use a microwave oven to do so because microwave ovens do not heat evenly and hot portions of formula can seriously burn your baby. Formula can be heated safely by standing a container of it in the middle of a pot of water while the pot is heated on a medium-high setting on the stove. Many mothers also find that containers of formula can be warmed by holding them under hot running tap water, but this method takes longer.

BFAR mothers often wonder if it is acceptable to mix formula and human milk in the same container. The concern seems to be that the proteins, iron, or some other components of the formula would somehow harm the quality of the human milk. There is no scientific or practical basis to this concern, however. The human milk and the formula will be mixed in the digestive system of the baby, and in the case of at-breast supplementation, it is combined in the mouth of the baby as he nurses.

Stools from Formula Ingestion

When formula is introduced into the digestive system of a baby who was previously breastfed exclusively, his stools will change as a result of differences between the curding factors of the formula and alterations in his intestinal flora (helpful organisms that aid in digestion). The stools will typically become less frequent, thicker, and will smell worse. Interestingly, many BFAR mothers have found that combining breastfeeding with formula supplementation can result in "layered" stools—they will see a portion of the stool that is classically from human milk (yellow, thin, seedy) and then they will see a portion that is classically from formula (brown, thick, pungent). The stool can sometimes also be a mixture, thinned and lightened by the presence of human milk.

Unacceptable Foods for Human Infant Feeding

Among the foods that are inappropriate for feeding infants under the age of at least six months (and in the case of some foods until twelve months) are:

- Informally donated human milk,
- Unaltered milk from other species (diluted or full-strength),
- Soy beverages,
- Homemade formula,
- Water, glucose water, juice, tea.

Informally Donated Human Milk

Informally donated human milk is not recommended because it carries a risk of transmission of bacterial and viral contaminants. Even though you may know the donor well, it is still nonetheless possible for her to be carrying a potentially devastating disease. She may not have any symptoms and so may not even know she is infected. For this reason, the US Centers for Disease Control and Prevention specifically recommend against informally donated human milk. Additional reasons not to accept informally donated milk are the tremendous emotional and legal ramifications that would result if a disease were transmitted to your child.

Unaltered Milk from Non-Human Species

Human Milk Composition[4]	Goat Milk Composition[5]	Cow Milk Composition[5]
Energy=700 kcal/L,	Energy=685 Kcal/L,	Energy=627 kcal/L,
Protein=9 g/L,	Protein=34 g/L,	Protein=32 g/L,
Fat=42 g/L,	Fat=41g/L,	Fat=35 g/L,
Carbohydrate=73 g/L,	Carbohydrate=45 g/L,	Carbohydrate=46 g/L,
Calcium=280 mg/L,	Calcium=1205 mg/L,	Calcium=1150 mg/L,
Phosphorus=150 mg/L,	Phosphorus=1020 mg/L,	Phosphorus=910 mg/L,
Sodium=150 mg/L,	Sodium=415 mg/L,	Sodium=515 mg/L,
Chlorine=400 mg/L,	Chloride=1540 mg/L,	Chloride=970 mg/L,
Potassium=580 mg/L,	Potassium=1845 mg/L,	Potassium=1400 mg/L,
Magnesium=30 mg/L,	Magnesium=130 mg/L,	Magnesium=96 mg/L,
PRSL=93 mosm/L	PRSL=339 mosm/L	PRSL=298 mosm/L

Unaltered milk from other species—milk that is either fresh or pasteurized, but which has not been compositionally altered—is not generally recommended for feeding to human infants under the age of one year of age because it does not contain some of the nutrients critical for human growth, and of those it does contain, most are not in the correct proportions.[6]

Cow's milk given in the first year has been linked to insulin-dependent diabetes mellitus.[7] It is also low in iron, linoleic acid, vitamin E, and vitamin C, while having excessive amounts of sodium, calcium, phosphorus, potassium, and protein. The protein in cow's milk is irritating to the infant digestive system and can cause an allergic reaction in those infants at risk for food allergies.

While goat's milk is more easily digested than cow's milk because the milk curds that result from it are softer, it is still much closer to the composition of cow's milk than it is to human milk. Before the development of commercial formula, goat's milk was often given to babies who did not have access to human milk and many babies survived on it. While some babies who are sensitive to cow's milk do seem to be able to tolerate goat's milk better, a recent research study concluded that those infants who have a true allergy to cow's milk will also be allergic to goat's milk.[8]

Soy Beverages

Soy beverages are occasionally incorrectly labeled as "soy milk," which has led to confusion on the part of some consumers who mistake them for soy-based infant formulas. In fact, soy beverages and soy-based infant formulas are wholly different products. Soy beverages are deficient in many of the crucial nutritional elements essential for human infant growth. For this reason, the FDA has requested that all manufacturers, importers, and distributors of soy beverages have a warning on labels that such products are not appropriate for use as infant formula.

Homemade Formulas

Formulas derived from common food products and prepared in a consumer's home kitchen are not adequate foods for promoting human growth. They cannot meet the specific nutritional and caloric needs of human infants and can cause serious, sometimes irreparable, damage to developing organs. The FDA has strongly warned against the use of homemade formula for infant feeding, stressing that there is no private kitchen that has the capabilities of creating a formula that contains the complex nutritional components necessary for adequate infant growth.

Water, Glucose Water, Juice, and Tea

Before the age of six months, human infants should derive all of their nutrition and hydration requirements from human milk or commercially prepared synthetic formula. Only these foods have the proper calories and nutritional balance. Water, glucose water, juice, and teas are all deficient in nutritional adequacy for human infant growth. Using them as supplementation merely fills space in a baby's tummy; it does not give him more than a few empty calories.

How to Supplement

The BFAR Golden Rule

If you do choose to supplement by any means other than using an at-breast supplementer, follow the BFAR Golden Rule: breast first, supplement after. This means that you will allow the baby to feed at your breast first for as long as he is willing to nurse. If he becomes overly fussy, stop breastfeeding and give him the supplement. If he falls asleep at the breast, try to wake him to feed him the supplement.

This advice may sound simple, but it is actually emotionally complex for BFAR mothers who are in the throes of trying to feed a frustrated and distressed baby. Our hearts are torn by our babies' discomfort and hunger and we don't always give enough credit to the value of the milk in our breasts. It can be easy to begin to believe that because we have a lesser quantity of milk, the quality of our milk is poor and that the formula is better. Of course, this is far from the truth; the formula is certainly not better, it is simply more readily available.

This kind of erroneous thinking, though, can prompt a well-meaning BFAR mother to reverse her feeding system and begin giving formula first until the baby is satisfied, and then offering the breast as a top-off. This greatly decreases the milk supply, though, because the baby simply will not nurse as long or as effectively at the breast when he is already full. By removing less milk from the breast, less milk will be made and available at the next feeding, thus creating a downward spiral of decreasing milk until very little milk is left and the baby is entirely formula-fed.

Supplementation at Night

When you first begin supplementing, you will need to offer supplements at every feeding, even during the night. Later, though, when your baby has begun gaining well and is rehydrated, and depending upon how much milk you have, it may be possible to forgo supplementing at night. It will be easier to do this after your baby is four months old and able to go longer between feedings at night. Of course, whether or not this will be possible for you will depend on your individual circumstances. Even if it is not currently possible, though, it very well may work a few months from now.

Supplementation Away from Home

How you choose to go about supplementing when you are away from home largely depends upon the supplementation device you choose to use. Some devices are easier to use than others, but convenience is not the highest factor to consider when deciding which supplementation device to use away from home. It is important to choose a device, such as an at-breast supplementer, finger feeder, or cup feeder, that does not introduce poor suckling techniques, which may make your normal supplementation routine more difficult, as well as adding obstacles to effective breastfeeding.

How Much to Supplement

As you can guess, the trick is supplementing as little as possible to permit the mammary system to produce milk to its fullest capacity, while still assuring that the baby is provided sufficient nutrition and hydration to gain well. Calculating how much supplement to give to your baby is often difficult to do when you are not exactly sure how much milk you are producing. You are supplementing because you know that you do not have a full supply, but you have no precise way of knowing how much is lacking.

If you are supplementing at the breast with an at-breast supplementer, you can largely skip this section because you are saved the worry of determining how much supplement to give since the at-breast supplementer flows more readily when less milk is being produced and slows down when more milk is produced, making the amount of supplement given fairly automatic. For those BFAR mothers who supplement with other feeding devices, however, it is necessary to prepare and give the proper amount of supplement to ensure that you are meeting your baby's nutritional needs.

How Much Should Your Baby Eat to Gain and Develop Well?

The calculation for determining how much food to give an infant is based upon the fact that babies generally need an average of two-and-one-half ounces (75 ml) of human milk/supplement for each pound they weigh in every 24-hour period. Thus, if you have a 16-pound (7.2 kg) baby, you multiply 16 by 2.5 (or 16 by 75) to find that you'll need to give him about 40 ounces (1200 ml) per day. Then it is only a matter of dividing the 40 ounces (1200 ml) by the number of feedings per day to know how much milk or formula supplement to give at each feeding. This amount can vary by a few ounces in either direction, but gives you a general idea of about how much your baby will need. [4]

When you are breastfeeding in conjunction with supplementing, though, you can not just divide the total amount of nutrition needed each day because there is also the factor of the milk that you are producing yourself. While we can determine how much

Human Milk Intake Guideline by Weight[+]

Weight	Amount in ounces/ml per 24 hours
5 lbs	13 oz/371 ml
6 lbs	16 oz/457 ml
7 lbs	19 oz/542 ml
8 lbs	21 oz/600 ml
9 lbs	24 oz/685 ml
10 lbs	27 oz/771 ml
11 lbs	29 oz/828 ml
12 lbs	32 oz/914 ml
14 lbs	37 oz/1057 ml
16 lbs	43 oz/1228 ml

Method of Determining Human Milk Production while Supplementing[+]

1) Determine daily milk requirement according to infant weight (round weight up or down as necessary) using Intake Guidelines table above.
2) Determine average amount of supplement in ounces that is ingested each day.
3) Subtract result of step 2 from result of step 1. The answer will be the approximate number of ounces of human milk that is being ingested by the baby each day.

To Determine Necessary Amount of Increased Supplementary Milk Needed per Feeding to Achieve a Gain of 4-6 ounces/week[+]

4) Convert the baby's weight into ounces (1 pound = 16 ounces).
5) Divide the baby's weight in ounces by 6.
6) The result is the total amount of milk (human or artificial) that is necessary in 24 hours for gaining 4-6 ounces/week.
7) Subtract the final result of Step 3 (above) from the result of step 6.
8) Divide this number by the usual number of feedings to determine the amount to supplement at each feeding.

milk we are producing in retrospect once we know how much supplement is taken in a given timeframe, we cannot know beforehand what that figure will be.

So the only true way to know how much to supplement your baby when you are also breastfeeding is to put aside the scientific calculations and simply tune in to your baby and watch his cues. Feed him at your breast first, listening to the manner and frequency of his suckling and his general behavior at your breast. When his suckling slows down and he seems less interested or fussy, unlatch him and offer him the supplement with the artificial feeding device that you've chosen to use. Be sure not to overfeed him by urging him to take more than he really wants to. Follow his lead and eventually you will know how much supplement he really needs. Of course, you must also continue to carefully assess his dehydration status and weight gain to make sure that he stays hydrated and gains well.

Once you know how much supplement your baby seems to need, you can then determine how much human milk you are producing by subtracting the total amount of supplement given in a 24-hour time period from the total amount needed in that same time period. For instance, if your baby is 16 pounds and takes 12 ounces per day, you would subtract the 12 ounces from the 40 ounces that you already calculated he needs. The resulting figure of 28 ounces is the amount of milk that you are producing, which is an impressive seventy percent of your baby's nutritional needs.

The charts on page 161 are adapted from *Breastfeeding and Human Lactation*. They will give you some intake guidelines and objective means for evaluating your baby's growth progress. Keep in mind that all babies have unique nutritional needs, so that these amounts can only be general guidelines and must be considered in the context of your unique circumstances. A link to a website that provides a milk intake calculator is provided in Appendix 1.

Supplementation Devices

- At-Breast Supplementers
- Finger-Feeding
- Cups and Spoons
- Eyedroppers, Medicine Droppers, and Feeding Syringes
- Bottles

There are advantages and disadvantages to each of these devices. While you may want to use more than one device at different stages and under varying circumstances, it will help to understand the benefits and drawbacks of the devices to help you to determine which devices will work best for you and your baby.

The most important function in a supplementation device for BFAR is its ability to preserve the breastfeeding relationship, which is dependent upon two factors: avoiding nipple confusion/preference and obtaining maximum stimulation of the lactation system. The list of devices above is presented in the order of this ability, from best to worst. Clearly, because no artificial nipple is used and because supplementation is given at the same time the baby nurses from the breast, an at-breast supplementer is the best device for BFAR.

Using artificial nipples can lead to nipple confusion and nipple preference so BFAR mothers must be particularly careful to avoid them. Ideally, supplementation will incorporate as much feeding at the breast as possible so that your lactation system will be stimulated to its maximum potential, which will result in production of the maximum quantity of milk possible.

Sometimes it is difficult to understand why these two factors are so critical, especially when bottle-feeding can seem more convenient. There is a sucking exercise that some lactation consultants have used to demonstrate the difference between feeding from a breast and feeding from a bottle. Try it yourself—put your index finger in your mouth, with the first knuckle resting on your lips, and try to suck. Notice that your tongue is pushing your fingertip up to the roof of your mouth. Now feel your lips and how tightly they close around your finger. Then feel your upper jaw and your teeth pressing on your finger. This type of sucking is similar to how a baby with an incorrect latch would nipple-feed (not breastfeed). It is also how a baby sucks an artificial nipple with a small nipple and a base that is too wide to take into the mouth.

Next, put your index finger in your mouth so that the second knuckle is resting on your lip. Feel how the tip of your finger is much farther back in your mouth, almost to the soft palate. Try sucking and feel how your tongue now massages your finger. Notice that your lips are now relaxed and may be slightly open. Feel how your jaw is more open and relaxed so that your teeth on your finger are not pressing as hard. This type of sucking is similar to breastfeeding when the whole nipple and areola are taken into the mouth.

Some artificial nipples are shaped to be accepted into the mouth more in this fashion, such as the Avent and Munchkin nipples. Still none have the structural or physiological ability to prompt the tongue to roll against the nipple/areola as it does in breastfeeding. Instead, when a baby nurses from an artificial nipple, his tongue presses up and down in a pistonlike fashion, controlling the flow of the milk by squeezing the nipple and even pressing against the end of the nipple to stop the flow. (This behavior pushes the nipple out of the baby's mouth during breastfeeding.)

From this demonstration, you can see that only supplementing at the breast will maintain the proper suckling technique necessary to effectively stimulate the lactation system. Also, supplementing at the breast allows the maximum amount of stimulation to the milk supply, prompting production of the greatest quantity of milk possible.

There are times and certain circumstances, however, in which supplementing with another type of supplementation device is necessary. The type of device you use can also be a matter of your baby's personality and your own preferences. Ultimately, only you will be able to determine the best supplemental device for you and your baby at any given time.

At-Breast Supplementers

The basic elements of an at-breast supplementer are a receptacle to contain the supplement and a thin, clear, plastic tube that leads from the receptacle to just past the mother's nipple.

Although the at-breast supplementer is the best supplementation device to use for the purpose of preventing nipple confusion/preference and maximizing the milk supply, it does pose some challenges. Using it requires more effort in preparation, setup, and cleaning than unsupplemented breastfeeding or bottle-feeding. Supplementing at the breast is a learned skill and it can take several nursing sessions to learn the technique well enough to feel comfortable using an at-breast supplementer. Sometimes they can leak when not properly assembled. At-breast supplementers are not as easy to use in public or with nursing clothes. Still, all-in-all, at-breast supplementers are a superior method of supplementation and most mothers find that these challenges are easily overcome.

At-breast supplementers can be made at home using special tubing, tops, and containers. However, it is not easy to devise such a contraption on a regular basis, and it will not work nearly as effectively as a commercially manufactured at-breast supplementer. Even though commercial at-breast supplementers are an added expense, a BFAR mother who chooses to supplement using this device can reassure herself that this expense is still far less than the cost of formula feeding (the estimated 2001 yearly average cost of exclusively feeding powdered formula was $1,850 US).

There are four commercially manufactured at-breast supplementers; two brands are marketed in North America, one is marketed in Australia, and one is marketed in

England. The North American brands are the Medela Supplemental Nursing System (SNS) and the Lact-Aid Nursing Trainer System, commonly known as the Lact-Aid. The Australian brand is the Supply Line Mark II and is marketed by the Nursing Mothers' Association of Australia (NMAA). The British brand is the Axicare Nursing Aid. The SNS and the Lact-Aid, however, comprise the largest international market-share of at-breast supplementers, and so the discussion of at-breast supplementers in this book will center around these two brands. Information on how to obtain these products is provided in Appendix 1.

Deciding which brand of at-breast supplementer to use is a personal decision and will depend on several factors, including availability, convenience, product effectiveness, nursing style, personal preference, and cost. Each of the two brands that are discussed in this book have advantages and disadvantages. Some BFAR mothers find that they like to have one of each brand to use in different situations.

The Medela SNS

Medela has two at-breast supplemental feeding devices. One is the Starter SNS for short-term feeding and the other is the SNS for long-term feeding. The term "SNS" used in this book refers to the product for long-term feeding because, between the two Medela at-breast supplementation products, it is the one used most commonly for BFAR.

The Medela SNS consists of a rigid rectangular-shaped plastic bottle that can contain up to five ounces of supplement and is hung upside down around the mother's neck from an attached cord. The cap for the bottle has a plastic insert that allows two tubes to extend from the bottle. This cap also allows one or both of the tubes to be clamped shut to stop the supplement flow. This insert can accommodate three different sized tubes, which helps regulate the flow of the supplement. The SNS is designed with two tubes so that one tube can be positioned in place at each nipple with a special medical tape prior to the nursing session. The SNS bottle can easily be filled with supplement and transported in a cooled container, which makes outings convenient.

The SNS product works upon a principle of gravity so that the supplement is continually dispensed from an unclamped tube, even when the baby is not actively suckling. For this reason a mother must either be sitting upright to use it, or hold the container upright while she lies down. The rate of the flow can be controlled somewhat by the size of the tubing, which makes it important to have the correct size tubing so that the baby is not overwhelmed by the flow and volume of supplement. This continual flow of supplement can cause ineffective suckling habits, which must be monitored carefully.

The size of the tube that is used is determined by the physical condition and nursing abilities of the baby. A baby who is seriously underweight and dehydrated would be given the larger tube, while a baby who is gaining well and is well hydrated would use the smaller tube. Many mothers start with the medium tubing when their babies are not in serious condition, but they want them to get enough supplement to remain contented at the breast. The rate of supplement flow can also be controlled by clamping or unclamping the unused tube. To increase the rate of flow, unclamp the unused tube; to decrease the flow, clamp it. These clamping changes can be made as needed during the feeding. For instance, it may help to have the unused tube unclamped to encourage a reluctant nurser, or the tube can be unclamped at the end of a feeding to prolong it.

To use the SNS, the clean and sterilized bottle is filled with human milk or formula. The insert, with the attached tubes of the desired width, is then placed inside the cap so that the tubes lead away from the top of the cap and the cap is screwed on tightly to the bottle. Both tubes must be clamped shut. The bottle is then hung from the mother's neck and adjusted for length (it should be above the top of her breasts). The tubes are then taped in place above the areola so that each tube protrudes about a quarter inch (.625 cm) beyond the tip of each nipple. When the baby is latched on correctly, the tube leading to the side from which the baby is nursing is unclamped. When the baby has finished nursing from that side, the tube is reclamped, the baby is switched to the other breast, and the tube for that breast is unclamped.

The SNS sometimes makes a gurgling sound as the supplement drains from the bottle. Some mothers find that this sound helps them know when the supplement is actively flowing, but other mothers have remarked that the sound can be a distraction for both the baby and themselves.

The SNS is cleaned by filling it first with hot, soapy water, screwing on the cap with both tubes attached, and squeezing the water through the tubes. This is then repeated with cold water. If formula remains in the bottle, it can be scrubbed with a small bottle brush. Formula remaining inside the tubes can usually be removed by squeezing vinegar through them. In cases of stubborn residue, a piece of yarn or a pipe cleaner can be threaded and worked back and forth to scrub the residue away. Optionally, using distilled water to clean the parts will ensure that no mineral deposits accumulate inside the tubing.

The Lact-Aid

The Lact-Aid at-breast supplementer consists of a disposable sterile plastic bag to hold the supplement. The bags are available in a four-and-one-half ounce (135 ml) size, as well as a larger seven ounce (210 ml) size. The bag is positioned with the opening at the top and attached to the body/nursing tube with the clamp ring. An extension tube runs from the body/nursing tube into the bag. The thin, flexible nursing tube extends from the top of the assembled unit to one-quarter inch (.625 cm) beyond the mother's nipple. The bag containing the supplement, which has been "burped" so that no air remains in the bag, is suspended from the mother's neck by an adjustable neck strap. The nursing tube can be held in place with tape above the areola if desired, but it is not necessary to do so.

The Lact-Aid does not work on a principle of gravity, but rather uses a vacuum naturally produced by the baby's suckling to draw the supplement out of the container. This is why the bag is upright, rather than upside down. When the baby is actively suckling the nipple/areola complex and the breast is expelling milk, the baby's jaw is relaxed and there is very little vacuum, so very little supplement is drawn from the Lact-Aid. When less milk is flowing and the baby's mouth naturally creates more suction, more supplement is drawn from the Lact-Aid. This inherently reinforces proper suckling behaviors and ensures that the mother's milk supply will be maximized. Although there is a clamp on the side of the valve for stopping the flow of the supplement in the nursing tube, it is generally not necessary to use because the

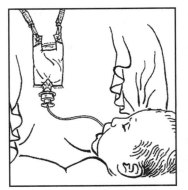

Mother and baby using the Lact-Aid at-breast supplementer.

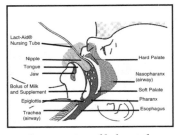

Cross-section of baby at the breast showing proper placement of the nursing tube.

supplement is only drawn through the tube with the baby's suction. For this reason, it is also possible to nurse lying down with the Lact-Aid without fear of leakage.

Rather than using different sized tubing to control the flow of the supplement through the Lact-Aid, it is controlled by adjusting the neck strap. Positioning the bag higher on the chest speeds the flow, and lowering it below the height of the baby's chin slows the flow. Normally, though, it is not necessary to either raise or lower the bag from the normal position. If you feel that an adjustment is necessary, it is a good idea to check with your LLL Leader or lactation consultant to make certain that the baby is nursing effectively and that the device is properly set up.

Cleaning the Lact-Aid consists of disposing of the plastic bag and washing the permanent parts and other accessories in hot, soapy water. The tubes are cleaned by forcing hot, soapy water through them with a special cleaning syringe, then rinsing with a mix of equal parts white vinegar and water, followed by a final rinse with distilled water. If it cannot be cleaned immediately after a feeding, dispose of the bag and place the other parts in a container of soapy water to prevent supplement from drying and caking. Occasionally, small brushes or cotton swabs may be necessary to removed caked matter.

Practical Tips for Using Your At-Breast Supplementer

The following practical tips apply in most cases to both brands of at-breast supplementers, although tips that apply to only one brand are noted specifically.

Formula Type

Some types and brands of formula do work better with at-breast supplementers than others because thicker types and brands tend to clog in the tubing. In general, concentrated and ready-to-feed formula types work better than powdered types, although powdered types work well when they are sufficiently blended with water. Shaking for several minutes is usually enough to achieve this. The Lact-Aid comes with a strainer for use with powdered formula, however if you should use this and find that a significant quantity of formula is kept in the strainer, you will need to re-blend the formula so that the supplement that is given to your baby is not over-diluted and contains the proper nutrition and calories.

Warming Formula

It is important not to position the supplementer in advance and use your body heat to warm up the supplement. Heating the supplement slowly promotes bacteria growth. A much better method is to warm the supplement under hot running water or in another container inside a pot of boiling water. Be careful not to warm it too much so that there is a risk of burning you or your baby—it should be about body temperature.

Tube Positioning

In most cases, it is best to put the tube in place on the nipple and then latch the baby onto the nipple/areola complex. Babies usually become used to having the tube on the nipple fairly quickly. If you should find, though, that your baby is confused by the tube or that it causes him not to latch on easily, you can latch him on first and then slip the clamped tube (so that the supplement is not yet flowing) into the corner of his mouth when he seems settled. The tube should be aimed toward the back and top of his mouth and should extend only a quarter inch (.625 cm) beyond where you anticipate that your nipple is, taking into account that nursing stretches the nipple further into the mouth. Once you are satisfied with the position of the tube, you can release the clamp and allow the supplement to flow.

If you find, as some BFAR mothers do, that your baby is beginning to suck on the end of the tube rather than properly nursing from your breast, you can move the tube to the exact end of the nipple. This will prevent him from being able to suck only the tube. If he pushes the tube out of position with his tongue, simply hold it in place with your finger just above his mouth.

If you have large breasts and find that they must be supported in order to allow your baby to maintain his latch properly, be certain to support them from underneath the breasts (U hold), rather than by using a sideways (C) hold or a finger (V hold). Supporting the breasts with a sideways or finger hold could cause the tube to curl out of proper position.

Length of Nursing Session

It usually takes between twenty to thirty minutes for a baby to consume four ounces (120 ml) of supplement at the breast. If you are finding that it is taking longer than this, one of several things may be happening. You may actually be producing more milk that you thought you were so that there is not enough suction to draw the supplement from the at-breast supplementer. If this is not the case, it may be that the nursing tube may not be correctly positioned on your nipple/areola complex or in your baby's mouth. He may also be latched-on improperly. Take some time to carefully reposition the tube and pay close attention to your baby's latch-on. If this does not solve the problem, have an LLL Leader or lactation consultant observe your at-breast supplementing technique and your baby's latch-on to correct the source of the problem.

Storing Filled Containers in Batches

To save setup and preparation time, many mothers who use at-breast supplementers fill several containers with supplement each day and refrigerate them so that they can be used throughout the day, eliminating the need to prepare them individually. It is important, though, to use them within a 24-hour time period so that the supplement is fresh.

When using the SNS, this means that several bottles must be purchased (they can be purchased individually as an accessory). For the Lact-Aid, the regular disposable baggies are opened (rub sides together for easy opening), filled, tied with a twist-tie or clamp and stored upright in a rigid container, such as a mug. Lact-Aid also makes a storage rack for storing filled bags in the refrigerator. Some mothers who use the Lact-Aid prefer to have multiple units so that they can have them fully assembled and ready to use, saving even more time.

Preparing containers of supplement is easier to accomplish when you are able to take your time and don't feel anxiety at meeting the needs of your hungry baby. From the baby's perspective, it is also a way to minimize the time your baby has to wait or cry to be fed, which reinforces his trust that his needs are readily met and maximizes the harmony of your breastfeeding relationship.

Transporting Filled Containers
The efficiency of storing filled containers for later use in the day can be extended to transporting pre-filled containers for outings outside the home. The SNS containers can be stored in any insulated cooler, even the ones built into some diaper bags. The Lact-Aid units can be transported in the special insulated cooler offered by the manufacturer for transporting filled bags, or they can be put into plastic containers that have screw- or snap-on lids to keep them upright and placed inside a regular insulated cooler.

Using At-Breast Supplementers in Public
While it may be tempting to set up your at-breast supplementer before you leave the house, wearing a filled container so that you can easily nurse at will in public, it is not safe for you to do so when it will be more than an hour before feeding because bacteria quickly grows in such an environment. It is very important that your supplement remains chilled in an insulated cooler until it is ready to be used. If your baby prefers that the supplement be warm, it is usually easy to warm the container under hot running water in a sink right before you are ready to use it.

Using the SNS discreetly in public can be somewhat of a challenge because the container is large enough that it can be obvious under clothing. Nonetheless, many BFAR mothers have found innovative ways to use their SNS supplementers in public, such as wearing multiple layers that make the container less visible. It is usually necessary, though, to set up the container and tubes in a private place, such as a public bathroom, baby feeding room, or changing room, before feeding the baby in a public area.

Because the Lact-Aid uses a soft bag that is thin and flat when filled with supplement, it can be hidden under clothing so that nursing discreetly in public is fairly easy to accomplish. Some BFAR mothers make decorative cloth pouches to contain the unit so that nursing in public is even more discreet. A small metal clip can be sewn onto the pouch so that the pouch can be attached to your bra, eliminating the need for the strap. Filled units can then be removed from their storage container and placed into the pouch through a nursing slit or from the bottom of a blouse.

Securing Tubes

Using medical-grade tape to hold the nursing tubes in place for either brand of supplementer can be irritating to the skin, especially when it is being placed and removed up to 12 times a day. Of course, it is not really necessary to use the tape at all, but some users of at-breast supplementers find that the system works better when the tubes are secured.

To prevent irritation to their skin, there is a nifty little trick that many BFAR mothers use to hold the tubes in place—Band-Aids! They place the Band-Aid horizontally where they would place tape and slip the tubing under the gauze portion of the adhesive bandage. The Band-Aid can be left in place as long as it stays secure, which most mothers who use them in this way say is about a week.

Other mothers prefer to use hair setting tape (which can be found at a beauty supply store or a drug store) because it stays in place nicely during the feeding, but does not cause discomfort with repeated applications and removal. An alternative to using tape or Band-Aids is to simply use your nursing bra to keep the tubing in place by slipping it between the panel of the bra and your skin.

Tube Grabbing

When babies get a little older and gain dexterity with their hands, they sometimes like to pull or play with the at-breast supplementer tubing. When they do this, the tubing can be pulled out of place. Here are a few ideas some mothers have used to minimize tube grabbing:

- Tuck his lower arm between his body and yours so that only one hand is free.
- Hold your baby's upper arm with the hand of the arm you are cradling him with.
- Cover the tube with your hand as your baby begins to nurse and until he settles. Once he is settled and nursing well, move your hand away from the tube and gently hold his upper hand.
- Cover the tube with your thumb and the palm of your hand so that he cannot see it at all.
- Wear a brightly colored neck scarf to attract baby's eyes and roaming hands.
- Give him something else to hold in his hand while nursing, such as a soft toy.

Choosing an At-Breast Supplementer

As mentioned earlier, the brand of at-breast supplementer you choose to use is an entirely personal decision and will be based on many factors. After some experience with at-breast supplementers, you will almost certainly develop your own preferences. Over the years, mothers who have used both brands have made comments about them to LLL Leaders, lactation consultants, and on Internet bulletin boards and email lists. The following are the most common comments made about the two brands of at-breast supplementers:

Some mothers like the SNS because the container is similar to a bottle and is easier to set up. They like that the units are less expensive and can be re-used. They also like that switching sides can be easier when both tubes are already taped in place.

Other mothers, though, feel the SNS can be cumbersome when trying to manage the baby at the breast. The second tube can get in the way and be an enticement to play. Because it operates on gravity rather than vacuum pressure, the supplement can continue to drip from the tubes after the baby has unexpectedly let go of the breast. They find that the SNS is also less discreet for public nursings.

A mother who wants to use just one supplementer and does not mind repeated cleaning and filling may choose the SNS over a product that uses disposable bags, which, although more sterile, are an additional, ongoing expense. However, for those who want the convenience of cleaning and filling several at-breast supplementers at a time, the cost for six Lact-Aid units, plus a six-month supply of bags, would be about the same as six SNS supplementers. When supplementing for several feedings, but not every feeding, the cost for bags is even less.

Fans of the Lact-Aid say they like it because it is less bulky and less noisy. The bag feels softer and more comfortable and the main unit is easier to clean. Many mothers believe that the Lact-Aid preserves and maximizes their lactation better than the SNS because it operates on a principle of vacuum rather than gravity.

Finger Feeding

There are times when supplementation must be away from the breast. Finger feeding can be used to feed the supplement with a supplementation device attached to your finger. This allows you to avoid giving your baby an artificial nipple, while still allowing him to suck, which is very important physiologically and psychologically. It also allows the baby to have the special feeling of human skin during his feeding, which can be very comforting. Moreover, it allows him to suck in a similar way to breast-feeding by keeping his tongue down and forward over his gums, with his mouth wide and jaw forward.

Supplementation can be fed with a finger feeder by either you or another caregiver. It is, however, more time consuming than using a cup or other supplementation device and for this reason is best used as a temporary method until you can get him to use an at-breast supplementer. For occasional feedings by other caregivers, a cup may be a better device.

A finger feeder can be made at home using a narrow feeding tube and a regular baby bottle that has had the opening in the nipple enlarged to snugly accept the feeding tube. The end of the tube should extend midway into the bottle.

Medela markets a commercially manufactured finger feeder, called the Hazelbaker. Some mothers have also successfully used the Medela SNS or the Lact-Aid at-breast supplementers to finger feed. The container can be hung around the neck as usual and the tube can be attached to the finger and fed to the baby as described below.

How to Finger Feed

First, wash your hands thoroughly, and, if necessary, trim the nail of the finger you will be using as short as possible. The best finger to use is either your index finger or your middle finger. Next, assemble the finger feeder and put it onto your finger, allowing it to extend just to the end of your finger. You can tape the tube to the upper portion of your finger with medical-grade tape if you prefer (or you can use a Band-Aid, slipping the tube under the gauze), but this is not necessary as the tube can also be held securely with your thumb.

Now, pick up your baby and sit in a chair that is comfortable for both of you. There are two good positions for finger feeding, although any position that feels right to you is fine. One position is to hold your baby in your lap in a half-seated position, facing you. Support his head, neck, and upper back with the hand that will not be feeding him. The other position is to hold him cradled in your arms as you would if you were breastfeeding him, snuggled close, ideally with his tummy turned toward yours.

The container filled with supplement needs to be held or suspended in some way about at the height of the baby's head or just a bit above it.

Next, turn your feeding finger upside down so that the pad of your finger is turned toward the ceiling and your finger is straight. Gently tickle his lower lip with your feeding finger to prompt him to open his mouth for the feeding. You can gently insert your finger, but allowing him the control of opening his own mouth is usually best. Keep your finger straight and allow him to begin sucking on your finger and pulling it deeply into his mouth. If you see him sucking in his upper or lower lip, gently flip the lips back out. If he persists in sucking in his lower lip, especially, gently pressing downward on his chin will teach him to rely more on the action of his tongue than on suction to nurse.

If you find that he seems to be working hard to suck the supplement, or if the feeding seems to be taking a very long time, you can raise the container of supplement a bit higher, but not so far that the supplement flows too quickly, which can cause the baby to gag and choke.

To clean the finger feeding supplementation device, wash the container with hot, soapy water. Occasionally, you may need to run vinegar through the tubing to clean it thoroughly.

Cups and Spoons

Although drinking from a cup can appear to be an advanced skill beyond the capabilities of infants, it can be surprising to know that babies of all ages, even preterm babies, have been successfully fed by cups throughout history. In fact, a 1994 English research study demonstrated that babies as young as those born ten weeks prematurely can feed well from a cup, long before they can effectively breastfeed or bottle-feed. Cup feeding stimulates tongue movements that are important in breastfeeding so that babies who are cup fed transition well to breastfeeding. It also takes less energy and allows the baby more control over his feeding than does bottle-feeding.[9] Contrary to popular belief, it does not take longer than bottle-feeding, and for many babies experienced at cup feeding it can be a faster feeding method.[10] Some parents worry that choking can be a hazard with cup feeding, but it is only a danger when fluid is poured into a baby's mouth, which is not the proper method of cup feeding.

Any clean small plastic or glass cup or bowl can be used. Many mothers find that a flexible plastic cup, such as a condiment cup or "Dixie" cup, allows them more control over the flow of supplement. You may prefer to feed your baby with a cup that is specially designed for feeding small babies. Medela markets two such cup feeding products, the SoftFeeder and the Baby Cup Feeder. Ameda also markets a cup, as does the Foley Company, and other companies. The Medela Softfeeder and the Foley Cup

Feeder work especially well because they feature a small self-filling reservoir that allows control over the amount of supplement offered at the babies' lips.

- Be sure your baby is awake and alert—do not attempt to feed him when he is sleepy.
- Swaddle your baby to keep his hands from bumping the cup.
- You may find it helpful to protect your and your baby's clothing from spills with a cloth.
- Hold your baby in an upright position in your lap, either facing you or cradled against you, paying careful attention to supporting his head, neck, and shoulders.
- Fill the container at least half full with the supplement.
- Bring the container to your baby's lips, gently tilting it so that when he opens his mouth the cup rests lightly on his lower lip and the milk just touches his lips.
- Tip the cup slightly so that a few drops of milk flow onto the baby's lips.
- Do not pour the milk into his mouth, as this can cause coughing and sputtering.
- Leave the cup in this position and let the baby set his own sipping rhythm, pause when needed, and end the feeding when satisfied.
- Stop to burp from time to time if necessary.

Spoon feeding is very similar to cup feeding, except that it can take longer to give the same amount of supplement and the shape of a spoon does not give you as much control over the flow of the supplement into your baby's mouth as does a cup. The process of spoon feeding differs from cup feeding in that you will need to allow for periodic refilling of the spoon.

Eyedroppers, Medicine Droppers, and Feeding Syringes

Eyedroppers, medicine droppers, and feeding syringes all work in a similar way and can be an effective means of giving supplemental feedings to your baby without compromising his sucking technique. This process does not, however, reinforce the tongue movements of breastfeeding or give the baby the control over the feeding as cup feeding does.

Eyedroppers work best for very small babies because they hold such a small amount of supplement at a time. The best type of eyedropper to use is the soft plastic type that can be purchased in most drug stores. When using an eyedropper, do not allow the baby to suck from the dropper.

Medicine droppers that use a bulb on one end work very well for most babies, and have the added advantage of holding more supplement, up to two teaspoons at a time.

Feeding syringes, also known as periodontal, orthodontic, or oral syringes, also work well for most babies and hold a fair amount of supplement. A feeding syringe can be used at the breast if supplement is needed before the mother can obtain an at-breast supplementer. It is important to use a feeding syringe with a soft tip to avoid hurting the baby's gums.

To feed your baby with an eyedropper, medicine dropper, or feeding syringe:

- Be sure your baby is awake and alert—do not attempt to feed him when he is sleepy.

- Swaddle your baby to keep his hands from bumping the dropper.
- You may find it helpful to protect your and your baby's clothing from spills with a cloth.
- Hold your baby in an upright position in your lap, either facing you or cradled against you, paying careful attention to supporting his head, neck, and shoulders.
- Fill the dropper with the supplement from a nearby container.
- Bring the dropper to your baby's mouth, gently dripping in the milk slowly enough so that he has a chance to swallow it before more is given.

You can also finger feed your baby with the feeding syringe:

- First, wash your hands thoroughly
- If necessary, trim the nail of the finger you will be using as short as possible.
- Ideally, the best finger to use is either your index finger or your middle finger.
- Turn your feeding finger upside down so that the pad of your finger is turned toward the ceiling.
- Gently tickle his lower lip with your feeding finger to prompt him to open his mouth for the feeding. You can gently insert your finger, but allowing him the control to open his own mouth is usually best.
- Keep your finger straight and allow him to begin suckling on your finger and pulling it deeply into his mouth.
- Insert the syringe into the corner of his mouth.
- As he suckles, depress the plunger on the syringe slowly to give him the supplement.
- When his suckling pauses, stop depressing the syringe.
- Resume depressing the syringe when suckling resumes.

Bottles

Avoiding artificial nipples is absolutely critical for the BFAR nursing couple in order to avoid nipple confusion/preference. Nonetheless, some BFAR mothers feel that using bottles is the best choice for them and they do so even though they are aware of the risk. And there are some babies who do not seem to have any trouble switching back and forth from bottle to breast. Nipple confusion/preference never happens to them. For some nursing couples, nipple confusion/preference seems to be less likely to occur when the mother has long, rigid nipples and a strong milk supply. Unfortunately, there is no way for you to know beforehand, but by being vigilant and watching for changes in the way your baby takes the breast, you may be able to catch the "confusion" before it becomes entrenched and change your strategy if you need to.

For BFAR mothers who have decided to supplement with bottles, it is important to use nipples closest in form to the human breast. Artificial nipples that BFAR mothers have used with success are the Avent nipple (newborn slow-flow), the Munchkin nipple, and the Medela Haberman feeder, which is a special bottle and nipple device that is designed to minimally interfere with proper breastfeeding techniques.

Although the Gerber Nuk nipple is frequently recommended for use by nursing mothers, many of the cases of nipple confusion that lactation specialists have worked with have been a result of using the Gerber Nuk nipple. A bit of research into the Gerber company's design of the nipple and their recommendations for use while nursing has revealed that this nipple is effective in preserving proper sucking habits only when the baby is taught to suck on the higher, wider portion of the nipple, which most babies won't do because the actual "nipple" part is so large, even in the newborn size.

When supplementing with a bottle, it is important to always do so in a tummy-to-tummy position. This may come naturally when you're supplementing with an at-breast supplementer, but should you choose to use bottles, be sure to supplement in cuddle position, with your baby's tummy against your own. Aside from maximizing closeness and intimacy, this reinforces the correct touches that prompt rooting behavior and preserves the optimal breastfeeding positioning technique to ensure that you and the baby will not develop habits that make it difficult for him to go back to feeding effectively at the breast.

Some BFAR mothers have had the experience of deciding to supplement by bottle and finding that the baby will initially consume a large quantity of supplement from the bottle. This may not be entirely because the baby is hungry/thirsty. Up to that point, the baby has learned that nursing from the breast requires a strong tongue and jaw movement. Using this technique on an artificial nipple will rapidly yield a large quantity. This can leave a mother with the conclusion that her poor baby was starving and she really must not have had much milk at all. In most cases, this is not accurate and even more reason to avoid bottles, especially in the early weeks.

Other mothers have come to the conclusion that their babies liked feeding from a bottle better than breastfeeding because they seemed to fuss less when feeding from a bottle. What they are observing is classic nipple preference, although they may not think of it in those terms. While it may be true that some babies prefer bottle-feeding because the flow of supplement is quicker and gives them more immediate satisfaction, it is a vastly inferior feeding method. Bottle-feeding deprives babies of all the structural and psychological benefits of breastfeeding discussed in Chapter 3, not even taking into account the benefits of the human milk. It is natural and right for you to feel empathy for his preferences, but for such an important and far-reaching issue, the bottom line is that you have knowledge about what is best for your baby that he does not have at such a young age, and so you may need to make this critical decision for him in his best interest.

REFERENCES:

1. Lawrence, A. and R. Lawrence. *Breastfeeding: A Guide for the Medical Profession*, 5th edition. St. Louis, Missouri: Mosby, 1999; 224, 412.

2. World Health Organization and United Children's Fund. *Joint World Health Organization/United Children's Fund Meeting on Infant and Young Child Feeding*. Geneva, Switzerland: 1979 (1981 printing); 55.

3. American Academy of Pediatrics. Breastfeeding and the use of human milk (RE9729). *Pediatrics* 1997; 100(6):1035-1039.

4. Riordan, J. and K. Auerbach. *Breastfeeding and Human Lactation*, 2nd edition. Sudbury, MA: Jones and Bartlett Publishers, 1999; 698, 322, 123-33, 361, 362.

5. Fomon, S. *Nutrition of Normal Infants*. Iowa City, Iowa: B C Decker. 1993.

6. American Academy of Pediatrics. Work group on cow's milk protein and diabetes mellitus. *Pediatrics* 1994;4:752-54.

7. American Academy of Pediatrics. The use of whole cow's milk in infancy (RE9251). *Pediatrics* 1992; 89(6):1105-9.

8. Bellioni, B., R. Paganelli, P. Lucenti, et al. Allergenicity of goat's milk in children with cow's milk allergy. *J Allergy and Clin Immunol* 1999; 103(6):1191-94.

9. Lang, S. et al. Cup feeding: an alternative method of infant feeding. *Arch Dis Child* 1994; 71:365-69.

10. Howard, C., E. de Blieck, C. ten Hoopen, et al. Physiologic stability of newborns during cup- and bottle-feeding. *Pediatrics* Nov 1999; 104(5) Pt 2:1204-7.

WENDY'S STORY

I am the mother of three children. Two were born and breastfed before my breast reduction surgery. The first weaned at twelve months, the second weaned at 22 months. I went into surgery under the impression that if I ever had another baby, breastfeeding wouldn't be an issue because my surgeon was leaving the nipple intact and doing everything he could to preserve my ability to breastfeed. I was told that all I needed to breastfeed was the ability to feel my nipple area. My nipples are very sensitive, so I conceived this baby never doubting I would breastfeed. While pregnant, I heard stories about babies who had been sick because of a mother's low milk supply because of breast reduction surgery, but a call to my doctor or lactation consultant or surgeon would put all my concerns to rest. I was completely assured that I could breastfeed.

I leaked colostrum during the pregnancy, and my nipples and breasts were incredibly sensitive. I also grew two bra sizes. These were confirmations of the fact that I could breastfeed my baby. My baby was born and put right to breast. My milk came in on the second day; I was thrilled. I was engorged and excited because everyone had been right; I was going to be able to breastfeed this baby. At her two-week checkup, she had gained five ounces over birth weight. She was thriving!

At about three weeks old she started crying a lot, and I decided she had colic. I use cloth diapers and became convinced that they were not getting wet enough. They were getting wet, and she was having bowel movements, but I felt something wasn't right. I called my lactation consultant, my doctor, and the hospital nursery. Everyone told me that she was fine. She had had a great weight gain at her two-week checkup. I had milk, I could breastfeed. I was just a new mother who was overly concerned about normal behavior. Yet, I couldn't shake the feeling that something was wrong. At four weeks, I took my daughter to my lactation consultant for a weight check. She had lost twelve ounces in two weeks. I was devastated! There were other mothers there for weight checks, I was shocked as I compared my baby to the others. My baby looked like a concentration camp baby. I had called her my "peanut," but I had no idea that I had been starving her. My lactation consultant gave me a Supplemental Nursing System (SNS) and I went home with a rented pump, ready to increase my supply.

My lactation consultant convinced me that stress was causing my low milk supply and that I needed to simplify my life and focus only on my baby. I found help for my older children, I used the SNS and Lact-Aid, and I let clutter pile up around me. I began to take fenugreek, and drink herbal teas. My doctor prescribed Reglan. I pumped for hours a day. I was doing everything my lactation consultant suggested to increase my supply, but it wasn't increasing as much as my baby required.

In desperation, I called Jimmie Lynne Avery at the Lact-Aid company and cried to her about what I was going through. She told me about the BFAR.org website. I was shocked as I read that what I was experiencing was common to BFAR. Stress wasn't the issue, surgery was. At that point I realized I would be using the Lact-Aid and the SNS for a long *time and that there wasn't much I could do to increase my supply beyond where it already was. I could breastfeed; I would just need to always supplement at the breast. I was so relieved to find BFAR.org and the support group of women who truly understood my feelings and the efforts I was going through to breastfeed this baby. For the first time*

I could relax and begin to accept my breastfeeding reality. I could focus on building an enjoyable breastfeeding relationship, instead of trying so hard to build my milk supply. I knew if I kept my baby at the breast, that she would get whatever milk I had to offer.

My baby is now ten months old. She has never had a bottle! All her supplementation has been at the breast. This was not always easy, but it got much easier with time. At first my baby would get all wrapped up in the tubing and I had a hard time keeping the tubing in her mouth. My skin was terribly sore from taping the tubes down. I wondered at times why I was trying so hard. But I just couldn't give my baby less then I gave her siblings. I wanted that special loving bond that only a mother can share with her baby; the same nurturing bond I had shared with my other two. I knew that feeding with a bottle would seem so artificial to me. I did get used to the supplemental systems and really began to enjoy our breastfeeding times together. I also started using Band-Aids to keep the tubing in place. That little trick went a long way toward making our breastfeeding relationship enjoyable because I no longer hurt. I also began to believe that giving my baby some human milk was better then giving her none at all. Keeping her at the breast was the best way to ensure she got what I had to give.

I still supplement using the Lact-Aid device, giving my baby donated human milk. Giving donated breast milk to my baby was initially very hard to do, but I feel good knowing I am giving her the best. I started taking domperidone under the watchful eye of my doctor and saw a significant increase in supply. I calculate that I make about 22 ounces of milk per day because of it. We co-sleep so she has access to my breast at night, maximizing the milk she receives. My supply has always been best during the sleeping hours, when prolactin levels are naturally high.

How do I feel about the breast reduction surgery I had? I regret it more then anything in my life. The breastfeeding experience for my baby is not much different than it was for her siblings. But for me it is night and day different. At ten months, I still occasionally fight back tears as I watch her feed with a tube in her mouth. I try not to let my sadness get in the way of our breastfeeding relationship, but sometimes I just want to scream because she deserves so much better. For the most part I feel "successful" because I haven't quit when others would. I am proud that I have done all I could to give this baby a healthy start. I am convinced that the relationship that has been fostered through breastfeeding is well worth all my struggles. I have enjoyed nurturing my daughter during the hours we have spent breastfeeding. If we have more children, I will do the same for them.

C H A P T E R 9

INCREASING YOUR MILK SUPPLY

Once the milk supply has been established to its maximum capacity, increasing it by external means is the most compelling goal of BFAR mothers. As with all breastfeeding mothers, the milk supply can be increased by specific breastfeeding techniques as well as by mechanical and chemical devices that stimulate the lactation system to higher milk production.

The mammary system operates on a principle of "supply and demand," whereby it will seek to replenish as much milk as was taken from it. If more is "demanded" than it can supply, it will increase production to meet that demand. If less is demanded than it has made available, less will be produced for future feedings. It typically takes two to three days for the mammary system to increase production to meet increased demands, although some research studies show that the response can be more immediate.

Many BFAR mothers wonder if their milk supplies can have an upper limit, a ceiling as it were, as a result of their breast surgeries. The answer to that question will vary according to each woman, her surgical experience, and her approach to breastfeeding after the surgery. This common question is most likely prompted by a theory that all normal breasts have the same amount of functioning lactiferous lobes and each of those lobes has an inherent limited production capacity. Those women who have less than the "normal" amount of functioning lobes might be expected to have a milk supply capacity correspondingly reduced by the proportion of functioning lobes that remain. In actuality, there are two flaws in this theory. First, all women do not have the same amount of lobes; there are between 15 to 25 lobes per breast and the size of the lobes vary. Second, and most importantly, there is no inherent limitation to the production capacity of a lobe. The alveoli in the lobes produce milk in direct response to the amount of milk that is removed from them according to the principle of supply and demand. The more milk that is removed from them, the more milk they will make. This is why there have been mothers who have nursed triplets or quadruplets, wet nurses who have fed up to six children at one time, and mothers who have nursed successfully from only one breast.

The problem for a BFAR mother is that her milk supply may be limited not only by the number of functioning lobes; there may also be nerve damage that can significantly inhibit the production of prolactin, which drives the milk supply. But as long as there are any functioning lobes, evidenced by the presence of any quantity of milk, the milk supply can be increased. The amount of the increase, though, depends upon the amount of functional lobes and the condition of the nerve supply to the nipple/areola complex. For some BFAR mothers, it may not be possible to increase their milk supply to the point that supplementation is no longer needed. Other BFAR mothers may be able to achieve this.

Increasing the BFAR milk supply can be accomplished by a myriad of techniques, as well as with the aid of mechanical and chemical devices, such as pumps and galactagogues. Most BFAR mothers who seek to increase their milk supplies do so using varying combinations of these techniques and devices. Determining which methods will be most appropriate and effective for your unique BFAR circumstance will be a matter of some experimentation and your personal comfort level with the technique or device. There is no single blueprint to increasing the milk supply because we all respond differently to different stimuli. Use the method that feels most comfortable and makes the most sense for you at the moment, knowing that you can move on to another method when you feel that you need to do so.

The following techniques to increase your milk supply are not BFAR-specific. They are commonly recommended for any breastfeeding mother who needs to increase her milk supply. In effect, each of these techniques prompts the lactiferous lobes to make more milk in at least one of the following three ways: by utilizing the mind's ability to increase lactation through psychological techniques, by placing an actual higher physical demand on the lobes, or through the use of galactagogues.

Psychological Techniques

The mind has a tremendous influence over the body's physiological processes. When we are worried or stressed, the tension that results can significantly inhibit let-downs. We cannot always avoid being worried or stressed because these are natural, normal, and quite appropriate feelings. We must therefore find techniques that help us minimize the impact our feelings have on lactation. The following techniques have worked successfully for many BFAR mothers.

Distraction

Reading books and magazines while nursing or pumping, either for pleasure or intellectual edification, can be wonderfully effective in taking your mind off of immediate concerns such as how much milk you are producing or how long the nursing/pumping session has lasted. Talking on the phone to good friends (about topics other than BFAR), watching television, and listening to the radio or music can also serve to ease stress and relax your tension.

Create a Relaxing Environment

Our environment is very important to our ability to feel safe and at peace, which can greatly influence the let-down reflex. When you are breastfeeding or pumping, try to minimize things in your immediate surroundings that cause you any sort of distress. This may mean that you need to be in a quiet room away from the rest of the family, especially any family members who are not entirely supportive of BFAR. The room should be pleasant, warm, and comfortable, with soothing lighting. Soft background music can really help to melt away your tension and concerns. Before you begin nursing or pumping, take a few slow, deep breaths to clear your mind and body of any remaining tension. Practice any relaxation techniques that feel right to you (see Appendix 4). Be sure to have a snack and drink by your side. Ideally, you will be able to create a place you can regularly go to that is set up as a nursing station with all your needs within reach.

Biofeedback and Autogenics

The following biofeedback and autogenic exercise can help mothers increase their milk supplies while pumping or nursing. This technique was contributed by Diane O'Brien Juve. She credits the technique to her father, Chuck Stroebel, a board-certified psychiatrist, who is also a senior fellow of The Biofeedback Society of America.

How to Become a Great Pumper

I don't claim to be an expert in most areas of mothering, but I was a dynamite pumper. Pumping is a learned skill, not a talent, and you, too, can do it well! I know it's tough getting time to yourself when you have little ones, but I can guarantee that if you do these exercises faithfully for two to three weeks you'll notice a significant increase in let-downs and you'll be able to do it without having to spend so long getting into that relaxed state.

I taught biofeedback for three years. Biofeedback teaches relaxation techniques combined with feedback to teach people to retrain injured muscles, prevent headaches, etc. It's used in most major medical centers now, and helps with stroke rehabilitation, among other things.

In addition to biofeedback, this technique relies upon "autogenics," which warms your hands, so your fingertips actually become warm and tingly. The warm hands are the easiest measure of the autonomic nervous system, which controls our fight or flight response. When you worry about pumping enough, for instance, you don't let down any milk at all. Right? That's because worrying sets off your fight or flight response, which shuts down excess circulation to the extremities (causing cold hands!), sending adrenaline through your system, slowing or shutting down your digestive tract, and basically stopping "unnecessary" functions (such as milk let-down!) in order to send more blood rushing to the heart and running muscles.

Practicing biofeedback and autogenic techniques enabled me to be a great pumper by allowing me to truly relax and let my right brain do its thing. Soon I had milk literally squirting into the bottle!

This skill is learned first without pumping. Once it is mastered, you can then begin using it as you pump. Begin practicing this routine at least once or twice a day for five to fifteen minutes until your body becomes accustomed to dropping into a relaxed state. After your brain has learned how to do this, and you learn how it feels to be in a relaxed state, you'll be able to relax enough to pump with just three or four slow abdominal breaths. And the nice thing is, once you've learned this skill, you will have it forever, and with very little practice you can become proficient again at any time.

The specific routine is as follows:

1) *Start by taking 15-20 SLOW abdominal breaths. That means counting slowly to four when you inhale, and again when you exhale. Breathing is the single most important skill to practice, and should be done slowly and deliberately throughout the relaxation session.*

2) *Next, tense and relax, say, your fists, tensing for five to ten seconds while keeping the rest of your body entirely relaxed, and BREATHING. You can tense and relax as many different muscle groups throughout your body as you want (top to toes, or working your way from your toes to your head, whatever is comfortable for you), concentrating on deep, relaxed breathing as you do it. (This is an extremely brief description of Jacobsen's Progressive Relaxation exercises, which have been around for many years; better descriptions can be found elsewhere.)*

Finally, begin autogenics by using your imagination to visualize tremendous warmth and security. Try imagining yourself lying in the warm sun, or perhaps moving a warm cloth over your body. Feel how the warmth radiates through your entire body, further relaxing you and making even your hands feel thoroughly warm and tingly.

Increased Demand Techniques

Breastfeed More Frequently

Encourage the baby to breastfeed as frequently as possible. Especially in the first few weeks, babies should not be allowed to go any longer than two hours between feedings and should be encouraged to nurse every three or four hours at night. Remember that shorter, more frequent feedings result in producing milk that is higher in fat and thus higher in calories than longer, less frequent feedings.

Take a Nursing Vacation

Take a "nursing vacation" (not a vacation from nursing) by spending the weekend in bed with your baby, doing nothing but cuddling and nursing. Have your partner bring all your necessities to you in bed, and leave only to use the bathroom. This "vacation" will not only help to encourage frequent nursing, but it will also result in enhanced bonding and a better rested baby and mother. Having the undivided attention of your baby can have a wonderfully positive effect on both of you. Of course, such a vacation is difficult, if not impossible, in many circumstances, but if it's at all feasible, it can really be nice.

If you can't take a whole weekend off, do try to rest and relax whenever you can. Don't do anything you don't have to. Take frequent naps and pamper yourself at every opportunity. Your milk supply will be able to respond most effectively when you are well rested and not stressed. It will also help to allow your baby to nurse for comfort between feedings when he wishes to so that your lactation system will have extra stimulation.

Breast Compression

A very effective means of inducing the breast to produce more milk is by a method called "breast compression." It achieves increased milk production by heightening the neural stimulation of the lactiferous system and manually forcing milk though the ducts, both of which prompt the let-down to occur. In addition to increasing the amount of milk that is produced, the milk will be a greater proportion of the higher calorie hindmilk.

The following breast compression technique has been developed and written by Dr. Jack Newman. Many BFAR mothers have employed this method with significant results. Breast compression can be utilized at any time milk is being expressed, including while the baby is actively nursing or during pumping.

- Hold the baby with one arm.
- Hold the breast with the opposite hand, cupping the breast from underneath with your thumb on one side of the breast and your fingers on the other, fairly far back from the nipple.
- Watch for the baby's drinking, though there is no need to be obsessive about catching every suck. The baby gets substantial amounts of milk when he is drinking with an open—pause—close type of suck (open—pause—close is one suck, the pause is not a pause between sucks).
- When the baby is nibbling or no longer drinking with the open—pause—close type of suck, compress the breast (not so hard that it hurts) and try not to change the shape of the areola (the part of the breast near the baby's mouth). With the compression, the baby should start drinking again with the open—pause—close type of suck.
- Keep the pressure up until the baby no longer drinks even with the compression, then release the pressure. Often the baby will stop sucking altogether when the pressure is released, but will start again shortly as milk starts to flow again. If the baby does not stop sucking with the release of pressure, wait a short time before compressing again.
- The reason to release the pressure is to allow your hand to rest and to allow milk to start flowing to the baby again. If the baby stops sucking when you release the pressure, he will start again when he starts to taste milk.
- When the baby starts sucking again, he may drink (open—pause—close). If not compress again as above.
- Continue on the first side until the baby does not drink even with the compression. You should allow the baby to stay on the side for a short time longer,

as you may occasionally get another let-down reflex and the baby will start drinking again, on his own. If the baby no longer drinks, however, allow him to come off or take him off the breast.

- If the baby wants more, offer the other side and repeat the process.
- You may wish to switch sides back and forth in this way several times.
- Work on improving the baby's latch-on.
- If you find a way which works better at keeping the baby sucking with an open—pause—close type of suck, use whatever works best for you and your baby. As long as it does not hurt your breast to compress, and as long as the baby is "drinking" (open—pause—close type of suck), breast compression is working.[1]

Stimulating the Let-Down Reflex

Many mothers find that moist warm compresses applied to the breasts just prior to nursing or pumping greatly facilitates the let-down reflex. There are many commercial products for moist heat, but you can make your own by filling a tube sock with uncooked (not instant) rice, and sewing or tying the end closed. Lightly dampen the sock and microwave for 30 seconds or so, testing to make sure the sock is not too hot. The shape of the sock allows itself to be wrapped comfortably around the breasts.

If you are experiencing any pain for any reason, be sure to speak to your health care provider about pain relievers you can safely take while nursing. It is very important that you not feel pain while nursing because pain can greatly inhibit your let-down response. If you or your physician is unsure about the effects of a specific drug while nursing, you can find specific information about it in Dr. Thomas Hale's book, *Medications and Mothers' Milk*. It is updated yearly and contains accurate, well-documented information on the synthesis of medication through human milk. Many LLL Leaders have access to a copy of this book and can share information from it about the drug you are interested in. Appendix 1 also contains information about obtaining your own copy.

There are many external and psychological stimuli that can be used to enhance and stimulate the let-down. Some can be used while either nursing or pumping, while others are specifically suited for pumping without your baby present.

While Nursing or Pumping

Visualization is a very powerful technique for increasing let-downs. To do this, you need to be very relaxed. Then create an image in your mind of whatever seems to connote a dramatic supply of milk. For many mothers, this is a waterfall-type image. Try to make the image as detailed and rich as possible; see it in vivid color, smell it, and hear it.

Having a special nursing station where you take the baby to nurse creates a psychological routine that helps to train the let-down response. Just as we see delicious food on TV and our salivary glands activate, "letting down" saliva into our mouths, we can condition ourselves to let down our milk when we are in specific situations and places.

While Pumping without Baby

Pumping without your baby present can sometimes make it difficult to let down your milk. Many mothers find that in order to pump well, they need to make pumping as much like nursing as possible. They make sure that they are comfortable and have all their needs within easy reach. You may find that it helps to make and listen to a recording of your baby's gurgling, coos, or gentle cries. If you have a special song that you often sing to your baby, try humming it to yourself as you pump. The sense of smell is very powerful–try holding your baby's unwashed blanket or piece of clothing next to your face as you pump.

Hand Expression

For the same reason that pumping is effective in increasing the milk supply, hand expression of your milk can be an effective alternative to using a mechanical device. Learning to express your milk by hand is an art that comes naturally to some women, but is more difficult to learn for others. Description of the two most common techniques can be found in Chapter 5 and Appendix 6. The frequency and duration of hand expression is the same as pumping, which is discussed in great detail in the following section.

Marmet Technique of Assisting the Milk Ejection Reflex

Chele Marmet, an LLL Leader and Co-Director of the Lactation Institute, developed this technique (see Appendix 6 for full instructions) using massage of the lactiferous lobes to stimulate milk ejection and move the milk through the ducts to the lactiferous sinuses so that it can be easily expressed. It can be performed in conjunction with nursing or pumping. The entire procedure should take approximately 20 to 30 minutes.

Using a Breast Pump

The principle behind pumping is to place a greater demand upon the mammary system so that it responds by producing more milk according to the supply and demand principle of lactation. While the supply and demand principle does not work as well for BFAR mothers because they may have impaired mammary systems, removing more milk from the breasts does stimulate further milk production in most cases.

There are advantages, as well as disadvantages, to pumping and many ways to go about pumping. Should you determine that pumping is a technique that is appropriate to your circumstances, you can experiment to develop the methods that work best for you and your baby.

Why (and Why Not) to Pump

Although pumping can potentially increase your milk supply, it is not the best way to increase the milk supply in all BFAR situations. If your baby is nursing often and well and also likes to comfort nurse in between feedings, his suckling is stimulating your lactation system more effectively than a pump could. Pumping in the short amount of time you have between feedings can be exhausting. Mothers with more than one child often feel especially overwhelmed at the amount of time that frequent nursing and then pumping between feedings can consume. It is natural to feel resentful of the amount of time that is involved, which can make it very tempting to simply give up and bot-tle-feed. Pumping also introduces a very mechanical, unnatural aspect to your breast-feeding relationship.

Pumping, however, can be helpful in providing additional stimulation to the lactation system to increase the milk supply when your baby is not nursing often or well, or when he does not seem to want to nurse for comfort in between feedings. It should only be done, though, when you feel that it is not overtaxing yourself physically. Above all, it should not interfere with the time you need to nurture and bond with your baby.

When to Pump

Should you decide to pump to provide extra stimulation to your lactation system, it is best to pump after daytime feedings so that your baby receives the majority of the avail-able milk at your breast. Pumping after nighttime feedings is certainly good if you can do it, but getting adequate sleep is actually more important to your overall health and well-being, which can significantly impact your milk supply.

Veteran "pumpers" have also found that pumping one breast while the baby nurses from the other can be a very effective means of increasing the number and strength of the let-downs, providing excellent stimulation. It is most important, though, that the baby be given the first priority at the breast since his stimulation will always be more effective than that of a pump.

When pumping for additional stimulation to increase the milk supply, rather than to remove milk from the breasts to maintain the milk supply, it is recommended that each breast be pumped for ten to fifteen minutes every two to three hours, after daytime feedings.

What Kind of Pump to Use

There are many classifications of breast pumps available to nursing mothers, both through rental and purchase:

- Automatic Electric Piston Pumps
- Automatic Electric Diaphragm Pumps
- Semi-Automatic Diaphragm Pumps
- Small Motorized Pumps
- Manual Pumps

There are many brands of breast pumps on the market. It is not always easy to determine which classification describes the different brands. The following table presents an overview of the classifications of the most common brands available in North America.

Automatic Electric Piston Pumps
Medela Classic
Medela Lactina Select
Ameda SMB
Ameda Lact-e
Ameda Elite
White River Concepts Model 9600

Automatic Electric Diaphragm Pumps
Medela Pump In Style
Ameda Purely Yours
White River Concepts Model 9050

Semi-Automatic Diaphragm Pumps
Ameda Nurture III
Evenflo Personal Comfort

Small Motorized Pumps
Medela DoubleEase
Medela Mini-Electric
Lumiscope Gentle Expressions
Omron MagMag
Evenflo Soft Touch Ultra
Evenflo Personal Comfort
Gerber Battery or Electric Breast Pump
Evenflo Press & Pump
The First Years Portable Breast Pump
The First Years Natural Rhythm Breast Pump
The First Years Simplicity

Manual Pumps
Pedal Pump
Medela PedalPump
VersaPed

Cylinder Pumps
Kaneson Comfort Plus
White River Concepts Model 500
Medela SpringExpress
Medela ManualEase
Medela Manualectric
Ameda Cylinder Hand Breast Pump
Lansinoh Easy Express
Evenflo Manual Breast Pump

Handle Squeeze Pumps
Avent Isis
Ameda One-Hand Breast Pump (also branded as Lansinoh Ameda
One-Hand Breast Pump)
Gerber Manual Breast Pump

In addition to the pumps listed above, there are also manual pumps that use a bicycle-horn-rubber bulb or trigger-squeeze mechanism and a maternal-suction device. Commercial brands for these product types are not widely marketed. The bicycle-horn-rubber bulb type is never recommended.

Recommended Pumps for BFAR

A BFAR mother must use a pump that will compel the mammary system to produce more milk beyond what the baby is able to extract. The most effective pump to do this is an automatic electric piston pump, also known as a hospital-grade pump. This is because the effectiveness of a pump is largely determined by two factors: the number of suction and release cycles it can consistently generate and the strength of the suction.

To be most effective, the suction and release cycles should be similar to the suckling pattern of baby at the breast, which averages between 40-60 cycles per minute. Automatic electric piston pumps automatically generate 30-60 cycles per minute, compared with small motorized pumps that generate only 4-7 cycles per minute. Pumps that provide fewer pump cycles per minute draw the nipple into the nipple tunnel of the pump flange for a longer time before it is released, which can cause significant nipple tissue damage and pain. They also provide less breast stimulation, and therefore less milk production. The strength of the suction is an important criteria for pumping, and automatic electric piston pumps have the correct level of suction for properly stimulating the milk supply, which is neither too weak nor too strong. Small motorized pumps that do not cycle automatically, but rather rely on the mother to press a button or bar for cycling, create increasing suction until safe levels are exceeded and breast tissue can be damaged. Automatic electric piston pumps, on the other hand, have been shown to pump milk that is higher in fat content as a result of correct cycling and suction rates.

Automatic electric piston pumps are usually not purchased outright by mothers because they are expensive ($700 to $1500 US). Typically, they are rented from local rental stations for a small monthly fee. When rented long-term and used regularly, an automatic electric piston pump may cost less to use than a battery-operated small motorized pump, which may need the batteries replaced every couple of days and will wear out quickly necessitating replacement.

Features of Automatic Electric Piston Pumps

Among the brands of automatic electric piston pumps, there are some variations of features. For instance, the Medela Classic and Ameda SMB models are larger and less portable than the Medela Lactina Select, Ameda Lact-e, or Ameda Elite. The parts for the Medela products and the Ameda products are slightly different, but equally effective. Even though they have similar mechanical specifications, different mothers have different favorites among the models. You may need to look at a few of them in person at your local rental station to determine which will be best for you.

How to Pump

Before your first pumping session, take some time to thoroughly read and understand the instruction manual that comes with your pump. Look at all the accessories and learn how the parts fit together. Some parts need to be sterilized before you use them for the first time. The manual should give clear instructions on the best way to do this.

When the parts have been sterilized, wash your hands and then reassemble the parts on the pump. It is always a good idea to wash your hands before each pumping session. How often you will need to sterilize the parts varies according to your unique situation and the age of your baby. Your health care provider will be able to give you advice appropriate to your circumstances.

Before turning the pump on, you may wish to moisten your breasts slightly to improve the fit and suction of the flange on your breasts. Be sure to center the flange over your nipple so that your nipple can move into the tube without rubbing against the sides. Always begin pumping with the suction level on the minimum setting and the cycling rate on the middle setting. As the pumping session progresses, and if you feel comfortable doing so, you can gradually increase the suction setting. Do not increase it to the point of discomfort, however, as that can damage your nipple/areola tissue, which can impact your milk supply.

When you are finished pumping, all the parts that come in contact with milk must be thoroughly washed in warm, soapy water. If you do not have the time to wash them right then, immerse them in a bowl of soapy water until they can be washed later. Ordinarily, there is no need to clean the plastic tubing, however if milk backs up into it, it can be washed and hung to drip-dry so that no moisture remains in it for the next pumping session.

Single vs. Double Pumping

Most of the automatic electric piston pumps allow either single or double pumping, meaning that either one breast or both breasts can be pumped at a time. There are advantages to each method.

Single pumping is often a more comfortable choice for BFAR mothers who have a much greater yield in one breast than the other as the lower yield breast can hurt when it is producing very little milk. Single pumping also maximizes the suction, which is fine as long as pumping at a higher level of suction is comfortable and does not result in damage to your nipple/areola complex. Many mothers find that alternating breasts while single pumping results in a higher volume of milk. This is similar to the principle of switch-nursing.

Double pumping, however, is usually more effective in stimulating the breasts toward a higher yield because it results in the production of higher levels of prolactin. It is also much faster. Working out the logistics of pumping both breasts at once can take some practice, but most mothers find that they can develop a technique fairly easily. Medela also sells a device that attaches the pump horns to your bra to allow hands-free pumping.

Pumping Tips

You will almost certainly find that the general techniques described to increase milk supply, including massage, breast compression, visualization, biofeedback, relaxation, warm compresses, conditioning, and reminding yourself of your baby through pictures, sounds, and smells, will be very effective in increasing your pumping yield. You may also find that gentle nipple stimulation before and periodically during pumping will help you let down your milk. Holding your baby while you pump may be the best stimulation of all.

Some mothers rearrange the flanges periodically so that the nipple is off-center, which can stimulate different glands. Along the same lines, you might try using the removable flange inserts for small breasts during the later portion of the pumping session to provide additional stimulation to the areolar nerves. It is important, however, to only use these special techniques so long as no pain is experienced, which might indicate tissue damage.

Pumping Yield Amounts and Expectations

Whatever amount of milk you are able to extract by using a breast pump is *not* an accurate gauge of your milk supply because a pump extracts milk by a different mechanism than a baby does. Pumps can only create a rhythmic vacuum to withdraw milk that is easily available in the ducts and encourage a let-down. A baby, on the other hand, compresses the special reservoirs within the areola called the lactiferous sinuses with a combined action of tongue and jaw movement, which acts to efficiently draw out the milk and induce effective let-downs. Some lactation specialists estimate that a pump is only able to extract 25 percent of a breast's actual milk-producing capability. Ideally, you are also pumping after a full feeding. So collection of only a quarter of an ounce (7 ml) after thirty minutes of pumping *does not* mean that is all you are capable of producing.

It is also important to remember that the human lactation system is not designed to provide eight ounces of milk from the moment a mother's milk comes in. A normally functioning breast will only produce an average of one to three ounces (30-90 ml) per feeding in the first week, which increases gradually as the baby's needs increase. *This is exactly what the baby needs at this stage.* So do not be at all disappointed if you are unable to pump more at first.

It may be helpful to know beforehand that the milk that you express will not look pure white and will soon separate as the cream rises to the top (shaking it gently will redistribute the fat particles throughout the milk). In fact, human milk rarely looks the same from one day to another or even from one time of day to another. In the first two weeks, especially, it will look yellowish as colostrum transitions to mature milk. The foods that we eat and even the medications that we take can impart colors to our milk. A pink shade of milk may mean that blood is present, but this is not dangerous to your baby. It may mean, however, that you have cracked nipples that need attention. If there are no visible cracks and the pink shade in your milk continues for more than two weeks after delivery, a lactation specialist or health care provider should be consulted.

Collection Materials

One problem that many BFAR mothers find with pumping is that because it is so convenient to pump milk directly into bottles (most pumps are designed to screw directly onto the rims of bottles), it can be very tempting to attach an artificial nipple and feed the baby the bottle of milk that was pumped. Nipple confusion/preference, then, becomes a very real danger. This happens because the baby must use a different sucking method for breast and bottle and many babies come to prefer the easier bottle technique and forget how to nurse effectively at the breast. Many BFAR nursing relationships have been ended prematurely as a result of nipple confusion/preference.

Using plastic bags designed for the collection of human milk will help you to avoid this problem. The disposable bags manufactured for use in bottles are not made to withstand the freezing and thawing process. Several companies sell a pre-sterilized bag that is specially designed for human milk and has markings that help measure the amount you've pumped. They are generally more expensive, but given the dangers of nipple confusion, they are well worth the cost.

Should you need, however, to use a rigid container instead of a bag, you can be assured that there is not much, if any, difference between glass, clear plastic (polycarbonate), and cloudy plastic (polypropylene) containers. The most recent research indicates that there is no significant nutrient loss from any of these materials, as had been previously theorized.[2]

Storing Expressed Milk

At Room Temperature
There is no need to refrigerate milk if it will be fed to the baby in only a few hours. This is because the immunological factors in milk resist bacterial growth. If the milk is stored in a room at a temperature of between 66 to 71.6 degrees Fahrenheit (19-22 degrees Celsius), it can be safely used for up to ten hours.[3] If the room temperature is no higher than 79 degrees Fahrenheit (25 degrees Celsius), it can kept safely for between four and six hours.[4]

Non-Electric Insulated Containers
There may be times when you are unable to refrigerate your milk and wish to keep it in an insulated container. There are several such containers on the market especially for transporting milk. Any insulated container, though, will be sufficient. Surrounding the expressed milk container with ice may be a necessary precaution depending on the temperature outside of the cooler.

When human milk is stored in a container that keeps it between 59-60 degrees Fahrenheit (15 degrees Celsius), it can be safely used for up to 24 hours.[4]

Refrigerating
When you will be able to use your milk within eight days after you pump it, it is better to refrigerate it than to freeze it so that the immunological factors can be better preserved. Be sure to place it in the middle or rear of your refrigerator so that it will be maintained at the appropriate cool temperature between 32-39 degrees Farenheit (0-4 degrees Celsius).

As a convenience, it may help to know that it is just fine to combine warm milk with previously pumped milk that has been refrigerated.

Freezing
When you cannot use the milk within eight days, it can be safely frozen for later use. Human milk can be safely stored in a freezer compartment inside a refrigerator for up to two weeks. If the freezer has a separate door from the refrigerator, it will be good for up to four months. It is important, though, to keep the milk in the center of the compartment if your freezer is a self-defrosting model. A deep-freezer that keeps milk at 0°F (-18°C) can keep milk fresh for six to 12 months.

Many mothers find that when they have enough milk to freeze, it is best to do so in two to four ounce quantities so that there will be no waste if a batch is thawed and the baby does not take it all. It is also very useful to label frozen batches with the collection date so that you can tell the older containers from the more recent.

Thawing Milk

To prepare milk that has been frozen for feeding to your baby, you can either hold it under warm, running water or place it in the middle of a pan of heated water. Be careful, though, not to allow the milk to get too hot, especially not to boil. Never use a microwave to heat human milk because it will do so unevenly and can burn your baby. Always test the temperature of the thawed milk on the inside of your wrist—if it is uncomfortable, it is too hot. Gently shake the milk before feeding so that the cream is remixed into the milk.

Milk that has been frozen and then thawed can be safely stored in the refrigerator for up to 24 hours. It cannot, however, be refrozen.[5]

Pumping Exclusively

Sometimes BFAR doesn't go smoothly and, as a result of poor advice or breastfeeding mismanagement, a baby can develop such severe nipple confusion/preference that feeding him at the breast is no longer possible. When this has happened to some BFAR mothers, the idea of giving up lactation is unthinkable after all that we know about the value of human milk and all that we have already gone through to maximize our milk supplies. So, many mothers have chosen to pump their milk and feed it to their babies in bottles.

Depending on your level of lactation, how often and regularly you pump, and other measures that you take to maximize your milk supply, you should be able to maintain your milk supply through pumping alone without much difficulty. Some BFAR mothers have maintained a consistent yield pumping only two or three times a day.

Exclusive pumping for an extended time period takes a true dedication to giving our babies the best our bodies can provide. One comes to value highly every drop of human milk that can be collected and given to our babies.

Pumping Problems

Pumping is not always easy and it does not always go smoothly. Most difficulties, though, can be resolved with some perseverance and appropriate assistance.

One difficulty that some BFAR mothers experience is that their breast mounds, the area under the nipple/areola complex, are somewhat flat and do not fit well into a pump. It may be difficult to form a good seal in order to get adequate suction. Moistening the areola skin can help, as can compressing the breast tissue in a sideways C-hold so that more tissue is pressed into the pump flange.

Pumping should never be painful. If you find that it is painful, it most likely means that there is a problem with your pumping technique or the pump itself. First, rule out a problem with the pump. Make sure that the pump is properly assembled and that all connections are dry. Linda Smith, a board certified lactation consultant, recommends the following steps to rule out a weak, damaged, or ineffective pump:

- First, try putting the flange against your cheek and using the pump. You should feel a very strong, almost painful pinch.

- Next, test it using a vacuum gauge. (Your lactation consultant may have one.) A baby uses pressures of 100-250 mm Hg. Your pump should get to at least 100 mm Hg pressure in 1-2 seconds.

- If the tests show that the pump is too weak and it is a new pump, return it to where you purchased or rented it. Get a more effective one.

- If the tests show that the pump is fine, especially if it used to work fine and this is a new problem, take a look at the pump parts.

- Clean all parts that touch the milk with warm soapy water. If a part is gummy with dried milk, soak it in vinegar for several hours then wash and rinse well.

- Check all parts for cracks and looseness. Hairline cracks will affect suction. If there is a white filter between the tubing and motor, it must be bone-dry and CLEAN. Double-check pressure settings.[6]

Once you have completely ruled out a problem with the pump, it will be necessary to have an LLL Leader or a lactation consultant evaluate your pumping technique to determine the source of the pain. Contacting her sooner rather than later is essential because the pain you are experiencing can significantly impact your milk supply.

Finally, one of the most difficult aspects of pumping for many BFAR mothers is wondering what to do when your baby cries or fusses in the middle of a pumping session. It can seem so important to finish the pumping session, but doing so while listening to your baby cry can be agonizing. If this should happen to you, remember that your baby's emotional needs come first and that nothing is as important as comforting a miserable child. You can always resume pumping later. Pumping should never cause you or your baby emotional stress.

Galactagogues

There are many substances that have been reported to have the ability to increase the human milk supply. These substances, which are typically herbal or prescription drugs, are known as *galactagogues* (pronounced ga-lack-ta-gogs). The practice of ingesting galactagogues to increase the milk supply has been employed by nursing women in almost every traditional and civilized culture. The degree of effectiveness and safety of the galactagogues that have been used vary and have led to a large anecdotal base of information. Because we have very little scientific data about the actual effectiveness of the many supposed galactagogues, we must rely instead upon anecdotal and traditional information to derive reasonable conclusions.

When considering the possibility of using galactagogues, it makes good sense for a breastfeeding mother to be cautious about ingesting any substance in therapeutic doses to achieve a physiological result because there is always the danger of unintended side effects and negative interaction with other medications. Therefore, the following information about galactagogues is provided not as a recommendation of medicinal galactagogues, but rather to provide you with accurate information so that you can make informed decisions on using galactagogues in conjunction with your health care provider. It is always prudent to consult your physician prior to taking any pharmaceutical substances. In addition, you may also wish to consult a trained herbalist if you should choose to use medicinal herbs.

Galactagogues may be beneficial in increasing a BFAR mother's milk supply because they may act to bridge the gap created by the damaged nerves that are unable to signal the body to produce prolactin or oxytocin. Galactagogues should only be used when you are already experiencing a low milk supply–they should not be taken proactively. You may not need them at all. If you do find that you have an insufficient milk supply, the first step would be to try the non-chemical ways to increase it. You may want to consider using galactagogues only after other methods of increasing the milk supply have been given a fair opportunity to work.

Galactagogues must never be taken during pregnancy because, aside from toxicity issues for the developing fetus, many of them have the potential of stimulating contractions and leading to premature labor. The very earliest appropriate time to begin therapeutic use of galactagogues is after your initial engorgement has subsided.

Galactagogue Myths

Before beginning the discussion of the galactagogues that have a verifiable effect, it is important to bring to light a few of those that do not. Among the folklore of galactagogue use, several myths persist. The most prevalent of these is that water, milk, and beer have the ability to affect a mother's milk supply.

Water

Nursing mothers have long been told that they have to stay excessively hydrated to make enough milk. While it is generally true that adequate hydration is important, quantities of water greater than 80 ounces (2.3 liters) a day can actually reduce necessary potassium levels and have a negative effect upon the milk volume. Moderate degrees of insufficient hydration, on the other hand, will normally only reduce the mother's urinary output and her own levels of hydration; it will not decrease her milk supply. The best rule of thumb is to simply "drink to thirst." Drink when you feel thirsty, and as much as you need to quench your thirst. Many mothers find that sipping a glass of water each time they nurse helps to keep them automatically hydrated.

Milk

One of the oldest myths about lactation is that a mother has to drink milk (generally meaning cow's milk) to make milk. This, of course, is completely untrue. Cows most certainly do not drink milk and lactate very well. In fact, other than humans, no mammals drink milk beyond childhood. Biologically, of course, we know that production of milk is not directly related to nor dependent upon the ingestion of any foods or liquids. It is a product synthesized from blood-borne particles produced and conveyed by the mother's body.

Beer

Beer has enjoyed a legendary status in many cultures for having the ability to increase a mother's milk supply. While brewer's yeast indeed seems to have galactogenic qualities, beer, particularly beer containing alcohol, does not have any galactogenic ability to increase the production of human milk. Although occasional alcohol consumption in moderate amounts is generally considered to be safe for most nursing mothers, alcohol is known to temporarily reduce both milk production and the infant's milk consumption. For BFAR mothers, this poses a significant, albeit transient, risk to their milk supplies and their babies' nutritional intake.

Herbal Galactagogues

Safety of Herbal Galactagogues

Large-scale research studies to determine the effects of most of the herbs thought to be galactagogues have not yet been conducted, although toxicology studies have shown the more widely available herbs to be relatively safe, demonstrating that the occurrence of side-effects or toxic reactions are relatively rare in the general population. [6,8] The formal research studies that do exist have been performed largely in the context of bovine (cow) milk production and show that many herbs thought to be galactagogues demonstrate estrogenic (estrogen-producing), oxytocic (oxytocin-producing), or other hormonal effects.

Unfortunately, there are no federal laws in the US to regulate the manufacture, processing, distribution, or marketing of herbs as there are in Europe. The Food and Drug Administration does provide general guidelines on natural herbs, but has no authority over commercially marketed herbal products. It is up to the consumer, then, to become knowledgeable about the nature and risks of the different herbs and to obtain them from reputable sources.

Many of the popular herbal galactagogues are also culinary herbs and have been used to flavor foods for much longer than they have been used as galactagogues. Because they have been used safely as foods, it is common to think of these culinary herbs as completely safe. Indeed, when used in the quantities required for seasoning foods, they generally are safe. However, in order to have a galactogenic effect, it is often (although not always) necessary to ingest the herbs in significantly larger doses. The larger amounts, then, can potentially cause side effects that were unknown in the lower culinary doses. Side effects seen from culinary herbs used in this fashion seem to be quite rare, however, it is important for nursing mothers to understand that simply because an herb is well-known and extensively used as a culinary herb, it does not mean that it is without any risk of toxicity.

Another concern for nursing mothers is that some herbs that do not have an inherent toxicity can nonetheless cause allergic reactions by means of their close botanical relationship to common allergenic plants. Several herbs, for instance, including chamomile, feverfew, and yarrow, are related to the sunflower (*Compositae*) or aster (*Asteraceae*) family and can cause reactions in those allergic to ragweed. Other herbs are related to different common allergens and so must be used with caution by those allergic to the families to which they are related. Even when the mother does not exhibit any obvious allergic reactions, a baby may be sensitive to the allergen and have a reaction. It is thus very important to be vigilant of the real possibility of maternal or infant allergic reactions as a side-effect of galactagogue use.

Transfer of Herbal Galactagogues into Human Milk

The definition of a medicine is any substance used in treating disease, healing, relieving pain, or improving health. The term "medicine," then, includes not only pharmaceutical medications (drugs), but also all the herbs that are used for this purpose. Thus they are known as *medicinal herbs*. The effectiveness of a given herb is often a result of a combination of many active ingredients that are each only present in minute amounts. When these active ingredients individually pass into human milk, assuming they do so according to the usual average transfer rate of one percent, only a very small amount of each active ingredient will be present in the milk. Of course, any amount of an ingredient carries the potential for a negative side effect, and logically, the combination of ingredients that produced the herb's effectiveness for the mother could produce a similar effect on the baby, although to a substantially lesser degree.

Fortunately, more and more research is being conducted to evaluate the transfer rates of all medicinal substances, including many herbs, into human milk. Dr. Thomas Hale has compiled a well-documented, annually updated reference book on this subject called *Medications and Mothers' Milk* (see Appendix 1). Consulting this book for specific information on the effect of any medicine, particularly galactagogues, is one of the best ways to have objective information about the safety of the substance in question.

Standardization and Quality Control of Herbal Remedies

Prepared medicinal herbs are generally available in teas, tinctures, syrups, gelatin capsules, and tablets. It is not safe to assume, though, that one form of the prepared herb is more potent than another because the manner in which an herb is prepared for medicinal use bears a significant relationship to its effectiveness. For instance, some teas are brewed longer than others and are thus stronger, making it inaccurate to assume that a tea is necessarily a weak dilution of the herb. Some herbs in tablet form have a small proportion of active ingredients, while others are quite potent. The plant itself can also vary in potency.

Interest in and market demand for safe, effective medicinal herbs in North America have resulted in an industry movement toward standardized herbal products, such as those available in Europe. Quality control programs to eliminate bacterial, fungal, and other contaminants, as well as to ensure that the correct plants are used in preparation of the herbal product, are now fairly standard among the larger brand names.

Specific Herbal Galactagogues and Their Uses

The most popular and readily available herbal galactagogues with known effectiveness are: Fenugreek, Blessed Thistle, Goat's Rue, Brewer's Yeast, Alfalfa, Marshmallow, Nettle, Vervain, and Dill Seed.

Although Vitex (Chaste Berry), Fennel, and Anise Seed are also popular galactagogues, they are not recommended for BFAR mothers because studies have shown that they may inhibit prolactin production.[9, 10]

The herbal galactagogues listed below can be purchased in capsule, tincture, and raw (tea) form in most health food stores, many drug stores or pharmacies, and even some grocery stores. They can also be purchased in capsule or bulk form through mail-order and internet companies. Capsules can be made by filling empty size "00" gelatin capsules with seed, ground, or powdered versions of the herbs. Tinctures can be made from galactogenic herbs; if you are not familiar with tincture-making, commercial tinctures are available for most galactagogues. Teas can also be brewed from the herbs, but teas are usually less potent than capsules or tinctures.

Herbal teas are a very comforting way to ingest galactagogues, but it is important to prepare teas containing only herbs that are known to be safe during lactation. The strength of the tea, too, is very important. If left to steep beyond the recommended time, the dose of the galactagogue may become inappropriately strong. Likewise, steeping for too short a time will result in a weak tea with little galactogenic properties.

Tinctures, which are herbs steeped in alcohol or glycerin for a specific period of weeks or months, are a potent way of preparing medicinal herbs that are easily ingested and well assimilated into the body. This preparation process avoids the use of heat, which can harm the active quality of an herb. Most tinctures are prepared in small colored vials to prevent light from altering the herb's potency and will remain potent for at least a year. They must be kept away from sunlight and heat. The alcohol contained in a normal dose of tincture is usually quite small, although some mothers may prefer to use glycerin tinctures to prevent any exposure to alcohol. Tinctures are usually taken by putting drops under the tongue or adding to water or juice.

Mothers often wonder if they can use two or more herbs simultaneously. Most herbalists agree that this is safe to do. There are no known negative interactions between the following galactogenic herbs, which are listed here in order of reported potency beginning with the most potent.

Fenugreek (*Trigonella foenum-graecum*)

Dr. Jack Newman and Kathleen Huggins have written favorably about fenugreek in their popular breastfeeding books, *The Ultimate Breastfeeding Book of Answers* and *The Nursing Mothers' Companion*, respectively. They describe using it in clinical practice with significant success. In fact, Huggins has recommended it specifically for BFAR. Many other physicians and lactation consultants support fenugreek as an effective galactagogue. It is also discussed quite widely among lay breastfeeding counselors and breastfeeding mothers as one of the most popular galactagogues.

Fenugreek is among the oldest of documented medicinal herbs. References to it have been found in Greek, Roman, Indian, and Egyptian writings, including those authored by Hippocrates, the father of modern medicine. It has been used with varying degrees of success to treat a wide variety of illnesses, injuries, and diseases, including fevers, respiratory distress, digestive disorders, rheumatic pains, boils, wounds, rashes, coughs, sore throats, depression, female hormonal disturbances, childbirth pain, and male impotence. It has also been used as a galactagogue for both human mothers and dairy cows throughout the world. It was, in fact, the principle ingredient of Lydia E. Pinkham's mass-produced and widely distributed Vegetable Compound in the 1800s, which was said to cure "all female complaints."

Fenugreek is included in the FDA's list of herbs that are "generally regarded as safe."[11] It has been widely researched in the context of its non-galactogenic medicinal properties and has been found to reduce cholesterol, lipid, and glucose levels, reduce tissue inflammation, and affect reproductive hormonal levels.

Although very little research has been conducted on fenugreek's galactogenic quality, one Egyptian study in 1945 concluded that it is a "potent stimulator of breast milk production," claiming increases in milk production up to 900 percent.[12]

In addition to being a medicinal herb, fenugreek seeds have been enjoyed in all parts of the world as a culinary herb, lending its distinct flavor to a wide variety of baked goods and foods, including curry and imitation maple syrup. Other portions of the fenugreek plant have been cooked as vegetables or eaten fresh in salads. It has also been roasted and used in a hot drink. It is known to be quite nutritious, containing protein, vitamin C, niacin, and potassium.

The galactogenic effects of fenugreek are most often seen within 24-72 hours after therapeutic dosing has begun. Coinciding with increased milk production, most mothers notice a maple syrup smell to their sweat and urine.

Capsule Therapeutic Dose

2-4 capsules (580-610 mg capsules), 3 times per day

Tincture Therapeutic Dose

1 ml, 3 times per day

Seeds/Powder Therapeutic Dose

1/2 – 1 teaspoon (1 capsule = 1/4 teaspoon), 3x/day — can be mixed with liquids and foods, such as water, juice, applesauce

Tea Therapeutic Dose

1 cup of tea, 2-3 times per day. 1 teaspoon of whole fenugreek seeds steeped in boiling water for 15 minutes – can be sweetened with sugar/honey to mask bitterness

Potential Side Effects

- Maple syrup odor in sweat and urine
- Therapeutic doses can cause baby to smell like maple syrup, which can be misdiagnosed as the metabolic disorder "maple syrup urine disease"
- Loose stools/diarrhea
- Hypoglycemia can occur with doses higher than the therapeutic dose
- Stomach upset can occur with doses higher than the therapeutic dose
- Uterine contractions (contraindicated in pregnancy)
- Low blood glucose levels in diabetic mothers
- Maternal and infant allergic reactions when sensitive to peanuts[13-17]

Blessed Thistle (*Cnicus Benedictus*)

The use of blessed thistle has been recorded as far back as the early sixteenth century for treating smallpox, fever, anorexia, dyspepsia, indigestion, constipation, and flatulence. It is also a popular galactagogue and has been reported anecdotally to be most effective when taken in conjunction with fenugreek. No formal research studies exist to document its effectiveness. Most mothers prefer to take blessed thistle in capsule form as the teas and tinctures are quite bitter.

<u>Capsule Therapeutic Dose</u>

3-4 capsules, 3 times per day

<u>Tincture Therapeutic Dose</u>

10-20 drops (2 ml), 2-4 times per day

<u>Potential Side Effects</u>

- Maternal and infant allergic reactions when sensitive to daisies
- Mild diuretic (can increase urinary output)[14, 15, 17]

Goat's Rue (*Galega Officinalis*)

Goat's Rue was first mentioned by dairy farmer Gillet-Damitte in 1873 in a letter to the French Academy in which he described milk production increases in his cows of between 35-50 percent when given this herb. Drs. Cerisoli and Millbank subsequently confirmed empirical evidence that goat's rue is indeed a powerful galactagogue.[17]

<u>Tincture Therapeutic Dose</u>

1-2 ml, 3 times per day

<u>Tea Therapeutic Dose</u>

Steep 1 teaspoon in 1 cup water for 10-15 minutes. Drink 1 cup 2 times per day.

<u>Potential Side Effects</u>

- diaphoretic (can increase sweating)
- hypoglycemic (can cause a drop in blood sugar)
- diuretic (can increase urinary output)[15, 17, 18]

Alfalfa (Medicago sativa)

Alfalfa, a popular and commonly used galactagogue, is often taken in combination with blessed thistle, marshmallow, and fenugreek. It is rated as "generally regarded as safe" by the FDA.

<u>Capsule Therapeutic Dose</u>

2 capsules, 4 times per day

<u>Potential Side Effects</u>

- Loose stools
- Contraindicated for persons with a history of systemic lupus erythematosus (SLE)
- Large quantities (greater than therapeutic dose) of alfalfa can produce a reversible pancytopenia in humans [15, 17, 19]

Marshmallow (*Althaea officinalis*)

Although it is not actually a galactagogue itself, marshmallow has a long anecdotal history of boosting the galactogenic effectiveness of fenugreek, blessed thistle, and alfalfa. There are records of its use as a food and medicinal herb in the earliest civilizations. It has been used to promote tissue healing, treat indigestion, kidney and bladder dysfunction, and as an expectorant. It contains high levels of vitamin A, calcium, and zinc, as well as lesser levels of iron, sodium, iodine, and B-complex vitamins.

<u>**Capsule Therapeutic Dose**</u>

2-4 capsules, 3 times per day

<u>**Tincture Therapeutic Dose**</u>

1/2 ml, 3 times per day

<u>**Potential Side Effects**</u>

- Allergic reactions possible, but extremely rare [15, 17, 20]

Nettle (*Urtica urens or Urtica dioica*)

Nettle is an herb that also has enjoyed a long tradition of medicinal use dating back to ancient Greece. It has been used to treat coughs, tuberculosis, arthritis, alopecia, benign prostatic hyperplasia (BPH), allergy symptoms, muscle spasms, parasitic infestation, kidney disease, gout, sciatica, hemorrhoids, and diarrhea. It is said to be particularly useful in the treatment of chronic eczema.

Most importantly for BFAR purposes, however, it has a consistent history of being a powerful galactagogue. It is a significant component of most commercial galactagogue products. It is rich in iron, calcium, vitamin K, silica, potassium, lectins, phenols, sterols, lignans, and histamines.

The freeze-dried version of the herb, which is used in capsules and tinctures, is the safest form of the galactagogue as leaves that have been dried in the usual fashion can contain mold spores, which could cause an allergic reaction in those sensitive to mold. The freeze-dried leaves are also more potent.

<u>**Capsule Therapeutic Dose**</u>

1-2 300 mg capsule, 3 times per day

<u>**Tincture Therapeutic Dose**</u>

1/2 – 1 teaspoon root or leaf tincture, 3 times per day

<u>**Tea Therapeutic Dose**</u>

Steep nettle 2-3 teaspoons in 1cup water for 10 minutes. Drink 1 cup 2-3 times per day.

<u>**Potential Side Effects**</u>

- Mild diuretic
- Mild gastrointestinal upset[15, 17]

European Vervain (*Verbena officinalis*)

European vervain has been used as an astringent, diuretic, emmenagogue, galactagogue, stimulant, tonic, wound healer, and aphrodisiac, as well as for treating eczema and other skin conditions. It is not one of the more commonly used galactagogues in North America, but it does have an anecdotal reputation for having the ability to increase the milk supply.

<u>**Tincture Therapeutic Dose**</u>

20-40 drops, 1-2 times per day

<u>**Potential Side Effects**</u>

- Contraindicated during pregnancy[15, 17]

Dill Seed (*Peucedanum graveolens* or *Anethum graveolens*)

Dill seed was widely used by the ancient Babylonians, Syrians, Greeks, Chinese, Romans, and Egyptians. Hippocrates included it in a prescription for oral cleansing. It has been used as a digestive aid and mild sedative for both adults and children. It has also been used in love potions and protective potions against witchcraft. In the 700s, Charlemagne had crystal vials of dill seed placed on his banquet tables to cure his guests' hiccups. Gripe Water, a common pediatric home remedy, is made from dill. Because of its soothing properties, dill's name is derived from the Norse word "dilla," which means to lull.

Dill seed is also a natural preservative and is widely used in canning and pickling. It is rich in calcium, vitamin C, and flavanoids. It is commonly used as a culinary spice in many German, Russian, and Scandinavian recipes.

Dill seed has enjoyed an additional popularity as a galactagogue. It is included in many popular commercial galactagogue products because it seems to work especially well when combined with other galactagogues. Dill seed is also one of the herbs thought to facilitate letdowns.

Tincture Therapeutic Dose

1/2 to 1 teaspoon, 1-3 times per day

Tea Therapeutic Dose

Steep 2 teaspoons of crushed seeds in 1 cup water for 10-15 min. Drink 1 cup 2-3 times per day.

Potential Side Effects

- None known[15, 17]

Commercial Products

There are several commercially prepared galactogenic products on the market in North America. Although they are not generally regulated by the FDA, the products listed below are made only from well-known herbs under high quality manufacturing processes. In most cases, the herbs used are deemed "generally regarded as safe" by the FDA.

Nursing Teas

Teas prepared with galactogenic herbs specifically for increasing the milk supply in nursing mothers are marketed by different companies under names such as "Mother's Milk Tea" or "Nursing Mother's Tea." Most brands contain a blend of fenugreek, blessed thistle, nettle, fennel seed, and anise seed.

Nursing Tinctures

There are several galactogenic tinctures on the market. Some are tinctures of just one galactogenic herb and others are blends of herbs specifically combined for their galactogenic properties. "More Milk" and "More Milk Plus" manufactured by the Motherlove Herbal Company are two popular brands that contain such a combination of galactogenic herbs. Many mothers have found galactogenic tinctures to be highly and rapidly effective in increasing their milk supplies.

There is another tincture called "Rescue Remedy" that is not specifically galactogenic in nature, but which many mothers find has a calming effect, facilitating letdown. It contains the flower essences of cherry plum, impatiens, rock rose, and star of Bethlehem. Although it is quite mild, because it has a sedative quality, it is important to use it only in moderation and monitor yourself and your baby carefully for excessive sleepiness.

Nutritional Galactagogues

There are some galactagogues that are neither herbal nor prescription, but rather derived from everyday foods and nutrients. Different cultures have various customs about galactogenic foods, but the following foods are those that are believed to have a galactogenic ability.

Protein

Research has shown that increasing protein in a mother's diet will increase the volume of her milk supply to a certain degree. [21] The increase does not seem to be profound, but is nonetheless observable. In some regions of China, it is the tradition that nursing mothers eat five to ten eggs per day in order to have a plentiful milk supply. A diet rich in protein is important for the nutritional health of all nursing mothers.

Calcium

Calcium seems to have a moderate ability to increase the milk supply by facilitating the role of oxytocin in the let-down reflex.[22] Eating a diet rich in dairy, legumes, and green leafy vegetables is an excellent way to increase your intake of calcium. Many orange juice brands have added calcium and there are also many calcium supplements on the market, including some in the form of chocolate candy.

B Complex Vitamins

The North American diet is commonly deficit in B vitamins. Increasing the intake of B complex vitamins has been shown to increase the milk supply and the nursing mother's energy level. Meats, dairy products, eggs, whole grains, beans, peanuts, bananas, and dark green leafy vegetables are all rich sources of B vitamins.

Brewer's Yeast

Brewer's yeast contains large amounts of B vitamins, as well as protein, iron, and other minerals, and so is considered to be an effective galactagogue. Many mothers find that taking supplements of brewer's yeast is a good way to include these nutrients in their diets. It is important, though, to be alert to the possibility of fussiness in the baby as the yeast can cause intestinal discomfort. Those who are susceptible to thrush may wish to avoid introducing additional yeast into their systems.

Capsule Therapeutic Dose

3-5 tablets, 3 times per day

Powder Therapeutic Dose

1.5-2.5 tablespoons, 3 times per day – can be added to juice

Potential Side Effects

- May cause gassiness
- Can exacerbate thrush
- Stool can have odor of yeast[23]

Oatmeal

It has long been believed that oatmeal has the ability to increase a nursing mother's milk supply. Many working nursing mothers, in fact, have noticed that eating oatmeal for breakfast results in a greater volume of pumped milk later in the day. Why this would be so is unclear. Oatmeal affects cholesterol absorption and is high in iron, but these are not known galactogenic qualities. It may be that oatmeal is a "comfort food," and is merely soothing, which facilitates let-down. Or perhaps there is indeed a galactogenic quality that has not yet been detected. Either way, oatmeal is nutritious and comforting, both of which are excellent for nursing mothers.

Prescription Galactagogues

There are no prescription drugs that have been specifically designated by the FDA as galactagogues. Several drugs that are marketed for other disorders do, however, have the side effect of increasing the milk supply. In most cases, the use of prescription galactogenic drugs will result in a significantly greater increase in the milk supply than will the use of medicinal herbs. Domperidone and metoclopramide, in particular, have the ability to increase the milk supply dramatically.

Domperidone (Motilium)

Domperidone, brand name Motilium, is a prescription drug that is generally used for adult and pediatric gastrointestinal disorders, but which has been clinically and anecdotally shown to also have a dramatic effect upon the milk supply.[13-14, 24-31] It achieves this effect by suppressing the neurotransmitter dopamine, which is a prolactin inhibitor. Prolactin, then, is produced in significantly greater quantities, compensating for nerve damage in BFAR mothers.

Many BFAR mothers choose to use domperidone because it is dramatically effective in increasing the milk supply and does not have the negative central nervous system (CNS) effects common to other prescription galactogogues such as metoclopramide (Reglan). The reason that domperidone does not have these side effects is because, unlike metoclopramide, it does not cross the blood-brain barrier. Drugs that cross the blood-brain barrier are more likely to cause detrimental CNS side effects.

Dr. Jack Newman has prescribed domperidone for many years in his clinic in Toronto, Canada, for appropriate breastfeeding situations when normal prolactin stimulation cannot be achieved. Many other physicians also prescribe domperidone for this purpose.

Unfortunately, it cannot be purchased in the United States, although it is readily available by mail-order from pharmacies in Canada, New Zealand, Germany, Australia, and Mexico (contact information is included in Appendix 1). The fact that domperidone is not available in US pharmacies, however, should *not* be mistaken as an indication that the drug is unsafe. In fact, the American Academy of Pediatrics (AAP) has approved it for use in breastfeeding mothers. Metoclopramide (Reglan), the prescription galactagogue that is available in the US, on the other hand, has been classified by the AAP as a drug, "whose effect on nursing infants is unknown but may be of concern."[13]

The reason domperidone is not available in the US may be due to competition between similar drugs used primarily to treat gastrointestinal disorders or inadequate funding for the drug approval process, rather than for any concerns of safety. It is hoped that the FDA will soon become aware of the market demand for a safe prescription galactagogue and will approve domperidone for this purpose.

Side effects of domperidone at the therapeutic dose are rare and minimal for both nursing mothers and infants. It is transferred into the milk in minute quantities, far below the therapeutic dose that is commonly prescribed for infants for gastrointestinal disorders.

Most mothers report an increase in their milk supplies within three to four days after beginning domperidone, although the response may occur sooner.[43] The increase, however, builds over the first few weeks and does not reach the maximum effect until around the third week. The galactogenic effect will subside when the drug is discontinued.

Tablet Therapeutic Dose

* 20-40mg, 3-4 times per day during daytime

Potential Side Effects

* Dry mouth (quite rare)
* Headache which disappeared when the dose was reduced (quite rare)
* Abdominal cramps (quite rare)
* Has caused breast tumors in rodents when given in vast quantities over exceedingly long periods of time – this effect has never been documented in humans [13]

Metoclopramide (Reglan, Maxeran)

As discussed above, metoclopramide, brand name Reglan (US) and Maxeran (Canada), also has a galactogenic effect of increasing milk production.[12, 16, 26, 29-37] It is commonly prescribed for adults, children, and infants for short-term treatment of gastrointestinal disorders, including reflux. Metoclopramide acts as a galactagogue in lactating women by blocking dopamine from inhibiting the production of prolactin. Clinical studies have shown that metoclopramide increases prolactin levels 66 to 800 percent within one hour of ingestion, and can sustain this rate for up to eight hours. Metoclopramide does, however, cross the blood-brain barrier and thus can cause significant CNS side effects, which are listed below. Clinical studies have also shown that it can accelerate the transition of colostrum into mature milk.[38]

It is transferred into human milk, although at a rate that is substantially less (1-5 percent) than that which is commonly prescribed therapeutically for gastrointestinal distress in an infant.[13]

An increase in the milk supply is usually noticed by mothers within two to four days of beginning therapeutic doses of metoclopramide. It should not be taken beyond four weeks, and the dosage is usually tapered off after the first week. The effect completely disappears when it is discontinued.[13]

Tablet Therapeutic Dose

10mg, 3-4 times per day during daytime for one week, then tapered off over following week

Potential Side Effects

- Fatigue (common)
- Nervousness (common)
- Sleepiness (common)
- Lassitude (common)
- Irritability (common)
- Depression (common)
- Sleeplessness (rare)
- Headache (rare)
- Bowel disturbances (rare)
- Acute dystonic reaction (quite rare)
- Side-effects can be greatly exacerbated after two weeks[13]

Antipsychotic Drugs

Several drugs that treat psychosis by blocking dopamine release have the ability, as a side effect, of increasing prolactin levels and thus enhancing the milk supply. These drugs include sulpiride (Dolmatil, Sulparex, Eglonyl), reserpine (Serpasil, Raudixin), trifluoperazine (Stelazine), thioridazine (Mellaril), and chlorpromazine (Thorazine). Unfortunately, these are strong neuroleptic antipsychotic drugs that cross the blood-brain barrier. They have a significant risk of maternal side effects, ranging from tardive dyskinesia (hyperkinetic involuntary movements) to extreme sedation, and are transferred in varying amounts into human milk, which potentially exposes the infant to these significant side effects as well.

Use of antipsychotic drugs to enhance lactation is not recommended.

Oxytocin Sprays (Syntocinon)

In some circumstances, synthetic oxytocin sprays have been used effectively by nursing mothers to induce let-down. Increasing the rate of occurrence of let-downs does not, however, necessarily result in higher milk production. In fact, consistent use over a period of weeks has been shown to suppress lactation.[16] The use of oxytocin sprays can also become chemically and emotionally habit-forming.

Oxytocin sprays are not useful in increasing the volume of milk production, but can be helpful in overcoming temporary psychological inhibitions that prevent let-down.

There are no commercial synthetic oxytocin spray products currently available in the United States, however, a pharmacist who is trained in compounding can make it by prescription by combining other ingredients. See Appendix 1 for more information.

Anti-Galactagogues

There are several substances that are known to decrease the milk supply, and so should be carefully avoided by BFAR mothers. These substances include culinary and medicinal herbs, as well as antihistamines, decongestants, and high-estrogen contraceptives.

It is important to understand that herbs known to be anti-galactogenic are only so when ingested in significant amounts. When used as seasoning and ingested on infrequent occasions, there will usually be no significant impact to the milk supply. The herbs that can cause a decrease of the milk supply when consumed in large quantities are: Parsley (*Petroselinum crispum*), Herb robert (*Geranium robertianum*), Lemon balm (*Melissa officinalis* L.), Oregano (*Origanum vulgare*), Peppermint (*Mentha piperita*), Periwinkle herb (*Vinca minor*), Sage (*Salvia officinalis*),[26] Sorrel (*Rumex acetosa*), and Spearmint (*Mentha spicata*).

Hormonal contraceptives have been found to negatively affect milk supply. Progestin-only methods of contraception, which include the minipill and the vaginal ring, and low-estrogen methods are considered compatible with breastfeeding by the American Academy of Pediatrics. However, research and anecdotal reports suggest waiting until breastfeeding is well established before starting these methods. Hormonal contraceptive methods that contain high levels of estrogen can reduce the milk supply by 20-40 percent.[39,40] For this reason, hormonal contraceptives may not be the best choice of birth control for a BFAR mother.

Conclusion

Using the specific breastfeeding techniques and mechanical and chemical devices described in this chapter to stimulate the lactation system to higher milk production is an excellent way for a BFAR mother to increase the benefits of breastfeeding her baby. Although the effectiveness of each of these techniques and devices will vary according to your unique needs, circumstances, and physiological capabilities, there is almost always a method of increasing the milk supply that will provide a sufficiently significant result to encourage you to continue breastfeeding your baby longer than you might have with a lesser milk supply. And, as you know, the longer you are able to breastfeed your baby, the greater the benefits will be for both of you.

For further information and assistance with any of these methods of increasing the milk supply, you are encouraged to contact your LLL Leader, lactation consultant, or health care provider.

REFERENCES:

1. Newman, J. *Breast Compression*. Handout #15: Jan 2000.

2. Lawrence, R. Storage of human milk and the influence of procedures on immunological components of human milk. *Acta Paediatr Suppl* Aug 1999; 88(430):14-28.

3. Barger, J. and P. Bull. A comparison of bacterial composition of breast milk stored at room temperature and stored in the refrigerator. IJCE 1987; 2:29-30.

4. Hamosh, M., L. Ellis, D. Pollock, et al. Breastfeeding and the working mother: effect of time and temperature of short-term storage on proteolysis, lipolysis, and bacterial growth in milk. *Pediatrics* 1996; 97(4):492-98.

5. The Human Milk Banking Association of America. *Recommendations for Collection, Storage, and Handling of a Mother's Milk for Her Own Infant in the Hospital Setting.* West Hartford, CT, 1993.

6. Smith, L. *My Pump Isn't Working!! Troubleshooting for Breastpump Users.* Bright Future Lactation Resource Centre website. http://www.bflrc.com/ljs/breastfeeding/pumpwork.htm

7. Farnsworth, N. Relative safety of herbal medicines. *Herbalgram* 1993; 29:36A-H.

8. Humphrey, S. and D. McKenna. Herbs and breastfeeding. BREASTFEEDING ABSTRACTS, Nov 1997; 17(2):11-12.

9. Sliutz G., P. Speiser, A. Schultz, et al. Agnus castus extracts inhibit prolactin secretion of rat pituitary cells. *Horm Metab Res* May 1993; 25(5): 253-55.

10. Tanira, M., A. Shah, A. Mohsin, et al. Pharmacological and toxicological investigations on Foeniculum vulgare dried fruit extract in experimental animals. *Phytother Res* 1996; 10:33-36.

11. Food and Drug Administration. *List of Herbs Generally Regarded as Safe.* 1995, U.S. Government Publications Office.

12. Fleiss P. Herbal remedies for the breastfeeding mother. *Mothering* Summer1988; 48(68).

13. Hale, T. *Medications and Mothers' Milk,* 9th edition. Amarillo, TX: Pharmasoft Publishing, 2000; 442-43, 260, 77, 217.

14. Newman, J. and T. Pitman. *The Ultimate Breastfeeding Book of Answers.* Roseville, CA: Prima Publishing, 2000; 85, 86-89.

15. *Physicians' Desk Reference for Herbal Medicines,* 1st edition. Montvale, NJ: Medical Economics Company, 1998; 1188-89, 761-62, 857, 963-64, 635-36, 1197-98, 1211-22, 646-47.

16. Lawrence, A. and R. Lawrence. *Breastfeeding: A Guide for the Medical Profession,* 5th edition. St. Louis, Missouri: Mosby, 1999; 376, 637.

17. Lust, J. *The Herb Book.* New York, NY: Bantam Books, 1974; 191, 394, 172, 89, 93-94, 291, 186. 173.

18. Grieve, M. *A Modern Herbal,* Vol. 1. New York, NY: Dover Publications, 1981.

19. McIntyre, A. *The Complete Woman's Herbal.* New York, NY: Henry Holt Company, 1994; 172.

20. Malinow M., E. Bardana, B. Profsky, et al. Systemic lupus erythematosus-like syndrome in monkeys fed alfalfa sprouts: Role of a nonprotein amino acid. *Science* 1982; 216:415–17.

21. Edozien, J., M. Khan, C. Waslien. Human protein deficiency: results of a Nigerian village study. *J Nutr* 1976; 106:312.

22. Newton, N. and C. Modahl. New frontiers of oxytocin research. 1980. In: van Hall, E. and W. Everaerd, Eds. *The Free Woman: Women's Health in the 1990's.* Park Ridge, NJ: The Parthenon Publishing Group, 1989.

23. THE WOMANLY ART OF BREASTFEEDING, 6th edition. Schaumburg, IL: LLLI, 1997; 226.

24. Da Silva, O., D. Knoppert, M. Angelini, et al. Effect of domperidone on milk production in mothers of premature newborns: a randomized, double-blind, placebo-controlled trial. *CMAJ* 2001; 164(1):17-21.

25. Maddern, G. Galactorhoea due to domperidone. *Med J Aust* 1983; 2:539-40.

26. Riordan, J. and K. Auerbach. *Breastfeeding and Human Lactation,* 2nd edition. Sudbury, MA: Jones and Bartlett Publishers, 1999; 167, 175.

27. Hofmeyr, G., and B. van Iddeking. Domperidone and lactation. *Lancet* 1983; I: 647.

28. Petraglia, F., V. De Leo, S. Sardelli, et al. Domperidone in defective and insufficient lactation. *Eur J Obstet Gynecol Reprod Biol* May 1985; 19(5):281-87.

29. Brown, T., P. Fernandes, L. Grant, et al. Effect of parity on pituitary prolactin response to metoclopramide and domperidone: implications for the enhancement of lactation. *J Soc Gynecol Investig* Jan-Feb 2000; 7(1):65-69.

30. De Leo, V., F. Petraglia, S. Sardelli, et al. Use of domperidone in the induction and maintenance of maternal breast feeding. *Minerva Ginecol* Apr 1986; 38(4): 311-15.

31. Cann, P., N. Read, C. Holdsworth. Galactorrhoea as side effect of domperidone. *Br Med J (Clin Res Ed)* Apr 30 1983; 286(6375):1395-96.

32. Budd, S., S. Erdman, D. Long, et al. Improved lactation with metoclopramide: a case report. *Clin Pediatr* 1993; 32:53.

33. Ehrenkrantz, R. and B. Ackerman. Metoclopramide effect on faltering milk production by mothers of premature infants. *Pediatrics* 1986; 78:614.

34. Gupta, A. and P. Gupta. Metoclopramide as a lactogogue. *Clin Pediatr* 1985; 24(5):269-272.

35. Kramer, P. Breastfeeding of adopted infants (letter). *Br Med J* 1995; 310:188.

36. McNeilly, A., M. Thorner, G. Volans, et al. Metoclopramide and prolactin. *Br Med J* 1974; 2:729.

37. *Physicians' Desk Reference*, 49th edition. Montvale, NJ: Medical Economics, 1995.

38. De Gezelle, H., W. Ooghe, M. Thiery, et al. Metoclopramide and breast milk. *Eur J Obstet Gynecol Reprod Biol* Apr 1983; 15(1):31-36.

39. Fraser, I. A review of the use of progestogen-only minipills for contraception during lactation. *Reprod Fertil Dev* 1991; 3:245-54.

40. Coxatto, H., et al. Fertility regulation on nursing women: IV. Long-term influence of a low-dose combined oral contraceptive initiated at day 30 postpartum upon lactation and infant growth. *Contraception* 1983; 27:13-25.

JANNA'S STORY

I had a breast reduction when I was 18. I asked my surgeon if I would be able to breastfeed, and his response was, "Maybe, maybe not." At 18 I knew I wanted to breastfeed, but the prospect of not being able to nurse wasn't a large factor in my decision.

I had my first child when I was 32. I had an easy birth, and my son spent four days nursing. I went to the pediatrician's office on about day two or three and met with a physician's assistant, who helped me with breastfeeding. I told her about my surgery, but she didn't seem concerned, and suggested that I cup feed Jared if he didn't seem to be getting enough. On the fourth day, my milk came in, and I was painfully engorged. I was concerned at this point that Jared wasn't getting very much milk, and I was still having difficulty nursing. I called a friend of a friend who was a nurse and had lots of breastfeeding experience. She came to my house for the next feeding, looked at my scars, and promptly told me I wouldn't be able to get any milk to my son. She said because the scars went around the nipple, there was no way for him to get any milk. I didn't know enough to ask any other questions. She told me I could get a supplementing nursing system (SNS), but I didn't think that it was possible to get one at 6:00 PM on a Friday. Little did I know I probably could have called a lactation consultant who would have shown up at my door with one an hour later. So, on the fourth day after my son was born, I gave up breastfeeding.

I drank sage tea to help my milk dry up, but I noticed that I sometimes had a few drops of milk. I would have small let-downs from time to time. I knew almost nothing about breastfeeding, and certainly nothing about breastfeeding after a reduction.

Before I got pregnant with my second child, I learned of an email list for mothers who were breastfeeding after reduction called BFAR. I wrote the list owner to ask questions, and I joined the list. I started attending La Leche League (LLL) meetings when I was five or six months pregnant, and learned everything I could about breastfeeding. I also read all the posts on the BFAR list. At the time, there was a mother who was exclusively nursing her second child, and it gave me great hope that I might be able to do the same. I met two women at LLL who had difficulty establishing their milk supplies, and both had used the SNS with their babies.

When Tauby was born, I had a lactation consultant (LC) lined up, I had a support system through LLL, and I felt prepared. Even so, I still wasn't prepared for BFAR! Tauby was 7 pounds, 12 ounces at birth. The LC had made a couple of visits in the first week to help with latch-on, and look at my very sore nipples.

I tried to exclusively breastfeed, but when Tauby was down to 6 pounds, 3 ounces at 12 days, and still not gaining, I decided to supplement. She was definitely hungry, and quickly drank what I gave her. I got a few bottles, and asked my LC for an SNS, which she brought over and demonstrated. It took me a few days to get used to it.

When Tauby was four or five weeks old, and my supply still seemed pretty minimal, I rented a pump. I pumped about a teaspoon the first time, and I was never able to pump much more than a half-ounce, so I quickly gave up on pumping. I started taking herbs and I used fenugreek with success. I also used vitex and blessed thistle. I drank a lot of water and used a protein supplement upon rising and before bed. I used breast compression and massage to improve the milk flow while I nursed, and I drank Mother's Milk tea with dill seeds every morning.

I used the SNS until Tauby was two months old, and then switched to just breast and bottles. Tauby was quite comfortable going between bottles and breast and it was much easier than the SNS. I offered the breast often, and she became a good comfort nurser. I never provided a very large milk supply for her, but we had a very nice nursing relationship. Our BFAR experience was a successful one, but it sure was hard during those first two months!

BREASTFEEDING PROBLEMS FROM THE BFAR PERSPECTIVE

Now that your BFAR experience is well underway, you may encounter breastfeeding problems that are not directly related to your surgery. This chapter addresses the common difficulties you may run into that specifically relate to BFAR. It is not a comprehensive analysis of all breastfeeding problems because many are not impacted by the post-surgical factor.

For common breastfeeding problems unrelated to BFAR, you can find excellent information in La Leche League International's THE WOMANLY ART OF BREASTFEEDING and other basic breastfeeding books. If your problem cannot be solved by the information in these books, it will be important for you to contact a La Leche League Leader or lactation consultant for personal assistance because sometimes the expertise, experience, and objectivity of a trained breastfeeding counselor is necessary to resolve a breastfeeding problem.

When you are experiencing breastfeeding difficulties, the advice you receive from others who are not knowledgeable about lactation can be very detrimental, even to the point of jeopardizing your breastfeeding relationship. Inaccurate and inappropriate advice from family members, friends, or even misinformed health professionals, can undermine your confidence and coerce you into making decisions that are counterproductive to your original BFAR goals.

By reviewing the information presented in this chapter and seeking out information from competent lactation specialists, especially those who are knowledgeable about BFAR, so that you will have the resources you need to maximize your BFAR success.

Nipple/Areola Problems

Nipple Soreness

It is not uncommon for any new mother to experience some nipple tenderness in the first few days after birth. This usually happens because the milk has not yet come in and the baby's sucking is causing negative pressure on the empty sinuses under the areola. When the sinuses are filled with milk, this kind of pressure cannot exist.[1] For this reason, BFAR mothers may experience tenderness past the newborn stage if milk is barely or not at all present. Many BFAR mothers find that their babies' non-nutritive sucking after they fall asleep can be especially painful in the early weeks. When this occurs, it is helpful to gently wake the baby and move him to the other side. Over a short period of time, the nipple and areola will adapt even though the milk supply may be scant, and, provided that latching-on, positioning, and sucking are correct, nursing will not be uncomfortable.

It is important not to confuse tenderness with actual nipple soreness. If you feel significant pain or discomfort at any time, especially if you see cracks or wounds, this indicates that the baby is not positioned or latched-on well, or he has an incorrect sucking technique. There may be other problems, such as a yeast infection, that can also cause pain. Any significant level of pain requires an immediate consultation with a lactation specialist. Suffering through it will only diminish your milk supply because pain inhibits the let-down reflex and can make you dread and delay feedings. It is not normal and it will not get better with time unless the problem is identified and treated accordingly.

Some BFAR mothers wonder if the results of the surgery itself can cause pain while breastfeeding. In some rare cases, scar tissue interior to the breast from the surgery can cause adhesions that create pain as they bind together tissue that normally would move independently. Such adhesions, though, which usually occur in the nipple/areolar complex, most often stretch and cease to cause pain after a very short time. If you should experience pain, it is best to completely rule out the normal latching-on, positioning, and sucking causes before assuming that adhesions are causing your pain. Adhesions cannot cause cracked, blistered, or bleeding nipples.

Nipple/areola soreness can also be caused by a bottle-supplemented baby who seems to nurse well from the breast but is actually nipple confused because he is using the technique that he learned from sucking artificial nipples, which also includes pacifiers. When this happens, the baby is not effectively milking the breasts, which means he is not getting all the milk that you are producing and your milk supply will ultimately diminish. If you are using bottles to supplement and are experiencing nipple soreness, you have two options. You can consult with a lactation specialist to try to teach your baby to consistently suckle your breast correctly while you continue to use bottles. Or you can stop using artificial nipples and exclusively supplement with an at-breast supplementer.

Nipple Shields

Nipple shields, which are thin latex or silicone coverings that fit over the nipple and areola, are occasionally recommended to help breastfeeding continue when significant nipple trauma has occurred. Unfortunately, nipple shields are no different from any artificial nipple in their ability to cause nipple confusion/preference. They, too, are an artificial nipple and the baby will suckle differently from them even though they are positioned on a human breast. It is important to keep in mind that the original nipple trauma is often caused by incorrect latching-on or suckling, so that using an artificial nipple merely reinforces the incorrect technique. Another danger is that some babies also become so used to a nipple shield that they will not nurse at the breast without it.

It is occasionally recommended that mothers use at-breast supplementers in combination with nipple shields to entice reluctant, nipple-confused nursers to take the breast. The thinking is that they will be more comfortable with the feel of the artificial nipple and the supplementer will supply enough flow to keep them interested. Unfortunately, as discussed above, this merely reinforces the reliance upon artificial nipples. It can also be messy and awkward, which can discourage an already stressed BFAR mother.

The most critical problem, though, is that, in addition to the danger of nipple confusion/preference, nipple shields significantly reduce stimulation to the breast, reducing prolactin secretion and ultimately resulting in a diminished milk supply, which some research studies show can be a consistent reduction of up to 58 percent.[2] Nipple shields, therefore, pose such a tremendous danger to the unstable BFAR milk supply that they are simply not recommended as a means of overcoming nipple trauma.

Nipple Blanching

Based on anecdotal evidence, it seems to be common for BFAR mothers to experience a phenomenon that is otherwise rare among breastfeeding mothers, called *blanching* or *nipple vasospasm*. Blanching occurs when either the tip of the nipple or the entire nipple becomes rigid, squeezing out all blood and turning completely white. After some time, it may turn blue, and then the nipple will relax and a deep purple-red color will flush the entire nipple as the blood returns. It is very painful, often including numbness, burning, and tingling. It can last several minutes and occur frequently, even in between feedings.

It is not known why BFAR mothers experience blanching so commonly. It may be a result of blood supply disruption or nerve trauma to the nipple/areola complex during the surgery.

Blanching can also be caused by many factors, however, that are unrelated to surgical trauma. At one time, it was thought that the phenomenon was a psychosomatic disorder (a manifestation of psychological disturbance).[3] It is now a well-known medical disorder, and is believed to be caused by physical factors, as well as external physical or chemical causes.[4]

Some cases of nipple blanching have been identified by numerous clinical studies as a manifestation of *Raynaud's Syndrome*, a disorder that causes blanching in the extremities.[5] Raynaud's Syndrome usually affects extremities such as fingers and toes in persons who are not lactating, but it can also affect coronary, pulmonary, ocular, gastrointestinal, penile, placental, and cerebral blood vessels. In nursing mothers, though, it seems to affect the nipples. Mothers who experience true Raynaud's Syndrome have experienced this disorder before breastfeeding as blanching in other parts of the body. They may have Primary Raynaud's Syndrome with no other symptoms or Secondary Raynaud's Syndrome, which is caused by an underlying autoimmune or connective tissue disorder.

In mothers who do not have Raynaud's Syndrome, blanching may be caused by either external physical or chemical factors. A vigorous suckling technique, with a tight jaw and clamping, can precipitate blanching, as can poor latching-on and positioning techniques. Exposure to cold can also precipitate nipple blanching. Some drugs, such as theophylline, terbutaline, epinephrine, norepinephrine, serotonin, nicotine, and caffeine are known to cause vasoconstriction, which can manifest in the nipple.[1]

The treatment of nipple blanching depends on the cause of the blanching. When it is caused by Raynaud's Syndrome, blanching can be improved by the use of food supplements such as calcium and magnesium, as well as evening primrose oil (gamma linoleic acid), and fish oil (eicosapentanoic acid and docosahexanoic acid). Unfortunately, it can take up to six weeks to see improvement with these supplements.

When the discomfort from nipple blanching is severe, a prescription medication may be warranted, despite the original cause of the blanching. The most commonly prescribed drug for the treatment of nipple blanching is nifedipine, which is a calcium channel blocker. It has been shown to be clinically effective in reducing nipple blanching fifty to ninety-one percent of the time. It passes into the milk at a rate of under five percent, which presents virtually no risk to the nursing child. The side effects that are most commonly seen from use of this drug are headache, flushing, dizziness, rapid heartbeat, and edema in the extremities.[5, 6]

Nipple blanching that is caused by poor positioning, latch-on, or suckling techniques is resolved by improvements to those techniques. Nipple blanching caused by exposure to cold can be prevented by keeping the entire body warm at all times as it is not enough to keep just the nipples warm. When it has already occurred, however, applying warm compresses to the nipple and gently squeezing blood back into the nipple can relax the spasm enough to stop the blanching.

Breast Problems

Engorgement

The issue of engorgement and methods to resolve it have been addressed in several places in this book because engorgement can be such a significant first hurdle in BFAR. Despite the cause or the extent of the engorgement and no matter when it is experienced, it is important to relieve the engorgement in a timely manner so as to avoid damage to functional alveoli, which can permanently reduce lactation capability. The discussion of engorgement management techniques in Chapter 7 will be helpful in coping with any engorgement that you may experience.

Most BFAR mothers with surviving lactational tissue will experience some degree of engorgement following delivery of their first babies. It is usually after delivery of the second baby, though, that engorgement becomes pronounced enough to cause serious discomfort and interfere with breastfeeding. This is because the first lactation experience prompted the recanalization and growth of additional lactational tissue, which is then subject to engorgement. Fortunately, it usually subsides more quickly the second time around.

The extent of recanalization bears a direct correlation between the degree of the first and subsequent engorgement episodes. BFAR mothers who have lactated longer with the first child will usually experience more engorgement following the next delivery as a result of recanalization than those BFAR mothers who lactated for only a short time. Engorgement following the third and subsequent births tends to be at least as pronounced as it was the previous time, and may even be more extensive as a result of further recanalization.

Apart from the pain and discomfort of engorgement, many BFAR mothers find that the engorgement experience is made more difficult by health care professionals who tend to refer to the engorgement as an inevitable result of severed ducts rather than as proof of functional lactational tissue. Instead of being reassured by the evidence of recanalization, the BFAR mother is warned about the unfounded risk of breast infections and the mistaken belief that the engorgement will take much longer than normal to resolve since the "milk has nowhere to go."

This is incorrect advice, of course, from the standpoint of both general lactation knowledge and BFAR physiology. From the general lactation perspective, engorgement is not a result of a large volume of milk so much as it is swelling of the tissues that surround the glands and ducts. Thus, the presence of milk in severed ducts is not responsible for the majority of the engorgement, and so will not have a bearing upon its progress. When the milk is not removed, the severed ducts atrophy almost immediately, so they do not become extended with "backed up" milk.

From the BFAR perspective, it is very rare, if it happens at all, that severed ducts become infected as a result of milk stagnation; in most cases they quickly dry up from lack of milk removal and stimulation. The anecdotal experience has consistently shown that severed ducts cannot be accessed by bacterial infection, and so do not become infected as a result of "stagnation."

Mastitis

Although mastitis caused by bacterial breast infections or lactiferous tissue inflammation rarely, if ever, occur as a result of postpartum engorgement, it does happen to some BFAR mothers, just as it can happen to any breastfeeding mother. Mastitis is usually experienced as fever, headache, and body aches, and a painful, red, hardened area on one breast. Fortunately, though, mastitis is fairly rare and many nursing mothers never experience it.

Mastitis often begins when milk has stagnated in the ducts because of a plugged duct (not a severed duct), an area of swollen tissue surrounding a duct, or infrequent or irregular removal of milk from the ducts. It can also be caused by introduction of bacteria from infected sores on the nipple, improperly strong suction from a breast pump, or any trauma to the breast.

One cause of mastitis that is directly related to BFAR is profound fluctuations in the milk supply caused by beginning, ending, or changing galactagogue use. The additional stress and fatigue that BFAR mothers experience can also cause them to be more susceptible to mastitis.

When mastitis occurs in BFAR mothers, it is a far more serious problem because aside from compounding an already complex and stressful situation, it can also temporarily decrease the milk supply.[7] Preventing mastitis and resolving it as quickly as possible if it does occur, are key to minimizing the impact mastitis can have upon BFAR.

Mastitis can be prevented in most cases by making sure that milk is completely and regularly removed from your breasts. If you are pumping, be sure to pump long enough to remove most of the existing foremilk from your breasts. When you are nursing, offer frequent, regular feedings, and avoid separations from your baby that can result in long intervals between feedings. If you must be away, pump or hand express your milk at the time of the regular feeding. During vacations and holidays, make sure that you maintain your regular schedule. Many cases of mastitis occur during holidays or visits from relatives because it is easy to become distracted and not nurse as frequently. Mastitis has also been known to occur from strenuous upper-body exercises.[8] Finally, avoid wearing constrictive clothing, especially bras that are too tight or press against breast tissue. Underwire bras in particular can be a source of pressure.

If you do develop symptoms that suggest you may have mastitis, contact your health care provider right away. The sooner treatment begins, the less impact the mastitis will have on your milk supply. In most cases, an antibiotic will be prescribed. You may wish to confirm that the drug that is prescribed is compatible with breastfeeding by consulting a reliable resource text such as *Medications and Mothers' Milk*. Most LLL Leaders have access to a copy of this book. You will also need to make sure that you take the entire prescribed course of the antibiotic and not simply stop taking it when you feel better. Even though the symptoms may no longer bother you, the bacteria is still present for a period of time afterward and could easily lead to another infection.

In addition to antibiotic treatment, it is also important that you slow down your activities for a few days and rest as much as possible. Your body needs a great deal of pampering and nurturing to help it heal from this serious infection. Drink an extra amount of fluids and try to eat as nutritiously as possible. Be sure to nurse as often as you can on the infected breast so that the milk has no opportunity to stagnate. Try to have your baby nurse in as many different positions as you can devise so that all the ducts are well-drained. If you have a sore spot on your breast, point his nose toward the spot, which will specifically drain the ducts that are in the affected area. Don't worry that the milk will hurt your baby; the bacteria that caused the infection will not be present in your milk.

Because you are a BFAR mother, if you experience pain, it is very important to talk to your health care provider about taking an appropriate pain medication to avoid any risk of the pain reducing your milk supply.

Surgical Adhesions

Adhesions formed after breast surgery are frequently discussed in medical literature and are often attributed as the cause of breast pain in BFAR mothers. The observed prevalence of adhesions, however, as a significant cause of post-surgical complications in BFAR mothers is fairly low.

Nonetheless, some breast pain felt by BFAR mothers, especially during their first lactation experience, can be attributed to adhesions. Adhesions are comprised of scar tissue that forms connections between layers of tissue after surgery. The binding together of the tissue layers that would normally move independently is painful. The adhesions can vary in severity, from thin, filmy adhesions, to thick, vascular adhesions, to dense cohesive adhesions. The thinner the adhesion, of course, the less pain it causes and the easier it is to break by exterior or surgical methods. Over time, adhesions shorten, and depending on the type of adhesion, can introduce pain that did not previously exist. This pain can significantly inhibit the let-down reflex, and thus reduce the milk supply.

When an adhesion is suspected, the first remedy is to try to move the layers of tissue by frequent, gentle massage, which will break the adhesions if they are not too dense. In the case of nipple adhesions, the nipples can be gently pulled outward. With time and active use of the breast, the adhesions will usually diminish in severity.

Unfortunately, when BFAR mothers have a sharp, stabbing breast pain, it is very common for their physicians to mistakenly attribute the cause of the pain to adhesions. The mothers are frequently told there is nothing that can be done about it and the pain is something to be suffered through. In fact, however, in many cases the actual cause of this type of pain is thrush, a yeast infection (*Candida*) which is treatable. Therefore, it is important to rule out the more common causes of breast pain in lactating women before attributing it conclusively to adhesions.

Silent Breast Wounds

It is important to regularly check the parts of your breasts that are not normally visible as part of your normal breast care. This suggestion is made because upon occasion BFAR mothers have been surprised to discover sores, abscesses, or wounds that were within the area of tissue that was still numb from the surgery, but which was out of the line of sight. Such wounds can become infected if not properly treated.

Itching

Many BFAR mothers find that the scar tissue around the perimeter of their areolas and on and under their breasts causes severe itching, which can inhibit the let-down reflex. The itching can come and go, with no clear precipitating factors. If you find that this is causing you discomfort and interfering with your nursing experience, it may be helpful to visit a dermatologist who can recommend an effective treatment.

Baby's Problems

Nipple Confusion/Preference

Nipple confusion/preference has been discussed in many sections of this book. It can manifest in many ways, ranging from a mildly improper sucking technique to complete rejection of the breast. Even though BFAR mothers may know it is a very real phenomenon, there are times that they feel it is a necessary risk or trade-off for the benefits of using artificial nipples. Fortunately, there are some babies who just never seem to have any difficulty switching back and forth from breast to artificial nipple. It is possible, though, that those babies have developed a nursing technique that allows them to extract milk from both sources, but which does not extract milk from the breast very effectively.

Signs of suck confusion may include:

- The baby opening his mouth, but not latching on;
- The baby shaking his head from side to side, rearing back, looking for the nipple and appearing puzzled;
- The baby reacting by screaming and/or arching his back;

- The baby not opening his mouth widely enough to latch on to the breast;
- The baby's tongue not extending to the lower gum line, but instead being retracted or raised;
- The tongue not curling around the nipple the way it should (like the bun around a hot dog);
- The baby seeming to latch on well but not suck.[9]

For those babies who do demonstrate clear nipple confusion/preference, getting them back to nursing well at the breast can be a challenge. Nipple confusion is more prone to occur in babies of BFAR mothers simply because supplementation is more likely during BFAR than during normal breastfeeding.

As suggested earlier in the section about nipple soreness, it is almost always necessary to work with a trained lactation specialist, such as an LLL Leader or a lactation consultant in order to resolve nipple confusion/preference. In most cases, the use of artificial nipples will be stopped and the baby will be encouraged to take all feedings at the breast using an at-breast supplementer.

Coaxing a baby back to the breast can sometimes be difficult, but most mothers find that lots of skin-to-skin contact helps to remind a baby of the pleasure of feeding from the breast. Many babies are also more receptive to breastfeeding when they are drowsy from a nap or during the night. Feeding an ounce (30 ml) of milk from a cup or other non-nipple feeding method before attempting breastfeeding can also help a baby become less frantic and more patient with nursing. Breast compression during breastfeeding helps increase the immediate milk flow, which gives babies more incentive to continue nursing. Your LLL Leader or lactation consultant will have more techniques to share with you that will help overcome your baby's nipple confusion/preference.

Sudden Refusal to Breastfeed (Nursing Strikes)

A sudden refusal by a baby to breastfeed is called a nursing strike. It can be disturbing to any mother, but it is especially worrisome to a BFAR mother who may already be feeling insecure or unsure about her breastfeeding relationship. It is very important for BFAR mothers to understand that a sudden refusal to nurse is a not rejection of the breastfeeding relationship and it is absolutely not indicative of your baby's decision to wean. True weaning is a slow, gradual process over many months. An abrupt nursing strike is your baby's way of telling you in the only way he knows that something is wrong. Determining exactly what this message means can sometimes take a bit of detective work.

An obvious cause for a nursing strike is nipple confusion/preference. If you have been using artificial nipples increasingly often, it is possible that this is the cause of the problem. In this case, your baby is not telling you that he prefers bottles to breastfeeding, but rather that he finds it just too difficult to do them both. It takes a specific sucking technique to make the milk flow well from a breast and yet a different technique altogether to feed from a bottle. Although breastfeeding is a far more pleasurable tactile activity for babies, sometimes babies will opt for the easier, faster flow of the bottle. They don't really prefer the bottle over the breast, they just don't find it as easy to feed well from the breast. Removing the option of the artificial nipples and teaching the baby how to properly nurse at the breast again is the way to get back on track. Until your baby is readily accepting the breast, though, you may need to feed him with a non-nipple feeder such as a cup, syringe, or spoon.

Babies can also have nursing strikes for other reasons, such as teething, nasal congestion, reactions to stress, being frightened by a mothers' involuntary reaction to biting, or any number of other causes. Despite the reason, though, patience, perseverance, and conviction of the absolute truth that feeding from the breast is best for your baby are key to resuming your breastfeeding relationship. There are many good ideas for overcoming nursing strikes in LLLI's THE WOMANLY ART OF BREASTFEEDING. Your LLL Leader or lactation consultant will also be helpful in showing you how to get past this obstacle.

Until your baby resumes his normal nursing pattern, it is important that you continue to remove your milk by pumping with an automatic electric pump at least as often as your baby had previously been nursing.

Refusal of One Breast

A variation on the nursing strike is a baby's refusal to nurse from one breast while he continues to nurse normally from the other. This seems to happen fairly often to BFAR mothers when babies prefer the significantly greater milk flow from the breast that was impacted least by the surgery, or when there are significant differences between the nipples as a result of the surgery.

Refusal to nurse from one breast can also be caused by issues that are unrelated to your surgery. For instance, an ear infection or an injury from the delivery, such as a shoulder dislocation, hernia, misaligned neck vertebrae, or broken clavicle, can be painful for the baby when he is placed to nurse in a certain position.[8] Occasionally, babies will refuse to nurse from one side because the milk suddenly tastes differently. This can be caused by mastitis [7] or the return of menses.[1] Although it is very rare, refusal to nurse from one breast can also indicate the presence of abnormal tissue growth, such as a cyst or a tumor.[10] For these reasons, it is recommended that you consult both your and your baby's health care provider to rule out any underlying physical problems that may be causing the refusal of the one breast.

Fortunately, resolving the problem and getting your baby back to nursing well on both breasts is almost always possible. Many BFAR mothers find that a good way to get their babies to nurse from the refused side is to first nurse the baby from the preferred side in the cradle hold until the baby is finished. Then, without changing the baby's position at all, slide him over to the other side, using a pillow to support your arm. The less his position is changed when you move him over, the better.

If your baby has an injury or ear infection, finding a position that does not cause him pain is especially important to reestablishing a pleasant nursing experience.

Coaxing your baby to nurse when he is sleepy, just as you would during a nursing strike, is also a good way to get him reaccustomed to nursing from both breasts. If these techniques are not effective, your LLL Leader or lactation consultant will be able to work with you to find an effective method.

Biting

Almost all nursing babies bite at one time or another, but when a BFAR mother is bitten, it can a problem for several reasons. First, depending on the sensitivity of her areola/nipple complex, she may not feel the bite until the skin is broken, which can lead to a topical infection and radiating pain that can be felt. If she does have sensitivity, the pain from the biting, combined with fear of future biting, may inhibit her let-down reflex.

Although the experience can be worse for BFAR mothers, nursing couples can almost always get past biting behavior without much difficulty. It is a matter of gently conveying the message to the baby that biting is simply not acceptable. There are several ways to teach this to your baby, including candid expressions of pain, removing him from the breast, or pulling him into the breast so that he unlatches himself. THE WOMANLY ART OF BREASTFEEDING has an excellent discussion of biting that will be helpful in working through this normal breastfeeding problem.

Breast Abrasions from Pinching

When the baby is a bit older, it is natural for him to begin gently kneading your breast with hands and fingers. This seems to be an almost instinctual behavior of most mammals to induce let-down. For this purpose, it can sometimes be very effective and should be encouraged, especially for BFAR mothers who may be worried or tense or having difficulties with let-down as a result of insufficient oxytocin.

Some children take kneading a bit further, though, and begin pinching. This can be painful for some mothers, but for many BFAR mothers, it actually may not be felt in the lower regions of the breast, which can lead to serious abrasions, especially when nails are a bit long. For this reason, it might be a good idea to keep an eye on your baby's hands, making sure you can see both of them at all times.

Monitoring Baby's Bowel Movements

As you monitor your baby's regular bowel movements, you may find, as many BFAR mothers do, that you have questions about the normalcy, appearance, and consistency of them that are not answered in the books about normal breastfeeding concerns. The following issues are commonly mentioned by BFAR mothers.

Green, Watery Stools

Occasionally, BFAR mothers will find that their babies have green, watery stools, that are sometimes even foamy. It is usually caused when the baby is not allowed to nurse long enough on at least one side to receive enough hindmilk and is called a *foremilk/hindmilk imbalance*. Such an imbalance is usually accompanied by slow weight gain and fussiness between feedings. It is not caused by damage to the lactation system–if you can make foremilk, you can make hindmilk (the higher fat, richer milk that is available later in a feeding).

There are several ways that a foremilk/hindmilk imbalance can occur. Probably the most frequent cause is the technique of switching back and forth between breasts every few minutes that is sometimes used to increase the milk supply. When this technique is used, the baby gets a lot of foremilk, but not much hindmilk. Use of this technique is not intended to be long term. It should be discontinued if baby shows signs of foremilk/hindmilk imbalance.

The key to solving a foremilk/hindmilk imbalance is to keep your baby on one side long enough so that he gets a good quantity of hindmilk. Rather than setting a specific time for him to feed at each breast, watching his cues and allowing him to determine the end of a feeding at the first side is a far better indicator of how much time he needs to get enough hindmilk and be satisfied. In general, it is best to allow him to finish the first breast completely before switching him over to the other side. For the second side, it does not matter how long he stays. Frequent feedings are also a good way to prevent too much foremilk production.

BFAR mothers who have significantly different milk supplies between their two breasts find that it is best to always begin nursing sessions with the higher volume breast, offering the second breast as "dessert."

If you've already tried the techniques described above and you don't find any difference in your baby's stools, consider whether you've begun eating anything different or more often. Green stools can also be caused by a food or drug allergy or a reaction to a nutritional supplement. Have you begun taking any new drugs or nutritional supplements? Iron supplements, in particular, can cause green stools. Such stools, however, are not usually watery or foamy. If you think that food, drugs, or nutritional supplements may be the cause of the green stools, it may be a good idea to consult with your baby's health care provider to determine the cause, as well as to rule out any other possibilities.

Infrequent Stooling

When BFAR mothers are carefully tracking wet and soiled diapers, it can be alarming to notice that their babies have begun stooling less frequently. After the first month, though, this is entirely normal and does not indicate that your milk supply has decreased. A fully breastfed baby may only have a bowel movement every few days or even once a week. In this case, the amount is copious.

When a mother is supplementing, it may be hard to determine whether the baby's stooling pattern is normal. Supplements of formula will often cause less frequent stooling. On the other hand, formula-fed babies can become constipated, which would be indicated if he has hard, dry stools. If you think something is wrong, a consultation with your baby's health care provider may be needed.

Baby Sleeping through the Night

The most frequent question asked of new mothers is whether their babies are "sleeping through the night yet." Somehow, this has come to be a sort of benchmark of maturity to some people. Or perhaps those who ask the question simply don't know much about babies and can't think of anything else to say. When a mother hears this over and over, though, she may begin to think long stretches of sleep are necessary.

The desirable length of a baby's main sleep period depends upon his age. Before the age of four months, babies are not physiologically able to go longer than four hours between feedings. Some need feedings even more frequently. Until he is four months old, then, you'll need to make sure he has at least one feeding during the night, even if you have to wake him to do it. For BFAR mothers, in particular, feeding frequently in the early months is key to increasing and maintaining an optimal milk supply.

When a baby is older, though, it is natural that his sleep patterns will begin to lengthen. Eventually, he will "sleep through the night," which is clinically defined as sleeping a five-hour period. At this point, it will be physiologically beneficial for him and will not harm your milk supply because he will simply begin taking more or longer feedings during the day. You will probably feel fullness or slight engorgement at first, but your supply will quickly adjust to providing mainly daytime feedings.

Normal vs. Abnormal Crying

As one quickly learns after becoming a parent, it is a fact of life that babies cry. At first, it can be difficult to know exactly why your baby is crying. Your first thought might be that he is hungry, but it is important to understand that babies cry for reasons other than hunger. They have no other way of communicating and have to get our attention to make things better. Your baby may be overstimulated from an active day or under-stimulated from a quiet day. He could be overtired and having difficulty settling to sleep. It's possible he has gas or is feeling an impending bowel movement. He may be too hot or too cold. His clothing may be uncomfortable; check for irritating tags or pins.

As a BFAR mother, though, it will be natural for you to discount the normal reasons for crying and be worried that your baby is crying because he is hungry. This is the time to go back to your assessment chart and reassure yourself that he is gaining well and is well hydrated. If all the basic criteria are met, you can let go of your worry that he is hungry and concentrate on other reasons for his distress. Sometimes putting him to the breast for comfort works, even if he is not hungry. Other soothing techniques to try are:

- wearing your baby in a sling or front carrier;
- walking with him around the house or outside;
- gently dancing or swaying from side to side;
- laying him face down across your lap;
- holding him face down with the heel of your hand against his tummy;
- driving;
- vacuuming;
- standing near the washer/dryer;
- singing to him;
- taking a warm bath with him.

If nothing works, after a while it may help to go back to first techniques you tried—they may work better now. If all else fails, allow someone else to have a try. Eventually, he will find peace.

Early Evening Fussiness / Colic

The most frequent phone call many LLL Leaders receive from new mothers is about regular fussiness in the early evenings. Starting around the end of the first month, a high proportion of breastfeeding mothers find that their babies are very fussy for one to three hours starting about dinnertime. It is amazing how common this phenomenon is. (It is not to be confused, however, with the fussiness that happens at three weeks, six weeks, three months, and six months when babies go through their regular growth spurts.)

Some mothers wonder if this fussiness is "colic" which is a catch-all term for regular periods of intense crying. The difference between "early evening fussiness" and "colic" is in the degree of the distress. Fussiness and persistent but gentle crying with a few bouts of hard crying are generally just "fussiness," while long stretches of hard crying with intense screams are characteristic of colic.

No one knows for sure why early evening fussiness happens, but because the breast is never fully emptied, it is unlikely to be caused by an absence of milk, even for BFAR mothers. In fact, it is very common for babies to demand to nurse during this time, but then to quickly become frustrated and pull off the breast. The problem is usually not that they aren't getting enough milk and are hungry, but rather that they are full and don't want any more milk—they just want to nurse for comfort. Of course, when this happens to a BFAR mother, it is natural for her to immediately conclude that the baby is hungry because she doesn't have enough milk and to overlook the fact that the baby has nursed happily all day until now.

When you are not already supplementing and you are worried about the well-being of your baby, it is easy to forget that the milk supply cannot suddenly drop. Feeling exhausted and vulnerable and wanting to soothe your distressed baby, you may be tempted to supplement him with formula. Before you take this drastic step, though, allow yourself a moment to breathe deeply and look over his assessment chart. Is he gaining at least three-fourths of an ounce (21 gm) a day? Is he having enough wet and soiled diapers? Is he well-hydrated? If you find that he meets all of these criteria, then you may be assured that supplementation is not necessary.

If you are already supplementing, it is equally important that you do not increase the supplement to soothe your baby's fussiness. Doing so would negatively impact your milk supply.

The true cause of early evening fussiness is probably that the baby is overtired and ready to sleep, but does not know how to make it happen. Eventually, he will learn how to relax and fall asleep when he is tired and regular evenings of crying will become a distant memory.

If your baby is regularly crying with more intensity than the crying pattern described above, it may be true colic, which is thought by some experts to be caused by spasmodic contractions of smooth muscles in the gastrointestinal tract. Typically, babies with colic will scream and pull away from the breast and only find comfort when being held upright or face down across a lap or arm. It is often helpful for someone other than the baby's mother to hold him because he will smell her milk, want to nurse, and then be in pain from the feeding. In most cases, babies suffering from colic can be comforted most easily by being held, carried, rocked, and cuddled. If your baby suffers from colic, it may be reassuring to know that it is experienced equally by breastfed babies and formula-fed babies. It is important to consult your baby's health care provider to try to determine the cause of your baby's distress so that neither you nor your baby have to suffer through such intense crying spells.

Physiological Dysfunction

Occasionally, babies suffer from physiological disorders that complicate the BFAR relationship and compound the difficulties a BFAR mother faces. The discussion of physiological dysfunctions in this section is not meant to be a comprehensive checklist, but rather is an overview of the more common infant physiological problems, particularly those that most commonly affect BFAR.

Food Allergies

Although most breastfeeding mothers can eat whatever they want, some babies are allergic to substances in their mothers' diets. Cow's milk, eggs, nuts, corn, and wheat are common culprits. The most frequent evidence of food allergies are gastrointestinal distress, stool changes, including blood in the stool, and eczema. Allergies can manifest in many ways, though, and it is sometimes necessary to have your child tested with either a skin test or a blood test to determine the source of his allergic reactions.

When a food is known to cause an allergic reaction in your baby, it will be necessary for you to completely remove it from your diet. This means that you will have to begin reading every label and taking great care when you dine out. The Food Allergy and Anaphylaxis Network (FAAN) is a helpful resource for learning to live with food allergies (See Appendix 1 for contact information). If you are supplementing and your child is diagnosed with an allergy to cow's milk protein, your baby's health care provider may recommend that you switch to a hypoallergenic protein hydrolysate formula. The protein in this type of formula is hydrolyzed, or broken down into smaller parts, and is less likely to cause an allergic reaction.

Occasionally, what is actually an allergy to cow's milk protein is mistakenly called "lactose intolerance," which can make a BFAR mother feel that something is wrong with her milk since human milk does contain lactose. Lactose, though, is a milk sugar that is essential for brain development and babies need it. True lactose intolerance, which is caused by a deficit of lactase, the enzyme that breaks down lactose, is not usually seen before early adulthood.

Gastroesophageal Reflux (GER)

Gastroesophageal Reflux (GER), which is also known simply as "reflux," occurs when the valve in the esophagus leading to the stomach does not close properly and contents of the stomach, including acids, rise into the esophagus and cause significant pain. Mothers usually notice this as "spitting up" in greater-than-normal amounts. All babies experience some degree of reflux because the esophageal valve is not mature at birth. It works more effectively in some babies than others, though. Those babies in whom it allows large amounts of stomach fluid to burn the esophagus are diagnosed as having "reflux." The problem may not be evident for several weeks until the esophagus has become irritated by repeated exposure to the acidic contents of the stomach. In most cases, reflux is not diagnosed until the baby begins to experience troublesome symptoms such as pain, difficulty feeding, or poor weight gain.

Reflux can be present even though the baby does not spit up an abnormal amount of feedings. This rare form of reflux, called "silent reflux," occurs when the stomach contents are brought up into the esophagus, but are reswallowed before exiting the mouth. This type of reflux is harder to diagnose without special x-ray tests.

In most babies with reflux, the esophageal valve matures at around six months of age when the baby begins sitting up and is vertical for longer periods in the day. It can, however, persist throughout or beyond the first year.

The most common symptoms of reflux are:

- Frequent/excessive spitting up and/or vomiting;
- Spitting up or vomiting hours after a feeding;
- Difficulty swallowing;
- Excessive crying;
- Crying out as if in sudden pain shortly after eating;
- Pulling away from the breast in distress;
- Arching back away from breast, or arching back while being held;
- Refusal to feed;
- Poor sleeping patterns;
- Foul, sour-smelling breath;
- Sudden gulping, gagging, or choking during a feed (not associated with let-down);
- Gulping, swallowing, or choking in between feeds;
- Gulping, choking, or coughing while sleeping;
- Frequent burping or hiccupping;
- Frequent red or sore throat;
- Rumination (chewing) between feeds;
- General difficulty with feeding;
- Slow weight gain;
- Frequent ear infections;
- Respiratory problems.[11]

A common scenario that many mothers with babies with reflux have experienced begins as she nurses her baby, who seems to feed well and is content after feeding. The baby may even drift off to sleep. After a short while (10 to 30 minutes), the baby begins fussing again, often quite vigorously. The mother may nurse again, or supplement, thinking that her baby is still hungry. The baby eats again, but spits up/vomits during this feeding or shortly after. The more the baby spits up/vomits the more the baby's esophagus becomes irritated, which causes more pain and crying. Because swallowing milk is soothing and helps stop the pain, the baby indicates a need to eat. But the stomach is full, so the baby continues to spit up/vomit, thus exacerbating the problem. Or, in a similar fashion, the baby may nurse well until the end of the feeding, then become upset, distressed, and pull off the breast. At this point the mother may think that her baby is not getting enough milk and is frustrated. In actuality, the baby may be experiencing reflux as the stomach fills up and milk leaks back up the esophagus.

Reflux can be especially problematic in BFAR because reflux babies often indicate that they want to eat even when they are not hungry in an attempt to soothe the burning pain in their throats. This frequently causes the BFAR mother to doubt the adequacy of her milk supply, since the baby may be fussy at the breast.

There are several treatments for infant reflux. One of the most effective is keeping the baby in a vertical position as often as possible, including during feedings, and especially after feedings, to use gravity to minimize regurgitation. Some mothers find that using a sling or front carrier allows them to position their babies at breast level so that they can nurse while standing or walking. To feed while sitting, it may be helpful to use a recliner or lean against several pillows on the sofa or in bed.

Another technique is to offer shorter, more frequent feedings, which prevent the baby's stomach from becoming too full, while at the same time increasing the amount of hindmilk that the baby receives. While at-breast supplementers are best when supplementation is necessary because they maximize the milk supply, if you are supplementing with bottles, it is best to use a very slow-flow nipple to better control the flow of the supplement.

If you are supplementing, your physician may suggest that you add cereal to the supplement to thicken it. Although research has not shown this treatment method to be effective, many doctors prefer to try it before prescribing medication. Even if you are not supplementing, your physician may recommend that you give your baby cereal by spoon.

In some babies, especially those who are supplemented with formula, reflux may be related to an allergy to cow's milk or soy. If this is the case for your baby, it may be necessary for you to eliminate all dairy products from your diet. Your baby's pediatrician may recommend using a hypoallergenic protein hydrolysate formula.

It is important to consult with your physician if you suspect that your child suffers from reflux. There are several drugs available by prescription that greatly improve infant reflux.

High Palate

A very small number of babies are born with very high palates (the roof of the mouth). These babies cannot suckle the nipple properly, and, as a result, not enough milk is expressed. Because the milk supply is not fully stimulated, the baby does not gain well. For BFAR mothers, of course, it is natural to place the blame on the breast surgery and overlook the problem of the high palate.

One way to rule out high palate as a cause of a low milk supply is to check to see if your baby's palate looks to be deeper than the curve of a teaspoon. Another way is to allow your baby to suck on your little finger with the nail side down. If he has a high palate, you will feel a frequent loss of suction between your finger and his tongue. You may also notice that your finger isn't in firm contact with the roof of his mouth.[12]

Since there is not much, if anything, that can be done about a baby's high palate, it may mean that a BFAR mother will need to use a pump or galactagogues to provide extra stimulation when she needs to increase her milk supply.

Ankyloglossia (Tongue Tie)

Another oral abnormality is *ankyloglossia*, commonly known as tongue tie. A baby with a tongue tie cannot extend the tip of his tongue over his gums because his tongue is connected to the bottom of his mouth by a membrane called a *frenulum*, which is shorter than normal. When babies with tied tongues cry, their tongues pull into the shape of a heart. Unfortunately, nursing is extremely difficult for babies with tied tongues because they cannot use their tongues to properly compress the nipple.

Most mothers first become aware of the problem when they develop sore nipples. Eventually, the milk supply is decreased because it does not receive adequate stimulation, which can cause a BFAR mother to mistakenly believe her low milk supply is due to her surgery.

It is important, then, to have a pedodontist (a pediatric dentist) or an ear, nose, and throat (ENT) physician specialist, evaluate a baby who is suspected of having a tongue tie. Fortunately, there is a simple treatment to cure a tongue tie. Short frenulums can be clipped to allow freer tongue movement. This procedure, called a *frenotomy*, is relatively simple and bloodless, and can be performed in the physician's office. Most babies are able to nurse immediately afterward, with dramatic improvement.[13-15]

Hospitalizing the BFAR Baby

Unfortunately, it is sometimes necessary for babies to be hospitalized. Should hospitalization be necessary for your child, you may find that you need to be very assertive about your need to supplement with an at-breast supplementer in order to avoid nipple confusion/preference. Not all pediatric specialists are familiar with this supplementation device, or they may not be aware of its importance. Being assertive at a time like this, though, can be very difficult. You may feel overwhelmed and vulnerable. You may also have limited access to your child which will increase your anxiety. But remember that you are your baby's mother, which is a very powerful position. You have a great deal more authority than you may realize and you have every right to think of yourself as an equal member of the team working to heal your baby.

A La Leche League Leader or a lactation consultant can be a great help to you at a time like this. She can listen to your concerns, offer emotional support, and give you accurate information about the best ways to manage feedings and supplementation while maximizing your milk supply during this difficult time.

Baby Addicted to the At-Breast Supplementer

Occasionally, a baby will refuse to nurse without an at-breast supplementer, even when a mother has a full milk supply. To him, having that tube present with the nipple is "normal" and he feels uncomfortable when it is not there, even though it may not be releasing any supplement. Weaning him away from needing the at-breast supplementer usually requires some ingenuity and a creative approach, similar to those necessary when overcoming nursing strikes. Many mothers find it helpful to nurse without the supplementer when their babies are sleepy, or to nurse in a warm bath with the lights down low. Eventually, your baby will grow past needing to have the at-breast supplementer and you will be able to move forward into an unencumbered breastfeeding relationship.

Mother's Problems

Sleep Deprivation

Motherhood seems to go hand-in-hand with some degree of sleep deprivation. For BFAR mothers, this lack of sleep can inhibit your milk supply, so it is important to try to minimize it, or at least its impact, as much as possible.

One way to do this is to try to avoid looking at the clock at night. Don't pay any attention to when you were awakened or how long you were up. Knowing those numbers can really add to your anxiety when you compare them to the "normal" amount of required sleep.

Many experts and mothering books recommend napping while the baby naps during the day. This is excellent advice and should be followed whenever possible, although it is not always practical. Still, try to do it when you can and do not worry about anything else that needs to be done. Your rest is very important.

For BFAR mothers who must supplement at night, you need to be awake longer for nighttime feedings because you have to prepare the supplement. Streamlining the process so that as little time as possible is spent preparing supplement will be helpful. Some mothers do this by using small coolers filled with ice or frozen blue-packs next to their bed in which they place already prepared at-breast supplementers or bottles. If warming a bottle is necessary, an electric bottle warmer can be used at the nightstand. It may be helpful to have a nightlight or bedside light with low wattage available so that you can see to prepare the supplement. Of course, for many mothers, the best way to conserve sleep is to have their partners prepare the supplement.

Many BFAR mothers find that sleeping with their babies is a helpful way to harmonize nighttime feedings. If you are able to avoid supplementation, at least at night, you will not need to fully awaken and leave your warm bed in order to meet your baby's needs. Once your baby is correctly latched on, you can fall back asleep. If you do need to supplement, you can do so in the comfort of your own bed, which will be less rousing for you than feeding your baby in another room. This can make a great difference in the amount of sleep you get each night. You will find a complete discussion of sleeping with your baby in LLLI's THE WOMANLY ART OF BREASTFEEDING, Tine Thevenin's book *The Family Bed*, and *Nighttime Parenting* by Dr. William Sears.

Fertility and BFAR

In the normal course of breastfeeding, when surgery has not been a factor, fertility is usually suppressed during the first few months of lactation when the baby is nursing exclusively, without any supplements, and feedings are never spaced longer than five hours. This is called *lactational amenorrhea* and is a result of the high level of prolactin present during lactation. Although there is no predictable timeframe for the return of menses in breastfeeding mothers, it usually occurs in the latter part of the baby's first year, and frequently even later. Of course, since ovulation can occur before menstruation, absence of menses cannot be interpreted as infertility. In general, though, most breastfeeding mothers who do not supplement and feed on demand, even at night, have diminished fertility.[16]

Many BFAR mothers wonder how BFAR affects fertility, especially when they are supplementing. While there are no hard and fast rules about fertility because each woman's physiology is different, fertility is definitely affected by three factors: the amount of supplementation, the frequency of feedings, and any galactogenic substances that affect the hormonal response.[1]

If you are supplementing, your body will not be receiving the same amount of stimulation that it would if you were exclusively breastfeeding. Therefore, your fertility will return sooner than it would if you were exclusively breastfeeding. Of course, this is also relative—if you are supplementing only a little, then your likely degree of fertility is increased only a small amount, whereas if you are supplementing a great deal, you are much more likely to become fertile sooner than a mother who is exclusively breastfeeding.[17]

The frequency of feedings also plays a part in fertility with BFAR, just as it does with normal breastfeeding. Longer stretches between feedings are more likely to hasten a return to fertility than frequent feedings.[17]

On the other hand, if you are taking galactagogues to increase your milk supply, they may have an effect of decreasing your fertility, especially if they act directly on prolactin production. Domperidone, in particular, is known to suppress ovulation.[18]

The bottom line, though, is that in most circumstances BFAR will not suppress fertility as effectively as exclusive breastfeeding, which entails no supplementation, solids, or regular intervals longer than five hours between feedings.

Supply Coinciding with Menstrual Cycle

Once their menstrual periods return, many mothers report that their babies are fussy at the time of the month they are menstruating. This could be related to hormonal effects or perhaps a mother is feeling more tense and this affects the let-down response. Many mothers may also find that their milk supplies decrease to a small degree during menstruation.[8] Because their milk supplies are so tenuous, BFAR mothers may choose to use the methods described in Chapter 9, such as additional use of herbal galactagogues or relaxation techniques, to enhance their let-down reflex during this time each month.

Pregnancy

BFAR mothers who are actively lactating and become pregnant are often concerned about the effect that the pregnancy may have upon their milk supplies. If they are using galactagogues, they may also be concerned about the effect such substances may have upon the pregnancy.

Most BFAR mothers find that their milk supplies begin to markedly decrease during the first trimester of pregnancy. Each woman is different, of course, and it also depends upon the amount of stimulation your lactation system is receiving, but it is safe to say that there is almost always some degree of decrease. And, of course, toward the middle of the pregnancy, your milk will begin converting back to colostrum, which will also significantly decrease the volume.

Most galactagogues are not safe to use during pregnancy, so if you are taking any when you discover that you are pregnant, it would be best to discontinue using them from that time forward. They can be resumed then the new baby is born.

If you should decide to continue nursing your older child during your pregnancy, you may find that you have a bit more nipple sensitivity due to the pregnancy than other mothers might have due to incomplete healing of the nerves in your nipple/areolar complex. You may also experience some discomfort as your lactation system expands and recanalizes during the pregnancy.

Tandem Nursing

When BFAR mothers choose to allow child-led weaning so that the child is allowed to nurse until he outgrows the need, which is usually between two and four years old, it occasionally happens that a new baby comes along before the older child is ready to wean. When this happens, many mothers choose to continue nursing the older child simultaneously with the newborn. This is commonly called tandem nursing. Although it is more taxing for them personally, these mothers choose to tandem nurse because they clearly understand the importance nursing holds for their older children and the benefits they will gain.

It is certainly possible for a BFAR mother to make tandem nursing work because in such a situation, the mother has lactated for a long period of time and is continuing to do so, which means that her breasts have probably recanalized and reinnervated quite a bit.

It is important when tandem nursing to take everything one day at a time; not to have preconceived ideas about how it will go or how you will feel about it. Some mothers find that they feel very protective of the newborn and actually just a little resentful of the older child's demands to nurse. Even though such feelings may seem difficult to identify with before the baby is born, it is hard to know how you will really feel after giving birth. If you do find yourself feeling this way, be tolerant, forgiving, and honest about your feelings. Acknowledge them and try find a balance between your feelings and your toddler's needs as much as you can.

If you are tandem nursing, you will need to be careful to meet your own needs. You will need to drink to thirst and eat nutritious food. In the first month, especially, you'll need help around the house so that your primary duty is nursing your children, without worry about keeping house. You may also want to consider sleeping with your new baby as a way to get as much sleep as possible.

Be forgiving of yourself if you find that you don't always feel positive about the tandem nursing experience. It can be very demanding on your body and emotional resources. There may be times when you just need a break. Be gentle with yourself during these times.

Many BFAR mothers who find themselves tandem nursing are delighted to discover MOTHERING YOUR NURSING TODDLER by Norma Jane Bumgarner. It is available through LLLI and is a wonderful resource for answering the special questions you may have.

There are some specific issues related to BFAR. You will naturally be keeping close watch on your new baby's weight gain, preferably by using a rental electronic scale at home and keeping track of his weight. It may help to understand that when the toddler nurses after the baby, it is much like pumping after a nursing session; it provides added stimulation without taking milk from the baby. In fact, tandem nursing is likely to have a very positive effect on your milk supply because the added demand of your older child's nursing will serve to increase your supply, just as pumping would, although far more effectively.

Try not to worry that the milk the toddler receives by nursing after the baby is milk taken away from the baby. The added stimulation your toddler is providing will serve to create a more abundant milk supply to replace at least as much, and quite possibly more, of the milk than he takes.

One issue that is commonly experienced by BFAR mothers is that the baby may need to nurse frequently, especially in the first month. When this happens, it can be a challenge to find time to allow the toddler to nurse, which can be emotionally difficult for the toddler to accept, particularly in this time of change and uncertainty. Provided you have two functional breasts, allowing the toddler to nurse from one breast simultaneously as the baby nurses from the fuller breast may be a way to meet both their needs. This will also provide excellent stimulation to your milk supply.

Coping with a baby's evening fussy periods while simultaneously nursing a toddler to sleep at bedtime can be especially difficult for a BFAR mother who is worried about her milk supply and meeting the needs of both her children. This may be the most important time of the day for your partner or another caregiver to help you out by taking the baby for a short while so that you can give your older child your undivided attention and a time of uninterrupted nursing and cuddling.

You may find that your physician is not supportive of tandem nursing, especially knowing that you are a BFAR mother. You will need to be confident in what you are doing to deflect negative criticism.

As long as you keep a careful eye on your new baby's weight and hydration, tandem nursing should be a wonderful way for you to meet the needs of both your children and introduce a special bond between them.

Breast Examinations

Performing a breast exam upon the BFAR breast can be difficult when the internal scarring is extensive. Self-exams, in particular, can be very difficult. It is not easy even for experts to differentiate scar tissue from suspicious tissue, especially during lactation. Benign fat necrosis is particularly prevalent after breast reduction surgery, and can simulate malignancies.[19] For this reason, as a BFAR mother, you are urged to become familiar with your breasts, especially when you are lactating, so that you can report and investigate any changes that occur. In addition, it would be wise to consider having mammograms as often as recommended by your health care professional. It is possible that your risk of breast cancer has been reduced by removal of a percentage of your breast tissue during your breast surgery[20] and research has shown that lactation lowers the risk of some types of breast cancer, but there are no guarantees.[21]

Changes in Breast Size—"I'm Huge Again!"

Finally, many BFAR mothers are distressed to discover that pregnancy, lactation, and weight gain have combined to increase their breast size, perhaps to an even larger size than they were before their reduction surgeries. Before you drive yourself crazy with self-recrimination and regrets, though, remember one very important factor: If you had not had the surgery, you would not be the size you are now—you would be that size *plus* all the breast tissue that was removed. Most mothers find peace with that realization.

Overcoming Severe Difficulties

If BFAR becomes so difficult and takes an emotional toll beyond what you or your baby can endure, you may be faced with the question of what changes you need to make to improve your situation. There are many options, depending on your circumstances. This is the time that it is important for you to remember that breastfeeding never needs to be "all-or-nothing." BFAR mothers who have had to come to terms with severe difficulties have found that there are many options available to them. In addition to those discussed in this section, there may be other options. With a little creativity and an open mind, there are really no limits to methods you can devise to feed your baby and meet both your needs.

Breastfeed for Comfort Rather than Nutrition

If your limited milk production is the problem but your baby is willing to nurse, you can continue to breastfeed just for comfort and be glad of any milk that gets passed along without worrying about it being his primary source of nutrition. You can then concentrate on feeding your baby formula or donated human milk, if you have access to it, using whatever supplemental device works best for you. Of course, depending on the age of your baby, you will need to make sure that he has adequate sucking opportunities if you choose not to use bottles.

Exclusive Pumping

When a BFAR mother has a good supply of milk, but nipple confusion/preference or other breastfeeding difficulties become so severe that the baby is no longer willing to breastfeed, the mother will be faced with two options: complete weaning to formula or donated human milk or exclusive pumping combined with supplementation as needed. Knowing that fresh human milk is superior to any other form of supplementation, many BFAR mothers have chosen to pump their milk as often as possible and give it to their babies in bottles. If necessary, additional supplementation can also be used.

Pumping full-time is an arduous task. There may be times when you will be pumping to fill a bottle even as your baby is crying in hunger. Good planning helps prevent this from happening very often, but despite your best efforts, there may be times when things do not go as smoothly as you may wish.

Managing your pumping schedule when you are away from home can also be difficult. You will need to plan to take your pump with you when you will be gone during the normal time to pump. Finding places to pump is not always easy, but many public bathrooms or baby care facilities have outlets and some automatic electric pumps have adapters to allow pumping in a car (of course, not while driving).

Exclusive pumping takes time and also requires an adherence to a regular schedule. How often you need to pump depends upon what works best for you. Some mothers pump every three hours and others pump only two or three times a day. Your milk supply will adjust to the schedule you set.

You should not have any trouble maintaining your supply so long as you continue to pump on a regular basis with an automatic electric pump. Having a high-quality pump is essential for exclusive pumping when the only stimulation the milk supply will be receiving is from the pump. Refer to the section about pumping in Chapter 8.

Many BFAR mothers who have exclusively pumped have found that using herbal and prescription galactagogues continues to be very helpful in maximizing their milk supplies.

Exclusive pumping is the most difficult form of BFAR. It requires commitment, determination, and perseverance. It has been done successfully, though, by many BFAR mothers for extended periods of time.

Weaning

Another option is simply to discontinue lactation entirely. Whether or not you are producing large amounts of milk, you will need to be careful not to expect your milk to dry up suddenly. Reducing your lactation output by a small amount each day will ensure a smooth weaning and avoid engorgement or other complications, such as plugged ducts or mastitis. If your baby will not nurse at the breast, it will be necessary to use a breast pump in order to reduce your milk supply without complications.

For BFAR mothers, weaning sooner than you might have originally planned to can be a difficult decision, full of mixed feelings. This is a time when it is especially important to remember that every drop of colostrum and milk that you gave your baby and every moment that he spent at your breast were priceless gifts. You owe it to yourself to realize that even though breastfeeding may not have worked out the way that you may have hoped it would, you put forth efforts that many women who have had reduction surgery do not. Your baby has benefited tremendously from your breastfeeding efforts.

During the weaning process, it is important to make time to give your baby additional attention and cuddling to establish new patterns of bonding that replace the intimacy of breastfeeding and allow you both to find new ways to discover and delight in each other.

If you decide that weaning is the best option for you, you may find it helpful to read Chapter 13, "Defining Your Success," in which the issues that surround finding peace with your BFAR experience are discussed.

Conclusion

Breastfeeding under any circumstances, but especially after breast reduction surgery, is a learned art that must be personalized and adapted to the individual needs of each nursing couple. All nursing mothers experience difficulties from time to time, which is why the information and support of mother-to-mother organizations like La Leche League have been instrumental in helping mothers find solutions to the problems they encounter so that they can go on to have fulfilling breastfeeding experiences.

Be assured that no matter what obstacles you face, you are in good company; other breastfeeding and BFAR mothers have experienced them as well and have felt the same feelings. Working through the difficulties and finding good solutions is almost always possible and tends to give mothers a sense of accomplishment and competency. Having been through a challenging breastfeeding experience, you will also now be able to empathize with and help other mothers who may be facing the same obstacles. Breastfeeding mothers are part of a unique sisterhood; no matter what our backgrounds and differences, we have an instant rapport and will go to great efforts to help and support each other.

R E F E R E N C E S :

1. Lawrence, R. and R. Lawrence. *Breastfeeding: A Guide for the Medical Profession*, 5th edition. St. Louis. Missouri: Mosby, 1999, 259, 275, 284, 653-57.

2. Woolridge, M., J. Baum, R. Drewett. Effect of a traditional and of a new nipple shield on sucking patterns and milk flow. *Early Human Dev* 1980; 4:357-64.

3. Gunther, M. *Infant Feeding*. London: Methuen, 1970.

4. Coates, M. Nipple pain related to vasospasm in the nipple? *J Hum Lact* 1992; 8(3):153.

5. Lawlor-Smith, L. and C. Lawlor-Smith. Vasospam of the nipple–a manifestation of Raynaud's Phenomenon. *BMJ* 1997; 314:644-45.

6. Hale, T. *Medications and Mothers' Milk*, 9th edition. Amarillo, TX: Pharmasoft Publishing, 2000; 482-83.

7. Riordan, J. and K. Auerbach. *Breastfeeding and Human Lactation*, 2nd edition. Sudbury, MA: Jones and Bartlett Publishers, 1999; 486, 328.

8. Mohrbacher, N. and J. Stock. THE BREASTFEEDING ANSWER BOOK, Schaumburg, IL: LLLI, 1997; 425, 106, 334.

9. Zeretzke, K. Helping a mother with a baby who is reluctant to nurse. LEAVEN Oct/Nov 1999; 99-103.

10. Goldsmith, H. Milk-rejection sign of breast cancer. *Am J Srg* 1974; 127:280.

11. Barmby, L. *Breastfeeding the Baby with Reflux*. LLLI, 2000. Publication No. 524-24.

12. Huggins, K. *Nursing Mothers' Companion*, 4th edition. Harvard Common Press, 1999; 67.

13. Conway, A. Ankylglossia – to snip or not to snip: Is that the question? *J Hum Lact* 1990; 6:101-2.

14. Fleiss, P., et al. Ankylglossia: A cause of breastfeeding problems? J Hum Lact 1990; 6:128-29.

15. Marmet, C., E. Shell, R. Marmet. Neonatal frenotomy may be necessary to correct breastfeeding problems. *J Hum Lact* 1990; 6:117-21.

16. Institute for Reproductive Health. *Guidelines: breastfeeding, family planning, and the Lactational Amenorrhea Method—LAM*. Washington, DC: Georgetown University, 1994.

17. Gray, R. et al. The risk of ovulation during lactation. *Lancet* 1990; 335:25-29.

18. Fujino, T., H. Kato, S. Yamashita, et al. Effects of domperidone on serum prolactin levels in human beings. *Endocrinol Jpn* Aug 1980; 27(4): 521-25.

19. Miller, J., S. Festa, M. Goldstein. Benign fat necrosis simulating bilateral breast malignancy after reduction mammoplasty. *South Med J* Aug 1998; 91(8): 765-67.

20. Brown, M., M. Weinberg, N. Chong, et al. A cohort study of breast cancer risk in breast reduction patients. *Plast Reconstr Surg* May 1999; 103(6): 1674-81.

21. Newcomb, P., B. Storer, M. Longnecker, et al. Lactation and a reduced risk of premenopausal breast cancer. *N Engl J Med* 1994; 330:81-87.

MISHA'S STORY

I had my breast reduction surgery when my first child was six months old. About a week after the surgery, I noticed my right areola had some dark spots on it. The doctor at first told us everything would be fine; after a few weeks it became obvious that I was losing the nipple. It was a two month process, at the end of which the surgeon grafted skin from my hip onto where my nipple and areola had been. Although I'd been told before the surgery that I could try to breastfeed future children, now the doctor told us that I would not be able to, because the milk on the right side would have nowhere to go. I was crushed.

I became pregnant late the next year, and called LLL immediately to find out whether or not I could breastfeed. The Leader I talked to told me that I could absolutely breastfeed on one side. I was thrilled. I miscarried that baby and the next, but went on to have my son in June 1999. I had found the BFAR email list quite a while before, and rejoined during my pregnancy with Sammy. Thanks to the knowledgeable women there, I was prepared with a Lact-Aid at-breast supplementer, herbs, and a lot of determination.

Sammy was a great nurser and we did fine until I switched to supplementing with bottles at about six weeks. He gradually developed nipple preference and spent less and less time at the breast. I'd gone from providing him with one-third to one-half of his nutrition, to providing him almost nothing. I quickly changed back to the Lact-Aid and used it until about five months of age, when he decided to nurse without it, so we started using bottles again. I had a very small supply after that, mostly due to becoming pregnant again, but we had a great nursing relationship and nursed right through the pregnancy. I weaned him at 17 months of age due to the nursing demands of my two-month-old, combined with being limited to only being able to nurse on one side.

Bridget was also an enthusiastic nurser from the start, but I decided I would not make the same mistake with bottles that I had with Sammy. I have exclusively used the Lact-Aid to nurse her (she also nurses without it, fortunately, which is great for comfort). I began taking domperidone at six weeks postpartum, and with the help of that plus fenugreek and some other herbs that I use in rotation, I have provided her with approximately half of her nutrition, give or take a little. Nursing on one side has presented some challenges, but I've learned that almost any breastfeeding difficulty can be overcome, and I feel very blessed by the wonderful experiences I've had nurturing my children at the breast.

BEYOND BFAR:
EVOLVING YOUR BFAR RELATIONSHIP

CHAPTER 11

BFAR AND THE OLDER BABY

The experience of BFAR is a dynamic process that evolves as we become more experienced with it. Many BFAR mothers who have had a difficult start find that once some time has passed and they have worked through the initial problems, BFAR becomes much easier. Of course, each stage poses its own challenges, and so most mothers have new questions as their children grow. This chapter has been written to address the concerns of BFAR and an older baby, which is defined in this context as a baby who is in the middle of his first year up to 18 months.

How BFAR Changes as Your Child Grows Older

By the time her baby is older, a BFAR mother has created a unique path for herself and her baby. She is usually strong in her convictions about the value of breastfeeding because she has had to work so hard to do so. Still, meeting the increasing needs of an older baby stretches one's patience and resources to new lengths.

An Active, Distracted Baby

The one constant about being a BFAR mother is that it is difficult for us to ever get far from the worry about our milk supply. Even mothers who have no need to supplement have occasional moments of panic and worry. Naturally, mothers worry that their milk supplies will not expand to meet the increased nutritional needs of an older baby. When this older baby becomes less cooperative during nursing sessions, concerns about getting enough milk into him become considerably greater. It is developmentally normal and appropriate, though, for babies in the middle of their first year to be very interested and excited about their surroundings. They are more coordinated and able to physically interact with their world and so they often do not have as much patience for nursing sessions. They just feel more playful than business-like about feeding.

If you should find yourself worried and frustrated by your baby's new approach to nursing, it may help to first cover the basics to make sure that he is well hydrated and getting enough nutrition to ensure adequate growth. This would be a good time to go back to keeping track of his diaper output and other physical criteria on an assessment chart. Do not become too involved in this record-keeping; just keep close enough track that you can know if there is any cause to be concerned about his hydration status and growth. Your health care provider will appreciate having this information, too, if there is any kind of problem.

When you are reassured of your child's level of hydration and continued growth, it will be possible for you to let go of some of your anxiety and take pleasure in your child's new abilities. This is not always easy to do, but as children get older, taking care of them becomes less and less about feeding and more and more about mothering. This applies to BFAR as much as to normal breastfeeding. As he develops into a little person and begins to interact with you, you may find that your relationship with your child grows and deepens. This is the beginning of the reward for all that you have invested in BFAR.

Mothers do not always feel relaxed and appreciative of this new stage; because they are human, they can sometimes feel annoyed by a child's lack of nursing cooperation. It is a normal feeling that can even co-exist with more positive feelings. And there are days when a mother simply does not have time for playing. To keep nursing sessions more to the point, many mothers find that minimizing distractions by nursing in a soothing, darkened room with either no sound or quiet, harmonious music is very helpful in settling a baby down to a serious nursing session. For babies who are highly active and distractible, it may be necessary for you to make a routine of having two or three of the nursing sessions each day be deliberately subdued in this way.

Growth Rates in Older Children

As a BFAR mother, it is normal to continue to be concerned about your child's growth rates, even when he is no longer an infant. It can be disturbing, then, to discover at around four months that your baby has begun to gain weight more slowly. When this happens, many BFAR mothers automatically blame their milk supplies and begin to work hard to increase them. What is most likely happening, though, is that these babies are following a normal growth pattern for breastfed babies, who tend to gain weight more slowly after four months. At this point, the head circumference becomes a more accurate gauge of reaching appropriate developmental milestones than does weight.

It may also put your mind at ease to know that the growth charts currently used by most physicians are not an accurate tool for assessing growth rates of breastfed children, including those who are formula-supplemented. The charts used most frequently were created by the National Center for Health Statistics (NCHS) and based upon the growth rates of a small sample of exclusively Caucasian, mostly formula-fed babies in Yellow Springs, Ohio, between 1929 and 1975. Fortunately, the Centers for Disease Control (CDC) has recently developed growth charts that are more accurate for evaluating childhood development, taking into account the differences between breastfed and bottle-fed children, as well as ethnic factors. The CDC charts can be found in Appendix 2.

As long as your baby continues to gain weight at a steady pace and is otherwise meeting his developmental milestones, there is usually no need to be concerned about your milk supply. Of course, a drop in weight is a definite danger sign that should be brought to your health care provider's attention.

Changes in Your Milk

One of the most fantastic qualities of human milk is that its composition changes over time to meet the changing developmental needs of growing babies. While the immunological and nutritional factors do not diminish over time, the proportions do change in order to better meet the needs of the older child. The amount of lysozyme, for instance, which destroys bacteria by degrading their cell walls, actually increases over the duration of breastfeeding, which is helpful to toddlers who are interacting more directly with their environment and thus being exposed to more germs. Most importantly for BFAR mothers, the immunological protection becomes more concentrated when the feedings become fewer.

Introducing Solids

The introduction of solids around the middle of the first year is an important milestone for BFAR. It is the beginning of the transition from complete nutritional dependence on human milk or formula. For this reason, it is often the point at which BFAR mothers are able to worry less about supplementation as the supplements are gradually replaced by solid foods. However, it is important to maintain your priority of giving your baby as much human milk as possible by focusing on replacing the supplements with solid foods rather than replacing the human milk with solid foods.

One perspective that is helpful for BFAR mothers to remember at this time is that human milk is the only perfect, nutritionally complete food for human babies. No other food or combination of foods can compare to the perfect nutrition of human milk. Also, only human milk has the immunological factors that protect your child from certain viruses and bacterial infections. Therefore, it is important that you not think of solids as the better, preferable food. This can be difficult to do, though, when our society places a high value on a baby's ability to eat solid food.

LLLI's THE WOMANLY ART OF BREASTFEEDING has excellent information on how to start solids, as well as which foods are most appropriate for introducing to breastfed babies. In general, introducing solids prepared from whole foods that have not been commercially processed or refined is the best way to ensure that your baby receives the highest quality nutrients. Margaret Kenda, one of the authors of *The Natural Baby Food Cookbook*, has written a new cookbook for La Leche League International WHOLE FOODS FOR BABIES AND TODDLERS. It contains helpful nutritional information and many recipes so that you can prepare meals from whole foods that are appropriate for your baby and are also enjoyable for the whole family.

The mechanics of replacing supplementation with solids requires a bit of flexibility and being in tune with your baby's mood and willingness to try new foods. If you are using an at-breast supplementer, you would first breastfeed without the supplementer and then offer small quantities of a soft minimally cooked food. If he still seems hungry, but refuses to eat more of the solid food, you can then offer to nurse him with the at-breast supplementer. Gradually, as he matures, he will begin to eat more and more of the solid foods and the supplement will not be necessary.

If you are supplementing with bottles or another type of supplementation device, you would follow the same pattern; breastfeeding first, offering solids, and finishing up with supplementation if the baby is still hungry.

Occasionally, a BFAR mother may have a baby who really delights in eating solids, sometimes to the point of seeming to prefer eating solids to nursing. It can sometimes feel like a rejection of the special bond you have worked so hard to have. This is not, though, your child's personal comment on breastfeeding, but rather it is simply an expression of his delight in a new experience. While it is natural and normal for a child's diet to evolve from nursing to eating regular foods, his initial enthusiasm may diminish after the novelty wears off and he may once again resume nursing with gusto. Until that time, though, the BFAR mother of such a child may worry about her milk supply. As long as there is not an abrupt cessation of breastfeeding to the point that she experiences engorgement, her milk supply will adjust to minor fluctuations. If there is an abrupt cessation, it will be necessary to pump or hand express milk if the mother wants to maintain her milk supply and relieve any engorgement.

Supplementing the Older BFAR Baby

The system that you, as the BFAR mother of an older baby past six months old, have devised to get to this point may be working fairly well, but it usually needs adjustments as your baby grows older and his and your needs change. As in the early days, flexibility and a willingness for innovation are key to finding a new system that works best for you.

Supplementing the Older Child in Public

BFAR in public when supplementing with an at-breast supplementer is not easy under most circumstances, but becomes even less so when the child grows older and is more active and distractible. Sometimes it can be difficult to keep the child latched on and the tube in place while still being discreet. Occasionally, BFAR mothers also find that the latching on and off that frequently occurs with an older baby's nursing can increase their painful symptoms of nipple blanching.

The key to supplementing an active baby in public is try to do so in places that have fewer distractions, especially when he is tired and more hungry. You may also find that keeping a finger on the tubing prevents him from pulling it out of position. Many mothers find that sometimes feeding an older baby a half-hour or so before he is normally hungry helps to keep his mood even so that he is more cooperative during the feeding.

Continued Need for At-Breast Supplementer after One Year

For a very small percentage of toddlers, supplementation will still be necessary at the one-year mark. Not all children are ready to regularly eat solids at this age and some children are also resistant to using sippy cups; they may continue to be dependent on supplementation at the breast to ensure that they remain hydrated.

It may no longer be necessary, though, to fill the at-breast supplementer with formula or donated human milk. Many children at this age are ready to transition to cow's milk, goat's milk, soy milk, or rice milk. It is important to consult with your child's physician, of course, before making this change.

Another difficulty that BFAR mothers sometimes experience is their babies' lessened acceptance of the at-breast supplementer. Some children will begin pulling out the tubing while nursing around the same time they start solids. It is a part of their natural development as they become more aware of and curious about everything. Keeping a finger on the tubing to keep it in place is just about all that can be done until your child outgrows this stage or supplementation is no longer needed.

Nipple Confusion/Preference Can Strike Even Older Babies

Most BFAR mothers are careful about using at-breast supplementers to avoid nipple confusion/preference in the early months. As time goes on, though, it is easy to become more casual about supplementation, and sometimes it seems more convenient to give a bottle. This is a time when you feel more confident about feeding your baby and you may believe that he is past the susceptible time for nipple confusion/preference. It can really be surprising, then, to discover that your baby has developed one of these difficulties.

The important thing to remember about nipple confusion/preference is that it can strike at any time. It is not a problem only of infants, although infants are much more likely to develop it. Nipple preference, especially, can even strike babies who had previously shown no difficulty in switching back and forth between breastfeeding and bottles.

If you feel that you must begin giving bottles, watch for signs that nipple confusion or nipple preference may be starting to happen. If you are not ready to stop breastfeeding, you may need to stop using bottles and consider other feeding methods instead. Fortunately, about the same time he is ready for solids, your baby will be able to drink from a sippy cup, which may make supplementation much easier.

The Effect of Longer Separations from Your Baby on Your Milk Supply

As your baby grows into a more independent toddler, there may be times when you are away from him during regular feeding times. The effect of these missed feedings on your milk supply will depend on how many feedings are missed at one time and how often it occurs.

One missed feeding here and there will not have a permanent impact on your milk supply. You may feel more full when you return or you may not; either way your milk supply will easily adjust. If this should happen repeatedly, though, your milk supply will correspondingly diminish to meet the reduced demand unless you pump during the time you are away. In most cases, however, it will not reduce your milk supply beyond the amount of the one feeding, and it is almost always possible to increase it again.

A longer separation beyond just a couple of feedings will seriously impact your milk supply, though, unless you pump in place of the missed feedings. Any sudden cessation of milk removal will result in damage to the alveoli and frequently some degree of uncomfortable engorgement, which could lead to plugged ducts and mastitis. If you must be away, pump or hand express your milk at the approximate times you would normally breastfeed.

Should you desire to rebuild your milk supply after a prolonged separation, you may need the help of an LLL Leader or lactation consultant to do so.

Weaning

Even though weaning is an inevitable end of the breastfeeding journey for every mother and child, there are many ways to approach it. You and your child must find the path that best meets your needs.

Criticism about Breastfeeding an Older Child

One of the ways that the issue of weaning is first introduced is by subtle (and not so subtle) inferences by friends and family members that the time has come. While they may have been accepting, or at least tolerant, of your earlier efforts to breastfeed, they may not understand the reasons for continuing it past a certain point. For some friends or family members, their perception of the appropriate timeframe for weaning is earlier than for others, but it is often sooner than when the nursing couple is actually ready.

For some reason, BFAR tends to make this issue more obvious than it is for other mothers. Perhaps this is so because supplementation makes the efforts of BFAR more apparent and friends and family members want things to be easier for you. No matter the reason, though, only you and your baby know when weaning is right for you. Weaning before you are ready due to the pressure of others will only cause emotional pain and deprive you of the joy of a natural end to your BFAR journey.

In responding to negative comments, it is important to convey that you appreciate the person's concern for you and understand that it is only the desire to help that has prompted such comments. At the same time, though, they need to see that you are confident in what you are doing and understand that you have studied the issues and made an informed decision to feed and parent your child in this way.

Talking to other breastfeeding mothers at mother-to-mother support groups such as La Leche League is an excellent way to learn strategies for coping with and responding to criticism about breastfeeding an older child. Other mothers will help reinforce your knowledge that the benefits of breastfeeding extend far beyond the first few months of life. They will also give you a safe place to express your hurt and frustration from the criticism you've received. Knowing you are not alone and being reminded that you are definitely doing the right thing for your child will help you feel stronger in the face of any further criticism.

How Long Should You Nurse?

BFAR mothers are often unsure about how long breastfeeding should continue. This is frequently because they only recently came to understand the value of human milk and breastfeeding and have not been exposed to many breastfeeding couples. Sometimes, though, there are other factors that make you wonder about the best time to wean.
Your baby has a biological and emotional need for breastfeeding for at least the first year of his life, and frequently longer. Ideally, breastfeeding should continue as long as both you and your baby enjoy it. The American Academy of Pediatrics (AAP) issued a statement in 1997 that recommended breastfeeding for at least the first year of life.[1] It

deliberately did not state a specific timeframe for weaning after that point. The United Nations Children's Fund (UNICEF) and the World Health Organization (WHO), in response to research that validates the benefits of extended breastfeeding, have recommended breastfeeding continue for at least the first two years of life.[2]

Although it can certainly be difficult to envision nursing a toddler when you have a newborn, it is important not to make definite decisions about the duration of your breastfeeding relationship. Until you get there, you can not know what is going to be right for you and your child. For many BFAR mothers, nursing into the toddler years is rewarding because supplementation is no longer necessary once baby is eating solids and drinking from a cup, and they can finally enjoy a relaxed approach to breastfeeding.

For some BFAR mothers, though, BFAR is such an added emotional and physical effort that even when the baby is doing well, there comes a time when they simply become too overwhelmed and frustrated to continue. They realize that they are not enjoying their babies and have come to dread feedings. It may be possible to get past these feelings by talking to an empathetic friend or lactation specialist. It is worth the effort to do this, even just for your own emotional health. If you find the feelings to be insurmountable, though, it may be the right time for you to wean. Follow your heart and trust your decision. And remember that every drop of human milk that you gave your baby and every moment at your breast was a tremendous gift that will benefit him throughout his entire life. Do not dwell on what you did not do—you have great reason to feel very proud for what you did do.

For many BFAR mothers, though, weaning is less desirable precisely because of the extra effort they have put into BFAR. After all the stress and hard work, you may find that you truly value what you've achieved and you are reluctant to wean prematurely. It has been observed that BFAR mothers who have been able to overcome the early challenges tend to nurse longer than some of their breastfeeding peers.

Natural (Child-Led) Weaning

When the breastfeeding relationship is allowed to run its course, weaning is gradual. Although weaning in the strict sense of the word begins with the first introduction of solid food, complete weaning from the breast will occur for most children between the ages of two and four years old. When weaning is a decision made by the child, it is usually more of a natural evolution of his development, occurring seamlessly and sometimes imperceptibly. In her book, MOTHERING YOUR NURSING TODDLER, Norma Jane Bumgarner makes this point beautifully by stating that "Every natural weaning is unique so that it is impossible to guarantee anything about it except that it will happen."[3]

Of course, many mothers of nursing toddlers wonder just how it will come about, especially when they see no signs of it on the horizon. Bumgarner, an experienced mother and grandmother of nursing toddlers, has reassured many such mothers in her book by describing the time of weaning as one in which

"*your child will not find nursing so absolutely essential to her well-being. She may stop asking so often. Or she may be distracted sometimes from nursing.... You will very naturally and with hardly a*

thought respond a little less quickly to her requests to nurse....
In time–how much time no one can say–your child will abandon all but
a few favorite nursing times." [3]

It is but a small step, then, for your child to nurse for shorter and shorter times until eventually he no longer asks to nurse. You may go several days before you realize that he hasn't asked in a while. It's not that he has forgotten about it so much as that he has simply grown beyond it. Your incredible child has weaned himself and your BFAR relationship has reached a natural conclusion.

For information on all the wonderful and sometimes puzzling non-BFAR aspects of nursing an older child, it is suggested that you read the newly revised, definitive book on this subject, MOTHERING YOUR NURSING TODDLER by Norma Jane Bumgarner.

R E F E R E N C E S :

1. American Academy of Pediatrics. Breastfeeding and the use of human milk (RE9729). *Pediatrics* 1997; 100(6):1035-1039.

2. United Nations Children's Fund. *Innocenti Declaration on the Protection, Promotion and Support of Breastfeeding*. Florence, Italy, 1990.

3. Bumgarner, N. *Mothering Your Nursing Toddler*. Schaumburg, IL: LLLI. 2000; 253, 252-53.

JENIFER'S STORY

I had a breast reduction when I was three months shy of my eighteenth birthday. It was the kind where my entire nipple and areola was moved. I have anchor-shaped scars which have almost entirely faded. I had no complications at all from the procedure and have often been told by doctors that mine is the best reduction result they have ever seen. I have always been very happy with it. I was told at the time of my reduction that I would have a 50 percent chance of being able to breastfeed.

Toward the end of my first pregnancy, I attended a breastfeeding information session given by the lactation consultant (LC) who worked with my obstetrician's practice. After that, I really wanted to be able to breastfeed and felt a great deal of guilt and sadness that my surgery might deprive my child of such important health and emotional benefits.

In a private consultation with that LC, she expressed doubt that I would be able to nurse. I was about eight months along, but had not had any leakage, although when my breast was compressed there was a slight glistening on the nipple. I arranged to have the LC meet with me at the hospital the day my baby was born.

My daughter, Isadora, was born after a long but healthy labor with minimal medical intervention. After I had had some private bonding time immediately after the birth with my husband and screaming child, my doula came into the room and said it sounded as though the baby was hungry. We put her to my breast where she latched on immediately, but didn't really know what to do once she got there. She didn't really know how to suck yet without "falling off" the breast. Later in the day, with the help of the LC, we taught her to suck on our fingers by putting an SNS (Supplemental Nutrition System) tube onto my finger. As soon as she felt the wetness, she immediately began to suck very well. She instantly became a terrific nurser. I had no significant pain or soreness.

My biggest hurdle in nursing this brand new baby was that I was so insecure about whether or not I would be able to successfully produce milk and deliver it to my child through my breast that I sought objective "proof" at every turn. I religiously recorded her nursing and elimination schedules for the first month. I met regularly with the LC to have the baby weighed before and after nursing to see what she was taking in. Everything went perfectly. Isadora nursed beautifully, she gained weight like a champ, and nursing was going well for both of us.

I returned to work full time as a criminal defense attorney when Isadora was twelve weeks old and continued to nurse exclusively. I attribute the success to a lot of external factors in addition to my own commitment to breastfeeding my baby. My husband stayed home with her full time and worked evenings, so he could bring her to me or call me home when it was necessary as we lived about ten minutes from my office. I also had a very supportive and understanding boss and an office with a lock on the door, and the help and support of two good LCs. My job required a fair amount of driving to different courts, which enabled me to pump in the car.

My child nursed exclusively until she was six months old and almost exclusively until she was nine months old. Of course, she continued to nurse frequently and fully. She was not a child who slept through the night (and only started doing this regularly at about 22 months), so we had a lot of nighttime nursing and she would nurse fairly often whenever I was home. She received pumped milk in a bottle at home until she was a year old when generally she would have juice or cow's milk while I was at work. Isadora has always slept in our bed and I have always allowed her to nurse on demand.

Isadora will be two next month and is still nursing, I am happy to say. Because of my new pregnancy, I have had to deal with the issue of whether or not to continue nursing after my baby is born. I have been advised by various people to stop by the time I am in my third trimester for various reasons. My own feelings were that my nursing style— co-sleeping, nursing on demand, and not taking my child off the breast for "non-nutritive sucking" if at all possible—was inconsistent with tandem nursing. However, I don't want to stop nursing abruptly as it has been such a huge and important part of my relationship with my child.

I have finally come up with a solution that I hope will make everyone happy. I am very slowly and gradually weaning Isadora to nursing only before bedtime. I plan to do this as I gradually put her into her own "big girl bed" as I feel she is showing signs of readiness for her own sleep space. She is currently nursing only in the morning and at night (while we are in bed). My husband remains very supportive and is participating in the weaning process by assisting in diverting her attention when she is nursing, or attempting to nurse, out of habit. So far, I have not had any tantrums or tears and although they may be coming, I think the gradual approach is working for us.

I can't begin to describe how I feel about nursing. It is part of how I mother that I wouldn't trade for anything. Because the odds I got for breastfeeding when I first became pregnant were far less than 50 percent that I would be able to do this, I also feel as though my children and I are incredibly fortunate. I see breastfeeding as a gift that I have received, as well as one I can give to my children. My husband's participation has been invaluable as well, as it allowed us the continuity and consistency we needed. It is just part of who we are as a family. I think the key to my success was a commitment to making it work, not giving up, and trying to fix any problems that came our way rather than seeing them as obstacles.

EMOTIONAL ISSUES

The diversity of emotions that a BFAR mother experiences can be quite surprising to her. Before her baby is born, it may be difficult for her to anticipate what she will feel, but even if she does have an inkling, actually encountering these emotions firsthand is probably much more intense than she could have imagined.

At the time of their surgeries, many women do not think being able to lactate will matter much to them or they are simply determined to cross that bridge when they come to it. They may not even have thought about or intended to try breastfeeding.

But when that precious baby comes along, many mothers who have had breast reduction surgery find that a fierce mothering instinct reaches up from the core of their beings and compels them to fight with every ounce of energy and determination they have to give their babies the very best that they are capable of giving them. That's how many of us became BFAR mothers.

As a BFAR mother, you will experience a wide range of emotions that are not felt by most breastfeeding mothers. You are never alone when you feel them, though, because every BFAR mother has experienced most of your emotions to some degree. One of the most valuable components of the online BFAR support group, in fact, has been the member's validation of and empathy with the unique emotions BFAR mothers feel.

The truth is that BFAR is seldom easy and is often emotionally painful. Some of the thoughts and feelings we have, in fact, are so painful that only another woman who has had a similar experience can understand them. Realizing that we are not alone in our feelings, painful as they may be, and knowing that other women all over the world feel them, too, can give us tremendous strength when we feel most vulnerable. Fortunately, the BFAR experience is not always emotionally painful. It also has a joyful side, which is often all the more so in light of the painful feelings we have experienced.

Many BFAR mothers have described BFAR as simultaneously the "worst of both worlds" and the "best of both worlds." They say this because in many ways BFAR is a middle ground between the world of breastfeeding and the world of formula feeding. At times, it can seem that BFAR mothers experience the worst of both worlds by having to supplement and watch their baby's progress so closely. At other times, it can seem that they have the best of both worlds by enjoying the intimacy and benefits of breastfeeding at the same time as having the advantages of supplementing, because someone else can help to feed the baby. Viewed as a whole, the very depth and range of the emotions felt during BFAR inevitably leave such a profound impression on a woman that it is likely to be one of the most important experiences in her life.

No matter what feelings you encounter during your BFAR experience, it is essential that you not only get the support you need from friends, family, La Leche League Leaders, or health professionals, but also that you are aware of some basic coping techniques that will help you along the way.

A Wide Range of Emotions

Anger about Your Surgery

After your baby is born and you begin to face the challenges of BFAR, it may be tempting to deny all the valid reasons you had for having your surgery. You may actually feel anger at yourself for deciding to do it or you may be angry toward others who talked you into it, including a physician who may have told you that the surgery would not impact breastfeeding. You can also feel frustrated by the irreversibility of the surgery.

It is easy to forget how miserable you may have been before your surgery and how much better you felt afterward. In retrospect, those emotional and physical discomforts caused by your original breast size may not seem important compared to your baby's well-being. But it simply isn't fair to yourself not to take into consideration that your decision to undergo reduction surgery was most likely made in the context of some very serious issues that were affecting your own quality of life. You did not undergo the surgery lightly.

Even if factors related to appearance seem trivial or vain to you now, remember that you made the decision to have the surgery in the context of what you were experiencing at that point in your life. You had no way of knowing what the future would hold.

When you feel anger and frustration about having had the surgery, go back to the first chapter of this book and remind yourself of the issues that led to your decision. And then feel compassion for your younger self and accept that you could not have understood at that time what breastfeeding would come to mean to you later in your life, especially if, like so many of us, you were not even sure that you would ever have children.

It is not surprising that so many of us did not know that breastfeeding would be profoundly important to us. Many societies are not completely comfortable with breastfeeding, even though all the physiological and psychological research has now clearly proven its value. In the United States, formula-feeding was considered far more culturally acceptable than breastfeeding for many decades. Unfortunately, resistance against breastfeeding still exists today. For example, some people equate breasts solely with sexuality and view breastfeeding as somewhat sexual; others think that breastfeeding is primitive and appropriate only for animals in a pasture. Many people believe that most women are not physically capable of producing enough milk to adequately meet their babies' nutritional needs. The formula industry has helped to reinforce these fallacies by launching continuous marketing campaigns throughout the world, suggesting subtly, and sometimes not so subtly, that their products contribute more than breastfeeding to happier, healthier, and more modern babies and mothers.

Anxiety about Your Baby

One of the most overwhelming emotions of BFAR is anxiety or worry about your baby's health. We feel pressured to maximize our milk supply but not allow our baby's health to suffer. We feel driven to produce as much milk as we can for our babies, but frequently feel anxiety about keeping up our supply, even when things seem to be going well. We also worry that we will supplement needlessly and jeopardize our tenuous milk supply.

We worry because we love our babies and we want them to have the best that we can possibly give them. BFAR definitely accentuates worry, but BFAR mothers do not have the corner on worrying. All mothers worry—some just have more to worry about than others. It is basic to the nature of motherhood and even if you had not had breast reduction surgery, you would not be able to escape having moments of doubt about your ability to care for your baby.

Realize that while worry has a purpose because it keeps you vigilant, it can also take up precious energy and impede your ability to enjoy breastfeeding your child. Try to counter your worry with faith in your body and your baby. Trust that you have the right information to make the best decisions for yourself and your family and that every bit of effort is a precious lifelong gift you are giving to your child.

Resentment about Your Situation

In almost every case, BFAR is hard work. So it is natural that at one time or another it has crossed the mind of most BFAR mothers that it just isn't fair that we have to work so much harder than other mothers in order to breastfeed our babies. Few of us want to work so hard—we'd much rather be spending our time snuggling with our babies and enjoying them. But because we want so much to breastfeed our babies, we go to the extra effort and try to stay away from self-pity. Sometimes, though, resentment creeps in and makes everything seem much more negative for a while.

Even though it is completely normal, resentment is a feeling that can only hinder your BFAR efforts. Honestly acknowledging your feelings of resentment, but then letting go of them and accepting your path with grace, is the best way to find peace with BFAR.

Feelings of Inadequacy

It is not uncommon for BFAR mothers to confide that they feel inadequate as a mother and that they feel deep in their hearts that their babies deserve better. The reality, of course, is that only a mother who loves her child so completely and is so dedicated to his well-being would feel that way. BFAR mothers are excellent mothers—they give so much of themselves and work so hard to provide a breastfeeding experience for their babies. Sadly, though, sometimes all their efforts aren't much consolation when they so passionately want their babies to have access to a full milk supply and it is not possible. Some mothers even think of themselves as failures for this reason. It is difficult to be objective when you are working so hard to provide a breastfeeding experience for your baby and loving him so deeply every step of the way.

If you should find yourself feeling this way, take a deep breath and remember one thing: no one loves this baby as deeply as you do and your tremendous love is every bit as important to this baby's well-being as nutrition. Many kinds of milk can nurture the body, but only your love can thoroughly nurture his soul.

Feeling Overwhelmed

There is no question that BFAR is a tremendous responsibility at a time in your life when you are emotionally and physically vulnerable. It is so easy to be worn down by lack of sleep and never-ending obligations that you feel as though you are sinking into an abyss. As soon as you realize that you are feeling this way, seek help and relief in any way that you can, so long as it does not jeopardize your BFAR efforts. For instance, many mothers find that having a nice hot cup of herbal tea all by themselves while the baby naps helps replenish their emotional energies. Other mothers enjoy a bubble bath or hot shower when someone else is able to take over caring for the baby. Or you might need to get out in the fresh air and take a walk. It is amazing what a few moments of self-pampering and indulging can do for your outlook.

Understand that it is very important for you to maintain an emotional balance so that you can have enough strength to meet the demanding challenges of BFAR. For some mothers, it may be helpful to turn to a supportive person or an organized support group for new mothers, breastfeeding mothers, or BFAR mothers. Knowing what other mothers are going through can really help you feel better about your experience. Beware, though, of advice that undermines your BFAR efforts.

To prevent BFAR from becoming overwhelming, it is important to find a balance between it and quality family time. Developing your family is very important now and having a strong family foundation will help you weather the difficulties of BFAR.

Guilt or Regret

One of the most prevalent and unproductive emotions felt by BFAR mothers is guilt. We can feel guilty about almost every aspect of BFAR, especially when we know that our decision to have surgery has affected our ability to make enough milk for our babies. What we really feel though is regret. We need to accept that we made the right decision at the time we had the surgery, but we regret that we were not fully aware that the outcome would affect our ability to give our child the very best. Essentially, though, what we may think of as guilt stems from our desire to give our children the very best, which is something that should make us feel proud.

Guilt can be very difficult to control because there is so little that is rational about it. Try, though, to be compassionate toward yourself and realize that there is nothing wrong with wanting the best for your child, which is the motivation behind all the efforts of BFAR.

Feeling Guilty about Previous Babies

A great number of women who have had breast reduction surgery do not try to breastfeed either because their surgeons told them definitively that they would not be able to or they made the assumption themselves that it would not be possible. In fact, due to lack of information, most physicians and many lactation consultants still do not believe that BFAR is possible.

Before the BFAR email support group, there was no organized resource to turn to for BFAR information. And until this book became available, there was no organized body of knowledge about BFAR.

So forgive yourself for not breastfeeding your previous children. You did not know you could and you did not have the support or resources to help you. You have, though, educated yourself about BFAR for this child now that information about it is available and that is the very best any BFAR mother could do.

Common Emotional Reactions

Feeling Selfish for Wanting to Breastfeed

Many BFAR mothers have admitted that they feel they might be selfish for wanting to breastfeed their babies. This, of course, is ironic when one considers the amount of work and sacrifice that BFAR entails. This feeling of selfishness can creep up on us, though, when we observe our babies' distress or frustration with supplementation and we begin to think that the stress and effort of BFAR could be harmful to our babies by depriving them of our full loving attention. At very vulnerable moments we may even think that they would be better off being completely bottle-fed with formula.

We are most susceptible to feeling this way when we are emotionally exhausted and see bottle-feeding mothers who are calmly and easily feeding their babies. This feeling can be crystallized if we should give the baby a bottle and observe his satisfaction with it. It is very easy to succumb to this way of thinking. In fact, formula companies have successfully honed their marketing tactics to this exact feeling for many decades. It can be further reinforced by negative questions about our motivation from well-meaning, but misguided, family members or friends.

We do feel that we have a strong personal investment—that we deeply want to succeed in being breastfeeding mothers. Of course, there is also nothing wrong with the fact that breastfeeding has special benefits for the mother, too, but this does not mean that you are only doing it to help yourself. With all the time, effort, stress, and personal sacrifices of BFAR, the benefits to us frankly are not enough to keep most BFAR mothers sufficiently motivated for any length of time.

The early months of BFAR can indeed be very difficult and that is when most BFAR mothers are susceptible to feeling that they are seeking this accomplishment more for their own sake than for the benefit of their babies. Without seeing direct, immediate evidence that your baby is benefiting from breastfeeding, it is hard to believe it really is making any kind of difference.

If you find yourself beginning to think this way, take some time to re-examine your motives for BFAR. Be as honest with yourself as you can. Naturally, you will find that BFAR has benefits for you. But almost definitely you will find that your deepest reasons for wanting to breastfeed your child are that you want to give him the lifelong benefit of the unique nutrition and immunities of human milk, as well as the special closeness and bonding of feeding him at your breast. These are benefits that you will not necessarily see today or tomorrow—but it really won't be long until you have a moment when you know that this special experience has been worth every bit of stress and effort for both of you, but especially for your baby.

Worry about the Expense of BFAR

Not only does breastfeeding provide the best source of nutrition, build immunity, and offer one of the best bonding experiences mother and child can have, but it is widely considered to be economical. This may not be true of BFAR because it can include frequent doctor visits, lactation consultant services, special supplemental devices, formula or donated human milk, the rental of pumps and scales, galactagogues, and other substances. These costs can make BFAR seem quite expensive in some cases and can be very disheartening for a new family that is already struggling with the tremendous costs of having its first baby. However, the costs of formula and doctors' visits required for babies who are not getting any of the health benefits of human milk also add up.

In many cases, insurance companies have been known to cover some of the costs of BFAR when specifically petitioned to do so and a thorough explanation of the necessity is provided. Insurance reimbursement is usually more likely when a physician writes a prescription or a referral. It also helps to remind the insurance company that the AAP recommends exclusive breastfeeding for the first six months of a baby's life. BFAR expenses that are often eligible for insurance coverage are lactation consultant services, pump and scale rentals, prescription galactagogues, and donated human milk.

The determination to give a new baby the very best makes BFAR costs more bearable. You are not alone in being concerned about the expense of BFAR, it is quite normal and realistic for you to address the issue and your feelings about it. It is a concern that is shared by most BFAR mothers to some degree.

Judging Other Mothers

The very nature of BFAR requires a mother to have a strong commitment to breastfeeding; she understands its benefits and fights hard to make it happen. It can be very disturbing to a BFAR mother to see other mothers with copious milk supplies put forth no more than a token effort to breastfeed. One BFAR mother told the BFAR email support group that she felt like screaming at all the formula-feeding mothers, "What are you thinking? You have FULL milk supplies!"

The reality is that we can never know what is in the hearts and life experiences of other mothers. Their reasons not to breastfeed, or what may look to you like a lack of persistence in the face of problems, may be related to serious personal issues that make breastfeeding as much a difficulty for them as BFAR is for you. On the other hand, it may be that they simply do not have accurate information about the benefits and joys of breastfeeding. While it may be understandable for you to feel jealous of a mother with a full milk supply and even to feel some anger as part of that jealousy, it is important not to allow those feelings to prevent you from appreciating the good and admirable qualities of that mother.

Striving for Perfection

BFAR mothers who do not have full milk supplies can often feel that they do not have control over their bodies. This lack of control can be very uncomfortable if they have been used to having control over most aspects of their lives. In compensation, then, it is common for BFAR mothers to feel a strong need to make all the other aspects of their babies' lives as perfect as possible. It may be that they want to prove to themselves and others that they can be highly successful at mothering even though they are not able to fully breastfeed.

The risk of doing this is in setting such high standards that you berate yourself for failing to meet your expectations and then feel even worse about yourself. It is also important not to drive yourself so hard that you become exhausted. Try to be compassionate toward yourself. Take inventory of what your accomplishments actually are. Mothering is not about proving yourself to anyone. It is about creating relationships. As a BFAR mother putting forth such great efforts to feed your baby, you deserve a great deal of kindness and gentleness.

Dealing with Painful Criticism

Few of us are immune to the pain of criticism and BFAR mothers can be especially sensitive when they are otherwise worn down by physical and emotional exhaustion and stress. Criticism from friends and family whom you would otherwise turn to for support can be especially painful—almost to the point of feeling like betrayal.

One of the best ways to cope with criticism is to look at the motivation of the person giving it and then to determine how much credibility he or she has in passing judgment. It may be, for instance, that your mother has criticized you for getting up often at night to breastfeed your baby. She has said this because she knows you are tired and feels that your need for adequate sleep is more important than breastfeeding at night. What she may not understand, though, is that breastfed babies do need to eat at least every four hours at night and that offering a bottle of formula will be very harmful to your breastfeeding efforts.

In most cases, the people who criticize or offer solutions mean well, but they do not have a complete understanding of the issues involved in BFAR. Don't spend time worrying about the best way to respond to their comments; it is usually best to just let them know in your most confident way that you really do appreciate their concern and that you have thoroughly researched the issues involved and have made the best choice for your family. If you think they are open to it, you might also offer to share the information in this book with them.

Some BFAR mothers have found that this approach, coupled with the person's willingness to learn about BFAR, has turned a critical person into a staunch supporter. Even if this does not happen, though, your confident demeanor and clear control of your BFAR efforts will make a very positive impression on most people.

Feeling Unable to Complain

Because we have chosen the road to BFAR when an easier alternative of exclusive formula-feeding is available to us, we sometimes do not feel that we have the right to complain when times are tough. We can especially feel this way when those around us are not supportive and seem eager for us to give up and formula-feed.

You not only have a right to complain about the difficult aspects of BFAR, it is very important that you do so to maintain your equilibrium and positive perspective. If you are not able to speak openly about your feelings to your family and friends, it will be helpful to find a supportive group of breastfeeding mothers, such as your local LLL group or the BFAR email support group, that will listen to your feelings, validate your right to have them, and help you work through them. For any mother, having a support network can make all the difference between a positive or an overwhelming experience.

Loneliness

BFAR is still a relatively new field in lactation and not many physicians or lactation specialists are familiar with it. With the best of intentions, they sometimes give incorrect information that leaves BFAR mothers feeling as though they are fighting in the dark.

Of course, you are ten steps ahead of most BFAR mothers who have begun their BFAR journey in this way because you have taken the time to read this book. Having accurate information is only half the battle, though. Without a support group, BFAR can still be difficult and lonely. That is why it is so important for you to develop relationships with other BFAR mothers. It is encouraging to know that other mothers are in similar situations, fighting the same battles. Most importantly, you can learn from each other and feel empowered by your shared objectives. You will no longer be alone.

Emotional Reactions to Specific Situations

Using the At-Breast Supplementer

Not all BFAR mothers feel entirely comfortable using an at-breast supplementer. To some BFAR mothers, an at-breast supplementer is a blatant reminder to them and to others that they do not have a complete milk supply and so need a device—almost like a prosthesis–in order to breastfeed. It makes them feel that they are "handicapped" because they cannot fully feed their babies without this device.

It is important to realize that not having a full milk supply is considered to be fairly common in our society. Amazingly, not having enough milk is cited as the number one reason for not breastfeeding among all mothers, despite the fact that only a small percentage of the female population truly has a physiologically insufficient milk supply. Over the past century, through many subtle marketing schemes, we have become convinced that human mothers no longer have the mammalian capability of feeding our young. This is preposterous, of course, but still the myth persists. The only positive aspect of this misconception is that it actually benefits BFAR mothers because they need not feel self-conscious for their insufficient milk supply.

Some BFAR mothers who use at-breast supplementers feel that it is not the point of supplementation that makes them feel uncomfortable, but just that supplementing in this way calls more attention to the fact that they are breastfeeding. Sadly, it is true that in many cultures bottle-feeding is so commonplace that it has become the prevalent norm for infant feeding and breastfeeding in public is not always accepted. If this is why it is uncomfortable for you, you may then have to simply consider the issue in terms of weighing the needs of your baby against the opinions of strangers. When you think of it that way, your baby's need to be breastfed will almost always be far more important than the needs of strangers.

Explaining why you are using an at-breast supplementer to a curious stranger can make many mothers feel embarrassed and self-conscious, but it can also be an opportunity to assert your purpose and enlighten them as to the breastfeeding possibilities that are made possible by this special device. When asked why they use it, some BFAR mothers have said simply that they don't make enough milk because of previous breast surgery. They do not volunteer details about the type of surgery, but rather focus on the point that they are deeply convinced of the benefits of breastfeeding and have chosen to supplement at the breast rather than using bottles because the special device keeps their babies happy at the breast. The usual reaction is complete amazement that such a device exists, followed by sincere admiration and warm acceptance of the mother for using it.

Feeling Self-Conscious about Using Bottles

While using bottles in public may be more acceptable than breastfeeding, BFAR mothers may find they feel uncomfortable supplementing with bottles among other breastfeeding mothers, especially mothers who feel strongly about breastfeeding. Because bottle-feeding is often thought to be in direct opposition to breastfeeding, it is understandable that some BFAR mothers can feel self-conscious about choosing to use them even when supplementation is necessary.

Hearing negative comments about formula can be especially hurtful if you are using formula for supplementation. BFAR mothers appreciate formula as viable nutrition for sustaining the health of their babies.

If you find yourself in a situation where you feel uncomfortable about supplementing, especially if you are using bottles, it can help to briefly explain that you must supplement because you had breast surgery that compromised your milk supply. Knowing that you are supplementing because you absolutely must is regarded differently by even the most adamant breastfeeding mothers. You will almost certainly find that once they understand your reason for using a bottle, they will be supportive and admiring of your BFAR efforts.

Feeling Discouraged because Supplementation Is Necessary

The necessity of supplementation can make many BFAR mothers feel very discouraged. They know intellectually that it is beyond their control, but on an emotional level, it can be disheartening, especially when they compare themselves to other breastfeeding mothers. After working so hard to provide half of your child's daily nutritional needs, it can make you want to just give up in complete frustration when your breastfeeding friend easily pumps eight ounces of milk in five minutes. Quantity can suddenly seem to mean so much more than quality. It can make all your efforts seem insignificant.

They aren't though! Every single drop of human milk is precious! Not a single one of your efforts is insignificant—on the contrary, every bit of effort is a tremendous gift to your child.

As BFAR mothers, our attitude toward the BFAR process is very critical to our success. We must try to maintain a positive perspective as much of the time as possible. A large part of that positive thinking is having a "glass is half full" philosophy, rather than a "glass is half empty" philosophy. This means that we must greatly value the milk that we can produce instead of regretting the milk we cannot produce.

When we adopt such a positive perspective, but work so hard for such a long time to produce such relatively small amounts, it is natural to cherish every single drop of our milk. In fact, it may be a cliché, but many BFAR mothers have cried over spilt milk. An overturned container of a mother's own milk is heartbreaking!

The frustration that we can feel when this happens is not only a feeling of distress that the baby will not have the benefits of that milk, which will have to be replaced by lesser-quality supplement, but it is also a deeper feeling of frustration over all the hard work that we have to put into making milk and how easily those efforts can be made futile by a careless elbow.

Having a Copious Milk Supply

Not all BFAR mothers have to supplement and for those who have a complete milk supply, there can be many conflicting emotions. On the one hand, it is natural to feel a tremendous sense of pride that your body is fully capable of nurturing your baby. Knowing that you can breastfeed normally and do not have to go through all the heartbreaking battles of supplementation can make one feel deeply thankful and blessed.

On the other hand, though, some BFAR mothers find that they occasionally feel almost a "survivor's guilt" that they have such a copious milk supply when so many other BFAR mothers do not. They may be reluctant to mention that they are not supplementing because they do not want to hurt the feelings of the other BFAR mothers or make them feel jealous. As a result, a fully breastfeeding BFAR mother might not feel that she belongs at a support group of BFAR mothers.

She is a BFAR mother, though, and as such has a natural place among other BFAR mothers. There will most certainly be times when she needs their advice and support. She also has a great deal to contribute to the group, including the factors that made her exclusive BFAR experience possible. She may indeed find that she is a source of inspiration to many of the mothers in her BFAR support group.

A Strong Commitment

Most BFAR mothers begin their journey intellectually convinced of the superiority of human milk and breastfeeding. They rationalize, though, that if they cannot breastfeed, they will accept it with grace and go on to bottle-feed. It is not usually until their babies are born that they discover a tremendous passion for breastfeeding that inspires them to persevere through all the bumps in the road.

While it is not fair to say that all BFAR mothers feel this way, it does seem true that most BFAR mothers come to feel very committed to breastfeed. They are tremendously motivated and go to great efforts to BFAR, possibly because they have discovered that the physical benefits of human milk and breastfeeding are only half of the rewards to be gained. They have realized that the most special qualities of breastfeeding are found in quiet moments that transcend merely feeding the baby nourishment, such as feeling our little warm baby curled close to our bodies, inhaling his special smell, and feeling enveloped by the tremendous spirit of mothering.

Baby Blues and Postpartum Depression

Most mothers feel some fluctuations in their emotions and some degree of depression around the third or fourth day following the birth of a baby, which is often referred to as the "baby blues." This is felt most often with the first baby. Even though she logically knows that all is well and that having a baby is a positive event in her life, a mother may feel sad and tearful. She may also feel unusually irritable and have either insomnia or fatigue. Most professionals believe that baby blues are caused by postpartum hormonal changes and the natural repercussions of the physical stress of labor. It is also likely to be a normal response to the sudden shift in self-image and identity as one becomes a mother and undertakes the great responsibility of parenting. Baby blues usually pass with adequate rest, nutrition, a healthy dose of self-pampering, and the support and empathetic listening of trusted friends and family members.

For some women, though, the depression they feel is so severe and persistent that it interferes with their abilities to adequately function or care for their babies. It may become serious enough to warrant a clinical diagnosis of postpartum depression (PPD). When this happens to a BFAR mother, her entire BFAR experience may be jeopardized. It is important for new mothers and those who work with new mothers to be aware of the symptoms of PPD and seek immediate treatment for it.

PPD is characterized by combinations of the following symptoms, although not all of the symptoms must be experienced in order to be diagnosed with PPD. The symptoms are usually felt with a significant amount of severity, last for more than two weeks, and do not seem to lessen in response to normal comfort measures.

Postpartum Depression Symptoms:

- Dysphoric mood (sadness, hopelessness, tearfulness, irritability, anxiety, crying spells)
- Loss of interest in normally pleasurable activities
- Excessive anxiety over child's health
- Difficulty concentrating or making decisions
- Psychomotor agitation or retardation
- Fatigue
- Changes in appetite or sleep patterns
- Deep feelings of worthlessness or guilt, especially failure at motherhood
- Recurrent thoughts of death/suicide

If you believe that you have one or more of these symptoms, you can be reassured that you are not alone as PPD affects between 10 to 15 percent of all new mothers. It is important, though, to promptly address your feelings of depression in order to minimize their impact upon your BFAR experience.

The appropriate treatment for PPD depends in great part upon the severity of your symptoms and may include medication and therapy. Discussing your depression with a health care provider is the first step to recovery. In most cases, drugs prescribed for PPD are compatible with breastfeeding, but you may need to check a specific medication with someone who is knowledgeable about lactation.

Coping Techniques

The chances are that as a BFAR mother you have experienced at least a few of the emotional issues that have been described. If so, then you have probably sought ways to effectively cope with them. Several of the coping techniques that have worked best for BFAR mothers are described in this section.

Attitude

The attitude with which we approach our world has a great deal to do with our perception of our BFAR experience. Throughout this book, a strong emphasis has been placed on the value of a positive attitude. To those who are feeling overwhelmed with BFAR, this kind of recommendation might not seem very helpful. But we always have a choice in the way that we choose to approach our experiences, and almost invariably those of us who decide to be as positive as possible find that our challenges are less stressful and more rewarding. When we deliberately choose to look at our BFAR experience in a positive light, we immediately begin to see the hidden benefits or the "silver lining."

Of course, we can't always be positive, but making a conscious decision to have a positive perspective will go a long way toward easing your stress and helping you to find an acceptance and peace with your BFAR experience.

Support Network

The most effective coping technique for BFAR is having a good support network. A mother simply can't do this alone. She needs to talk to other BFAR mothers and share her feelings and concerns with trusted friends, family members, counselors, or breastfeeding support groups, such as a local LLL Group. This book has covered many of the topics and concerns common to BFAR, but each BFAR mother is unique and will have her own special issues. Knowing that other breastfeeding mothers have felt the same way and faced the same challenges is reassuring and validating. If you are online, you may also find it helpful to share your experiences with the BFAR email support group or other online support groups.

Taking It One Day at a Time

Another coping technique that is helpful in keeping BFAR mothers from feeling overwhelmed is to take each day of BFAR at a time. Especially in the beginning, a single day can seem to go on forever and we wonder how we will ever manage months and months (or even years) of BFAR. On days like that, it's hard to believe that in just a month or two most of the rough spots will be behind you. So the only way to really keep from feeling completely overwhelmed now is to block out all thoughts of future weeks, months, and years and just think about today. Thinking of going to the effort of BFAR just for a day is much easier to handle emotionally than thinking of doing it over and over for a long time. Don't worry that what you are doing implies a binding contract to keep it up for any length of time beyond today.

It is even helpful for some BFAR mothers to say to themselves, "I'll wean tomorrow after I breastfeed today." Of course, in almost every instance, they don't wean the next day (or anytime soon), but knowing that they can wean gives them enough relief to have the strength to continue breastfeeding today. Eventually, each day will add to another and before you know it, the timeframe that overwhelmed you is past and you and your baby have come through beautifully.

Trusting Your Baby

One of the most powerful aspects of breastfeeding is developing an intuitive relationship with your baby so that you and he form a mutual trust. He trusts you to meet his needs and you trust him to let you know what his needs are. As BFAR mothers, it can sometimes be hard for us to feel we have the luxury of trusting our babies to let us know what they need because we are so worried we will miss their signals and undernourish them.

Especially when we are supplementing them, it can be easy to just give them what we think they should have. But in a breastfeeding relationship, it is important to follow our baby's cues and allow him to take the lead. It is understandably hard to do this when we are so worried about whether or not our baby will get enough, but so long as the diaper count, hydration status, and weight gain are adequate, we can let go of some of the control and trust our babies to tell us what they want and need. On some days, they will want less than on other days, and that's okay. If we are in tune with their cues and trust them to know what they want and need and give it to them accordingly, they will receive exactly the right amount for their development.

For BFAR mothers that are supplementing with at-breast supplementation devices, this can mean that there may be times the baby repeatedly spits out the tubing. If you should find this happening, allow him to nurse without it for a while. You may be very surprised to find out that you are having great let-downs. He didn't want the tube because he was overwhelmed with milk!

Trust that your baby's wants and needs are genuine and do your best to meet them accordingly. The harmonious relationship that naturally develops will be rewarding to you both.

Fast Forwarding

One of the most powerful coping tools used by veteran mothers is a technique called "fast forwarding." This technique is most helpful when you are at your wit's end and completely overwhelmed with stress.

All you need to do to use "fast forwarding" is take a deep breath, and try to imagine as vividly as possible what things will be like in five, ten, or even twenty years. For instance, when your four-month-old baby has fussed and cried all day and you don't think you can take another minute, just form a mental picture of this same child ten years from now when he is an independent, perfectly charming boy, capable of heart-warming conversations and the excitement of discovering his own potential. You really won't remember all the stress you were feeling when he was four months old. And furthermore, all of the time, patience, and love that you gave him will turn out to be a very worthwhile investment.

Remember That Time Flies

Finally, always try to keep in mind that it most certainly will not always be as difficult as it seems today. Our babies are tiny for only a short time and that time will seem to fly past you, even though some days may drag a bit. Before long, you will look back and realize that the hardest days are far behind you and that it really has gotten easier. You are now a veteran BFAR mother yourself and you have a child who was well loved and well cared for every moment of the way. Allow yourself to be proud of all that you have accomplished.

Your Identity as a Breastfeeding Mother

When we become mothers for the first time, we undergo a personal identity transformation that requires us to completely adjust the ways in which we define ourselves. One of the most important aspects to this new identity is the way in which we feed our babies. For many women, being a breastfeeding mother is a distinct badge of honor. BFAR mothers who must supplement, though, do not always feel they have a right to that desirable label, even though they may be spending quite a bit of each day with babies at their breasts.

For the record, any mother who feeds her baby at her breast—no matter how much she is lactating or if she must also supplement away from the breast—is a breastfeeding mother. BFAR mothers by definition are breastfeeding mothers. You are a breastfeeding mother.

Conclusion

Because of the need for continuous assessment, as BFAR mothers, we can begin to think of breastfeeding in very quantifiable terms, so that we are always evaluating our success against an arbitrary standard of what we define as our ultimate goal. Failing to reach that goal, despite the fact that it might simply be impossible to do so, induces deeply negative feelings that no logic can assuage. While comparing our experience to a breastfeeding ideal may be very natural, it is not at all helpful for us and is often detrimental by compelling us to feel negative emotions that obscure the many positive aspects of our BFAR experience.

Nonetheless, it is very important for a BFAR mother to have a sense of her "big picture" because it is this image that directly influences her perception of her capabilities and strengths and motivates her future endeavors. What she may not realize is that she has choices about how she perceives this broad image of her breastfeeding experience. Just as we must make a point of choosing a positive attitude toward our BFAR experience while it is happening, we can make a conscious choice to remember our BFAR history in terms of the benefits we and our baby received and the personal growth we would not have experienced without it.

In the next chapter, the concept of how we define the success of our BFAR experience is discussed. It is not enough to simply have experienced the unique journey of breastfeeding your baby after your reduction surgery. There are many factors that determine our understanding of our BFAR history and many ways that we can deliberately define it so that our memories and perceptions become beneficial to us. You are invited to elevate your BFAR experience to its most positive form by defining your own success in terms that are uniquely meaningful and gratifying to you.

LARA'S STORY

I had my surgery done when I was 18. I had just over four pounds of breast tissue removed, and went from an overflowing 38DD to a 36 B/C. At the time of my surgery, my surgeon told me I'd never be able to breastfeed. I knew nothing at the time about the benefits of breastfeeding and human milk, and never thought I'd get married and have children. I just wanted to look "normal" and get rid of the bra-strap grooves in my shoulders and the constant backaches.

When I was pregnant with my first son, Benjamin, I was able to express a drop or two of colostrum during the late stages of my pregnancy, so I was hopeful I'd be able to breastfeed. When my milk came in after Benjamin's birth on the second or third day following a long labor and an eventual cesarean birth, I was ecstatic. I exclusively breastfed him for two-and-a-half weeks until I started supplementing with formula. Benjamin was still down more than a pound from his nine pound, nine ounce birth weight and showing signs of dehydration (urate crystals in his not-very-wet diapers being the big one). I only supplemented after he had nursed for a long period of time before getting fussy at the breast. At the beginning, I let him nurse for an hour before I supplemented, but later I could tell when he wasn't getting enough from me and switched then. I was lucky that he always preferred me to the bottle. At our peak of supplementation, he was taking 12 to 14 ounces of formula a day. I was able to cut out the supplementation around six or seven months of age, when he was well-established on solids. I ended up nursing Benjamin for over three years—he even tried to nurse a few times after his brother was born.

With my second son, Evan, I supplemented only for the first two or three months, and at the peak I was giving him seven ounces per day of formula in either the SNS or Avent bottles. I started to cut back on the supplementation after he went through a period of time where he was gaining an average of 11.2 ounces a week. I figured if he was gaining that quickly, he didn't need as much supplement as I was giving him.

I think that I might have been able to exclusively nurse Evan, but I had two big things counting against us: 1) I had a cesarean birth and I lost quite a bit of blood so I was anemic. 2) Evan was born with a birth defect that required surgery when he was only nine days old. We had a delayed start to nursing on the day he was born until the local doctors spoke to a specialist who said we could handle him like a normal infant. The entire event was very stressful, and on the day of surgery I went almost 24 hours between nursings. I supplemented the most in the hospital. I do know that if I hadn't been nursing him, I wouldn't have been able to hold him nearly as much as I did in the hospital. Our nursing relationship allowed him a lot more cuddling and nurturing which I believe helped him to heal quicker.

Even though I've had wonderful nursing relationships with both of my boys, my supply was much better for Evan. Here's the list of what I did differently for Evan than with Benjamin, in the order I think they did the most good:

1. **Herbs/Reglan:** *I had Benjamin before I had heard about taking herbs to increase your milk supply. With Evan, I took fenugreek, blessed thistle, vitex (chastetree berry), More Milk tincture and brewer's yeast. I stopped taking the vitex after a few weeks and the brewer's yeast after a few months, but I took fenugreek and blessed thistle (with an occasional dose of More Milk when needed) for the first year following his birth. I also took a two week course of Reglan, but did not notice any change in my supply over what I was getting with the herbs. I didn't have any side effects, though I didn't take much time to notice them if I did (this was over Evan's surgery and recovery time). I also drink Mother's Milk tea by Traditional Medicinals when I feel like I need a boost.*

2. **Water, water, water!** *Make sure you are drinking adequate amounts of water every day, in addition to anything else you drink. It really does make a difference.*

3. **This was my second BFAR experience.** *I nursed Benjamin for over three years, so I think that helped me grow more milk-producing tissue and maximize the efficiency of what I do have. Plus, I was more relaxed in general and I knew what I was doing. Confidence and experience can make a huge difference! I also had the combined knowledge of all the wonderful women of BFAR over the years.*

4. **Properly fitting nursing bras;** *remember, women who don't nurse are often advised to bind their breasts to get rid of their milk quicker. Your bra should not be snug or uncomfortably tight.*

I was extremely disappointed when I had to start supplementing, but I realize that I've been amazingly successful considering that I originally thought I'd never be able to breastfeed at all. My husband is very supportive of breastfeeding and helped me through the tough times when Benjamin was a newborn when my mantra was "Two months! Two months!" My goal at the beginning was to make it to two months. When two months arrived, I was amazed that I ever considered stopping.... It does get better if you hang in there past the initial learning time and postpartum chaos. I am so grateful I didn't give up because my nursing relationships have been very special and have helped me to be a better mother.

For the record, I never got engorged when my milk came in and rarely ever felt engorged. I would get a slightly uncomfortable full feeling if we'd gone several hours without nursing, but nothing really painful. I have never felt a let-down, and most of the time instead of having the normal suck-swallow pattern, Benjamin does more of a suck, suck, suck, swallow. The only time I've ever leaked was the night my milk came in and I leaked a few drops from the side he wasn't nursing on (that's how I knew it had come in). I produce more milk on my left side even though that's the side that had the most tissue removed.

DEFINING YOUR OWN SUCCESS

Each BFAR experience is unique, even for each BFAR mother. Some experiences are deeply rewarding, others are tremendously disappointing, and many are somewhere in between. No matter what our experience was, though, it is important to thoroughly process our feelings about it so that we can then define our experience and remember it in the most positive way possible. It is important to find peace in your BFAR experience before too much time has passed so that any painful feelings do not have a negative effect on other aspects of your life.

As we always have a choice about approaching BFAR with a positive perspective, we also have a choice about how we define and remember our BFAR experience in retrospect. This is not to say that we should dismiss or ignore our negative feelings, but rather that we should be honest about them and thoroughly deal with them so that we can find peace and closure by developing a complete acceptance of our BFAR experience.

Exploring Your Feelings

Recognizing that Many Factors Were Beyond Your Control

BFAR is a deeply emotional experience. We pour our hearts and our souls into giving the best to our children, but are limited by our physical capabilities, environmental circumstances, access to information, and level of support. In coming to terms with our feelings about BFAR, it is important to separate out those things that we had control over and those we could not control. While some of the decisions we made along the way contributed directly to our outcome, there were many factors that were beyond our control.

As mothers, it is natural for us to feel completely responsible for our experiences, but BFAR is highly complex and dependent upon many interrelated factors. If you did not have access to correct information about BFAR, you could only make the best decisions possible from the information at hand. If you did not have a supportive environment, anything you could accomplish would be amazing. If you were not able to purchase some of the devices that can help, such as at-breast supplementers or galactagogues, you were handicapped beyond your control. And it may be that no matter what you did, your lactation system was too minimal. You can only accept responsibility for the portions of BFAR that you could directly control.

Celebrating the Rewarding Aspects

Coming to terms with feelings about a BFAR experience is not limited to negative emotions. For many BFAR mothers, their BFAR experience was largely rewarding and very pleasurable. Nursing a baby at her breast is often one of the most sublime moments of a mother's life.

It is very important to draw out and celebrate our pleasant memories from the more painful aspects of our experience so that we can see the balance and appreciate the good. Take time to think back over your BFAR experience and actively search your memory for beautiful moments and precious times of bonding. Remember, too, the insights, wisdom, and personal growth that you received as a direct result of BFAR. When you have gathered these aspects in your memory, you can then make a point of celebrating them with gratefulness. The pleasure that you receive from this exercise will help you to preserve the positive aspects of your BFAR experience and integrate them fully into your memories of this unique time.

Confronting Painful Feelings

Of course, for many BFAR mothers, breastfeeding has painful moments. No matter whether we were responsible or not, it just hurts to go through the anxiety, anger, worry, concern, guilt, regret, disappointment, and anguish of trying to give your baby the highest quality nutrition and nurturance when your body and other circumstances are incapable of allowing it to happen.

It is natural to suppress and deny yourself the indulgence of fully experiencing those feelings when they happen, but before you can move forward from your BFAR experience, you need to be honest about what you felt and allow yourself to grieve for what you couldn't have.

Take some time alone when you are not responsible for caring for your child and can be unobserved for a while. Make yourself comfortable and put a box of tissues by your side. Then allow all the hurtful feelings of your BFAR experience to slowly come to the surface. Feel compassion for yourself and complete entitlement to these feelings. You are an incredible mother who has been through a difficult experience because you wanted to give the best to your child.

It may take a good amount of time to thoroughly process all the painful feelings you experienced while breastfeeding. You may need to go through this cathartic process several times before you feel you have come to terms with all of them. But once you have and you are ready to move forward, you will then be able to make a satisfying peace with your BFAR experience.

Making Peace with Your BFAR Experience

Once we have processed the feelings we experienced during breastfeeding, the only hurdle that remains in order for us to have peace is to forgive ourselves for anything we regret that we had control over. We must be kind to ourselves and remember that we made the best decisions we could at the time and we had the best intentions. If they weren't the best choices in retrospect, there is nothing we can do about it now except to forgive ourselves and know that we have learned from the consequences of those decisions and will make better ones in the future.

It may also be necessary to forgive others who contributed to the negative aspects of your BFAR experience. This could include a surgeon who gave you incorrect information about BFAR prior to your surgery, a nurse or a physician who jeopardized your BFAR efforts, a lactation consultant who was inexperienced in BFAR, or friends and family members who were not supportive.

When we have honestly forgiven ourselves and others, we can have complete acceptance and soothing peace about the BFAR experiences that we leave behind us, and focus our attention upon our present mothering relationships, while we begin to think about any future BFAR experiences.

Make the Most of Your Current Relationship– Surround Your Baby with Love

Our BFAR babies are very special. They are patient with us while we try to do our best for them and they are very forgiving as we learn our way. With all the added stress and effort of BFAR, we sometimes don't relax enough during our quiet moments with our babies to simply stare at them in joyful wonder, appreciating their every nuance, and learning their special ways of communicating with us. But they are only this little for such a short period of time. Once past, these precious quiet moments are gone forever, unless we've imprinted them on our heart's memory.

Now is the time to immerse yourself in your baby and learn everything you can about his unique little self. In so many ways, he is unlike any other baby that has ever been born. And, as his mother, only you have the ability to see all that is truly wonderful about him.

Becoming a mother is a tremendous adjustment in identity and it is difficult even for those of us who are having our babies in the best of circumstances. But many BFAR mothers have found that the easiest way through this difficult time is to take comfort from our babies, and to give them comfort in return. Something very miraculous happens when a mother and her baby connect in this way. Suddenly it is as if they are inside each other's skin and they can understand and anticipate the other's needs with even the smallest cue.

You already know your baby better than any one else ever could and your love for each other will grow deeper and deeper as time goes on. By breastfeeding your baby, if only for a short while, you connected with him in a unique and intimate way that will always be a special bond between you. Above all, take as much time as you can to completely surround your baby with love. The love you give him now has more power than it will have at any other time of his life.

Continue to Participate in Breastfeeding Support Groups

Many BFAR mothers choose to continue participating in breastfeeding forums after they have ended their BFAR experience. They do this for the camaraderie of being among mothers who have come to understand and appreciate the road they've traveled. They also find it rewarding to share their hard-won wisdom and information with new mothers who are just beginning their BFAR journeys.

You can rest assured that you will always be welcome at breastfeeding support groups such as LLL meetings, as well as the BFAR email support group. A mother does not have to be actively breastfeeding to attend and you will not be judged, especially by BFAR mothers, for breastfeeding decisions that you made. We know that we are each doing the best we can for our babies and the choice one mother makes may not be the best choice for any other mother. BFAR mothers who choose to participate on the BFAR email support group even after breastfeeding has ended are warmly appreciated because the experience they gained from BFAR is so beneficial to new BFAR mothers.

Next Time Will Be Easier

Fortunately, if you should have another baby, breastfeeding after a breast reduction surgery is usually much, much easier the next time around. As you know, each lactation results in a process called "recanalization," whereby the lactation system actually regrows and reconnects. It is one of the few systems in the human body that has this capacity. Many BFAR mothers who were able to only provide a small amount of milk for their first babies are able to produce much more, sometimes even to the point of nursing without any supplementation. Additionally, subsequent breastfeeding usually goes much more smoothly because let-downs are stronger and easier as a result of better relaxation and enhanced confidence. And even if this is not the case for you, you will benefit by using the knowledge you have gained along the way to plan ahead and avoid some of the pitfalls you experienced during your previous BFAR journey.

Defining Your Own Success

Look at what an extraordinary gift you've given your baby! Defining your success is not about how much milk you were able to produce or how many months you were able to breastfeed. Defining your success means giving yourself credit for the commitment you made to giving your baby the best start in life and the tremendous effort you put into pursuing that goal. You and your baby have developed a bond that will continue throughout your ongoing parenting relationship. Even if BFAR didn't work out quite the way you may have hoped it would, you undoubtedly shared some special moments that you might not have otherwise had. And you learned a great deal more about yourself as you faced the challenges of BFAR.

There are two important messages of this book. One is that each mother must discover a system that best meets the needs of her baby, her family, and herself. The second is that you must view your experience with a deep appreciation of the mothering and lactation abilities you do have rather than feeling deprived of what you cannot have.

Defining your own success means looking beyond conventional definitions of breastfeeding success and determining for yourself, according to your own needs, abilities, and unique circumstances, the true value of your efforts. As you define your BFAR success, do not allow the amount of your milk supply or the duration of your breastfeeding experience to be part of your evaluation. It is far more important to recognize that any amount of human milk is an extraordinary gift for any baby. Every single drop of milk that your baby received from you will benefit him throughout his entire life. And the special moments you shared during nursing will always be a dear part of your relationship, forming the foundation for a deep and lasting bond between you.

In addition to the act of providing nutrition to your child at your breast, the success of the BFAR experience can be best measured by also considering the effects that this unique privilege of motherhood has had on your self-image and sense of self-worth. To most people, it is obvious that a BFAR mother is an exceptional mother. It may be difficult for some BFAR mothers to accept and agree with this because of their conflicting feelings of doubt, regret, and guilt. Most people do not expect a woman to breastfeed at all after a breast reduction surgery. It has taken a great deal of courage for you to undertake BFAR. You may not feel at all courageous, but true courage is not doing something without fear, but rather in spite of it. In recognizing your priorities, educating yourself about BFAR, and then going to the effort to breastfeed against the odds, you have many reasons to be proud of your journey and the choices that you have made. No matter what your experience turned out to be, you deserve to move on from it with an understanding of the true value of your efforts encompassing a conviction that you have given your baby the most precious gift you will ever give him.

You went to tremendous effort to give your child the very best, and you will continue to do that throughout your parenting relationship. The fact that you have breastfed in the face of difficulty and opposition demonstrates your deep love for your child and your deep sensitivity as a mother. Your commitment to your baby and his best interests sends a strong message of the profound love and devotion you have for him. You have set the stage to continue to make parenting choices that communicate this message and will help to form a solid foundation for him as he develops an understanding of himself and his worth.

Each BFAR mother is a heroine. By your experience, you have undoubtedly touched many lives and impressed many people with your determination to provide the best for your baby. Your exceptional efforts and deep devotion to your child add a new dimension to the definition of motherhood and inspire mothers everywhere to reach to greater heights of nurturing.

P A R T   I V

THE PROFESSIONAL PERSPECTIVE

ASSISTING THE BFAR MOTHER FROM THE PROFESSIONAL PERSPECTIVE

While the primary focus of this book has been directed toward the BFAR mother, the information contained herein is also relevant to all health care providers who treat BFAR women. This chapter thus provides specific information according to specialty on the optimal ways to facilitate BFAR from the clinical perspective.

In addition to the information that is provided in this book, LLLI publishes information about breastfeeding topics from the clinical perspective through its LACTATION CONSULTANT SERIES. Although there is no LACTATION CONSULTANT SERIES publication about BFAR as of the time of this writing, one will be published and made available to health care providers within the next few years. It is highly recommended that you obtain a copy when it becomes available in order to have access to the most recent developments in clinical management of BFAR, as well as current research findings.

All Health Care Providers (HCPs)

The following information is provided as a general address to all professional health care specialties. Depending on the context of the specific recommendation, it may apply more directly to some specialties than to others, but will be broadly applicable. Specific information according to specialization follows this section.

Identify Treatment Objectives

In order to ensure an optimal outcome for BFAR mothers and their babies, it is important to realistically identify the treatment objectives. It most cases, the goals will be that the baby receive sufficient amounts of the best quality nutrition possible, with as much time spent at the breast as possible to promote maternal-infant bonding. In order to achieve this objective, then, it is imperative to maximize the maternal milk supply and minimize supplementation away from the breast.

Discuss Your Approach to BFAR

BFAR mothers are particularly in need of reassurance by means of an explicit comment from their health care providers that asserts awareness of the superiority of breastfeeding and commitment to helping them successfully BFAR. In discussing BFAR with a BFAR mother, it is important to be neither overly optimistic about the chance of exclusive breastfeeding nor pessimistic regarding the mother's likelihood of breastfeeding at all.

A health care provider has a unique opportunity by virtue of the authority of his credentials to encourage BFAR mothers to understand that while it may not always be possible to breastfeed exclusively, most BFAR mothers can have a satisfying breastfeeding relationship even with supplementation. If the BFAR mother is not familiar with this book, making information about BFAR available to her, either in the form of a recommendation to read this book, giving her a pamphlet from LLLI about BFAR, or referral to a knowledgeable resource, will help her explore the many options that are available to make BFAR possible.

Become Knowledgeable about the Major Issues of BFAR

In order to achieve these objectives, HCPs must be knowledgeable about the major issues that surround BFAR. For many HCPs, it is unrealistic to read a comprehensive text such as this that has been written to a lay audience. Nonetheless, until a Lactation Consultant Series publication on BFAR is available, a skimming of the most relevant topics will provide a great deal of information and insight into the mechanics of successful BFAR.

BFAR Need Not Involve Risk

In some cases, BFAR from the clinical perspective can seem to involve a measure of risk that may be outside the realm of comfort for some HCPs. When administered according to the principles described in this text, however, no actual risk is incurred. The most important of these principles is that the patients comply with the recommendations of vigilant and constant monitoring of nutritional and hydration status of their babies in cooperation with a health care provider in order to provide early warning of impending infant deterioration.

Include Subjective Information as Criteria for Diagnosis and Treatment

In conjunction with objective, quantitative data, many health care professionals have found that it is beneficial in the process of diagnosis and treatment to include subjective or other qualitative factors, such as the mother's impressions, opinions, and insights, as this subjective information often reveals objective data that are critical to successful management of her case.

Drugs and Lactation

If drugs must be prescribed for a BFAR mother, it is recommended that HCPs refrain from reliance upon recommendations of the *Physician's Desk Reference* (PDR) as the final, authoritative source. In almost all cases, the information in this publication is not based upon actual research that specifies the action of a given drug upon lactation. Therefore, the PDR tends to recommend total exclusion of most discussed drugs in the context of lactation in order to avoid litigious liability. For this reason, the AAP has reviewed many common drugs and provided its own set of recommendations for their use for lactating mothers. Another consideration is that many drugs routinely used in the neonatal/pediatric context are not specifically approved for that purpose. Excellent resources for specific information on the effects of drugs upon lactation are Dr. Thomas Hale's annual publication, *Medications and Mothers' Milk* and *Drugs in Pregnancy and Lactation* by Gerald G. Briggs, B. Pharm, Roger K. Freeman, MD, and Sumner J. Yaffe, MD. Alternatively, Dr. Ruth Lawrence has provided a hotline for physician questions about the effects of specific drugs upon lactation. Information about each of these resources is provided in Appendix 1.

Facilitate Insurance Reimbursement

BFAR can be very expensive and the average household will find the associated costs to be fairly daunting. A health care provider can be of great assistance in facilitating insurance reimbursement by writing prescriptions, referrals, and letters of justification whenever appropriate. The onus of offering such prescriptions, referrals, or letters may be upon the health care provider, however, as the mother may not be aware that insurance reimbursement may be possible.

Provide Referrals to Competent HCPs Supportive of BFAR

As the process of BFAR almost always entails enlistment of multiple HCPs in a multi-visit approach beginning in the prenatal period, extending through the postpartum and pediatric visits, you may be called upon to provide a referral to a professional in another specialty. When doing so, it is important that the HCP most directly involved facilitate the continued success of BFAR by referring BFAR mothers preferentially to professionals that are likely to be supportive of BFAR.

One of the most important referrals that an HCP can make is to a competent local lactation consultant if the mother is not already working with one. It can be assumed that a lactation consultant is competent if she is board certified by the International Board of Lactation Consultant Examiners (IBLCE).

Plastic Surgeons

Be Realistic about Future Lactation Capabilities

It is very common for candidates for breast reduction surgery to ask about the effect of the proposed surgery upon their future lactation capabilities. It can be difficult to know how to respond, especially because there are so many factors beyond the surgery itself that affect lactation. A surgeon may also be very sensitive to the fact that most young women contemplating surgery do not understand how they may feel about breastfeeding a few years later when they begin their families. Many reduction mammoplasty candidates are typically young women, nulliparous, frequently still single and or seeking education, and have not settled into or considered maternal roles. In fact, it is common for young patients to assert that they have no interest in breastfeeding. In their textbook *Breastfeeding: A Guide for the Medical Profession,* Drs. Ruth and Robert Lawrence state that "Although plastic surgeons report that these women do not wish to breastfeed, it is our experience that many of them do wish to breastfeed later when they bear a child and are suddenly aware of their maternal role."[1]

For these reasons, it is best to be realistic in projections of post-surgical lactation potential, rather than falsely optimistic or falsely pessimistic. Avoid the overly simplistic statement that she "should be able to breastfeed," or an inaccurate statement such as "women with big breasts cannot usually breastfeed anyway." Instead, with every reduction candidate of childbearing years explain the practical range of BFAR scenarios as outlined in this book or refer them directly to this book. It may also be appropriate to include documentation of possible lactation outcomes along with the informed consent.

Employ Surgical Techniques that Best Preserve Lactation

Clearly, a surgeon who has sufficient interest in BFAR to read this section of this book will take great care to select a surgical technique that is conducive to BFAR, using techniques that do not completely sever the nipple/areolar complex from the breast and that preserve as much of the parenchyma as possible.

In a discussion of the best techniques to achieve these goals, John Little, in *Surgery of the Breast: Principles and Art*, states that

> "…we [should] develop mastery of a pedicle technique in breast
> reduction, one that I hope would be physiologic in the sense of favoring
> postoperative lactation and nipple sensation, as do the modified
> McKissock, central mound, and inferior pedicle techniques…. I have no
> desire to master or even attempt a pedicle technique that robs a patient
> of the hope for lactation or sensation when there are so many excellent
> techniques available that do not."[2]

In *Lactation, Physiology, Nutrition, and Breast-Feeding*, Drs. Neville and Neifert further elucidate the optimal criteria of a technique that preserves lactation:

> "The nipple and areolar complex are innervated solely by the inferior
> ramus of the fourth intercostal nerve, a point of considerable
> importance because interruption of this innervation may interfere with
> the afferent arm of the let-down reflex. Circular incisions around the
> lateral aspect of the areola should, for this reason, be avoided."[3]

Make Detailed Surgical Documentation Accessible

One of the best ways for a BFAR mother to begin preparation for BFAR is to obtain and decipher her surgical documentation. By having an understanding of the specific type of surgery she received and the events that transpired during the surgery, she will have realistic expectations about her lactation capability.

It is very important for the surgeon's office to make this information easily available to BFAR mothers who seek to understand their surgical histories. It may also be necessary for a surgeon to explain the charts to them in lay terms. Ideally, each woman of childbearing years would be given a copy her surgical report at her final post-surgical examination.

Obstetricians and Midwives

Incorporate Education and Discussion of BFAR at Prenatal Visits

The obstetrician or midwife frequently has a unique opportunity of introducing the concept of BFAR, as many post-reduction women may have never given breastfeeding serious consideration. Scheduled prenatal visits are an especially ideal setting to begin early BFAR education. This may be a casual discussion at any given individual appointment or referenced in a group setting such as a prenatal class. It is also important to encourage and support the BFAR mother-to-be to educate herself and investigate BFAR prior to delivery, providing referrals and reference material such as this book.

Minimize Interventions during Delivery

Research has now clearly shown that the mode of delivery can have a direct effect upon breastfeeding success. In *Breastfeeding: A Guide for the Medical Profession*, Drs. Lawrence and Lawrence state that:

> "The influence of mode of delivery on initiation of breastfeeding was
> examined in 370 primiparas. Cesarean birth and other surgical delivery
> procedures (e.g., vacuum extraction) were associated with a sleepy
> infant, late start to feeding after delivery, increased incidence of bottle
> supplementation, less frequent night feedings, and delayed milk
> production in the hospital." [1]

Many studies have shown that medications, including epidurals (especially epidurals containing bupivacaine),[1,4] during childbirth can significantly inhibit the sucking abilities of newborns. Of course, it would be unrealistic to assert that there are never circumstances that warrant administering drugs to a BFAR mother during labor. Rather, it is most conducive to BFAR to facilitate a birth that utilizes as few medical interventions as prudently possible in order to fully stimulate the baby's initial sucking reflex and the establishment of prolactin receptors during the critical first three hours after birth, which are essential to maximizing the BFAR milk supply.

For a complete discussion of the effect of prolactin receptors upon the BFAR milk supply, refer to Chapter 2.

Delay Prophylactic Eye Drops to Enable Bonding

While it is customary in most hospital settings to immediately administer prophylactic eye drops to the baby upon delivery, the resulting, albeit temporary, impairment of vision is a direct impediment to maternal- and paternal-infant bonding. A moderate delay in administration of the drops will not compromise the effectiveness of the treatment. Drs. Lawrence and Lawrence assert this point clearly by stating that:

> "It is important to delay instillation of prophylactic eye drops until after this time spent with the mother. If the drops are put into the eyes, blepharospasm will prevent the infant from opening the eyes and will mar the eye-to-eye contact. Only if there is a known risk of gonorrhea should the drops be put in immediately." [1]

Prevent Maternal-Infant Separation

Whenever possible, barring cases of severe postpartum or neonatal complications or sedation, BFAR mothers and babies should be kept in constant close proximity to facilitate demand nursing and maximum stimulation of the milk supply, even if such a practice is normally against hospital policy.

Be Knowledgeable about the Benefits of Galactagogues

The most profound influences for increasing the milk supply are often galactagogues, both herbal and prescription. Chapter 9 of this book provides a thorough explanation of their benefits and appropriate usage. The prescription drug domperidone, in particular, is likely to be most beneficial to your BFAR patients' milk supplies, although the better galactogenic herbs also have quite an impressive effect. Your patients may already be familiar with them or your information may be new to them. Discussing this option with them may be one of the most directly useful consultations they receive in regard to BFAR.

Treating Mastitis in the BFAR Mother

Mastitis in the context of BFAR is a very complex issue. There are many theories, but no concrete research to substantiate any of them. The best information at this point is that which is consistently empirically demonstrated.

One theory that is quite prevalent, but which cannot be substantiated either logically or empirically, is the belief that engorgement almost inevitably leads to mastitis since the "milk has nowhere to go." In terms of basic lactation physiology, engorgement is not a result of a large volume of milk so much as it is swelling of the tissues that surround the glands and ducts. Thus, the presence of milk in severed ducts is not responsible for the majority of the engorgement, and so will not have a bearing upon its progress. Lack of removal of the milk causes the ducts to atrophy almost immediately, so they do not become extended with "backed up" milk.

From the BFAR perspective, it is very rare, if it happens at all, that severed ducts become infected as a result of milk stagnation; in most cases they quickly dry up from lack of milk removal and stimulation. The anecdotal experience has consistently shown that severed ducts do not have access to bacterial infection, and so do not become infected as a result of "stagnation."

Nonetheless, BFAR mothers do seem to be particularly susceptible to mastitis. In some cases, the mastitis occurs chronically necessitating prophylactic antibiotics. The most current reasoning for this phenomenon is that the fluctuations in milk supply, to which the BFAR mothers' inherently tenuous milk supply is quite vulnerable, results in milk stagnation that leads to mastitis. If this is indeed the actual explanation for the phenomenon, the best prevention is thorough, regular draining of all ducts. This is best accomplished with a breastfeeding infant as pumping cannot compress the lactiferous sinuses, which is essential for effective let-down stimulation and milk removal. It is, therefore, essential to discourage the use of pumps and lengthy separations from the baby whenever possible. Galactagogues must be used consistently. Frequent variations in nursing position will ensure drainage of all ducts.

Watch for Postpartum Depression

Because BFAR is extraordinarily stressful at a time when the maternal physiology is most subject to hormonal fluctuations, BFAR inherently increases the risk for postpartum depression. Almost all BFAR mothers seem to experience some degree of depression, with most falling in the moderate range. Not all BFAR mothers will feel comfortable mentioning it to their obstetricians or midwives, though. They may think that it is normal and will subside on its own with time. They may not realize that it can be greatly moderated with appropriate temporary medication or cognitive therapy. Approaching the subject casually during a normal postpartum visit may be the best way to gauge the BFAR mother's degree of depression.

Breast Exams

Although recent research suggests that the risk of cancer is decreased by the event of reduction mammoplasty,[5] malignancies are still a risk factor for all women with breast tissue. Examining the post-surgical lactating breast, however, can be very arduous as it is often difficult to differentiate between scar tissue, active parenchyma, and suspicious formations. Mammograms are a less useful diagnostic tool in the post-surgical breast as the stroma is more dense. Awareness of her own internal breast strucure is often the best means of becoming aware of changes that necessitate further investigation. BFAR women, then, should be strongly urged to perform regular, thorough self-exams, even during lactation.

Maternity Nurses

A maternity nurse is often the first health care professional to interact with the BFAR mother when she begins actively nursing. The nurse's influence, then, carries an important potential benefit to the BFAR mother if her information is comprehensive and correct, while her demeanor is positive and supportive.

Help BFAR Mother and Baby Nurse Immediately after Delivery

Research has shown that prolactin receptors (see the discussion of prolactin receptors in Chapter 2) are most sensitive in the hour immediately after birth. It is very important for BFAR, then, to get the baby latched onto the breast correctly as soon after birth as possible. If the baby is not interested or other circumstances prevent this from happening, try to facilitate the initial nursing session as soon as it can be reasonably accomplished. Once nursing has successfully commenced, be as complimentary as possible, reassuring the mother that she "is a natural" (as all mothers basically are).

Minimize Maternal-Infant Separations

It is very important to keep BFAR mothers and their babies together at all times, barring, of course, cases of severe postpartum complications or sedation. By having the opportunity to establish a demand nursing schedule, the BFAR mother's milk supply will be stimulated to its greatest capacity.

Although it may seem kind, allowing a BFAR mother to sleep for an extended period of time, forgoing feedings, will negatively impact her sensitive milk supply and can sabotage her nursing relationship.

If the policy of the hospital is to have the baby taken to a nursery periodically, it would be prudent to enlist her physician's cooperation in writing an order to supercede this policy. At the very least, the baby should be taken to his mother immediately upon waking.

As a maternity nurse, you will also have a unique opportunity to reassure the new BFAR mother about the benefits of rooming-in with her baby and her ability to competently care for her new baby.

Encourage Nursing on Demand

Many BFAR mothers begin motherhood mindful of the stories they have heard from their mothers about convenient, scheduled feedings. They may not understand the benefits and desirability of nursing on demand. Now is a good time to gently mention these points and explain that allowing her baby to nurse on demand is the best way to ensure maximum stimulation of her milk supply, which is critical during the early postpartum weeks. It may also help to tell her that scheduled feedings are usually incompatible even in a normal breastfeeding relationship. If she still seems convinced that a schedule is desirable, reassure her that her baby can be coaxed into a schedule after the second month, after breastfeeding is well established.

Help BFAR Mothers Learn Alternative Nursing Positions

BFAR mothers need to be able to nurse in a variety of positions. Learning these positions early can be particularly helpful for them in stimulating the milk supply to its greatest capacity by exerting force on the ducts from different angles. They may also find, as many new mothers do, that some positions do not work well at first, and so they need viable alternatives. The side-lying position, football hold, and cross-cradle hold are particularly useful in BFAR.

Be Sensitive to the Dangers of Unnecessary Supplementation

It is important for caretakers of the baby to be sensitive to the dangers of supplementation while the baby is away from his mother. As explained above, it is not a kindness to allow a mother to sleep through the night. Unless supplementation has been deemed medically necessary by the baby's pediatrician, it will unnecessarily reduce the mother's milk supply.

For this reason, it is important to avoid enabling the mother to likewise sabotage her own milk supply by having formula samples readily accessible when she goes home. Unless she specifically requests them, do not volunteer unsolicited formula samples.

Do Not Give BFAR Babies Artificial Nipples

It is critical that BFAR babies not be given artificial nipples. Nipple confusion/preference is a very real phenomenon that is the leading reason for BFAR failure. According to Drs. Lawrence and Lawrence in their book, *Breastfeeding: A Guide for the Medical Profession*:

> *"An infant who is given a bottle or rubber nipple [pacifier] to suck can become confused because the milking action is different. The relatively inflexible rubber nipple may keep the tongue from its usual rhythmic action. In addition, the flow may be so rapid, even without sucking, that the infant learns to put the tongue against holes in the rubber nipple to slow down the flow. … When infants use the same tongue action needed for a rubber nipple while at the breast, they may even push the human nipple out of the mouth."* [1]

Alternatively, if supplementation is needed, it can be given at the breast with an at-breast supplementer, or by cup, syringe, eyedropper, or gavage tube (finger-feeder). All maternity nurses should have a least a peripheral knowledge of such feeding devices, or be able to refer the patient to an informed professional. This is especially important in a birthing facility where a full-time lactation consultant is not on staff.

Be Aware of "Information Overload"

In the first days after birth, especially in a hospital setting, it can be easy for a mother to become overwhelmed with information. So many different professional specialties are providing input and advice, occasionally in conflict with each other, that a mother may not know what to think. When a health care provider confides a personal opinion or experience, it is often especially confusing to a new mother. The advice that you give her, then, must be provided in small doses that are clear, reasonable, and consistent.

Be Supportive of BFAR Even When Apart from the BFAR Mother

It can be very difficult for a maternity nurse to see a new mother undertake BFAR. It is hard to know how educated she truly is about the process and how responsibly she will respond if it does not go well. Nonetheless, it is very important to convey complete support to her at this early stage.

It is also essential to convey support for her to all the staff with whom you interact. On more than one occasion, a husband of a BFAR mother has overheard a maternity nurse making a derisive comment about BFAR to other staff when she was ostensibly supportive in the mother's presence. Invariably, such comments are conveyed to the mother, who feels criticized, embarrassed, and less confident of her ability to BFAR.

Advocate Lactation Consultant Services

In almost all cases, BFAR mothers will need to work with competent lactation consultants. Not all BFAR mothers are aware that such services exist, however. Your comments about the value of having access to the expertise of a lactation consultant can make the concept seem more appealing to her.

If your hospital retains lactation consultants on staff, facilitate a referral so that she is able to spend time with her before her stay in the hospital ends. If one is not available, provide contact information to a qualified, preferably board-certified, lactation consultant in her area.

Educate and Document Teaching of Nutritional and Hydration Status of the Newborn

As stated previously, maternity nurses are often in the position to provide first-line, practical, day-by-day care of the newborn. This may be at some scheduled time during the postpartum stay or discussed in the discharge summary. As with any breastfeeding mother, if no prior education or documentation is present, the maternity nurse should educate the BFAR mother to monitor infant nutrition and hydration status as described in Chapter 7. This is of vital importance in a BFAR scenario to ensure the well-being of the newborn. It may also be helpful to include clinic and resource numbers for the mother to contact for further questions.

Lactation Consultants

Lactation consultants (LCs) are a health care specialty that has been working with BFAR mothers since improved reduction surgical techniques rendered breastfeeding a realistic option. LCs are often deferred to by other members of the health care team as the definitive voice on breastfeeding practice. By virtue of their very credentials, LCs can have the most influence on a BFAR mother during the critical time of establishing a breastfeeding relationship. For this reason, an LC should be mindful of the importance of her role and the value of demonstrating confident support. It is also useful to stay as up-to-date as possible about the developing research in this field.

However, with that said, much of the information in this book, in fact, is the culmination of the trial-and-error work of many lactation consultants. There is little, then, that can be recommended to this specialty in this context, with the minor exception of the following three points that have been mentioned by BFAR mothers as helpful to them when working with a lactation consultant.

Help the BFAR Mother Appreciate the Breast Milk She Produces

For many BFAR mothers, BFAR begins with an expectation that either she will produce a full milk supply or she will give up and bottle-feed. It can be very discouraging, then, when she discovers that she does have milk, but not a full supply. Helping her accept that supplementation is positive because it allows her to continue breastfeeding will be difficult until she understands that every drop of human milk and every moment spent at the breast are of unequaled value to her baby. Developing an appreciation for the superiority of human milk and breastfeeding in any amount is essential for her ability to maintain a sufficient level of motivation to persevere in BFAR. Educating the BFAR mother on ways to maximize her own supply also will empower her to gain some control over her unique breastfeeding situation, thereby decreasing her level of anxiety and fear.

Help the BFAR Mother Identify Her BFAR Goals

For many BFAR mothers, embarking upon the BFAR journey is a decision that is made without a great deal of information about what it entails, primarily because there are few sources for information about BFAR. As she progresses through the stages of BFAR, encountering difficulties that she did not know to anticipate, it can be very difficult for her to maintain her motivation.

One of the most important services a lactation consultant can give to a BFAR mother, is to help her understand and identify her BFAR goals. Taking the time to consider alternatives and decide what is important to her may be very enlightening. She may find that she has an unsuspected passion for breastfeeding, or she may find that deep in her heart she does not truly want to breastfeed. You may also be able to help her realize that BFAR is not an "all or nothing" prospect and that she can adjust the elements of BFAR so that it is comfortable for her. Becoming attuned to her own values will give her an outcome to work toward that is perfectly suited to her needs. Having the insight of the BFAR mother's values will also help you know how to tailor your lactation consulting perspective to most effectively help her meet her goals.

Facilitate Affordable Alternatives

BFAR can be very expensive at a time when new families are already experiencing the harsh realization that the costs of having a new baby can quickly mount. There may be ways that you can help BFAR families find affordable alternatives for the BFAR aids they require that may very well enable them to continue BFAR when they might not have been able to otherwise. Even something so simple as writing a letter to help her obtain insurance reimbursement for your services or supplies may make a tremendous difference in the budget of a new family.

LLL Leaders

As a mother-to-mother support organization with a reputation for empathy and expertise, LLL is often the first place new BFAR mothers turn when they realize they need help with BFAR. Fortunately, LLL Leaders are in an excellent position to be of genuine assistance because if they do not have personal knowledge about BFAR, they can turn to their Area Professional Liaison Leader, who will be able to research the topic and give her much of the information she needs to assist the BFAR mother. As a component of many local LLL Group libraries, this book also serves as a ready source of specific information about BFAR to educate both the LLL Leader and the BFAR mother.

Welcome the BFAR Mother

One of the most important services an LLL Leader can give to a new BFAR mother is actually one of the simplest. She can welcome her warmly and sincerely into the Group and make her feel comfortable to supplement at meetings should she need to, with whatever supplementation devices work best for her. This is not a time to try to educate her about the dangers of nipple confusion if she should use bottles. Instead, she should be made to feel completely welcome and among friends who would not judge her. Focusing entirely on the inspiring fact that she is a breastfeeding mother is the most important message that she needs when she first visits an LLL Group.

Inform Her of Breastfeeding Resources

If the mother should seek your help with her BFAR efforts, you can make her aware of the tremendous LLL resources of information and support that are available to her. Share an overview of your personal expertise, as well as the avenues that are available to you to access current information to help her overcome the issues that she is facing.

Use Your Own Resources

Fully utilize your resources to help the BFAR mother if you find that her needs extend beyond your personal expertise. Don't hesitate to contact your Area Professional Liaison Leader with your questions about BFAR. And if you should feel that her needs for breastfeeding counseling surpass your capabilities, available time, or emotional energy, then do not hesitate to recommend that she contact a board-certified lactation consultant. You can continue to support and encourage her, but it is important to be realistic when the extensive needs of a BFAR mother are beyond the scope of your role as an LLL Leader.

Encourage Her Every Step of the Way

As an LLL Leader, your most valuable gift to a BFAR mother is your enthusiasm for her decision to breastfeed and your encouragement and unflagging support along the way. Knowing that you are impressed and inspired by her extraordinary efforts to breastfeed can really bolster the often fragile self-esteem of a BFAR mother.

Volunteer to Counsel BFAR Mothers as a Specialty

If you have worked closely with a BFAR mother and acquired a level of expertise in BFAR, please consider officially listing your expertise with LLLI as a specialty. LLLI is frequently contacted by BFAR mothers for personal help with BFAR and it seeks to refer them to Leaders with BFAR expertise whenever possible. Unfortunately, there are few Leaders with this highly specialized expertise, so your help in meeting the special needs of BFAR mothers would be greatly valued and appreciated.

Pediatricians and Pediatric Nurses

As health care providers in the pediatric field, you are involved during the entire BFAR process and so will have an opportunity to make a very positive impact upon the success of BFAR for your pediatric patients. The most basic aspect of your role in working with a BFAR mother and her baby will be demonstrating your agreement with and support for the value of breastfeeding. The following broad guidelines were published in a recent issue of *Pediatrics*. Clearly, these guidelines extend far beyond the scope of BFAR, but are nonetheless relevant to establishing a foundation of support for breastfeeding that will directly facilitate BFAR.

The Role of Pediatricians in Promoting and Protecting Breastfeeding

- Promote and support breastfeeding enthusiastically.
- Become knowledgeable and skilled in both the physiology and the clinical management of breastfeeding.
- Work collaboratively with the obstetric community to fully inform women about infant feeding.
- Promote hospital policies and procedures that facilitate breastfeeding.
- Become familiar with local breastfeeding resources.
- Encourage routine insurance coverage for necessary breastfeeding services and supplies.
- Promote breastfeeding as a normal part of daily life.
- Promote breastfeeding education as a routine component of medical school and residency education.
- Encourage the media to portray breastfeeding as positive and the norm.
- Encourage employers to provide appropriate facilities and adequate time in the workplace for breast-pumping.[6]

The Limitations of Scales as a Means of Evaluating Nutrition and Hydration Status

While it is reasonable to rely upon an office scale for data to evaluate nutrition and hydration status, it is important to be aware that all scales are calibrated differently, and can therefore vary as much as five to eight ounces, which can be the determining difference between adequate and inadequate weight gain. For this reason, a baby must be weighed on the same scale that has remained in the same location, preferably at the same time of day, and without clothing. Many BFAR mothers have rental scales at home as a means of monitoring daily weight gain. This information should be used to observe developmental patterns, but should not be compared to the readings of the scale in the professional's office as these two scales cannot be calibrated identically.

Avoid using the technique of "before and after weighings" as a means of determining nutritional intake. For BFAR mothers, this process can greatly inhibit let-down, which fuels their fears. The almost inevitable result is a cyclical, downward spiraling phenomenon of worry inducing poor let-down, which results in a lowered milk supply, which in turn causes the mother to worry, repeating the process with ever diminishing lactation.

It is also important to remember that weight gain is only one criteria in determining nutritional and hydration status. Other dehydration criteria, such as the list provided to the BFAR mother in Chapters 5 and 7, must also be taken into account. After the third month, additional growth factors such as head circumference become equally if not more indicative of nutritional status.

Use Accurate Growth Charts

On average, a satisfactory weight gain for a BFAR baby is at least .75 ounce (22.5 ml) per day for the first three months. As you may know, however, the growth charts currently used in many pediatric offices do not reflect this standard and so are not an accurate tool for assessing growth rates of breastfed children, including those that are formula-supplemented. The charts used most frequently were created by the National Center for Health Statistics (NCHS) and based upon the growth rates of a small sample of exclusively Caucasian, mostly formula-fed babies in Yellow Springs, Ohio, between 1929 and 1975.

Fortunately, the Centers for Disease Control (CDC) has recently developed growth charts that are a far more accurate tool for evaluating childhood development, taking into account the differences between breastfed and bottle-fed children, as well as ethnic factors. The CDC charts can be found in Appendix 2.

Be Sensitive to the Dangers of Unnecessary Supplementation

Chapter 8 of this book provides a thorough overview of the issues of supplementation in the context of BFAR. Supplementation is not inevitable in BFAR; in fact, a significant portion of BFAR mothers do not need to supplement at all. But for a great many others, it is a necessary component of BFAR.

Fortunately, supplementation is not a decision that must be made in the first three to four days as almost all healthy full-term babies are born with sufficient fluid and fat reserves to forestall their need for significant additional hydration or nutrition for the first several days, until the mature milk comes in. Unless the mother's ducts under the nipple/areola complex were completely severed during the reduction surgery, the chances are excellent that she will be able to produce at least some colostrum. The baby should have the maximum opportunity to receive as much of this precious substance as possible. Nursing often will also allow her breasts to create as many prolactin receptors as possible, ensuring that her milk supply is maximized to its complete potential.

Barring neonatal complication, determining whether supplementation is necessary depends upon the baby's degree of dehydration or weight loss. The greater the degree of dehydration or weight loss, the more critical it is to begin immediate supplementation. Conversely, the less the dehydration and weight loss, the more latitude one has to determine if, when, and how much supplementation may be necessary.

If the baby is not gaining weight well, but is not showing signs of dehydration, supplementation may not yet be necessary. In fact, it may not be necessary at all if the mother can increase her milk supply. So long as the baby has not experienced significant weight loss and is well hydrated, the milk supply can be increased using the chemical and mechanical methods discussed in Chapter 9.

When weight gain is borderline and minor signs of dehydration are present, it may be appropriate to supplement small amounts to ensure that the baby does not deteriorate further. Should clear signs of dehydration or significant, rapid weight loss be present, immediate supplementation at higher amounts is, of course, warranted.

It is very important to note, however, that making formula samples available to a BFAR mother before the need for supplementation has been determined can be a direct sabotage of her breastfeeding efforts, as well as her self-confidence.

Do Not Give BFAR Babies Artificial Nipples

When supplementation is necessary, it is important to actively encourage the use of an at-breast supplementer and discourage the use of artificial nipples because every feeding that is supplemented away from the breast is a lost opportunity for stimulation of the sensitive lactation system and will result in a corresponding decrease in the milk supply. This loss of stimulation has an even greater negative impact during the first six weeks when the prolactin receptors are being established.

Nipple confusion/preference is also a very real phenomenon that occurs to many BFAR mothers without regard to the baby's age when artificial nipples are introduced. The most prevalent reason for BFAR failure is an inability to overcome nipple confusion/preference.

For these reasons, it is critical that BFAR mothers supplement at the breast using an at-breast supplementer.

Inform BFAR Mother of Alternative Supplements

Should supplementation be deemed necessary, it is important to make the BFAR mother aware of the realistic possibility of using banked human milk as an alternative to synthetic formula. A thorough discussion of the optimal substances for supplementation is provided in Chapter 8 and resources for obtaining banked human milk is included in Appendix 1.

Encourage Nursing on Demand

Nursing on demand without regard to a schedule is the optimal way to ensure maximum stimulation of the BFAR milk supply, which is critical during the early postpartum weeks. Many mothers worry, though, that caring for the baby will become overwhelming without a schedule. Such mothers are usually relieved to be told that nothing is as important as feeding their babies during this important time, and that most babies can be coaxed into a schedule after the second month, after breastfeeding is well established.

Prevent Maternal-Infant Separation in the Event of Hospitalization

Should it be necessary to hospitalize your pediatric patient for any reason, whenever possible it is critical to make accommodations for the BFAR mother to accompany her child so that BFAR can continue without impediment or interruption.

Discourage BFAR Mothers from Relying upon Mechanical Pumps to Measure Milk Output

It is common among many HCPs to rely upon electric, mechanical pumps to measure the full quantity of milk that a BFAR woman may produce. There are several disadvantages to this practice. First, many women will not be able to sufficiently let down into a pump. The ability to let down well into an artificial device is often a learned skill. Second, while an initial let-down may occur into a pump, additional let-downs may not if the mother does not have practiced, proficient pumping skills. Finally, a mechanical pump has approximately one-third to one-fifth the efficiency of a baby to extract milk from the lactiferous sinuses. Therefore, the expressed amount in the container will only be a fraction of what the woman is capable of producing. Pumping is occasionally useful in BFAR as a means of increasing the milk supply, but should not be the exclusive determining factor of a BFAR mother's general ability to produce milk. Rather, the status of the newborn should be the definitive measurement.

BFAR Topics for Future Research

The following issues are presented as potential topics for future research on BFAR. Conclusive data that addresses any of these issues would be a substantial contribution in this burgeoning field of lactation.

- *How does it psychologically impact a teenager or young woman to delay reduction surgery for the sake of nebulous future children?*

- *We know that "The total dose of such key components as immunoglobulins, which the infant receives from breast milk, remains relatively constant throughout lactation, regardless of the amount of breast milk provided by the mother. This happens because concentrations decrease as total volume increases as lactation is established; at weaning, concentration increases as total volume decreases."* [8] *How does this work for BFAR mothers?*

- *Does the concept of storage capacity have any beneficial implication for BFAR mothers with regard to fat content of the milk?*

- *Is there a relationship between the amount of tissue removed and lactational ability?*

- *Is length of time between surgery and first lactation predictive of milk volume when the surgical technique is the same? (With controls for surgeon, race, and geographic location)*

- *Can engorgement in non-connected lobes lead to mastitis?*

- *Why is mastitis more prevalent in BFAR women? Is it caused by fluctuations in the milk supply?*

- *What is the relationship of BFAR pumping yield to suckling yield?*

- *Many BFAR mothers wonder if their inherent milk supply can have an upper limit—a ceiling as it were—as a result of their breast surgery.*

- *Research into the use of galactogenic herbs as treatment for breastfeeding difficulties is needed in order to substantiate their use for clinical application.*

- *Why do BFAR mothers experience blanching so commonly? Is this a result of blood supply disruption or nerve trauma to the nipple/areola complex during the surgery?*

- *What is the correlation, if any, between milk production and prolactin receptors with relation to passage of time? Is there a way to prevent or overcome the frequently observed phenomenon of decreasing milk production as baby matures despite increased demand?*

REFERENCES:

1. Lawrence, R and R. Lawrence. *Breastfeeding A Guide For The Medical Profession*, 5th edition. St. Louis, Missouri: Mosby, 1999; 547-548, 252, 241, 250, 254.

2. Spear, S., ed. *Surgeries of the Breast: Principles and Art*. Philadelphia, PA: Lippincott-Raven, 1998.

3. Neville, M. and M. Neifert. *Lactation, Physiology, Nutrition, and Breast-Feeding*. New York: Plenum Publishing Corp., 1983.

4. Mohrbacher, N. and J. Stock. THE WOMANLY ART OF BREASTFEEDING, 6th edition. Schaumburg, IL: LLLI, 1997; 19.

5. Brown, M., M. Weinberg, N. Chong, et al. A cohort study of breast cancer risk in breast reduction patients. *Plast Reconstr Surg* May 1999; 103(6): 1674-81.

6. American Academy of Pediatrics. Breastfeeding and the Use of Human Milk (RE9729). *Pediatr* 1997; 100(6):1035-1039.

7. Riordan, J. and K. Auerbach. *Breastfeeding and Human Lactation*, 2nd edition. Sudbury, MA: Jones and Bartlett Publishers, 1999; 122.

RESOURCES

Mother-to-Mother BFAR Support and Information

La Leche League International
1400 N. Meacham Road
Schaumburg, Il 60173-4840 USA
(847) 519-7730
http://www.lalecheleague.org
To find an LLL Group in your area:
(800) LA LECHE

BFAR Website/Email Support Group
http://www.bfar.org/subscription.html

Pumping Support and Information

Pumping Moms
http://www.pumpingmoms.org

Lactation Consultants

The International Lactation Consultant Association(ILCA)
1500 Sunday Drive, Suite 102
Raleigh, NC 27607
Tel: 919-787-5181
http://www.ilca.org

US National Registry of International Board Certified Lactation Consultants
http://www.iblce.org/registr2.html

Breastfeeding.com's Lactation Consultant Directory
http://www.nursingmother.com/directory/lcdirectory.html

Doulas

Doulas of North America
1100 23rd Avenue, East
Seattle, WA 98112
(206) 324-5440
http://www.dona.com

Nursing Clothes

Motherwear
(800) 950-2500
http://www.motherwear.com

Motherhood Nursingwear
(800) 466-6223
http://motherhoodnursing.com

One Hot Mama
(323) 969-0790
http://www.onehotmama.com

Mother and Child, Etc.
(877) 858-6262
http://www.motherandchildetc.com

Nursing in Style
http://www.nursinginstyle.com

Nursing Bras

Jeunique International
(800) 732-9289

Bravado Bras
Sparrow's Nest
301-824-6378
http://www.nestmom.com/bravado.html

Medela
(800) TELL-YOU (800-835-5968)
http://www.medela.com/products/bras.html

Motherwear
(800) 950-2500
http://www.motherwear.com

Baby Friendly Hospitals

**The Baby Friendly Hospital
Initiative – USA**
8 Jan Sebastian Way #13
Sandwich, MA 02563
(508) 888-8044
http://www.aboutus.com/a100/bfusa

UNICEF UK Baby Friendly Initiative
http://www.babyfriendly.org.uk/home.htm

Human Milk Banking

**Human Milk Banking Association of
North America**
http://www.hmbana.org

*Human Milk Banks in
North America*

Mothers' Milk Bank
c/o Professional Group
PO Box 5730
San Jose, CA 85150
(408) 998-4550

Mothers' Milk Bank
HealthOne
1719 E. 19th Avenue
Denver, CO 80218
(303) 869-1888

Mothers' Milk Bank/SCN
Christiana Hospital
4755 Ogleton-Stanton Road
Newark, DE 19718
(302) 733-2340 or 1-800-NICU 101

Mothers' Milk Bank at WakeMed
3000 New Bern Avenue
Raleigh, NC 27610
(919) 350-8599

Mothers' Milk Bank at Austin
900 E. 30th St., Suite 101
Austin, TX 78705
(512) 494-0800
http://www.mmbaustin.org

Banco de Leche
Veracruz, Mexico
+ 52 55 14 45 51
C & W Milk Bank

BC Children's Hospital
Vancouver, BC Canada
(604) 875-2282
Hospital Grade Pumps

Medela™
(800) TELL-YOU (800-835-5968)
http://www.medela.com

Ameda® (formerly Ameda/Egnell)
(800) 323-4060
http://www.hollister.com/products/breast.htm

White River Concepts
(800) 342-3906
http://www.whiteriver.com

Electronic Infant Scales
Medela™ BabyChecker™ Scale
(800) TELL-YOU (800-835-5968)

Supplementation Devices

At-Breast Supplementers
Medela™ Supplemental
Nutrition System™ (SNS)
P.O. Box 660
McHenry, IL 60051-0660
http://www.medela.com

The Lact-Aid®
Lact-Aid International, Inc.
P.O. Box 1066
Athens TN 37371-1066
(423) 744-9090
http://www.lact-aid.com

Axicare Nursing Aid
Colgate Medical, Ltd
Fairacres Estate
Edworth Road
Windsor, Berks SL4LE
United Kingdom
Windsor 60378 (telephone)
http://www.intaventorthofix.com/
colgate_1.htm

Supply Line Mark II
Nursing Mothers' Association of
Australia
PO Box 231
Nunawading 3131
Victoria, Australia
61-3877-5011
61-3894-3270 (fax)
http://www.nmaa.asn.au

Finger Feeding Devices
Medela™ Hazelbaker™ FingerFeeder
(800) TELL-YOU (800-835-5968)
http://www.medela.com/products/
feedprod.html#hazelbaker

Cups
Medela™ SoftFeeder
(800) TELL-YOU (800-835-5968)
http://www.medela.com/products/
feedprod.html#softfeeder

Medela™ Baby Cup Feeder
(800) TELL-YOU (800-835-5968)
http://www.medela.com/products/
feedprod.html#babycupfeeder

Ameda Baby Cups
(877) 99 AMEDA (877-992-6332) USA
(800) 263-7400 Canada
(847) 680-1000 International
http://www.ameda.com/products/
accessories.htm

Foley Cup Feeder
Foley Development, Inc.
PO Box 50
Conway, Michigan 49722
(231) 439-9882

Flexi Cup
Equipment Shop
PO Box 33
Bedford, Massachusetts 01730
(800) 525-7681

Bottles

Medela Haberman™ Feeder
(800) TELL-YOU (800-835-5968)
 http://www.medela.com/products/feed-
prod.html#anchor465526

Avent, America, Inc.
(800) 542-8368
http://www.aventamerica.com

Munchkin, Inc.
(800) 344-2229
http://www.munchkininc.com

Relaxation Techniques

The Menopause Self-Help Book
Dr. Susan Lark
Celestial Arts
ISBN 0890875928

An Interactive Relaxation
http://www.darcynat.com/downrlx.htm

A Milk Intake Calculator

**Adoptive Breastfeeding
Resource Website**
http://www.fourfriends.com/
cgi-bin/milk.pl

Galactagogue Sources

Dancing Moon Herbs
http://www.DancingMoon-herbs.com

Garden of Grace
(800) 230-5166
http://www.gardenofgrace.com

Kerry's Herbals
(612) 827-4920
http://www.kerrysherbals.com

**Lvmyboy's Essentials
C and A Greenhouse Nursery**
7526 RT 415 N
Bath, NY 14810
(607) 776-0425
http://www.lvmyboysessentials.com

Snowbound Herbals
(603) 880-0911
http://www.sbherbals.com

Wise Woman Herbs
(800) 721-0200

Bulk Galactogenic Herbs

Stony Mountain Botanicals, Ltd.
155 N Water St
Loudonville OH 44842
419-994-4857
888-994-4857
www.wildroots.com

Ameriherb
PO Box 1968
Ames, IA 50010-1968
(800) 267-6141

More Milk and More Milk Plus Tinctures

Motherlove Herbal Company
(970) 493-2892
http://www.motherlove.com
Also available at many natural food stores in the US and Canada

Earthbaby
(877) 375-3600
http://www.earthbaby.com/motherlove.html

Mama's Herbs
1-888-747-MAMA
http://www.mamasherbs.com

Domperidone (Motilium™)

Although domperidone (Motilium™) is not available in US pharmacies, it is legal for US citizens to purchase it from other countries and have it mailed to them in the US. The three international pharmacies listed below have an excellent reputation of reliably exporting domperidone to the US.

It is usually least expensive when purchased from the pharmacy listed below that is located off-shore of New Zealand, slightly more expensive from the pharmacy in Canada, and most expensive from the pharmacy in Mexico. The domperidone products dispensed by any of these pharmacies are identical. They are manufactured by the same drug company (Janssen Pharmaceuticals) and packaged in tamper-proof blister-packs.

No prescription is required to purchase Domperidone from the pharmacy off-shore of New Zealand or the pharmacy in Mexico, however, a prescription from any US or Canadian physician or midwife is required to purchase Domperidone from a Canadian pharmacy.

The reason that the pharmacy in New Zealand is not actually located in New Zealand, but is actually located on a small island just off its shore, is because it is against New Zealand law to export prescription drugs from the New Zealand mainland, although it is quite legal for prescription drugs to be exported from off-shore islands.

New Zealand (off-shore)
Pharmacycare
(877) 271-6591
http//pharmacycare.co.nz

Mexico
Jose Rabay Pharmacy
011-526-654-1834
To order in English, ask for Oscar or Gabriel

Canada
Murray Shore Pharmacy
(800) 201-8590
(800) 201-8591 (fax number for prescriptions)
http//www.mshorepharmacy.com

Compounding Pharmacists

The International Academy of Compounding Pharmacists
PO Box 1365
Sugarland TX 77487
(800) 927-4227

Information about Drugs During Lactation

Medications and Mothers' Milk
By Dr. Thomas W. Hale, RPh, PhD
Pharmasoft Medical Publishing
www.perinatalpub.com

Dr. Thomas Hale's Breastfeeding Pharmacology Website
http://neonatal.ttuhsc.edu/lact

Drugs in Pregnancy and Lactation
By Gerald G. Briggs, B Pharm, Roger K. Freeman, MD, and Sumner J Yaffe, MD.

University of Rochester Lactation Study Center
Founded by Dr. Ruth Lawrence
(716) 275-0088

Videotape of Breast Reduction Surgery

Breast Reduction Surgery
The Learning Channel (TLC)
Approximately $50.00 US
(800) 257-5126

Additional Resource Publications

Breastfeeding

THE WOMANLY ART OF BREASTFEEDING
La Leche League International
ISBN 0912500247
http://www.lalecheleague.org/Web_store/
web_store.cgi

MOTHERING YOUR NURSING TODDLER
Norma Jane Bumgarner
La Leche League International
ISBN 0912500522
http://www.lalecheleague.org/Web_store/
web_store.cgi

The Nursing Mothers' Companion
Kathleen Huggins
Harvard Common Press
ISBN 1558321527

Bestfeeding: Getting Breastfeeding Right for You
Mary Renfrew, Chloe Fisher, and
Suzanne Arms
Celestial Arts
ISBN 0890875715

Nursing Your Baby
Karen Pryor and Gale Pryor
Pocket Books
ISBN 0671745484

The Ultimate Breastfeeding Book of Answers
Jack Newman and Teresa Pitman
Prima Publishing
ISBN 0761529969

Weaning

HOW WEANING HAPPENS
Diane Bengson
La Leche League International
ISBN 0912500549

The Nursing Mothers' Guide to Weaning
Kathleen Huggins and Linda Ziedrich
Harvard Common Press
ISBN 1558320652

Galactogenic Herbs

Herbal Remedies for the Breastfeeding Mother
Paul Fleiss, MD
Mothering Magazine, Summer 1988
(800) 984-8116
http://www.mothering.com

List of Herbs Generally Regarded as Safe Food and Drug Administration
U.S. Government Publications Office
HFE-88
Rockville, MD 20857
(301) 443-5006
http://vm.cfsan.fda.gov/%7Edms/eafus.html

Wise Woman Herbal for the Childbearing Years
Susan Weed
Ash Tree Publications
ISBN 0961462000

The Complete Woman's Herbal : A Manual of Healing Herbs and Nutrition for Personal Well-Being and Family Care
Anne McIntyre
Henry Holt Publications
ISBN 0805035370

The Herb Book
John Lust
Bantam Books
ISBN 0553267701

Herbally Yours
Penny Royal
Sound Nutrition
ISBN 096092261X

Earl Mindell's New Herb Bible
Earl Mindell
Fireside
ISBN 0684856395

**The Complete German Commission E
Monographs: Therapeutic Guide to
Herbal Medicines**
The American Botanical Council
Blumenthal, Busse, Goldberg,
Gruenwald. Hall, Klein, Riggins, &
Rister
ISBN 096555550X
abc@herbalgram.org

**Herbal Drugs and
Phytopharmaceuticals: A Handbook for
Practice on a Scientific Basis**
Medpharm Scientific Publishers
Norman Grainger Bisset
ISBN 0849371929
(202) 628-4410

The following charts have been adapted from the source developed by the National Center for Health Statistics in collaboration with the National Center for Chronic Disease Prevention and Health Promotion (2000) http://www.cdc.gov/growthcharts

Weight by Age for Girls From Birth to Age 3

To plot your baby's development on Chart A, weigh her on the day that corresponds to age on the chart, such as the day she turns three months old. Then locate the corresponding figures on the graph and draw a dot to where they intersect. When you record her weight at each age interval, draw a line connecting the new dot to the previous dot.

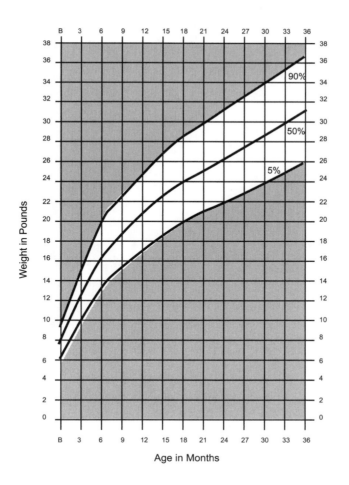

Age in Months

Weight by Age for Boys From Birth to Age 3

To plot your baby's development on Chart A, weigh him on the day that corresponds to age on the chart, such as the day he turns three months old. Then locate the corresponding figures on the graph and draw a dot to where they intersect. When you record his weight at each age interval, draw a line connecting the new dot to the previous dot.

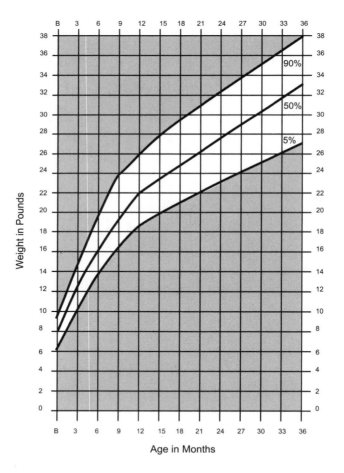

Length by Age for Girls From Birth to Age 3

To plot your baby's development on Chart B, measure her on the day that corresponds to age on the chart, such as the day she turns three months old. Then locate the corresponding figures on the graph and draw a dot to where they intersect. When you record her length at each age interval, draw a line connecting the new dot to the previous dot.

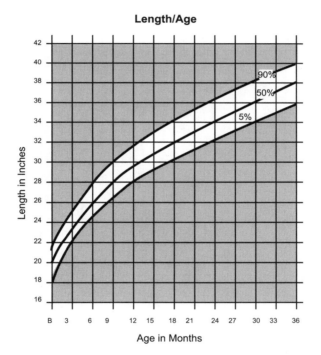

Length by Age for Boys From Birth to Age 3

To plot your baby's development on Chart B, measure him on the day that corresponds to age on the chart, such as the day he turns three months old. Then locate the corresponding figures on the graph and draw a dot to where they intersect. When you record his length at each age interval, draw a line connecting the new dot to the previous dot.

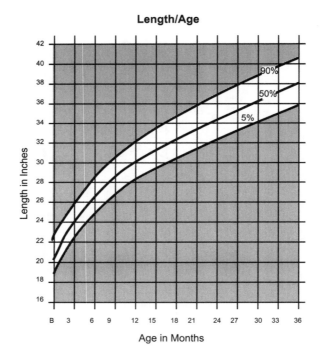

Length/Age

Date:

AM / PM (circle one)

Today's Weight:

Comments:

ASSESSMENT CHART

ABS=At-Breast Supplementer EBM=Expressed BreastMilk
DBM=Donated BreastMilk

TIME (during the hour of)	12:00	1:00	2:00	3:00	4:00	5:00	6:00	7:00	8:00	9:00	10:00	11:00	Total
Diaper (S=scant, M=moderate, H=heavy)													
Wet													
Stool													
Feeding (percentage or qty)													
Breast Only													
ABS													
Cup													
Bottle													
Other													
Supplement (Y/N)													
Amount													
Type of Supplement													
EBM													
DBM													
Formula													
Other													
How Feeding Went													
Well													
Acceptable													
Difficulties													
Baby's Behavior													
Happy													
Alert													
Quiet													
Sleepy													
Fussy													
Crying													
When Baby Slept													

SIGNS OF DEHYDRATION: Listlessness; weak cry; a depressed or sunken "soft spot" on top of the head (assess when the baby is lying down and not when standing); insufficient and infrequent wet and soiled diapers; dry mouth and eyes; cool and clammy hands and feet or fingers and toes; absence of tears in infants older than three months; gently pinched skin stays pinched looking; pressed skin stays dented.

RELAXATION TECHNIQUES

From *Living a Healthy Life with Chronic Conditions,* by Kate Lorig (Editor), Halsted Holman, David Sobel, Diana Laurent, Marian Minor, and Virginia Gonzalez. Reprinted with permission from Bull Publishing. Copyright © 1994 Bull Publishing Company.

Note: This presentation of relaxation techniques was originally written for the benefit of persons suffering from chronic illness. For this reason, terms like "symptom management" and "illness" are used, which do not apply to BFAR. Nonetheless, the techniques described are excellent for providing deep relaxation, which is very beneficial to BFAR.

While many of us have heard and read about relaxation, some of us are still confused as to what relaxation is, what are its benefits, and how to do it. We know relaxation is not a cure-all, but neither is it a hoax or a silly mind game. Rather, like other treatment methods, it has specific guidelines and specific uses. Some techniques are used only to achieve muscle relaxation, while others are aimed at reducing anxiety and emotional arousal, or diverting attention, all of which aid in [stress] management.

The term "relaxation" means different things to different people. We can all identify ways we relax. For example, we may walk, watch TV, play golf, knit, or garden. These methods, however, are different from the techniques discussed here because they include some form of physical activity that requires your mind's attention. Relaxation techniques are also different from napping in that they require us to use our minds actively, to help our bodies achieve a relaxed state.

The goal of relaxation is to turn off the outside world so the mind and body are at rest. This allows you to reduce the tension that increases the intensity of [stress].

Here are some guidelines to help you practice the cognitive techniques described in this section:

- *Pick a quiet place and time* during the day when you will not be disturbed for at least 15-20 minutes.
- Try to *practice the technique twice daily*, but in any event not less than four times a week.
- *Don't expect miracles.* Some techniques take time to acquire the needed skill, sometimes 3-4 weeks of practice before you really start to notice benefits.
- *Relaxation should be helpful.* At worst, you may find it boring, but if it is an unpleasant experience or makes you more nervous or anxious, then you might do better with other [stress] management techniques.

Muscle Relaxation

Muscle relaxation is one of the most commonly used cognitive techniques for [stress] management. It is popular because it makes sense to us. If we are told that physical stress or muscular tension intensifies our pain, shortness of breath or emotional distress, we are motivated to learn how to recognize this tension and release it.

In addition, muscle relaxation is easy to learn and recall for practice in different situations. It is also one technique from which we can recognize some immediate results, such as the positive sensations of reduced pain, stress or muscle tension, and calm, normal breathing. Muscle relaxation is not likely to fail because of distractions caused by symptoms or thoughts. It is a useful strategy to reduce pain, muscular tension and stress, while helping to control shortness of breath and to achieve a more restful sleep.

The following are two examples of muscle relaxation techniques. Try both techniques and choose the one that works best for you. Then you might want to tape record the script for that routine. Although this is not necessary, it is sometimes helpful if you find it hard to concentrate. Also, you won't be distracted by having to refer to the book when you are trying to relax.

Jacobson's Progressive Relaxation

Many years ago, a physiologist named Edmund Jacobson discovered that in order to relax, one must know how it feels to be tense, as well as relaxed. He believed that if one learned to recognize tension, then one could learn to let it go and relax. He designed a simple exercise to assist with this learning process.

To relax muscles, you need to know how to scan your body, recognize where you are holding tension, and release that tension. The first step is to become familiar with the difference between the feeling of tension and the feeling of relaxation. This brief exercise will allow you to compare those feelings and, with practice, spot and release tension anywhere in your body.

Progressive Muscle Relaxation

Make yourself as comfortable as possible. Loosen any clothing that feels tight. Uncross your legs and ankles. Allow your body to feel supported by the surface on which you are sitting or lying.

Close your eyes. Take a deep breath, filling your chest and breathing all the way down to the abdomen. Hold... Breathe out through pursed lips, and, as you breathe out, let as much tension as possible flow out with your breath. Let all your muscles feel heavy and let your whole body just sink into the surface beneath you... Good.

This exercise guides you through the major muscle groups, asking you to first tense and then relax those muscles. If you have pain in a particular area today, tense those muscles only gently or not at all and focus on relaxing them.

Become aware of the muscles in your feet and calves. Pull your toes back up toward your knees. Notice the tension in your feet and calves. Release and relax. Notice the discomfort leaving as relief and warmth replace it. That's it.

Now tighten the muscles of your *thighs and buttocks*. Hold and feel the tension. Let go and allow the muscles to relax. The relaxed muscles feel heavy and supported by the surface upon which you are sitting or lying.

Tense the muscles in your *abdomen and chest*. Notice a tendency to hold your breath as you tense. Relax, and notice that it is natural to want to take a deep breath to relieve the tension in this area. Take a deep breath now, breathing all the way down to the abdomen. As you breathe out, allow all the tension to flow out with your breath.

Now, stretching your fingers out straight, tense your fingers and tighten your *arm muscles.* Relax. Feel the tension flowing out as the circulation returns.

Press your shoulder blades together, tightening the muscles in your *shoulders and neck.* This is a place where many people carry a lot of tension. Hold... Now, let go. Notice how the muscles feel warmer and more alive.

Tighten all the muscles of your face and head. Notice the tension, especially around your eyes and in your jaw. Now relax, allowing your jaw to become slack and your mouth to remain slightly open... That's right. Note the difference.

Now take another deep breath, breathing all the way down to the abdomen. And, as you breathe out, allow your body to sink heavily into the surface beneath you, becoming even more deeply relaxed. Good.

Enjoy this comfortable feeling of relaxation... Remember it. With practice, you will become skilled at recognizing muscle tension and releasing it....

Prepare to come back into the here and now. Take three deep breaths. And, when you're ready, open your eyes.

As Jacobson emphasizes, the purpose of voluntarily tensing the muscles is to learn to recognize and locate tension in your body. You will then become aware of tension and use this same procedure of letting go. Once you learn the technique it will no longer be necessary to tense voluntarily; just locate the existing tension and let it go.

The Relaxation Response

In the early 1970s, Dr. Herbert Benson studied extensively what he calls the "relaxation response." According to Dr. Benson, our bodies have several natural states. One example is the "fight or flight" response experienced when faced with a great danger. Here, the body becomes quite tense, followed by the body's natural tendency to relax; this is the relaxation response. As our lives become more and more hectic, our bodies tend to stay in an extended or constant state of tension, and we lose our ability to relax. In order to help our bodies relieve this tension and elicit the relaxation response, we may consciously need to practice the following exercise, which consists of four basic elements:

1. *A quiet environment.* Turn off all external distractions and internal physical or emotional stimuli.

2. *Choose an object to dwell upon,* or a mental device. For example, repeat a word or sound like the word "one," gaze at a symbol like a flower, or concentrate on a feeling, such as peace.

3. *Adopt a passive attitude.* This is the most essential element. Empty all thoughts and distractions from your mind. Thoughts, images, and feelings may drift into awareness, but don't concentrate on them. Just allow them to pass on.

4. *Find a comfortable position.* You should be comfortable enough to remain in the same position for twenty minutes.

To elicit the relaxation response:

1. *Sit quietly* in a comfortable position.
2. Close your eyes.
3. *Relax all your muscles*, beginning at your feet and progressing up to your face. Keep them relaxed.
4. *Breathe in through your nose.* Become aware of your breathing. As you breathe out through your mouth, *say the word "one"* silently to yourself. Try to *empty all thoughts* from your mind; concentrate on "one."
5. *Continue* this for 10-20 minutes. You may open your eyes to check the time, but do not use an alarm. When you finish, sit quietly for several minutes, at first with your eyes closed. Do not stand up for a few minutes.
6. Do not worry about whether you are successful in achieving a deep level of relaxation. *Maintain a passive attitude* and let relaxation occur at its own pace. When distracting thoughts occur, ignore them by not dwelling upon them, and return to repeating the word "one."
7. *Practice* this once or twice daily, but ideally not within two hours after any meal. Digestive processes can interfere with relaxation responses.

This exercise is very much like meditation, which provides the principles on which the relaxation response is based.

While relaxation is the most common method for relieving muscle tension, other techniques can be used as supplements to provide additional emotional and/or cognitive benefits. These benefits include a reduction in fear and anxiety and a refocusing of attention away from the discomfort or unpleasantness of symptoms. These techniques include guided imagery and visualization.

Imagery

Guided Imagery

The guided imagery relaxation technique is like a guided daydream. It allows you to divert your attention, refocusing your mind away from your symptoms and transporting you to another time and place. It has the added dimension of helping you to achieve deep relaxation by picturing yourself in a peaceful environment.

The two guided imagery scripts presented here can help take you on this mental stroll. Again, depending on which exercise you prefer, consider each of the following ways to use them:

1. Read the script over several times to familiarize yourself with it. Then sit or lie down in a quiet place and try to reconstruct the scene in your mind. Each script should take 10-15 minutes to complete.
2. Have a family member or friend read you the script slowly, pausing for 5-10 seconds wherever there is a series of dots (...).
3. Make a tape of the script and play it to yourself whenever convenient.

Guided Imagery Script 1: A Walk in the Country

Make yourself as comfortable as possible, sitting or lying down. Loosen any constricting clothing. Uncross your arms, legs, and ankles. Allow your body to feel supported by the surface on which you are sitting or lying.

Close your eyes.

Take a deep breath in through your nose breathing all the way down to the abdomen. Hold... Breathe out slowly through slightly pursed lips and as you do relax your whole body allowing all your muscles to feel limp and heavy... Good.

Scan your body for any muscle tension, starting with your head and going all the way down to your toes.

Release any tension in your face, head and neck by letting your jaw become slack and your head feel heavy on your shoulders. Allow your shoulders to drop heavily. Take a deep breath and relax your chest and abdomen. Allow your arms and legs to feel heavy and to sink into the surface beneath you.

Now take a deep breath and become aware of any remaining tension in your body. As you breathe out, allow all the muscles of your body to sink heavily into the surface beneath you, becoming even more deeply relaxed... Good.

Imagine yourself walking along an old country road... the sun is warm on your back... the birds are singing... the air is calm and fragrant.

As you progress down the road, you come across an old gate... The gate creaks as you open it and go through.

You find yourself in an overgrown garden, flowers growing where they have seeded themselves, vines climbing over a fallen tree, green grass, shade trees.

Breathe deeply, smelling the flowers... listen to the birds and insects... feel the gentle breeze, warm against your skin.

As you walk leisurely up a gentle slope behind the garden, you come to a wooded area where the trees become denser, the sun is filtered through the leaves. The air feels mild and a bit cooler. You become aware of the sound and fragrance of a nearby brook. You breathe deeply of the cool and fragrant air several times, and with each breath, you feel more refreshed.

Soon, you come upon the brook. It is clear and clean as it tumbles over the rocks and some fallen logs. You follow the path along the brook for a way. The path takes you out into a sunlit clearing where you discover a small and picturesque waterfall... There is a rainbow in the mist....

You find a comfortable place to sit for a while, a perfect niche where you can feel completely relaxed.

You feel good as you allow yourself to just enjoy the warmth and solitude of this peaceful place.

It is now time to return. You walk back down the path, through the cool and fragrant trees, out into the sun-drenched overgrown garden... one last smell of the flowers, and out the creaky gate....

You leave this secret retreat for now and return down the country road. However, you know that you may visit this special place whenever you wish.

When you're ready, take three deep breaths, and open your eyes.

Guided Imagery Script 2: A Happy Time
Before imagining or listening to this scene, close your eyes and take three deep breaths... breathe slowly and easily, in through your nose and out through your mouth....

Now picture a happy, pleasant time, a time when you have little or no problems or worries about your health....

Fill in the details of that time... Look at the surroundings -- is it indoors?... outdoors?... who is there?... what are you doing?... Listen to the noises... even those in the background... are there any pleasant smells?... feel the temperature... now, just enjoy your surroundings... you are happy... your body feels good... enjoy your surroundings... fix this feeling in your mind... you can return any time you wish by just picturing this happy time....

When you are ready, take three deep breaths... with each breath say the word "relax"... imagine the word written in warm sand... now open your eyes— remain quiet for a few moments before slowly returning to your activities.

Visualization

This technique, also referred to as vivid imagery, is similar to guided imagery. It is another way of using the imagination to picture yourself any way you want, doing things you want to do. Visualization can be done in different ways and can be used for longer periods, or while you are engaged in other activities.

One way to use visualization is to recall pleasant scenes from your past or create new scenes in your mind. It allows you to create more of your own images than does the guided imagery technique. For example, try to remember every detail of a special holiday or party that made you happy. Who was there? What happened? What did you talk about? You can do the same sort of thing by remembering a vacation.

In fact, visualization can also be used to plan the details of some future event. In this case, try to fill in the details of a pleasant fantasy. For example, how would you spend a million dollars? What would be your ideal romantic encounter? What would your ideal home or garden look like? Where would you go and what would you do on your dream vacation?

Another form of visualization involves using your mind to think of symbols that represent the discomfort of pain felt in different parts of your body. For example, a painful joint might be red or a tight chest might have a constricting band around it. After forming these images, you then try to change them. The red color might fade until there is no more color, or the constricting band will stretch and stretch until it falls off.

Visualization is a useful technique to help you set and accomplish your personal goals. Studies have shown that this technique can help people cope better with stressful situations, master skills and accomplish personal goals. In fact, those people who have become skilled at visualization find they can actually reduce some of the discomfort and distress associated with symptoms by changing unpleasant images to pleasant ones.

All the relaxation techniques mentioned above can be used in conjunction with pursed-lip breathing and diaphragmatic breathing. These two breathing methods can help you achieve a more relaxed state.

Other Cognitive Strategies

While learning to relax is an important part of [stress] management, other cognitive strategies can also be useful. These techniques, however, may require more practice than relaxation before you notice the benefits; they include self-talk, distraction, dissociation, relabeling and prayer.

Self-Talk -- "I Know I Can"

All of us talk to ourselves all the time. For example, when waking up in the morning, we think, "I really don't want to get out of bed. I'm tired and don't want to go to work today." Or, at the end of an enjoyable evening, we think, "Gee, that was really fun. I should get out more often." These things we think or say to ourselves are referred to as "self-talk."

All of our self-talk is learned from others and becomes a part of us as we grow up. It comes in many forms, mostly negative. Negative self-statements are usually in the form of phrases that begin like these: "I just can't do..." "If only I could or didn't..." "I just don't have the energy..." This type of self-talk represents the doubts and fears we have about ourselves in general, and about our abilities to deal with a disease and its symptoms, in particular. In fact, negative self-talk can worsen symptoms like pain, depression and fatigue.

Because those things we learn in life influence our beliefs, attitudes, feelings, and actions, what we say to ourselves plays a major role in determining our success or failure in becoming good self managers. Therefore, learning to make self-talk work *for* you instead of *against* you, by changing those negative statements to positive ones, will help you manage symptoms more effectively. This change, as with any habit, requires practice and includes the following steps:

1. Listen carefully to what you say *to* or *about* yourself, both out loud and silently. Then write down all the negative self-talk statements. Pay special attention to the things you say during times that are particularly difficult for you. For example, what do you say to yourself when getting up in the morning with pain, while doing those exercises you don't really like, or at those times when you are feeling blue?

2. Work on *changing* each negative statement you identified to a positive one, and write these down. Positive statements should reflect the better you, and your decision to be in control. For example, negative statements such as, "I don't want to get up," "I'm too tired and I hurt," "I can't do the things I like anymore so why bother," or "I'm good for nothing," become positive mes-

sages such as, "I have the energy to get up and do the things I enjoy," or "I know I can do anything I believe I can," "People like me and I feel good about myself," or "Other people need and depend on me; I'm worthwhile."

3. *Read and rehearse* these positive statements, mentally or with another person. It is this conscious repetition or memorization of the positive self-talk that will help you replace those old, habitual negative statements.

4. *Practice these new statements in real situations.* This practice, along with time and patience will help the new patterns of thinking become automatic.

As with exercise and other acquired skills, using your mind to achieve relaxation requires both practice and time before you will begin to notice the benefits. Thus, if you feel you are not accomplishing anything, don't give up. Be patient and keep on trying.

ITEMS TO HAVE ON HAND

Note: Items marked with an asterisk should be taken with you if you give birth in a hospital where you will stay longer than 24 hours.

☐ *This DEFINING YOUR OWN SUCCESS book

☐ *Good general breastfeeding book, such as THE WOMANLY ART OF BREASTFEEDING

☐ *Print-out of the Signs of Dehydration (from Chapter 6 or Chapter 8)

☐ *Print-out of the Assessment Checklist (from Appendix 3)

☐ Rental scale

☐ Tissue to put in diaper to check for wetness

☐ *At-breast supplementer (SNS or Lact-Aid) (be familiar with how to use it)

☐ *Cup, syringe, or other type of feeder (as an alternative to at-breast supplementer)

☐ *If using SNS, a bottle brush (to clean)

☐ *If using SNS, medical grade paper tape (or Band-Aids or hair tape) for securing tubes to breast

☐ *Phone number of LLL leader

☐ *Phone number of a lactation consultant

☐ *Spill resistant water bottle for you (to avoid worry of spilling)

☐ *Purified lanolin (such as Lansinoh)

☐ *Comfort foods/special edible treats

☐ *An enjoyable book or magazine to read while nursing

☐ *Nursing nightgown

☐ *Nursing bra

☐ Nursing pads

☐ Nursing pillow

☐ Nursing stool

☐ Sling

☐ Arrangements for postpartum help

☐ Any herbal galactagogues that you may wish to use (do not take for first three days)

Do not have on hand:
- Prescription galactagogues (they are expensive and may not be needed, but can be obtained if necessary)
- Formula (can be obtained if needed, but is too tempting to have at hand)
- Bottles
- Pacifiers
- Hospital-Grade Rental Pump (if one is needed, it can be obtained)
- Inferior-Grade Pump (completely inappropriate and ineffective for BFAR)

THE MARMET TECHNIQUE OF MANUAL EXPRESSION

The Marmet Technique of Manual Expression

The Marmet Technique of manual expression and assisting the milk ejection reflex (MER), which was formerly called the let-down reflex, has worked for thousands of mothers—in a way that nothing has before. Even experienced breastfeeding mothers who have been able to hand express will find that this method produces more milk. Mothers who have previously been able to express only a small amount, or none at all, get excellent results with this technique.

Technique Is Important

When watching manual expression, the correct milking motion is difficult to see. In this case, the hand is quicker than the eye. Consequently, many mothers have found manual expression difficult—even after watching a demonstration or reading a brief description. Milk can be expressed when using less effective methods of hand expression. However, when used on a frequent and regular basis, these methods can easily lead to damaged breast tissue, bruised breasts, and even skin burns.

The Marmet technique of manual expression was developed by a mother who needed to express her milk over an extended period of time for medical reasons. She found that her milk ejection reflex did not work as well as when her baby breastfed, so she also developed a method of massage and stimulation to assist this reflex. The key to the success of this technique is the combination of the method of expression and this massage.

This technique is effective and should not cause problems. It can easily be learned by following this step by step guide. As with any manual skill, practice is important.

Advantages

There are many advantages to manual expression over mechanical methods of milking the breasts:

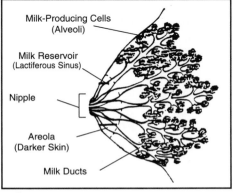

- Some mechanical pumps cause discomfort and are ineffective.
- Many mothers are more comfortable with manual expression because it is more natural.
- Skin-to-skin contact is more stimulating than the feel of a plastic shield, so manual expression usually allows for an easier milk ejection reflex.
- It's convenient.
- It's ecologically superior.
- It's portable. How can a mother forget her hands?
- Best of all, it's free!

©2000, 1997, 1988, 1981, 1979, 1978 Chele Marmet, used with permission.

How the Breast Works

The milk is produced in milk-producing cells (alveoli). A portion of the milk continuously comes down the ducts and collects in the milk reservoirs (Lactiferous sinuses). When the milk-producing cells are stimulated, they expel additional milk into the duct system (milk ejection reflex).

Expressing the Milk

Draining the Milk Reservoirs:

1. **Position** the thumb and first two fingers about 1" to 1 1/2" behind the nipple.
   - Use this measurement, which is not necessarily the outer edge of the areola, as a guide. The areola varies in size from one woman to another.
   - Place the thumb pad above the nipple at the 12 o'clock position and the finger pads below the nipple at the 6 o'clock position forming the letter "C" with the hand, as shown.
   - Note that the fingers are positioned so that the milk reservoirs lie beneath them.
   - Avoid cupping the breast.

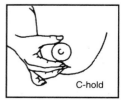

C-hold

2. **Push** straight into the chest wall.
   - Avoid spreading the fingers apart.
   - For large breasts, first lift and then push into the chestwall.

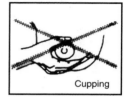

Cupping

3. **Roll** thumb forward as if taking a thumbprint.
   Change finger pressure from middle finger to index finger at the same time.
   - **Finish Roll.** The rolling motion of the thumb simulates the wave-like motion of the baby's tongue and the counter pressure of the fingers simulates the baby's palate. This milking motion imitates the baby's suck by compressing and draining the milk reservoirs without hurting sensitive breast tissue.
   - Note the moving position of the thumbnail and fingernails in the illustration.

4. **Repeat rhythmically** to drain the reservoirs.
   - Position, push, roll; position, push, roll . . .

5. **Rotate** the thumb and finger position to milk the other reservoirs. Use both hands on each breast. These pictures show hand positions on the right breast.

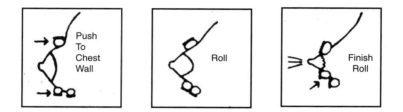

Avoid These Motions

- Squeezing the breast. This can cause bruising.
- Pulling out the nipple and breast. This can cause tissue damage.
- Sliding on the breast. This can cause skin burns.

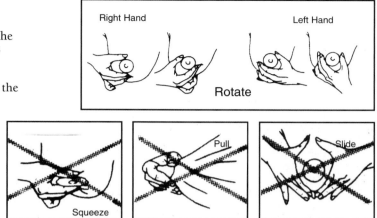

Assisting the Milk Ejection Reflex (MER)

Stimulating the flow of Milk:

1. **Massage** the milk-producing cells and ducts.
   - Start at the top of the breast. Press firmly into the chest wall. Move fingers in a circular motion on one spot on the skin.
   - After a few seconds move the fingers to the next area on the breast.
   - Spiral around the breast toward the areola using this massage.
   - The pressure and motion are similar to that used in a breast examination.

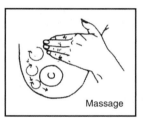

2. **Stroke** the breast area from the top of the breast to the nipple with a light tickle-like stroke.
   - Continue this stroking motion from the chest wall to the nipple around the whole breast.
   - This will help with relaxation and will help stimulate the milk ejection reflex.

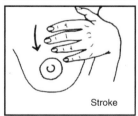

3. **Shake** the breast gently while leaning forward so that gravity will help the milk eject.

Procedure

This procedure should be followed by mothers who are expressing in place of a full feeding and those who need to establish, increase, or maintain their milk supply when the baby cannot breastfeed.

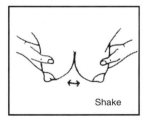

- Express each breast until the flow of milk slows down.
- Assist the milk ejection reflex (massage, stroke, shake) on both breasts. This can be done simultaneously, and only takes about a minute.

- Repeat the whole process of expressing each breast and assisting the milk ejection reflex once or twice more. The flow of milk usually slows down sooner the second and third time as the reservoirs are drained.

Timing

The *entire procedure* should take approximately 20-30 minutes when manual expression is replacing a feeding.

- Express each breast 5-7 minutes.
- Massage, stroke, shake.
- Express each breast 3-5 minutes.
- Massage, stroke, shake.
- Express each breast 2-3 minutes.

Note: If the milk supply is established, use the times given only as a guide. Watch the flow of milk and change breasts when the flow gets small. If little or no milk is present yet, follow these suggested times closely. Any portion of the procedure or timing may be used or repeated as necessary.

GLOSSARY

Adipose Tissue – Tissue comprised of fat cells (fatty tissue).

Alveoli (individually called alveolus) – The basic unit component of the mammary system, containing specialized cells that produce milk derived from elements of the adjacent bloodstream.

Ampullae (also known as lactiferous sinuses) – The pooling areas for milk at the end of the main ducts, beneath the areola.

Amylase – An enzyme necessary for the digestion of starch.

Arachidonic Acid (AA) – A long-chain polyunsaturated fatty acid derived from linoleic and linolenic acid that is abundant in human milk.

Areola Mammary (also known as the areola) – The darker pigmented circle of skin that surrounds the nipple on the end of the breast.

At-Breast Supplementer – A supplementation device that supplies supplemental nutrition at the breast while a child is suckling.

Autocrine Milk Removal (also known as supply-and-demand milk production) – The system of milk production that produces milk in direct response to the amount of milk that is removed. It is self-perpetuating and is not hormonally-driven.

Autologous Blood Donation – Donation of one's own blood for use during surgery.

BFAR– An acronym which stands for Breastfeeding After Breast Reduction.

Bifidus Factor – An antibody factor in human milk that promotes a low stool acidity, creating an inhospitable environment for harmful bacteria.

Bilirubin – The principal pigment of bile and a byproduct of the liver, it is accumulated in high levels immediately after birth because of the rapid synthesis of red blood cells.

Bioavailability – The degree to which a substance is well absorbed into the physiological system.

Biotinidase – An enzyme thought to aid in the digestion of the vitamin biotin, a deficit of which results in dermatitis.

Cannula – A suction tube used in liposuction surgeries.

Casein – A protein that is one of the main components of milk.

Cholecystokinin (CCK) – A hormone present in the gastrointestinal system that aids in digestion and conveys sensations of satiation, drowsiness, and well-being.

Colostrum – The first clear, yellowish milk produced by the breasts after birth.

Nipple/Areolar Complex – The combined anatomical structures of the nipple and areola.

Cooper's Ligaments – A type of connective tissue that figures prominently in the support structure of the breast.

Cortisol – A hormone that seems to affect maternal stress levels and may suppress some immunological responses.

Docosahexanoic Acid (DHA) – A long-chain polyunsaturated fatty acid derived from linoleic and linolenic acid that is abundant in human milk. It results in greater visual acuity and is necessary for formation of myelin.

Doula – A woman who is hired to provide labor or postpartum support and assistance to a mother.

Ducts – Conduits that convey milk through the breast from the milk-producing portions of the gland.

Ductules – Smaller branches of the ductal network.

Endocrine Milk Production – The initial postpartum lactation process that relies upon hormonal stimulation rather than milk removal for milk production.

Engorgement – The normal postpartum process whereby the mature milk appears in the first few days after birth, resulting in swelling in the breasts. Engorgement can also occur at any time during lactation when a larger amount of milk is produced than removed.

Epidermal Growth Factor (EGF) — A polypeptide that stimulates the production of the cellular tissue that lines the interior surfaces of the body.

Epithelium – The cellular tissue that lines the interior surfaces of the body and prevents the inappropriate internal transfer of microorganisms.

Estrogen – Any of a group of female hormones (estrone, ethinyl estradiol, and estriol) produced in the ovaries that control growth of the lining of the uterus during the first part of the menstrual cycle, affect lactation, and regulate various metabolic processes.

Fasciculi – The branches of the fourth intercostal nerve.

Foremilk – The milk the baby receives when he begins suckling. Thin and usually bluish, it is the milk that has accumulated since the last nursing and has a higher protein, but lower fat content than hindmilk.

Galactogenic – The ability of a substance to increase the milk supply.

Galactagogues – A substance that increases the milk supply.

Galactose – A sugar present in milk that is critical to human brain growth.

Glucose – A sugar that is critical to human brain growth.

Growth Hormone – A hormone that regulates and promotes tissue growth.

Growth Modulators – Polypeptides that promote human tissue growth.

Hindmilk – The milk actively produced during the feeding after most of the foremilk has been removed. Hindmilk is much higher in fat, which results in a thick, white appearance.

Human Growth Factors I, II, and III – Polypeptides that stimulate cell reproduction and growth.

Immunoglobulins – An immunological factor that protects against bacteria, viruses, and fungi.

Innervation – The conduction of nerve impulses through the neural network.

Insulin – A secretion of the pancreas that aids in the synthesis of sugar and carbohydrates.

Insulinlike Growth Factor – A hormone believed to promote cell growth.

Intercostal Spaces – The regions between the ribs.

Intermammary Fold – The line at the base of the breast where the breast meets the chest wall.

Intestinal Villi – The miniscule projections of the intestine that attract and absorb nutrients from passing food.

Lact-Aid (see at-breast supplementer)

Lactiferous Sinuses (see ampullae)

Lactobacillus Bifidus – A highly beneficial intestinal bacteria.

Lactoferrin – A powerful protein that binds to iron, thereby starving harmful organisms that rely on iron for their subsistence.

Lactoperoxidase – The enzyme that, in conjunction with sIgA, is particularly effective in killing the bacteria streptococci.

Lactose – The primary carbohydrate in human milk, it is a natural sugar that fosters brain and bone growth, aids in calcium absorption, and the growth of beneficial intestinal bacteria.

Lansinoh® – Purified, hypoallergenic lanolin, endorsed by LLLI for use to moisturize and aid in healing of wounds on the nipple/areolar complex.

Let-down (also known as the Milk Ejection Reflect [M.E.R.]) – The process by which milk is forcibly expelled from the milk-producing glands, through the ducts, and from the breast.

Lipase – A necessary enzyme for the completion of digestion.

Lipid – A fatty acid.

Lobe – A complete section of the lactation system, containing alveoli, ducts, and sinuses.

Lobuli – Clusters of alveoli.

Lymphatic System – A network of ducts throughout the body that convey digested fat from the intestine to the bloodstream, filter and eradicate toxic substances, and combat infection and disease.

Lysozyme – An enzyme that destroys alien cells by dissolving their cell walls.

Mammoplasty/Mammaplasty – Surgery of the breast (see also reduction mammoplasty).

Mature Milk – Milk that has fully transitioned from colostrum.

Milk Ejection Reflex (M.E.R.) (see let-down)

Montgomery Glands (also known as Montgomery's tubercles) – Raised bumps on the areola that appear in late pregnancy and may seep small amounts of a quasi-oily substance and milk throughout lactation. Thought to disinfect and lubricate the nipple/areola complex.

Mucosa – The cellular tissue that lines the interior surfaces of the body and prevents the inappropriate internal transfer of microorganisms.

Multipara – A woman who has been pregnant more than once.

Myelin – The material forming the myelin sheath; an outer layer that covers nerves and that transmits impulses among nerve cells.

Myoepithelial Cells – Minute muscles that squeeze milk from the alveoli cells.

Neural Pathways – The interlacing network of nerve fibers that allows a nerve impulse to follow a myriad number of pathways.

Nipple (see papilla mammary)

Nucleotides – Compounds formed from nitrogen that serve to reinforce the strength of tissue cells, while also prompting the growth of intestinal villi. They are also a component of the immune system, facilitating its defense against bacteria, viruses, parasites, and malignancies.

Nulliparous – A woman who has never been pregnant.

Oligosaccharides – Carbohydrates that deter harmful bacteria by aiding the bifidus factor and preventing microbial adhesion to intestinal tissues.

Oxytocin – A hormone produced by the pituitary gland that stimulates uterine and lactiferous muscle contractions.

Papilla Mammary (also known as a nipple) – A knob of very elastic skin at the tip of the breast from which milk is expressed by contraction of minute muscles surrounding ductal openings that lead to the milk-producing glands.

Parathyroid – A gland that secretes the hormone parathormone, which controls levels of calcium and phosphorus in the blood.

Parenchyma – The elements of an organ system, i.e. the mammary system.

Parous – Referring to a quantity of pregnancies (e.g., multiparous).

Phagocytes – White blood cells that ingest and destroy harmful cells, microorganisms, and bacteria.

Pituitary Gland – The endocrine gland that produces prolactin and oxytocin.

Placenta – A vascular organ present in the uterus during pregnancy through which the fetus is provided nourishment and hydration and by which waste matter is eliminated.

Postpartum – The period of time after giving birth.

Polypeptide – A combination of amino acids.

Primipara – A first time mother.

Progesterone – A hormone formed by the corpus luteum of the ovary. During pregnancy, it stimulates the formation of aveoli in the mammary gland, while preventing lactation by inhibiting the release of prolactin.

Prolactin – A hormone produced by the pituitary gland that influences and promotes lactation.

Prostaglandins – A type of lipid that is thought to convey anti-inflammatory properties.

Oncology – The medical specialization of cancer diagnosis and treatment.

Recanalization – The process by which severed ductule pathways reconnect.

Reduction Mammoplasty/Mammaplasty – Breast reduction surgery.

Reinneration – The process by which nerve segments are regrown between or around severed nerves.

Sebaceous Glands – Glands that produce fatty substances known as sebum.

Secretory Immunoglobulin A (sIgA) – An immunological factor that acts as a physical barrier in the mucus membranes of the throat, lungs, and intestines, where harmful bacteria, viruses, fungi, and proteins attempt to enter the bloodstream.

Stroma – Tissue that provides a formative structure to the breast.

Subareolar Plexus – A network of lymphatic nodes beneath the areola.

Supplemental Nursing System (SNS) (see at-breast supplementer)

Taurine – A neurotransmitter, naturally present only in human milk, that stimulates human brain cellular growth and interlacement, as well as retina development.

Thyroid – A gland that secretes a hormone that controls metabolism and growth.

Thyroxine – A hormone that is thought to play a role in intestinal maturation.

Transition Milk – The yellowish human milk that is in the process of transitioning from colostrum into mature milk.

Triglycerides – A beneficial fat contained in human milk.

Vascularization – The establishment of the network of blood veins and arteries.

Whey – The protein that forms soft curds during digestion, which allow efficient processing of nutrients. It also contains critical immunological elements.

INDEX